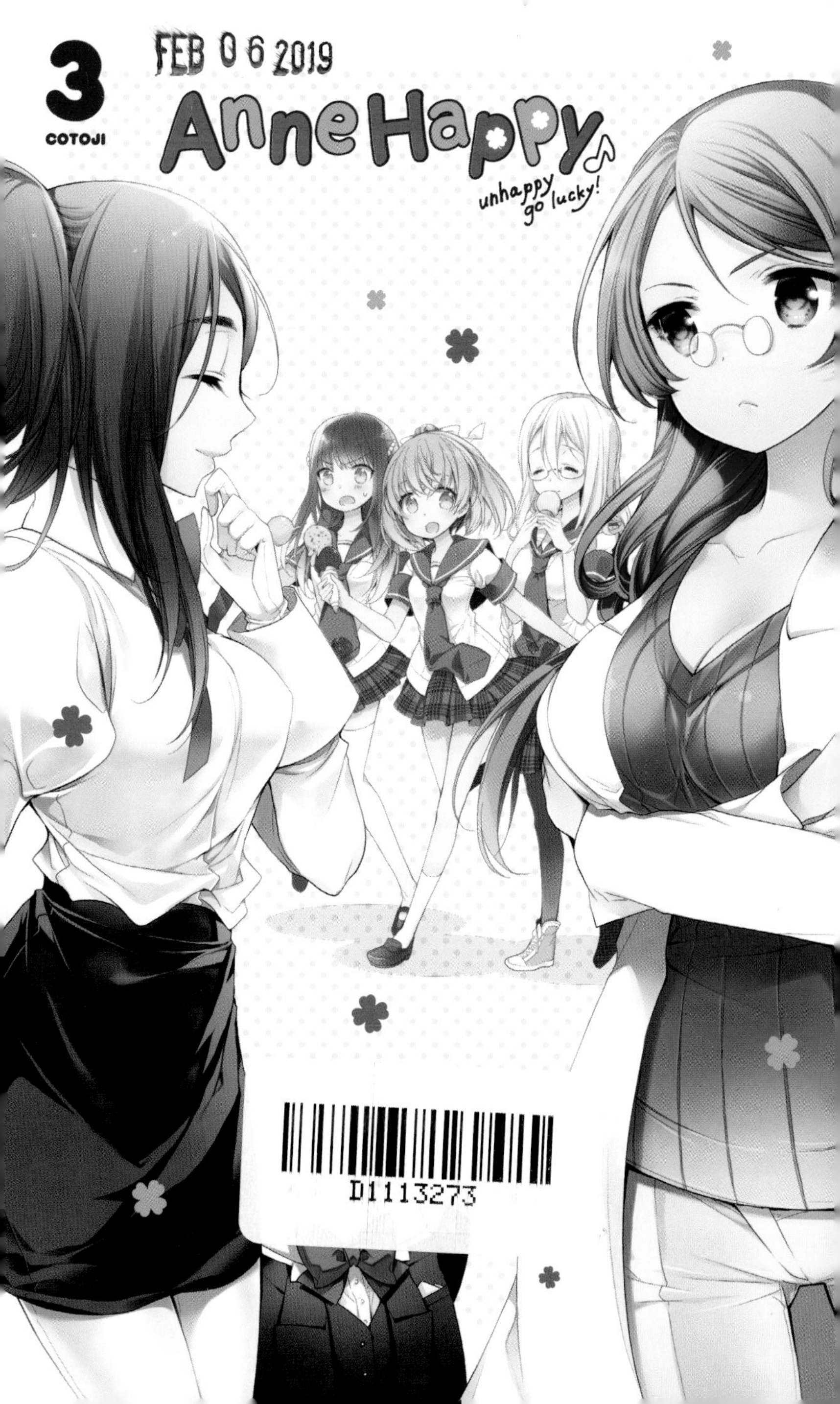
3
COTOJI
Anne Happy
unhappy go lucky!

Lucky. 15 003
Lucky. 16 027
Lucky. 17 043
Lucky. 18 059
Lucky. 19 077
Lucky. 20 103
Lucky. 21 127
Lucky. 22 153

CONTENTS

ANNE HAPPY
VOLUME THREE
COTOJI

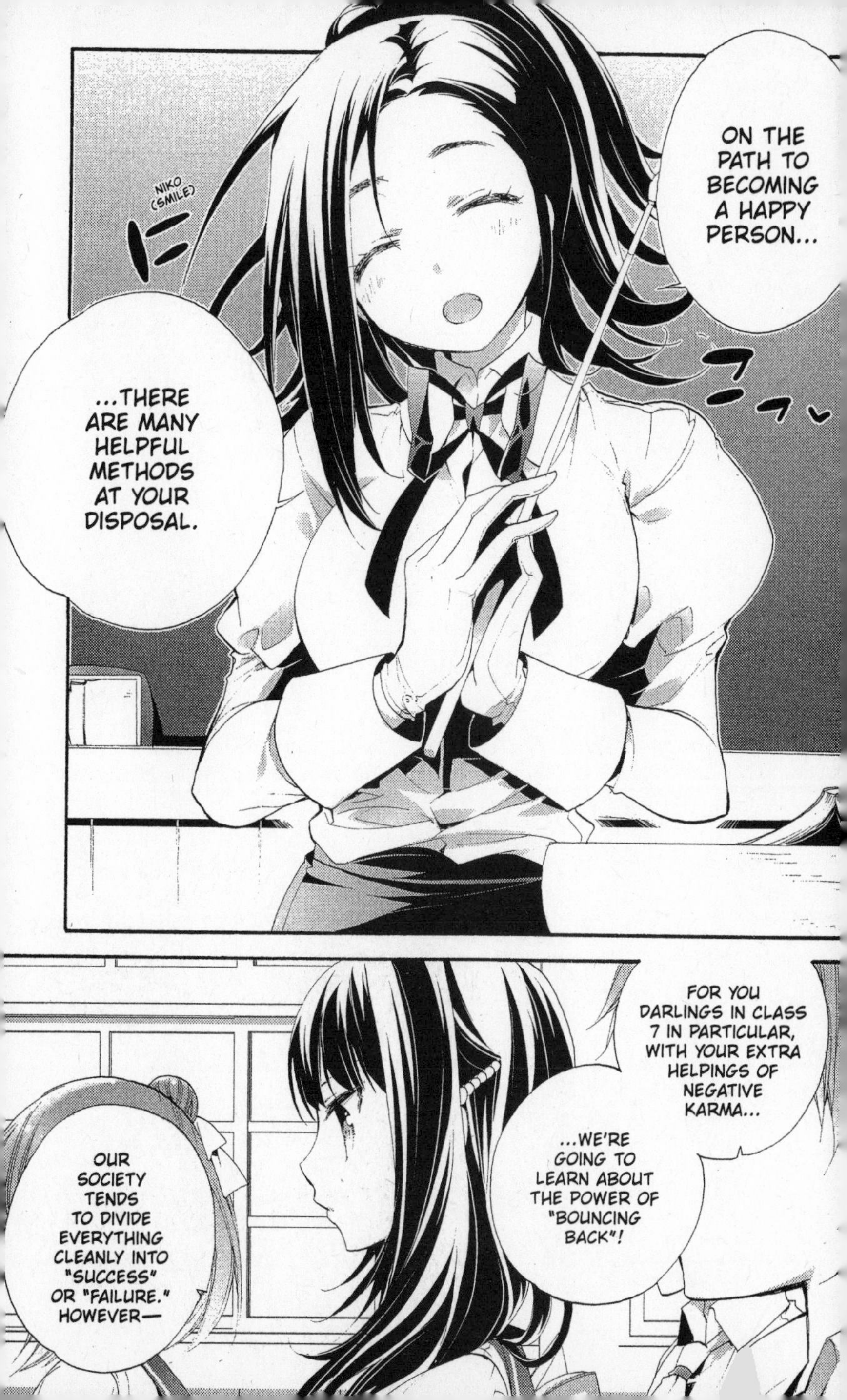
ON THE PATH TO BECOMING A HAPPY PERSON...
NIKO (SMILE)
...THERE ARE MANY HELPFUL METHODS AT YOUR DISPOSAL.
FOR YOU DARLINGS IN CLASS 7 IN PARTICULAR, WITH YOUR EXTRA HELPINGS OF NEGATIVE KARMA...
...WE'RE GOING TO LEARN ABOUT THE POWER OF "BOUNCING BACK"!
OUR SOCIETY TENDS TO DIVIDE EVERYTHING CLEANLY INTO "SUCCESS" OR "FAILURE." HOWEVER—

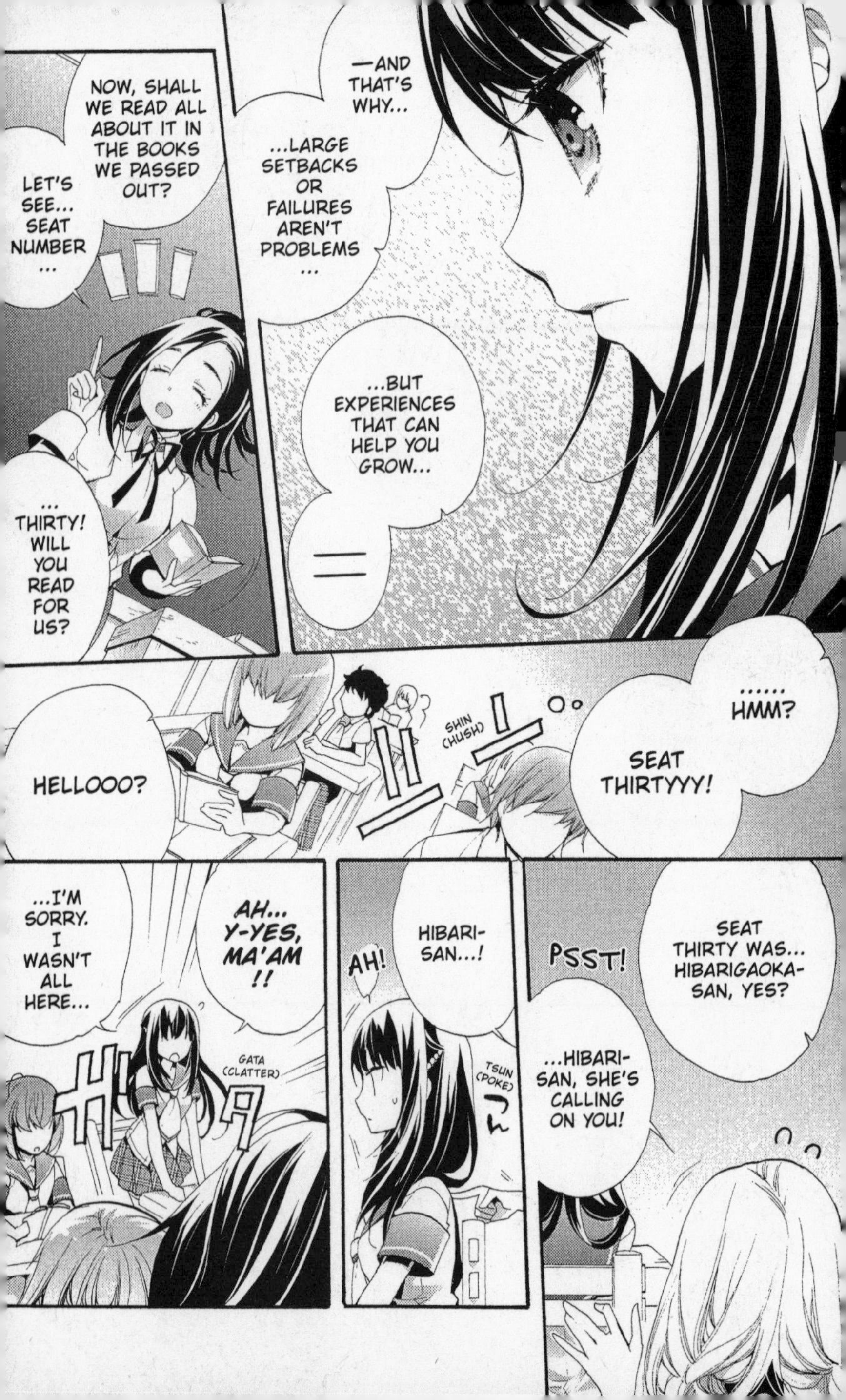
—AND THAT'S WHY...
...LARGE SETBACKS OR FAILURES AREN'T PROBLEMS...
...BUT EXPERIENCES THAT CAN HELP YOU GROW...
NOW, SHALL WE READ ALL ABOUT IT IN THE BOOKS WE PASSED OUT?
LET'S SEE... SEAT NUMBER ...
... THIRTY! WILL YOU READ FOR US?
......HMM?
SEAT THIRTYYY!
SHIN (HUSH)
HELLOOO?
SEAT THIRTY WAS... HIBARIGAOKA-SAN, YES?
PSST!
...HIBARI-SAN, SHE'S CALLING ON YOU!
HIBARI-SAN...!
AH!
TSUN (POKE)
AH... Y-YES, MA'AM!!
...I'M SORRY. I WASN'T ALL HERE...
GATA (CLATTER)

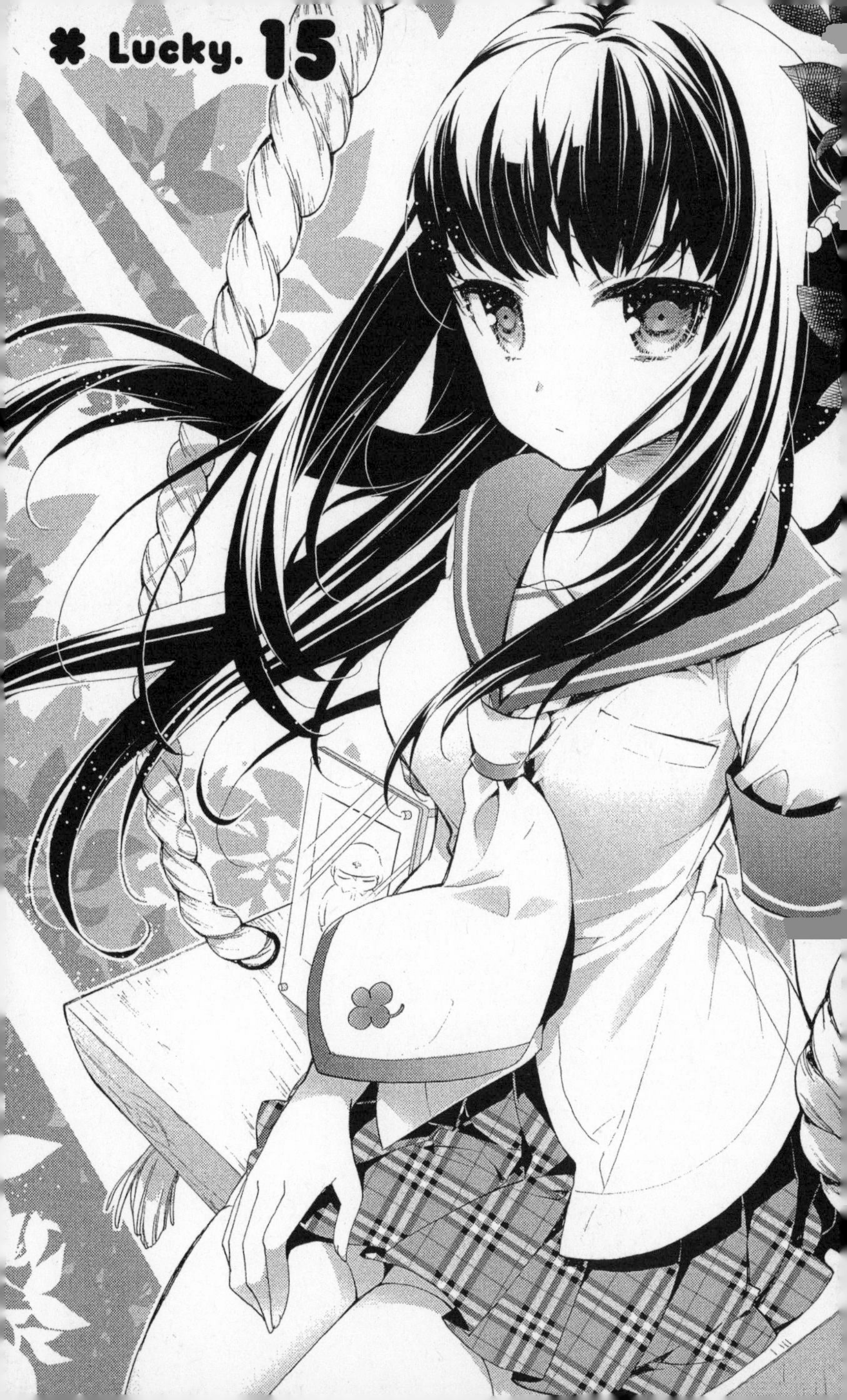
Lucky. 15

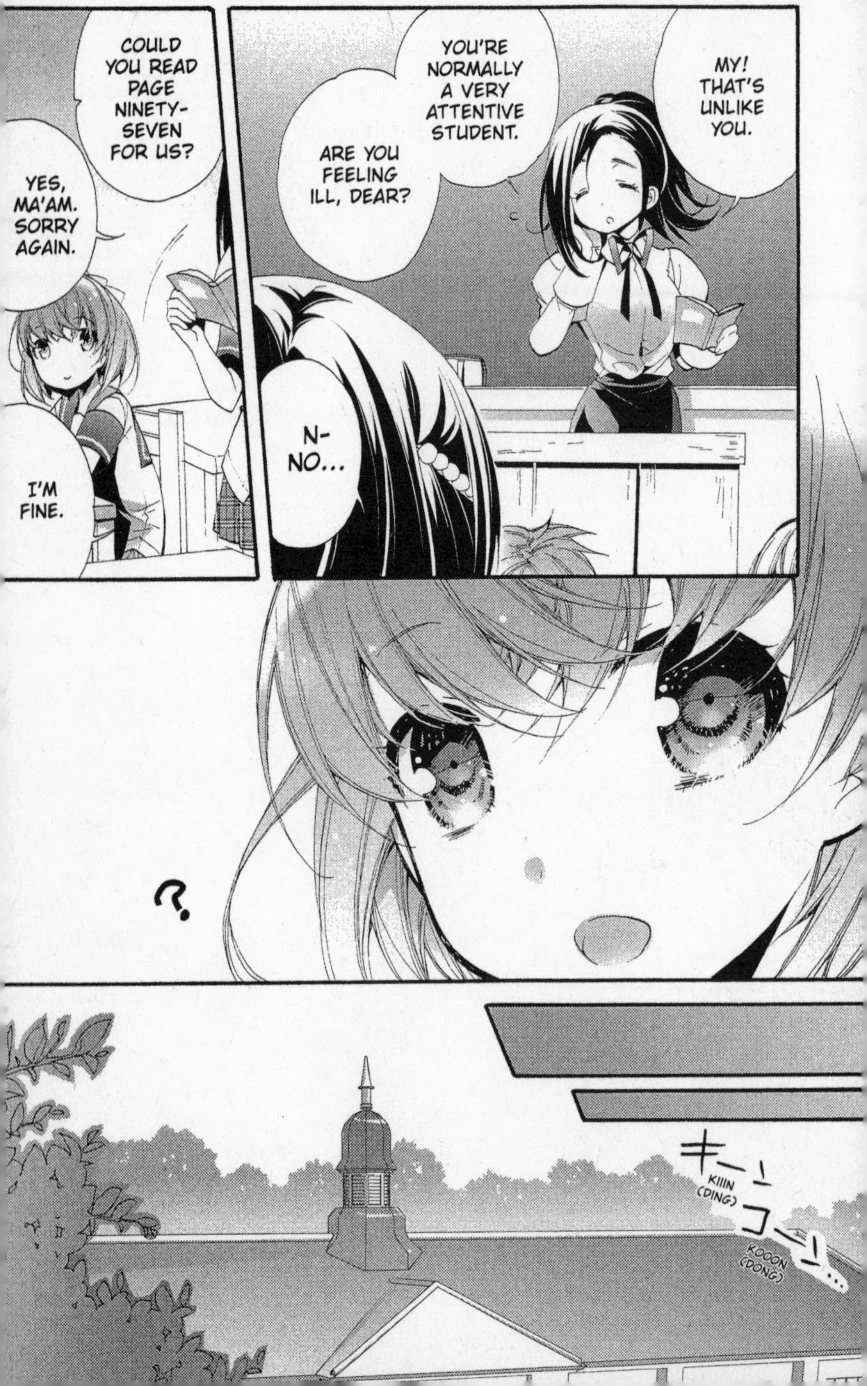
MY! THAT'S UNLIKE YOU.
YOU'RE NORMALLY A VERY ATTENTIVE STUDENT.
ARE YOU FEELING ILL, DEAR?
N-NO...
COULD YOU READ PAGE NINETY-SEVEN FOR US?
YES, MA'AM. SORRY AGAIN.
I'M FINE.
?
キーン
KIIIN (DING)
コーン…
KOOON (DONG)

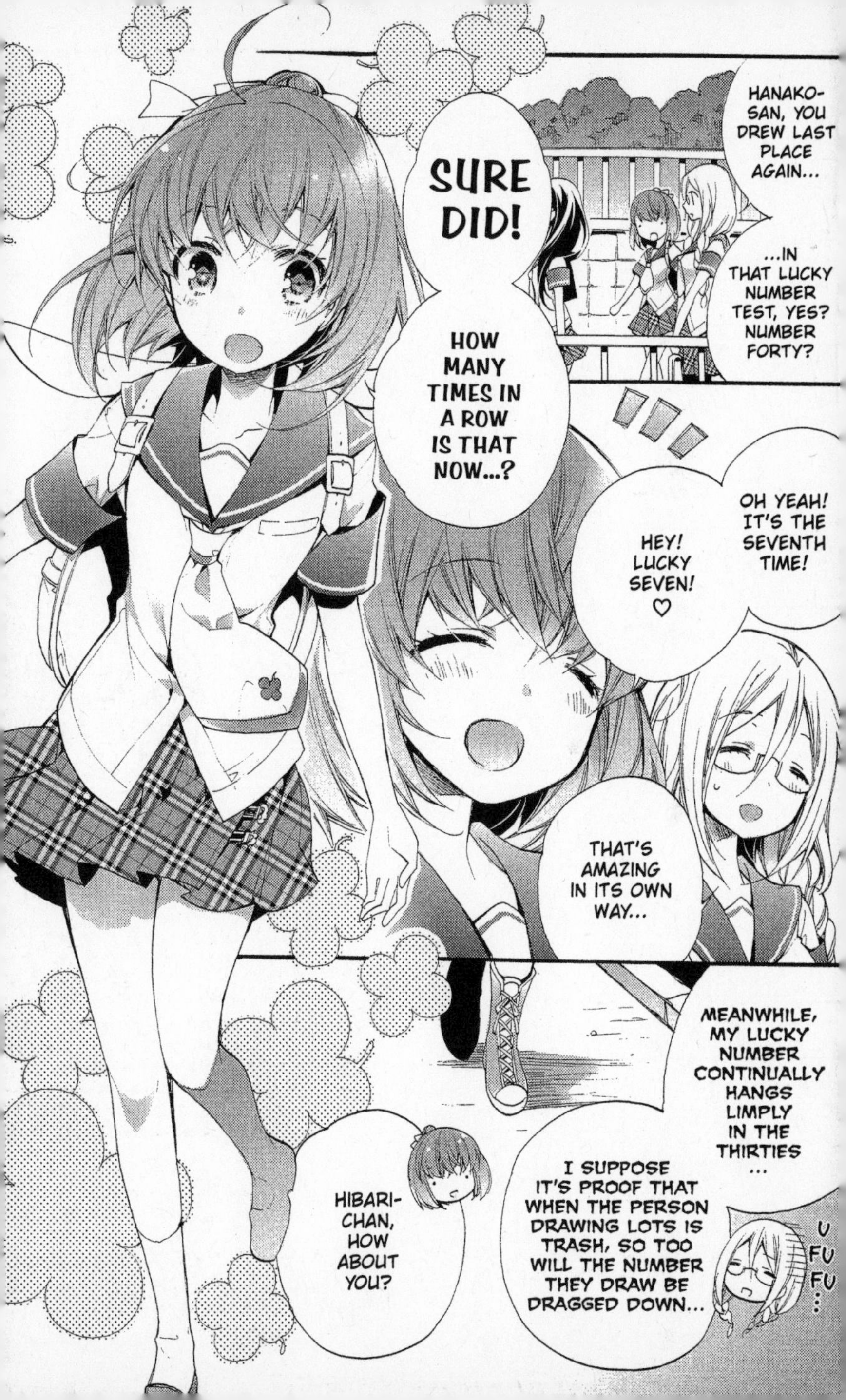

HANAKO-SAN, YOU DREW LAST PLACE AGAIN...
...IN THAT LUCKY NUMBER TEST, YES? NUMBER FORTY?
SURE DID!
HOW MANY TIMES IN A ROW IS THAT NOW...?
OH YEAH! IT'S THE SEVENTH TIME!
HEY! LUCKY SEVEN! ♡
THAT'S AMAZING IN ITS OWN WAY...
MEANWHILE, MY LUCKY NUMBER CONTINUALLY HANGS LIMPLY IN THE THIRTIES...
UFUFU...
I SUPPOSE IT'S PROOF THAT WHEN THE PERSON DRAWING LOTS IS TRASH, SO TOO WILL THE NUMBER THEY DRAW BE DRAGGED DOWN...
HIBARI-CHAN, HOW ABOUT YOU?

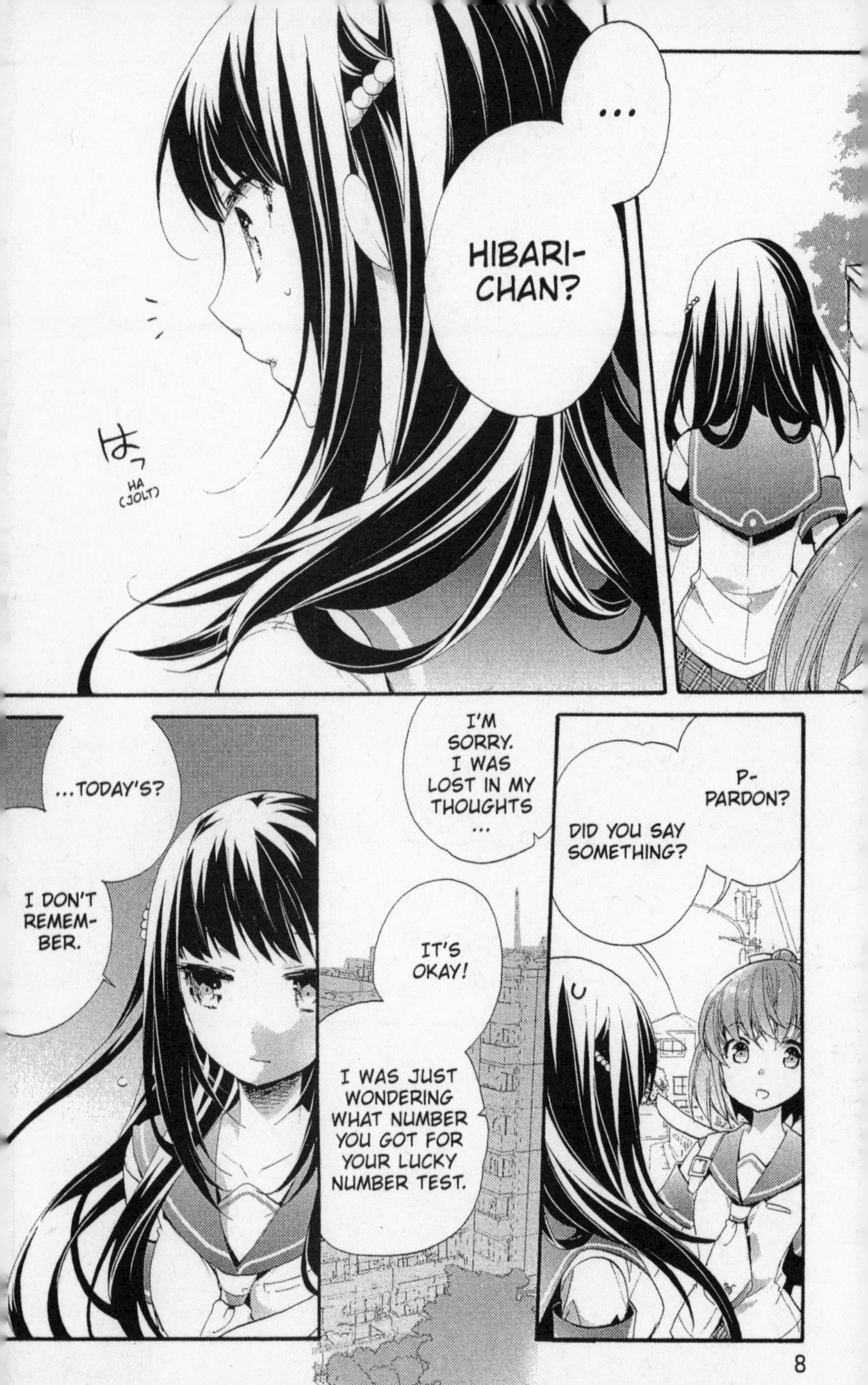
...
HIBARI-CHAN?
はっ
HA (JOLT)
P-PARDON?
DID YOU SAY SOMETHING?
I'M SORRY. I WAS LOST IN MY THOUGHTS...
IT'S OKAY!
I WAS JUST WONDERING WHAT NUMBER YOU GOT FOR YOUR LUCKY NUMBER TEST.
...TODAY'S?
I DON'T REMEMBER.

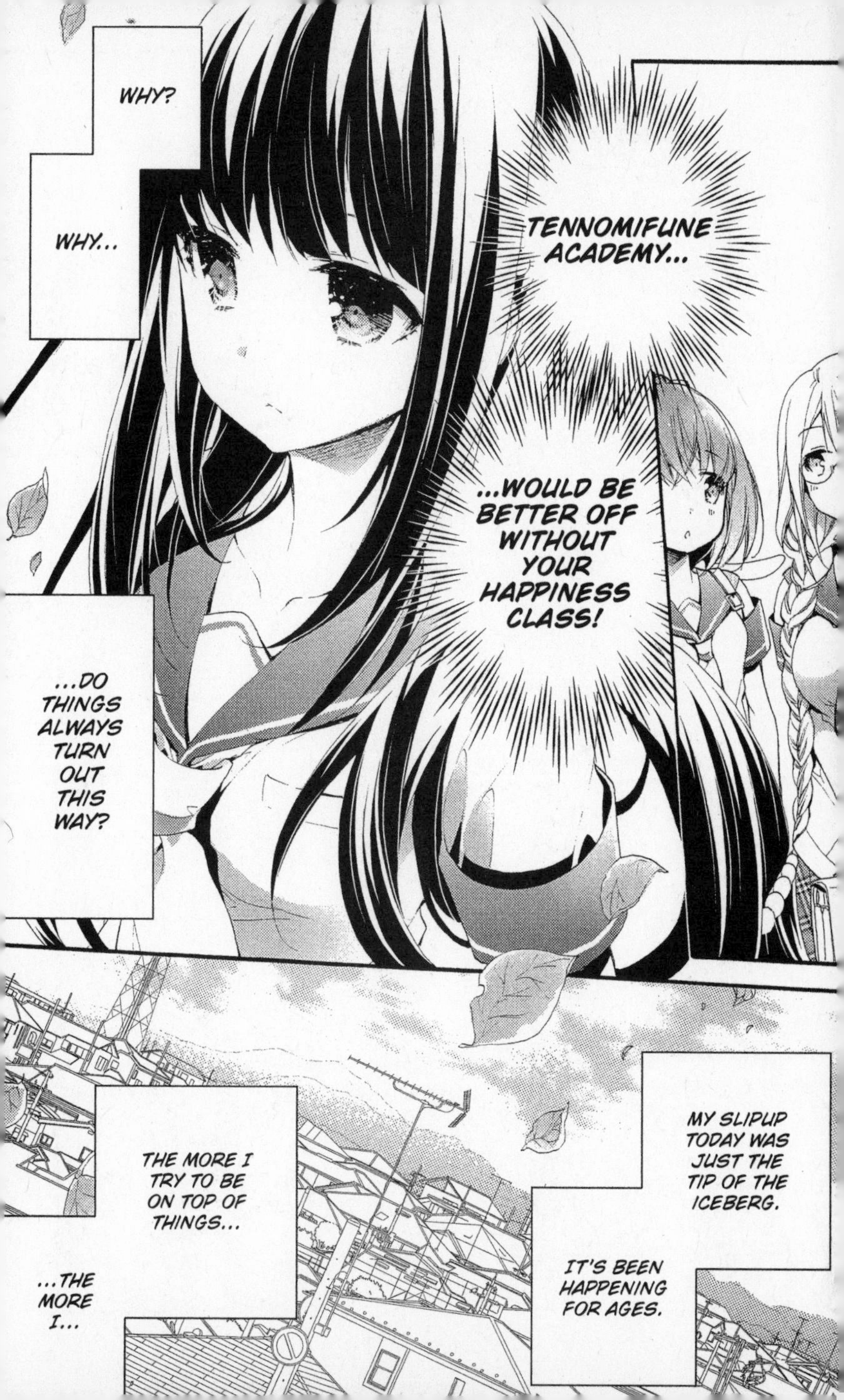
TENNOMIFUNE ACADEMY...
...WOULD BE BETTER OFF WITHOUT YOUR HAPPINESS CLASS!
WHY?
WHY...
...DO THINGS ALWAYS TURN OUT THIS WAY?
MY SLIPUP TODAY WAS JUST THE TIP OF THE ICEBERG.
IT'S BEEN HAPPENING FOR AGES.
THE MORE I TRY TO BE ON TOP OF THINGS...
...THE MORE I...

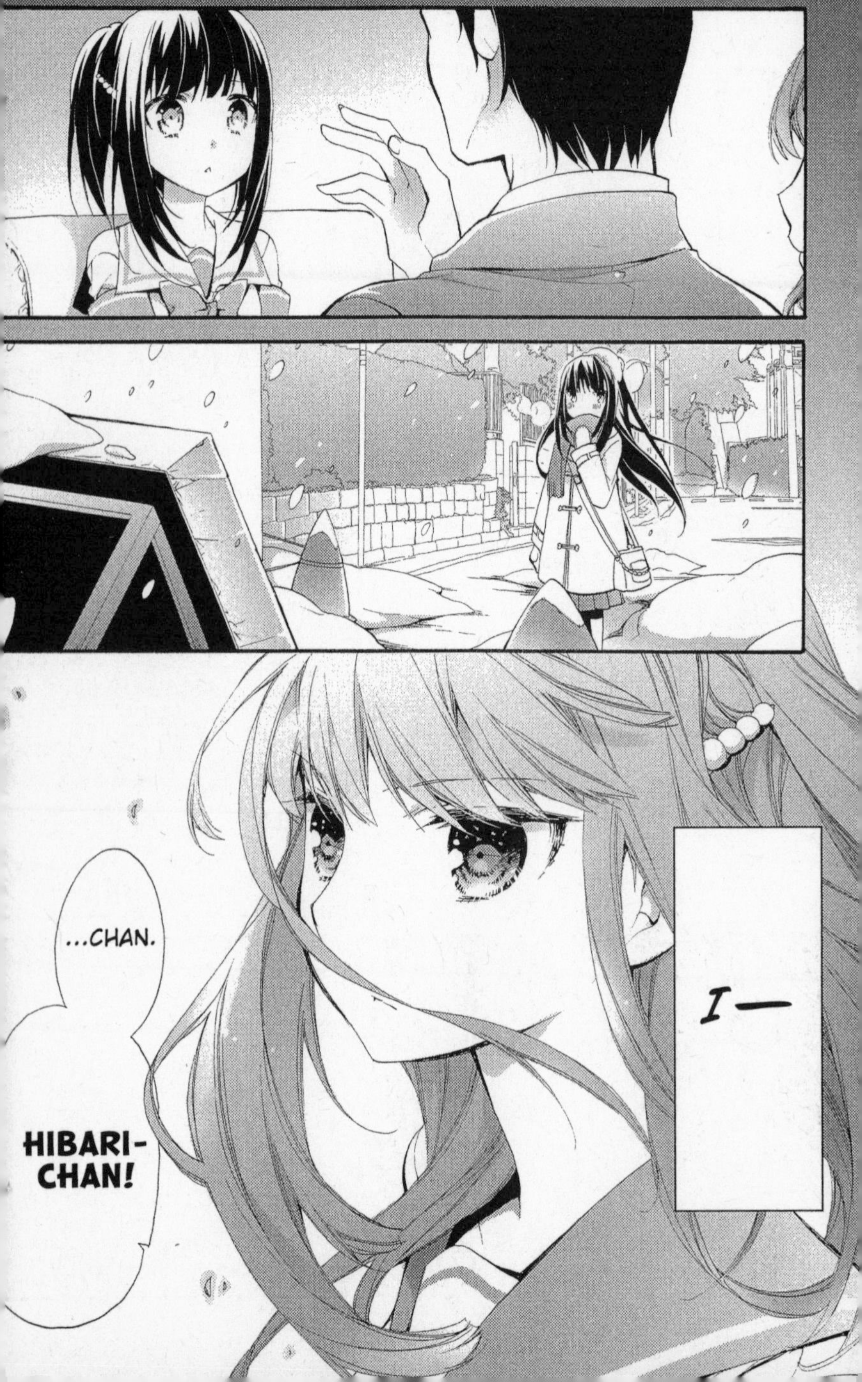
I—
...CHAN.
HIBARI-CHAN!

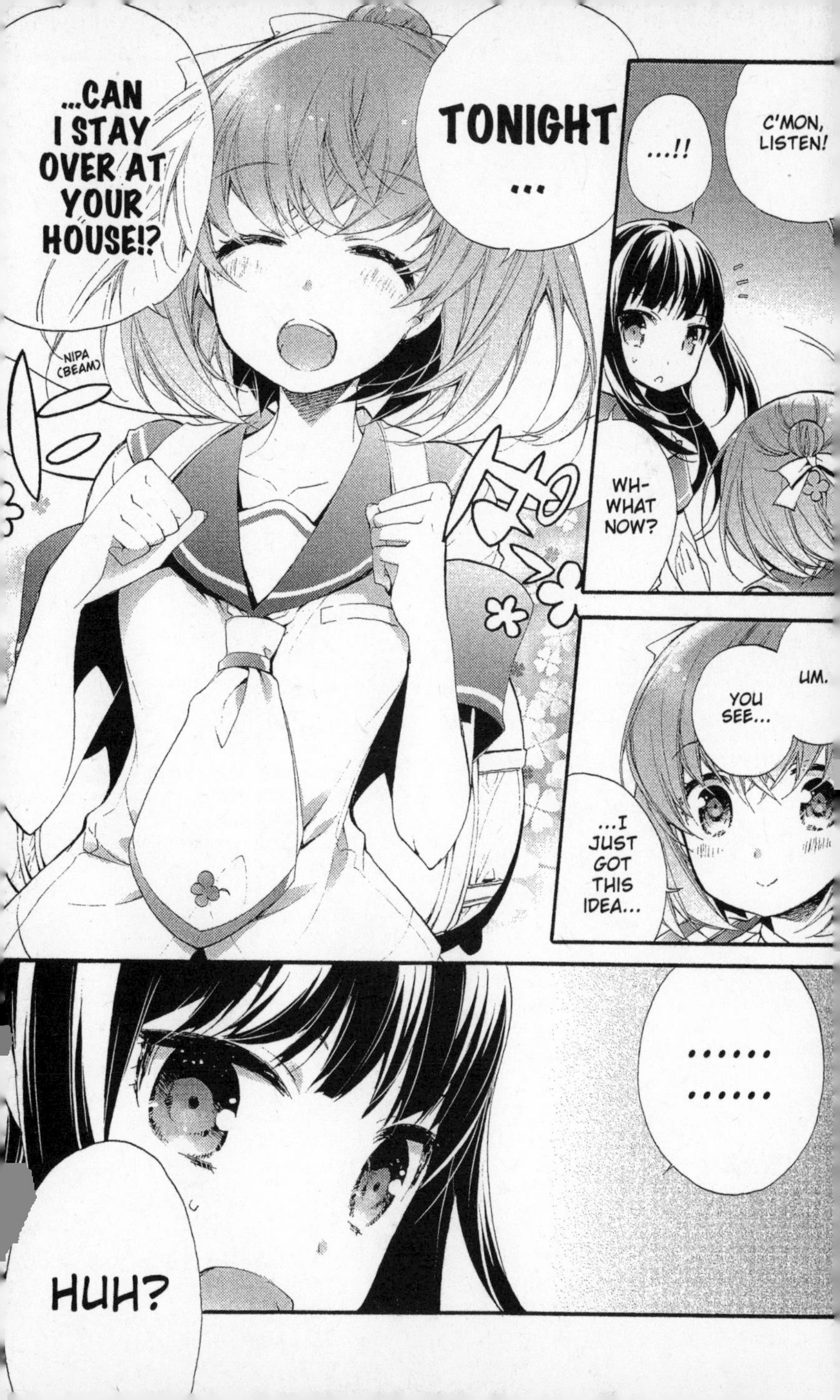
C'MON, LISTEN!
...!!
WH-WHAT NOW?
UM.
YOU SEE...
...I JUST GOT THIS IDEA...
TONIGHT ...
...CAN I STAY OVER AT YOUR HOUSE!?
NIPA (BEAM)
....
HUH?

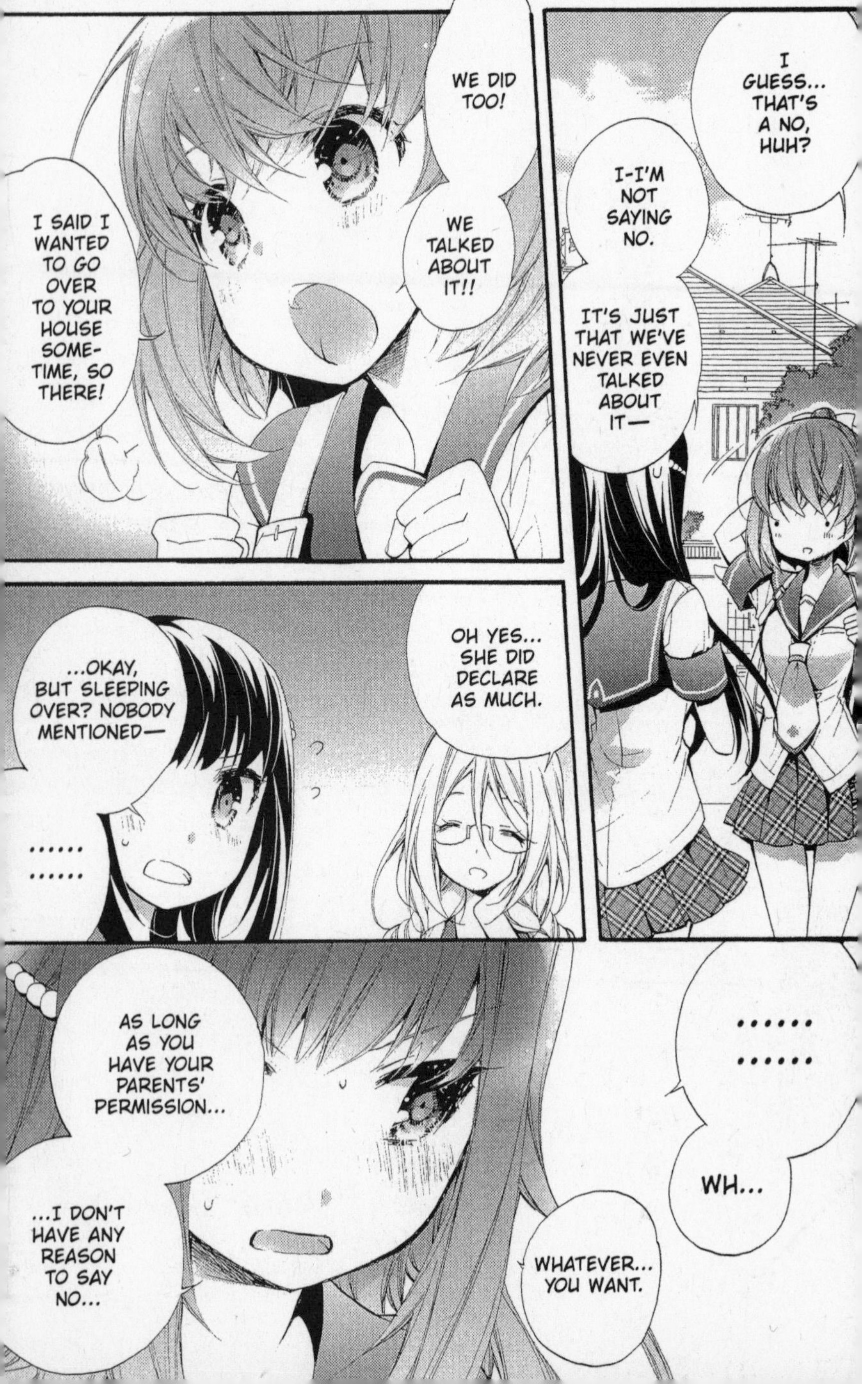
I GUESS... THAT'S A NO, HUH?
I-I'M NOT SAYING NO.
IT'S JUST THAT WE'VE NEVER EVEN TALKED ABOUT IT—
WE DID TOO!
WE TALKED ABOUT IT!!
I SAID I WANTED TO GO OVER TO YOUR HOUSE SOMETIME, SO THERE!
OH YES... SHE DID DECLARE AS MUCH.
...OKAY, BUT SLEEPING OVER? NOBODY MENTIONED—
....
....
WH...
AS LONG AS YOU HAVE YOUR PARENTS' PERMISSION...
...I DON'T HAVE ANY REASON TO SAY NO...
WHATEVER... YOU WANT.

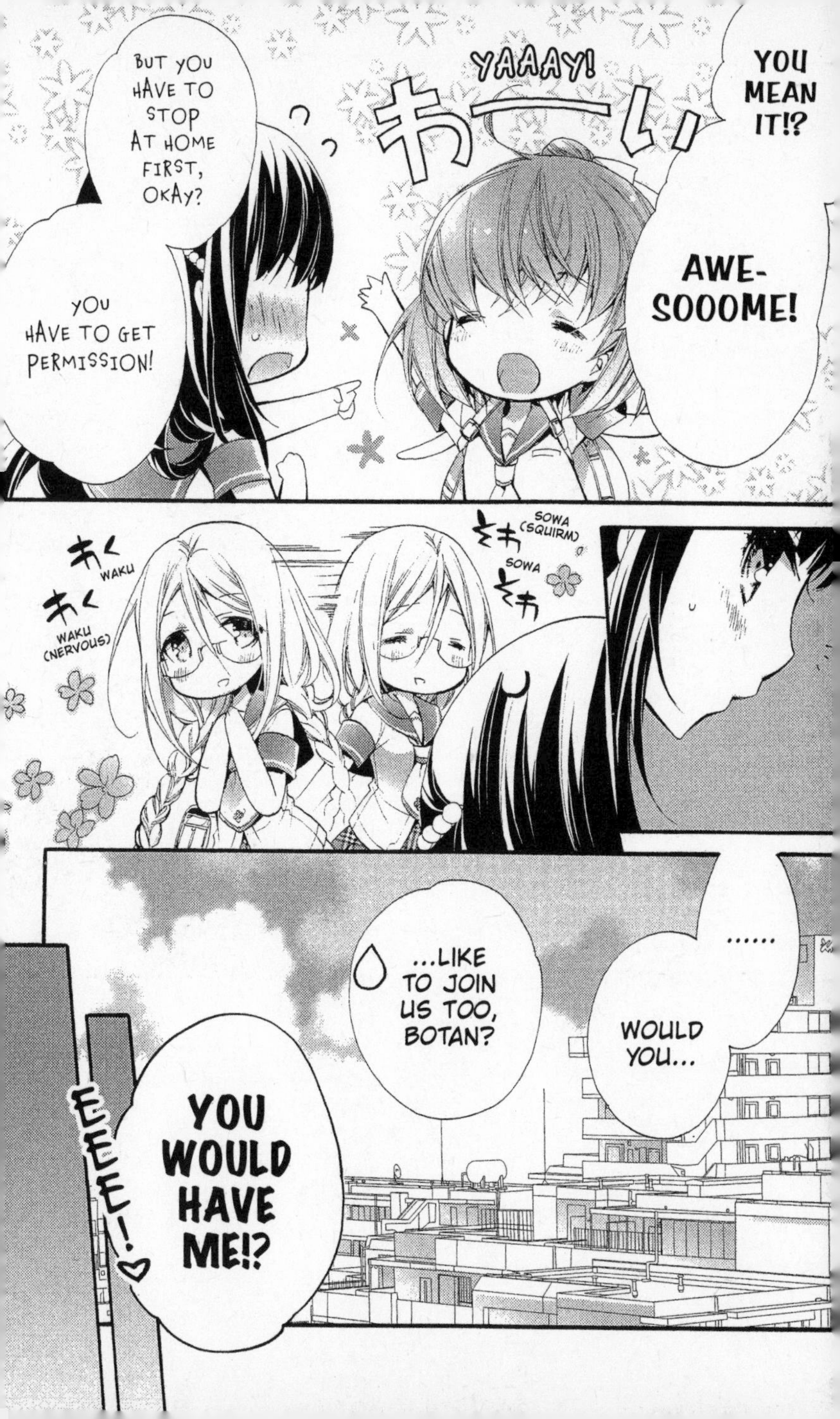
YOU MEAN IT!?
AWE-SOOOME!
YAAAY!
わーい
BUT YOU HAVE TO STOP AT HOME FIRST, OKAY?
YOU HAVE TO GET PERMISSION!
そわ SOWA (SQUIRM)
そわ SOWA
わく WAKU
わく WAKU (NERVOUS)
......
WOULD YOU...
...LIKE TO JOIN US TOO, BOTAN?
YOU WOULD HAVE ME!?
EEEE!♥

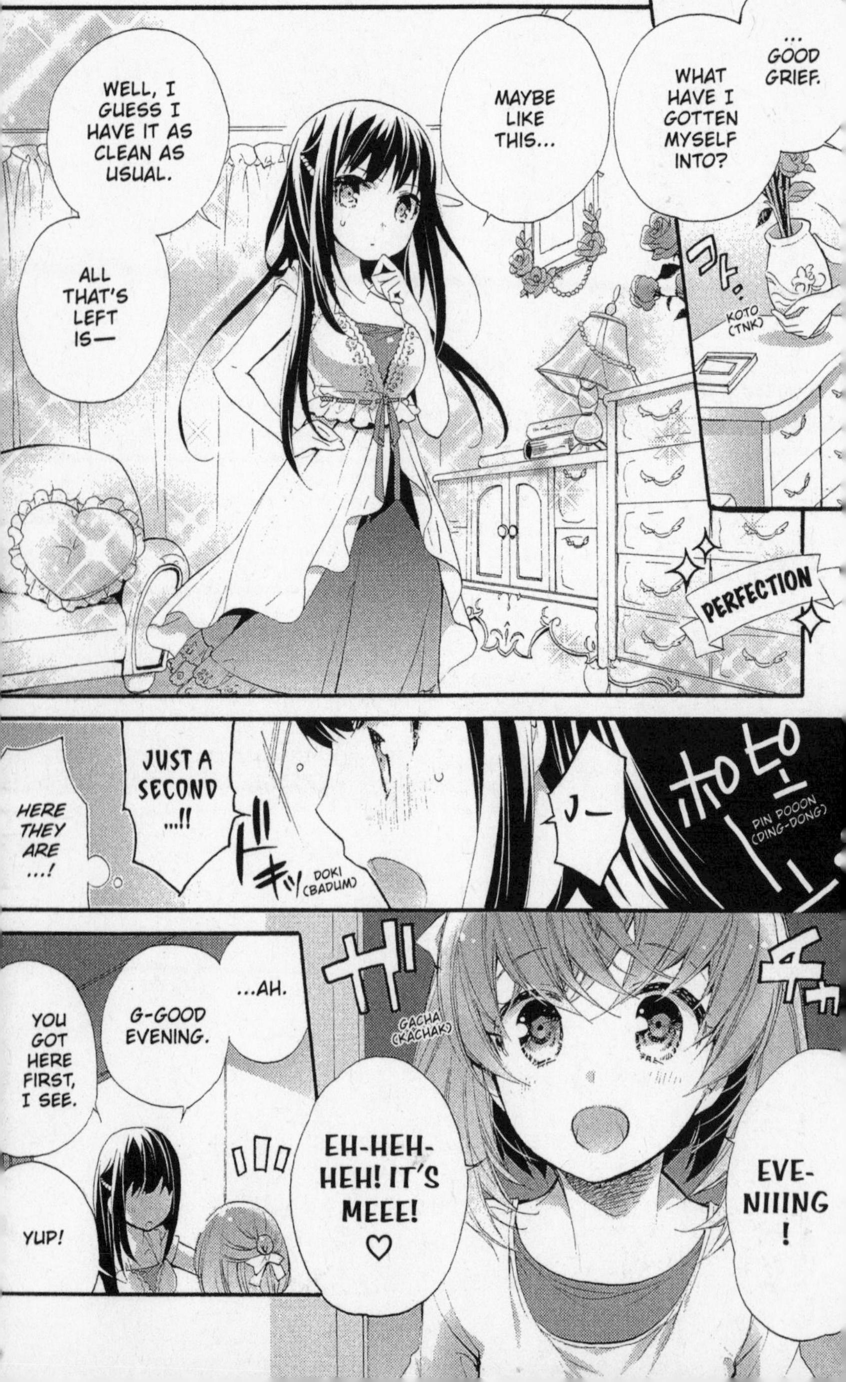
... GOOD GRIEF.
WHAT HAVE I GOTTEN MYSELF INTO?
コト。
KOTO (TNK)
MAYBE LIKE THIS...
WELL, I GUESS I HAVE IT AS CLEAN AS USUAL.
ALL THAT'S LEFT IS—
PERFECTION
ピンポーン
PIN POOON (DING-DONG)
J—
ドキッ
DOKI (BADUM)
JUST A SECOND ...!!
HERE THEY ARE ...!
ガチャ
GACHA (KACHAK)
EVE-NIIING!
EH-HEH-HEH! IT'S MEEE! ♡
...AH.
G-GOOD EVENING.
YOU GOT HERE FIRST, I SEE.
YUP!

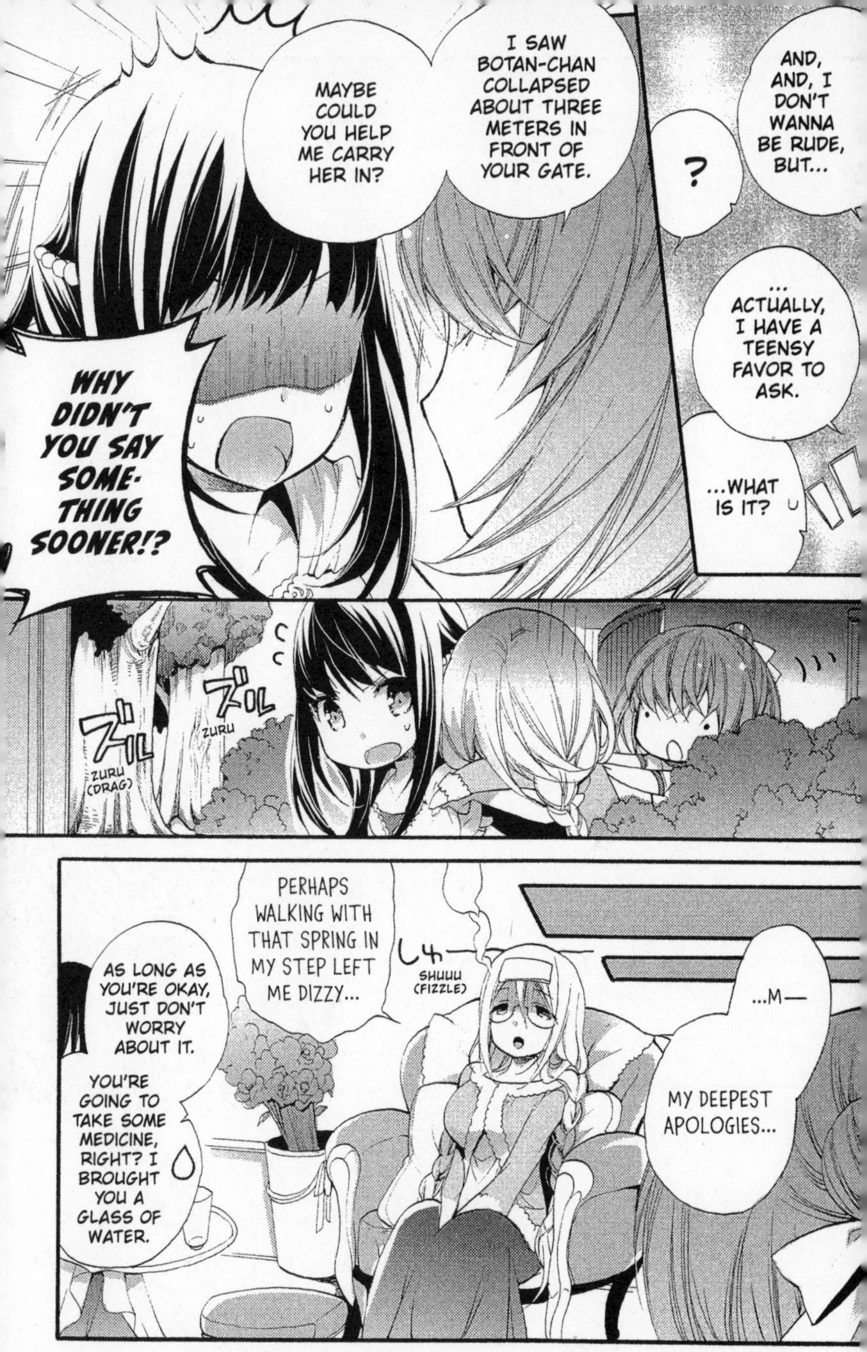
AND, AND, I DON'T WANNA BE RUDE, BUT...
?
... ACTUALLY, I HAVE A TEENSY FAVOR TO ASK.
...WHAT IS IT?
I SAW BOTAN-CHAN COLLAPSED ABOUT THREE METERS IN FRONT OF YOUR GATE.
MAYBE COULD YOU HELP ME CARRY HER IN?
WHY DIDN'T YOU SAY SOME-THING SOONER!?
ズル
ZURU
ズル
ZURU (DRAG)
...M—
MY DEEPEST APOLOGIES...
しゅー
SHUUU (FIZZLE)
PERHAPS WALKING WITH THAT SPRING IN MY STEP LEFT ME DIZZY...
AS LONG AS YOU'RE OKAY, JUST DON'T WORRY ABOUT IT.
YOU'RE GOING TO TAKE SOME MEDICINE, RIGHT? I BROUGHT YOU A GLASS OF WATER.

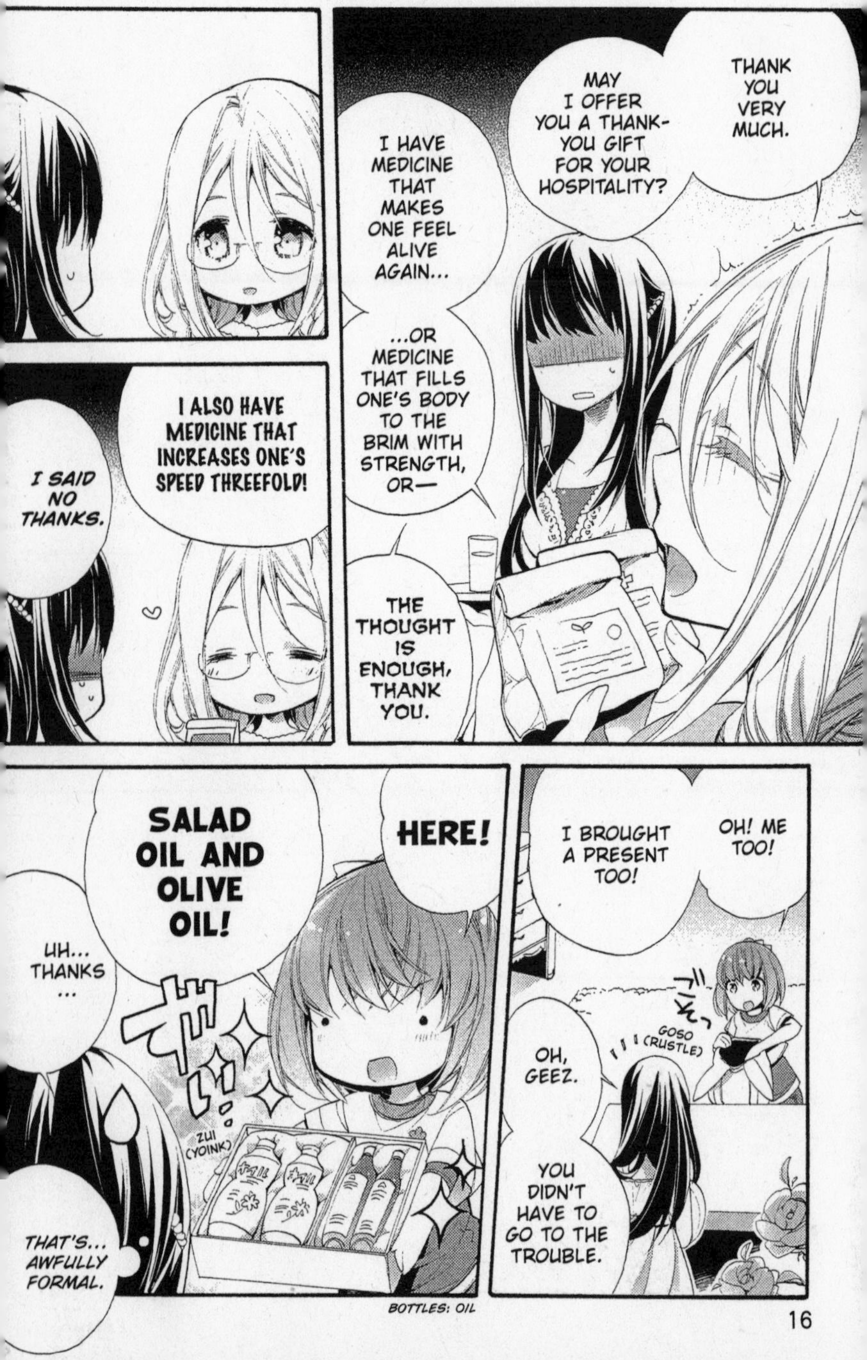
THANK YOU VERY MUCH.
MAY I OFFER YOU A THANK-YOU GIFT FOR YOUR HOSPITALITY?
I HAVE MEDICINE THAT MAKES ONE FEEL ALIVE AGAIN...
...OR MEDICINE THAT FILLS ONE'S BODY TO THE BRIM WITH STRENGTH, OR—
THE THOUGHT IS ENOUGH, THANK YOU.
I ALSO HAVE MEDICINE THAT INCREASES ONE'S SPEED THREEFOLD!
I SAID NO THANKS.
OH! ME TOO!
I BROUGHT A PRESENT TOO!
GOSO (RUSTLE)
OH, GEEZ.
YOU DIDN'T HAVE TO GO TO THE TROUBLE.
HERE!
SALAD OIL AND OLIVE OIL!
ZUI (YOINK)
UH... THANKS...
THAT'S... AWFULLY FORMAL.

BOTTLES: OIL

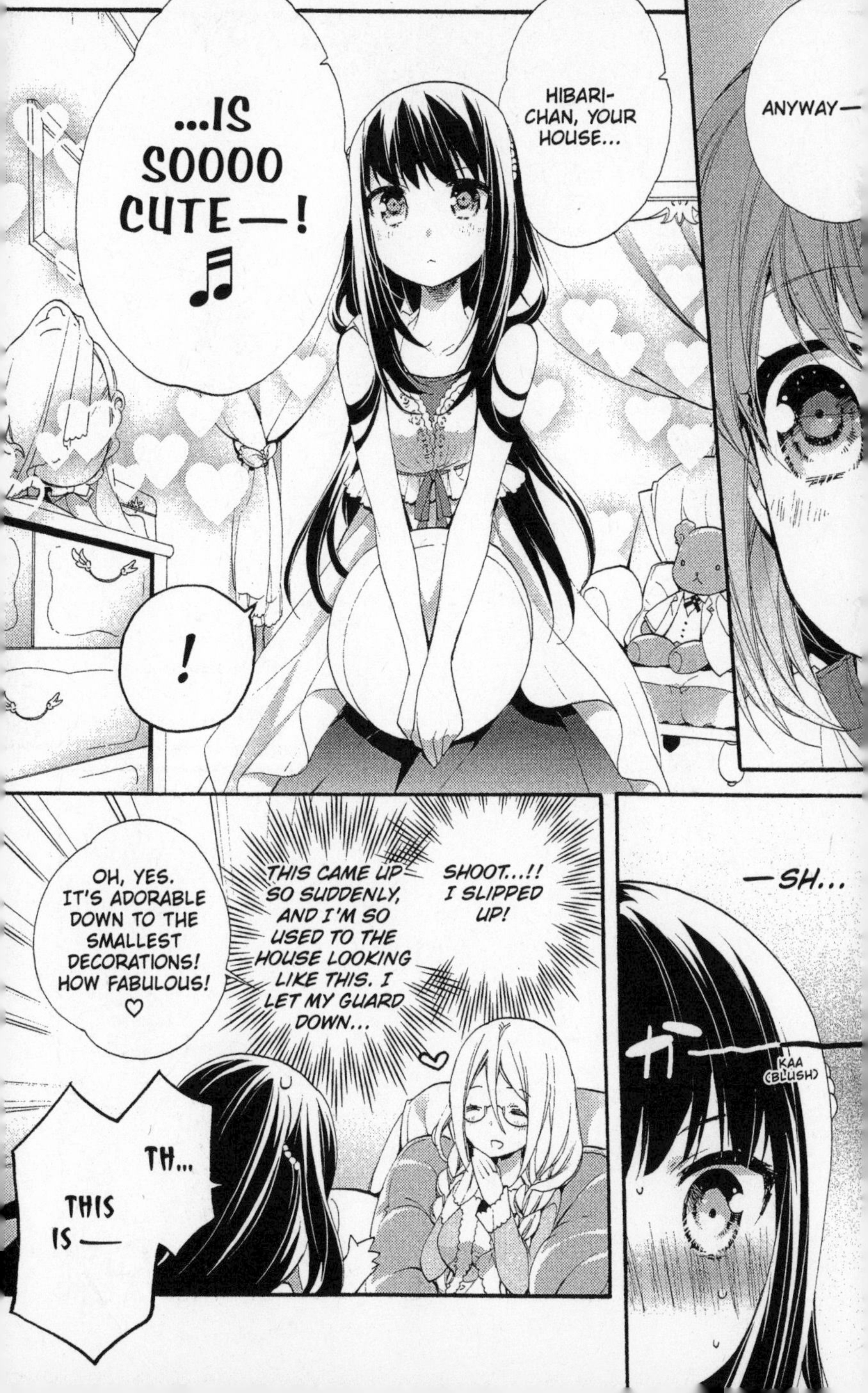
ANYWAY—
HIBARI-CHAN, YOUR HOUSE...
...IS SOOOO CUTE—! ♫
!
—SH...
KAA (BLUSH)
SHOOT...!! I SLIPPED UP!
THIS CAME UP SO SUDDENLY, AND I'M SO USED TO THE HOUSE LOOKING LIKE THIS. I LET MY GUARD DOWN...
OH, YES. IT'S ADORABLE DOWN TO THE SMALLEST DECORATIONS! HOW FABULOUS! ♡
TH... THIS IS—

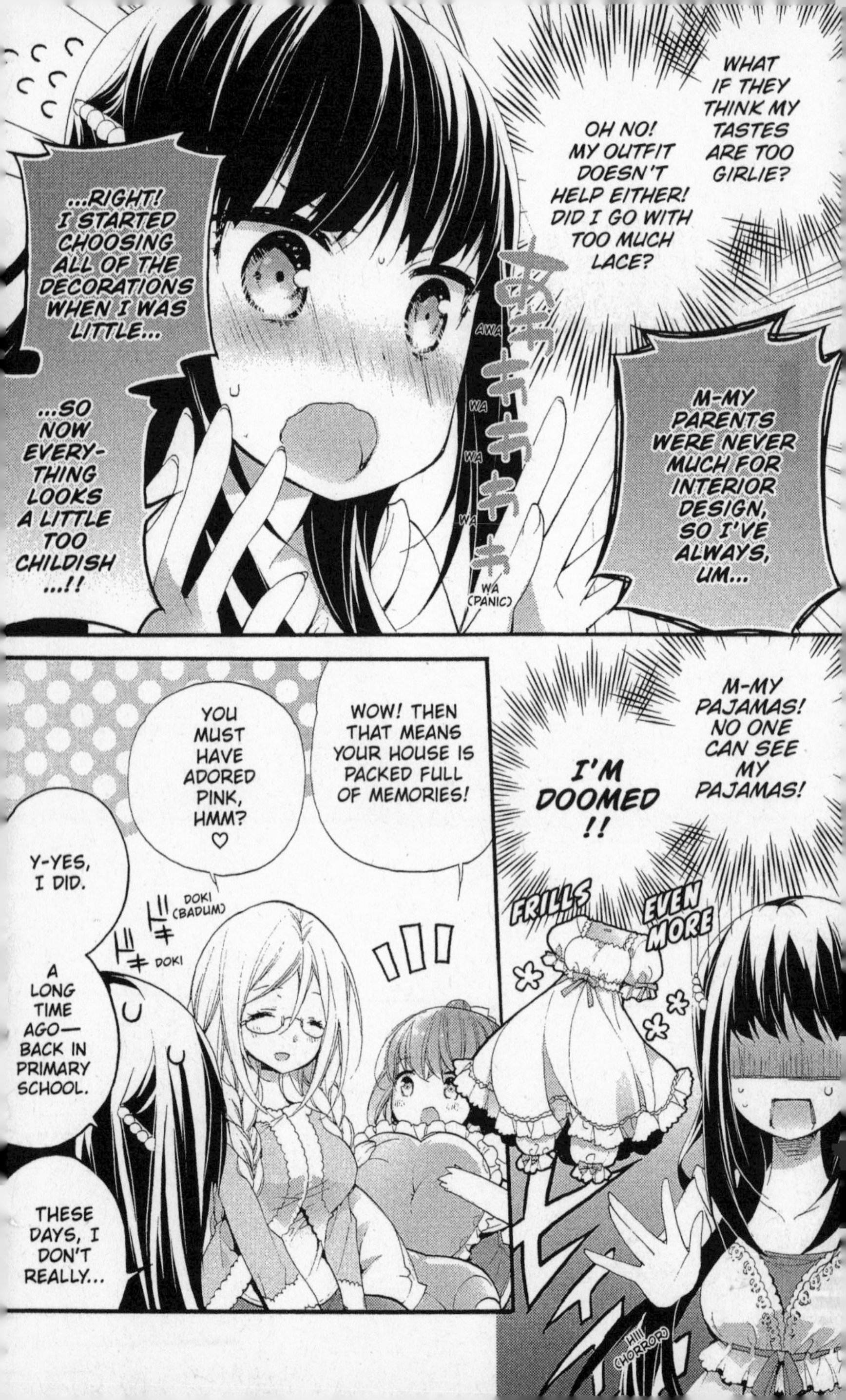
WHAT IF THEY THINK MY TASTES ARE TOO GIRLIE?
OH NO! MY OUTFIT DOESN'T HELP EITHER! DID I GO WITH TOO MUCH LACE?
M-MY PARENTS WERE NEVER MUCH FOR INTERIOR DESIGN, SO I'VE ALWAYS, UM...
AWA WA WA WA WA (PANIC)
...RIGHT! I STARTED CHOOSING ALL OF THE DECORATIONS WHEN I WAS LITTLE...
...SO NOW EVERY-THING LOOKS A LITTLE TOO CHILDISH ...!!
M-MY PAJAMAS! NO ONE CAN SEE MY PAJAMAS!
I'M DOOMED !!
EVEN MORE
FRILLS
HIII (HORROR)
WOW! THEN THAT MEANS YOUR HOUSE IS PACKED FULL OF MEMORIES!
YOU MUST HAVE ADORED PINK, HMM? ♡
DOKI (BADUM)
DOKI
!!!
Y-YES, I DID.
A LONG TIME AGO— BACK IN PRIMARY SCHOOL.
THESE DAYS, I DON'T REALLY...

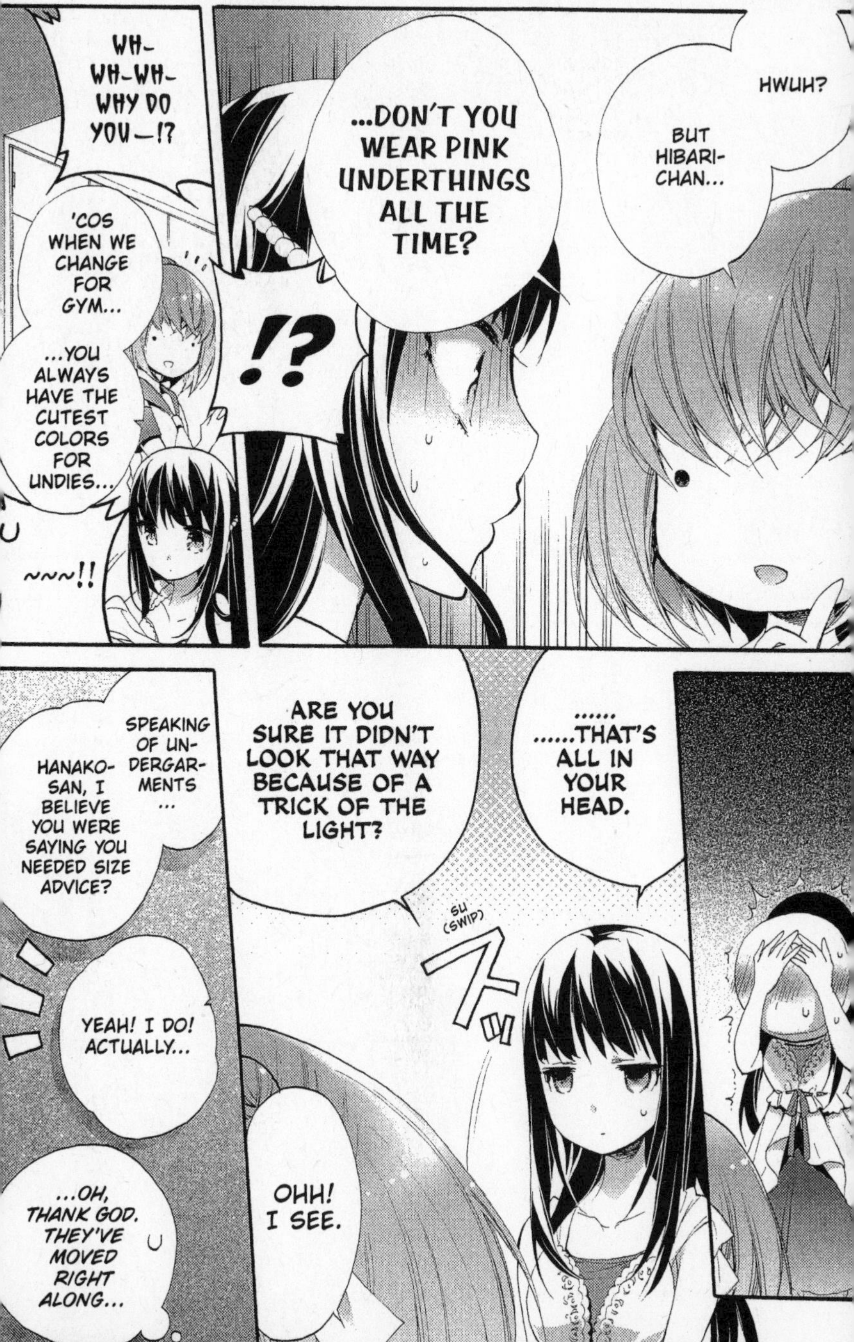
HWUH?
BUT HIBARI-CHAN...
...DON'T YOU WEAR PINK UNDERTHINGS ALL THE TIME?
!?
WH-WH-WH-WHY DO YOU—!?
'COS WHEN WE CHANGE FOR GYM...
...YOU ALWAYS HAVE THE CUTEST COLORS FOR UNDIES...
~~~!!
....THAT'S ALL IN YOUR HEAD.
ARE YOU SURE IT DIDN'T LOOK THAT WAY BECAUSE OF A TRICK OF THE LIGHT?
SU (SWIP)
OHH! I SEE.
SPEAKING OF UNDERGARMENTS...
HANAKO-SAN, I BELIEVE YOU WERE SAYING YOU NEEDED SIZE ADVICE?
YEAH! I DO! ACTUALLY...
...OH, THANK GOD. THEY'VE MOVED RIGHT ALONG...
~~~

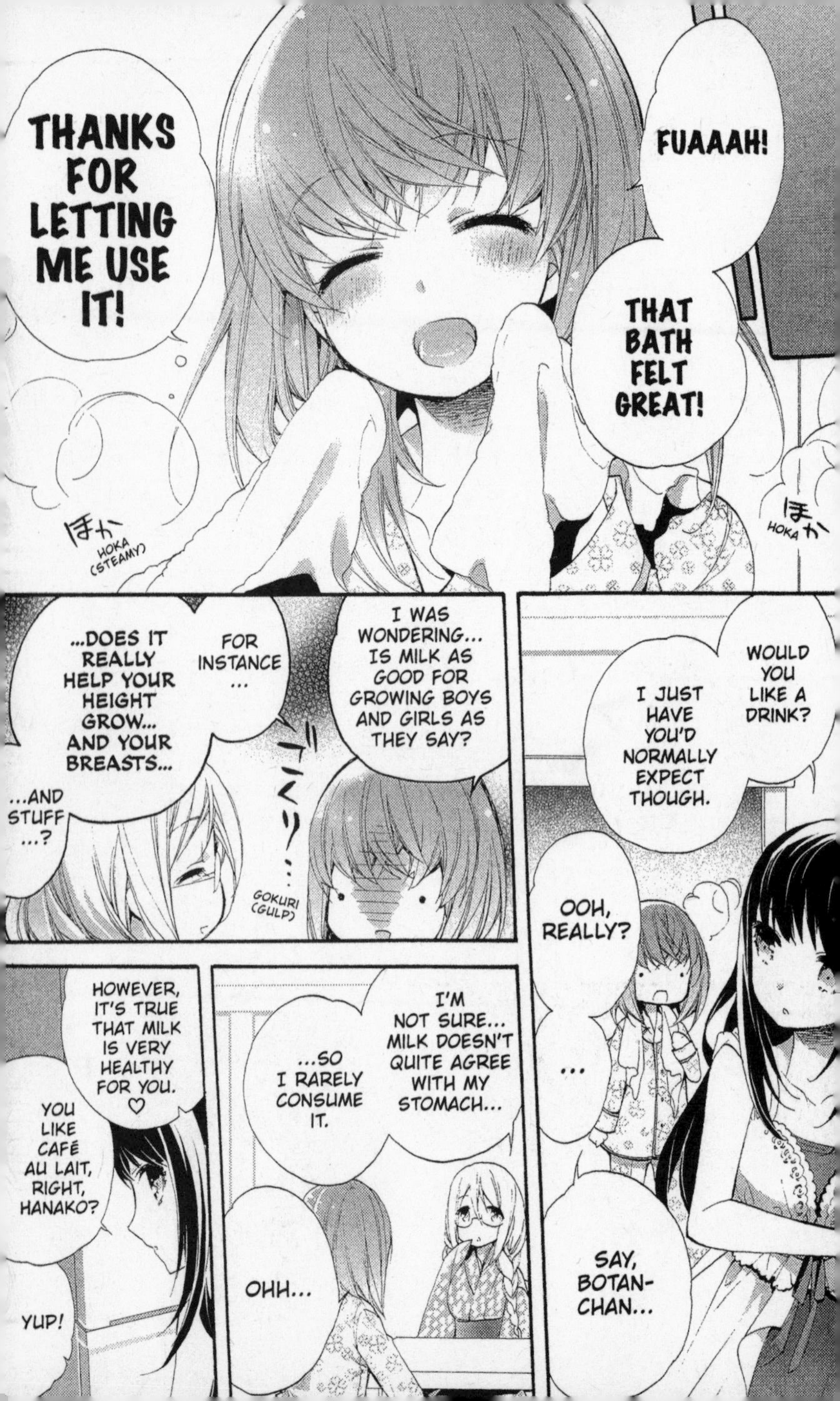
FUAAAH!
THAT BATH FELT GREAT!
THANKS FOR LETTING ME USE IT!
ほか
HOKA
ほか
HOKA (STEAMY)
WOULD YOU LIKE A DRINK?
I JUST HAVE YOU'D NORMALLY EXPECT THOUGH.
OOH, REALLY?
...
SAY, BOTAN-CHAN...
I WAS WONDERING... IS MILK AS GOOD FOR GROWING BOYS AND GIRLS AS THEY SAY?
FOR INSTANCE...
...DOES IT REALLY HELP YOUR HEIGHT GROW... AND YOUR BREASTS...
...AND STUFF...?
ゴくリ…
GOKURI (GULP)
I'M NOT SURE... MILK DOESN'T QUITE AGREE WITH MY STOMACH...
...SO I RARELY CONSUME IT.
OHH...
HOWEVER, IT'S TRUE THAT MILK IS VERY HEALTHY FOR YOU. ♡
YOU LIKE CAFÉ AU LAIT, RIGHT, HANAKO?
YUP!

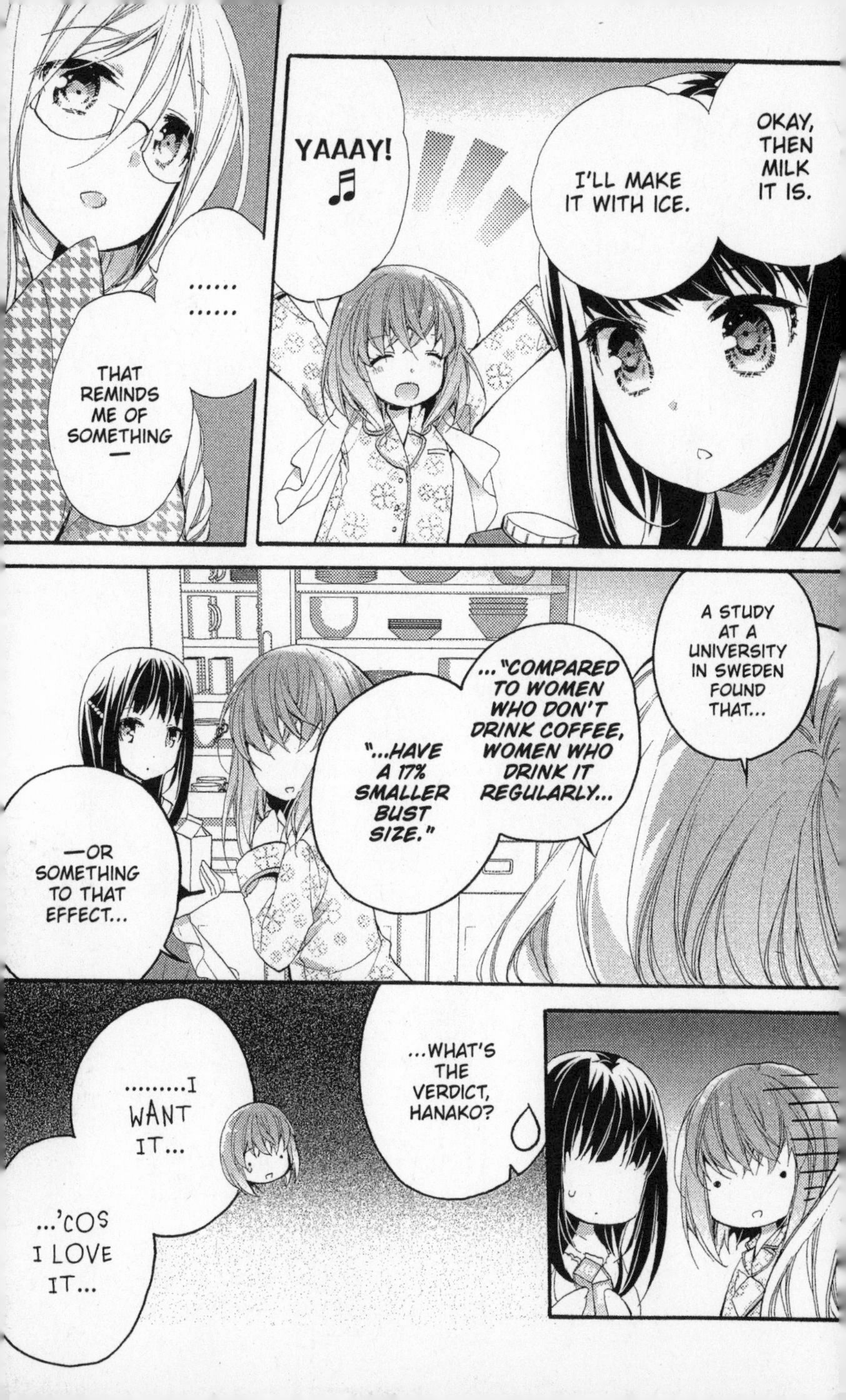
OKAY, THEN MILK IT IS.
I'LL MAKE IT WITH ICE.
YAAAY! ♬
......
......
THAT REMINDS ME OF SOMETHING—
A STUDY AT A UNIVERSITY IN SWEDEN FOUND THAT...
..."COMPARED TO WOMEN WHO DON'T DRINK COFFEE, WOMEN WHO DRINK IT REGULARLY...
"...HAVE A 17% SMALLER BUST SIZE."
—OR SOMETHING TO THAT EFFECT...
...WHAT'S THE VERDICT, HANAKO?
.........I WANT IT...
...'COS I LOVE IT...

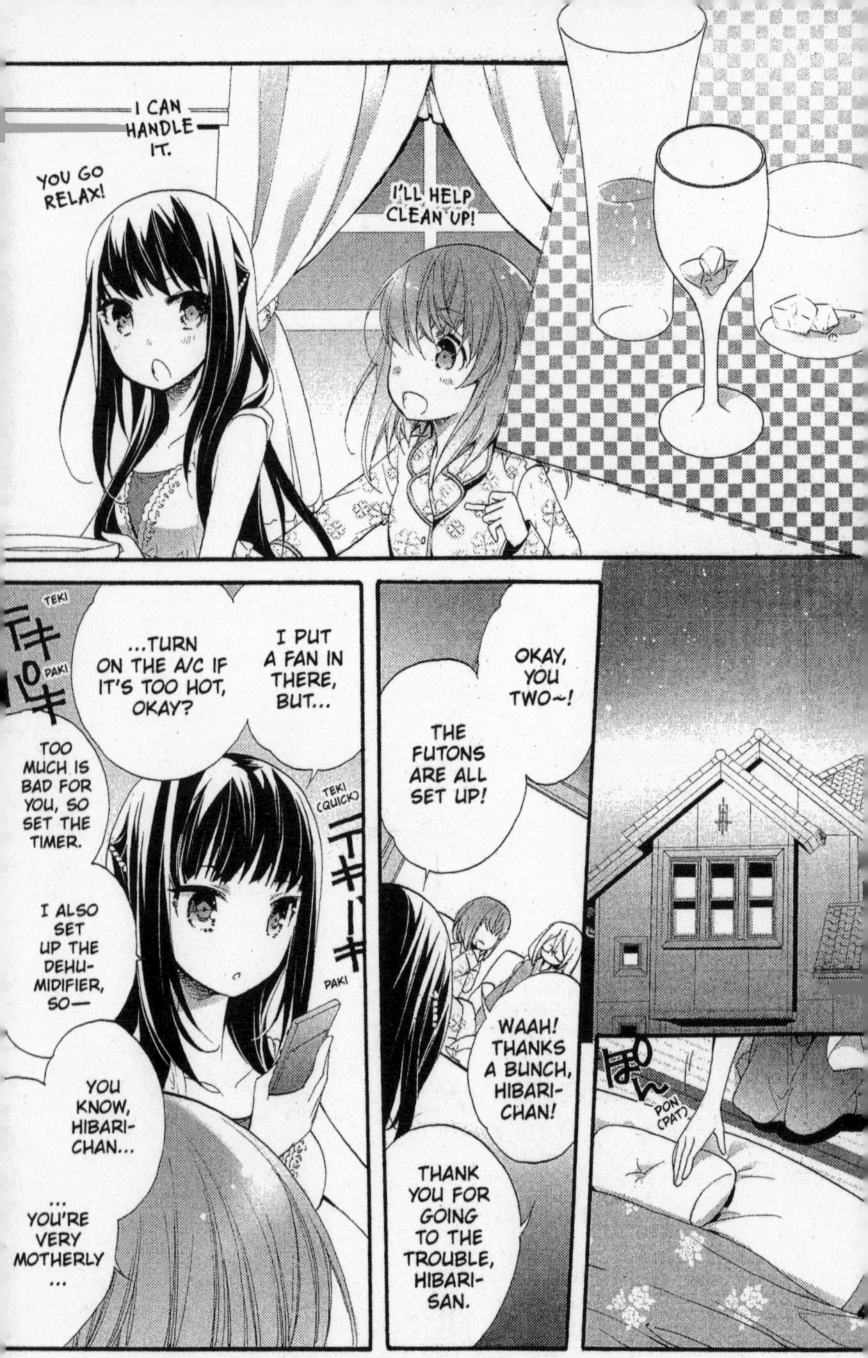
I'LL HELP CLEAN UP!
I CAN HANDLE IT.
YOU GO RELAX!
ぽん PON (PAT)
OKAY, YOU TWO~!
THE FUTONS ARE ALL SET UP!
WAAH! THANKS A BUNCH, HIBARI-CHAN!
THANK YOU FOR GOING TO THE TROUBLE, HIBARI-SAN.
I PUT A FAN IN THERE, BUT...
...TURN ON THE A/C IF IT'S TOO HOT, OKAY?
テキ TEKI (QUICK)
パキ PAKI
テキ TEKI
パキ PAKI
TOO MUCH IS BAD FOR YOU, SO SET THE TIMER.
I ALSO SET UP THE DEHU-MIDIFIER, SO—
YOU KNOW, HIBARI-CHAN...
...YOU'RE VERY MOTHERLY...

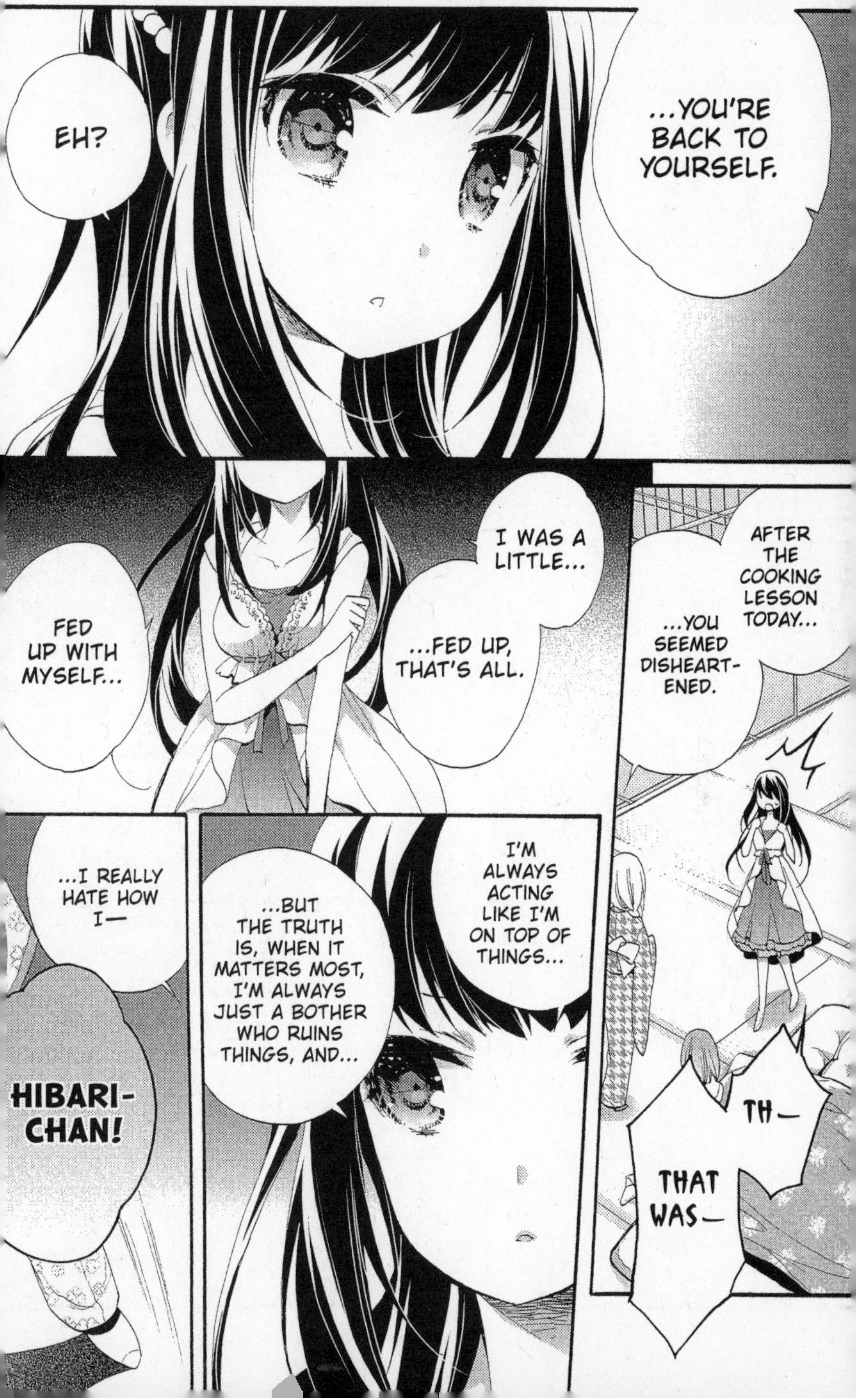
...YOU'RE BACK TO YOURSELF.
EH?
AFTER THE COOKING LESSON TODAY...
...YOU SEEMED DISHEART-ENED.
TH—
THAT WAS—
I WAS A LITTLE...
...FED UP, THAT'S ALL.
FED UP WITH MYSELF...
I'M ALWAYS ACTING LIKE I'M ON TOP OF THINGS...
...BUT THE TRUTH IS, WHEN IT MATTERS MOST, I'M ALWAYS JUST A BOTHER WHO RUINS THINGS, AND...
...I REALLY HATE HOW I—
HIBARI-CHAN!

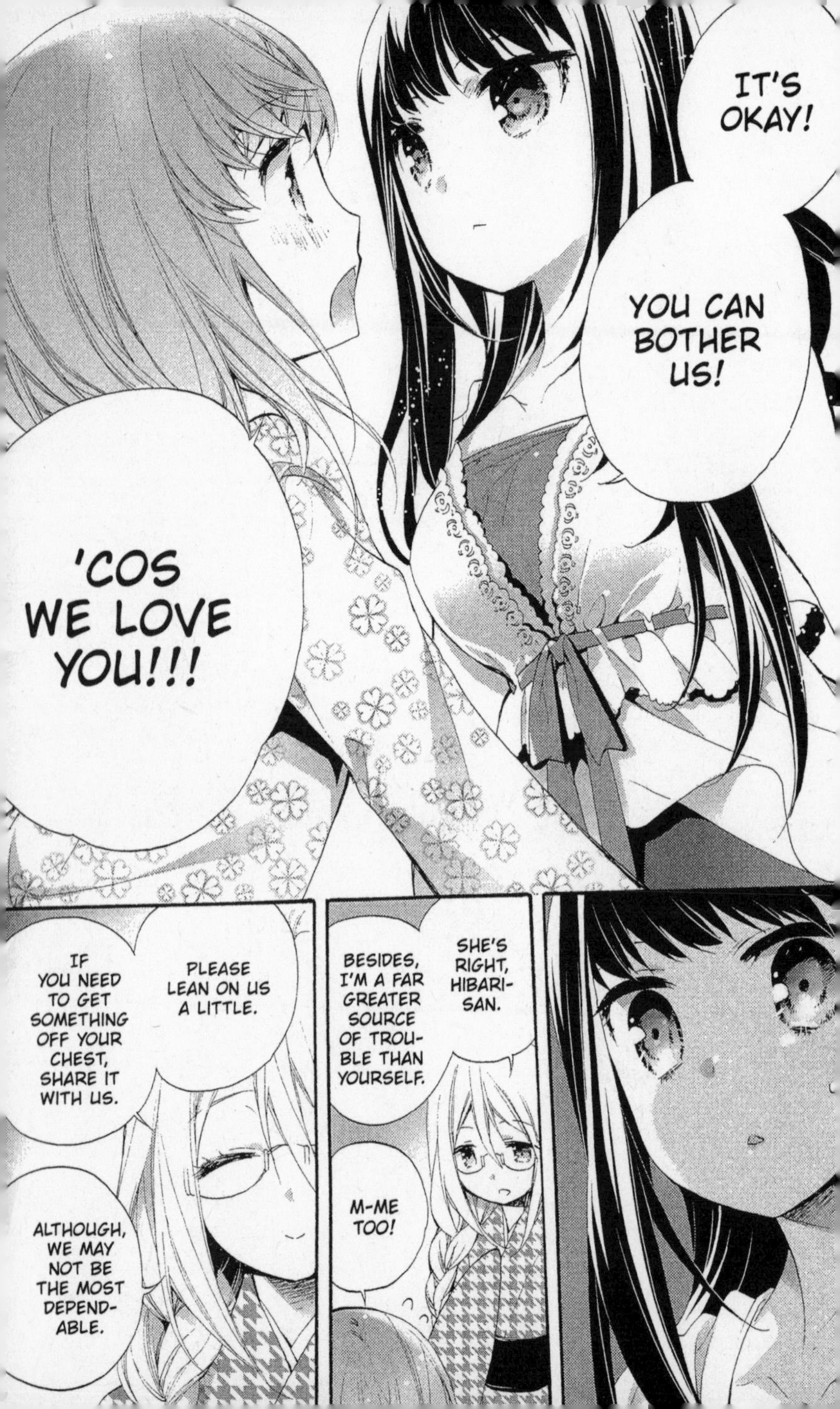
IT'S OKAY!
YOU CAN BOTHER US!
'COS WE LOVE YOU!!!
SHE'S RIGHT, HIBARI-SAN.
BESIDES, I'M A FAR GREATER SOURCE OF TROUBLE THAN YOURSELF.
M-ME TOO!
PLEASE LEAN ON US A LITTLE.
IF YOU NEED TO GET SOMETHING OFF YOUR CHEST, SHARE IT WITH US.
ALTHOUGH, WE MAY NOT BE THE MOST DEPENDABLE.

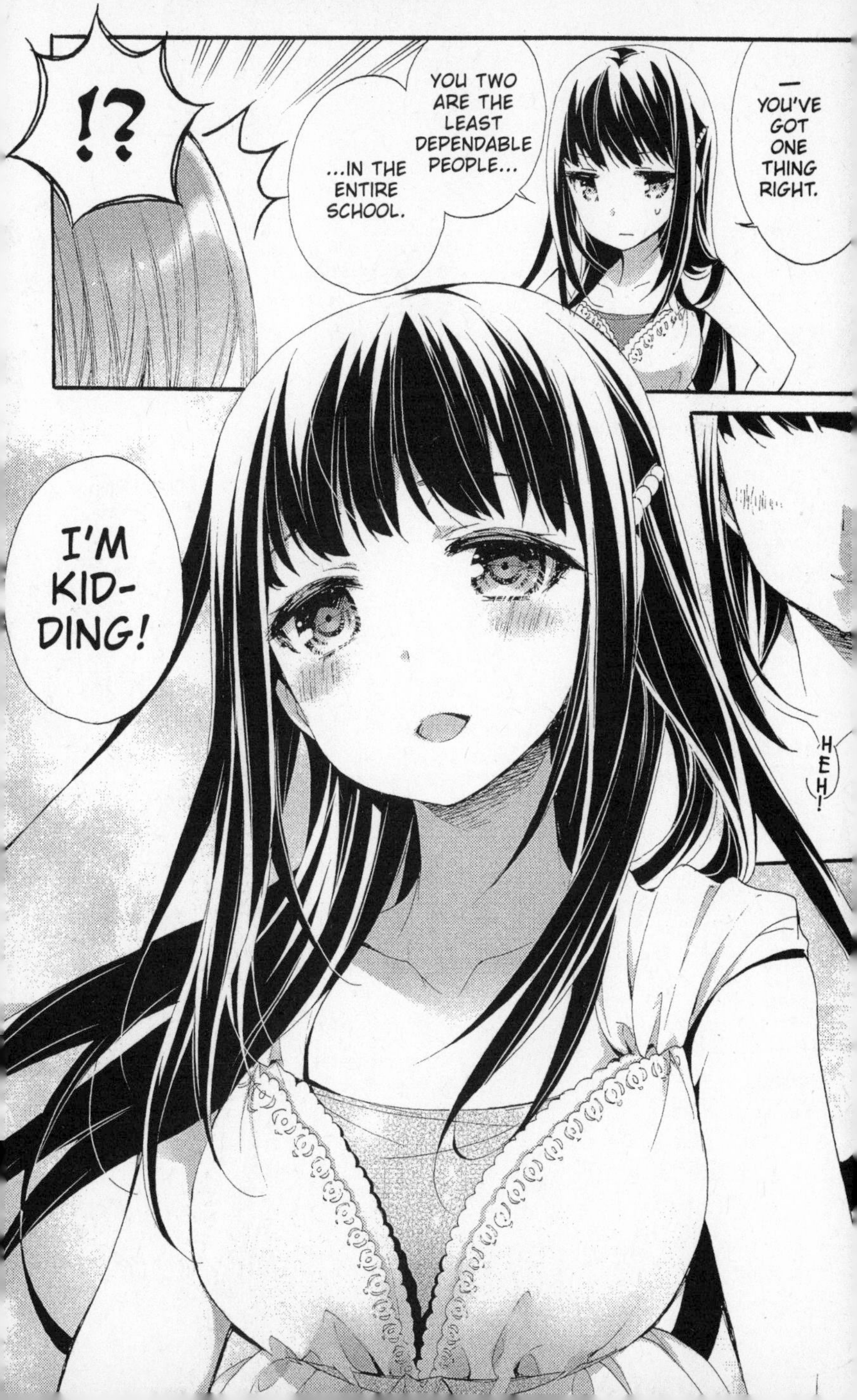
—YOU'VE GOT ONE THING RIGHT.
YOU TWO ARE THE LEAST DEPENDABLE PEOPLE...
...IN THE ENTIRE SCHOOL.
!?
I'M KID-DING!
HEH!

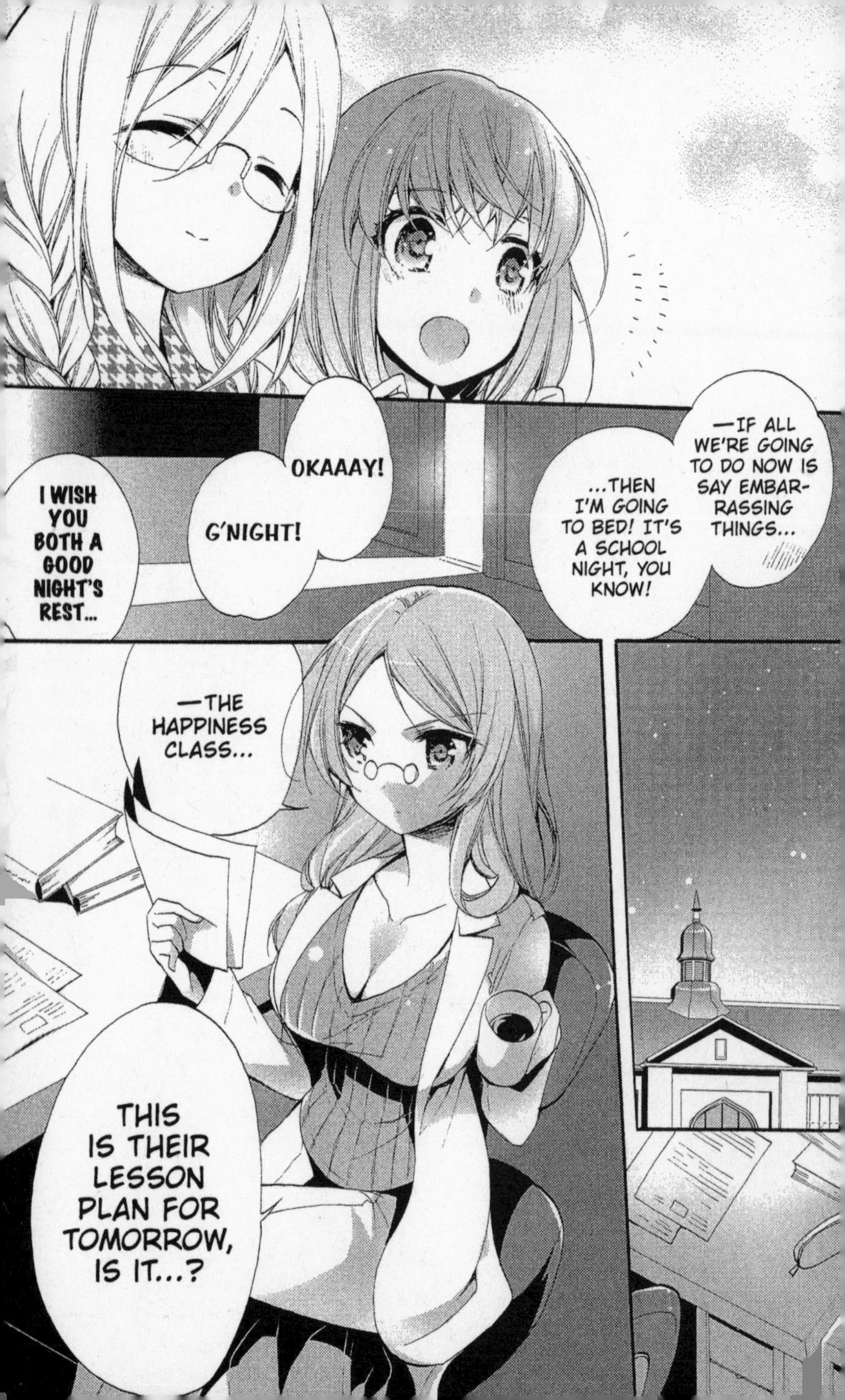
—IF ALL WE'RE GOING TO DO NOW IS SAY EMBAR-RASSING THINGS...
...THEN I'M GOING TO BED! IT'S A SCHOOL NIGHT, YOU KNOW!
OKAAAY!
G'NIGHT!
I WISH YOU BOTH A GOOD NIGHT'S REST...
—THE HAPPINESS CLASS...
THIS IS THEIR LESSON PLAN FOR TOMORROW, IS IT...?

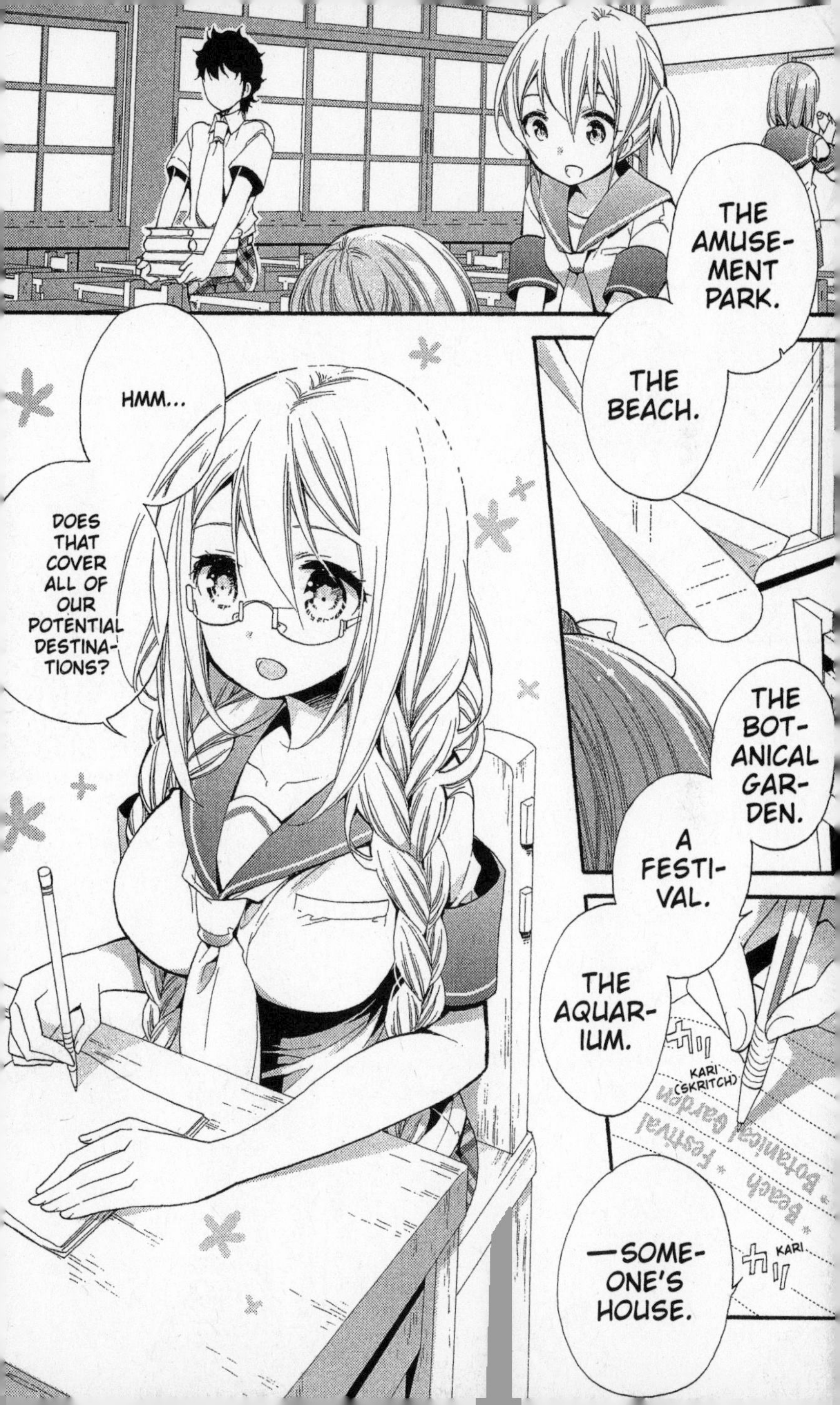
THE AMUSEMENT PARK.
THE BEACH.
THE BOTANICAL GARDEN.
A FESTIVAL.
THE AQUARIUM.
カリ KARI (SKRITCH)
Beach * Botanical Garden * Festival
—SOMEONE'S HOUSE.
カリ KARI
HMM...
DOES THAT COVER ALL OF OUR POTENTIAL DESTINATIONS?

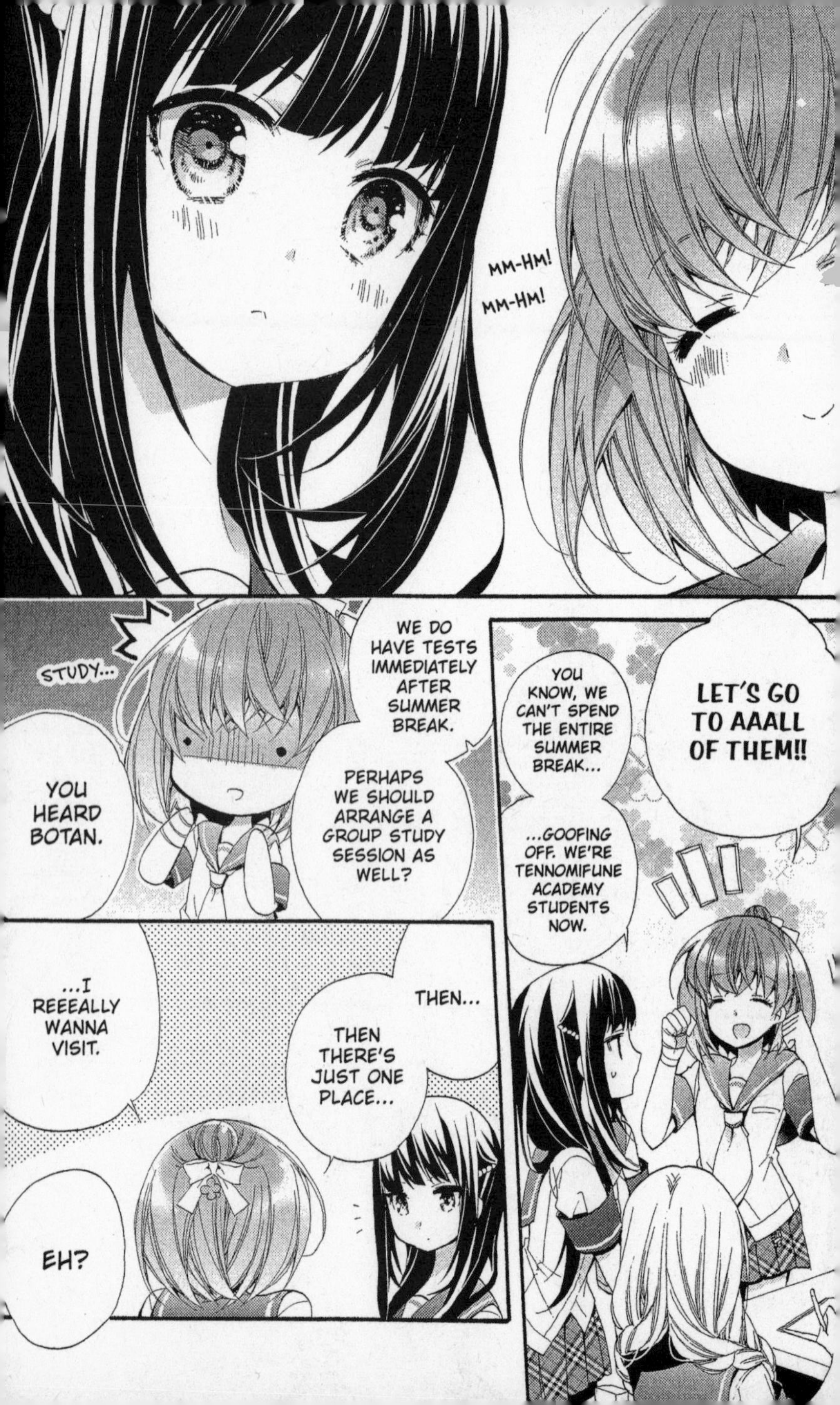
MM-HM!
MM-HM!
LET'S GO TO AAALL OF THEM!!
YOU KNOW, WE CAN'T SPEND THE ENTIRE SUMMER BREAK...
...GOOFING OFF. WE'RE TENNOMIFUNE ACADEMY STUDENTS NOW.
WE DO HAVE TESTS IMMEDIATELY AFTER SUMMER BREAK.
PERHAPS WE SHOULD ARRANGE A GROUP STUDY SESSION AS WELL?
STUDY...
YOU HEARD BOTAN.
THEN...
THEN THERE'S JUST ONE PLACE...
...I REEEALLY WANNA VISIT.
EH?

�֎ Lucky. **16**

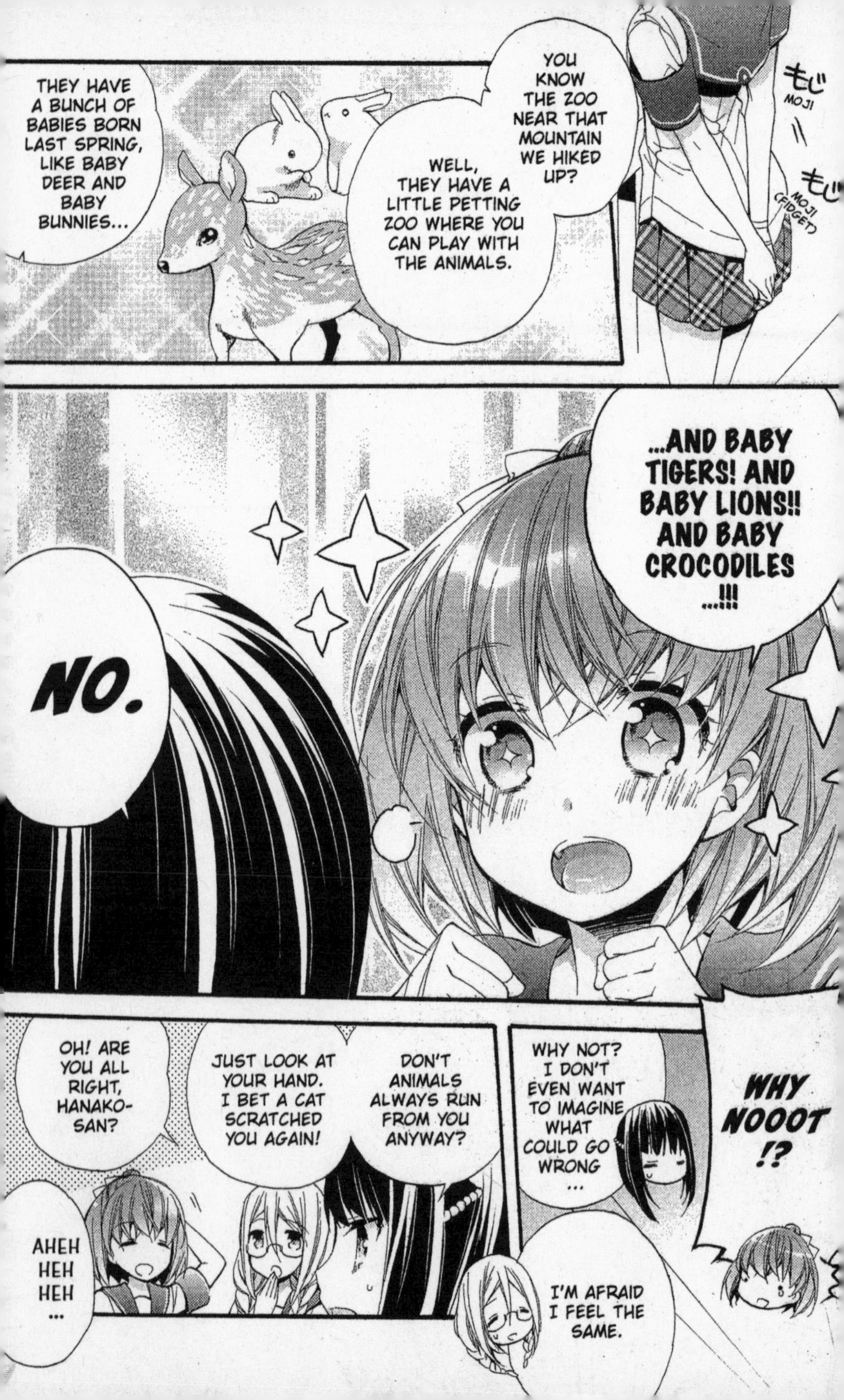

もじ MOJI
もじ MOJI (FIDGET)
YOU KNOW THE ZOO NEAR THAT MOUNTAIN WE HIKED UP?
WELL, THEY HAVE A LITTLE PETTING ZOO WHERE YOU CAN PLAY WITH THE ANIMALS.
THEY HAVE A BUNCH OF BABIES BORN LAST SPRING, LIKE BABY DEER AND BABY BUNNIES...
...AND BABY TIGERS! AND BABY LIONS!! AND BABY CROCODILES ...!!!
NO.
WHY NOOOT !?
WHY NOT? I DON'T EVEN WANT TO IMAGINE WHAT COULD GO WRONG ...
I'M AFRAID I FEEL THE SAME.
DON'T ANIMALS ALWAYS RUN FROM YOU ANYWAY?
JUST LOOK AT YOUR HAND. I BET A CAT SCRATCHED YOU AGAIN!
OH! ARE YOU ALL RIGHT, HANAKO-SAN?
AHEH HEH HEH ...

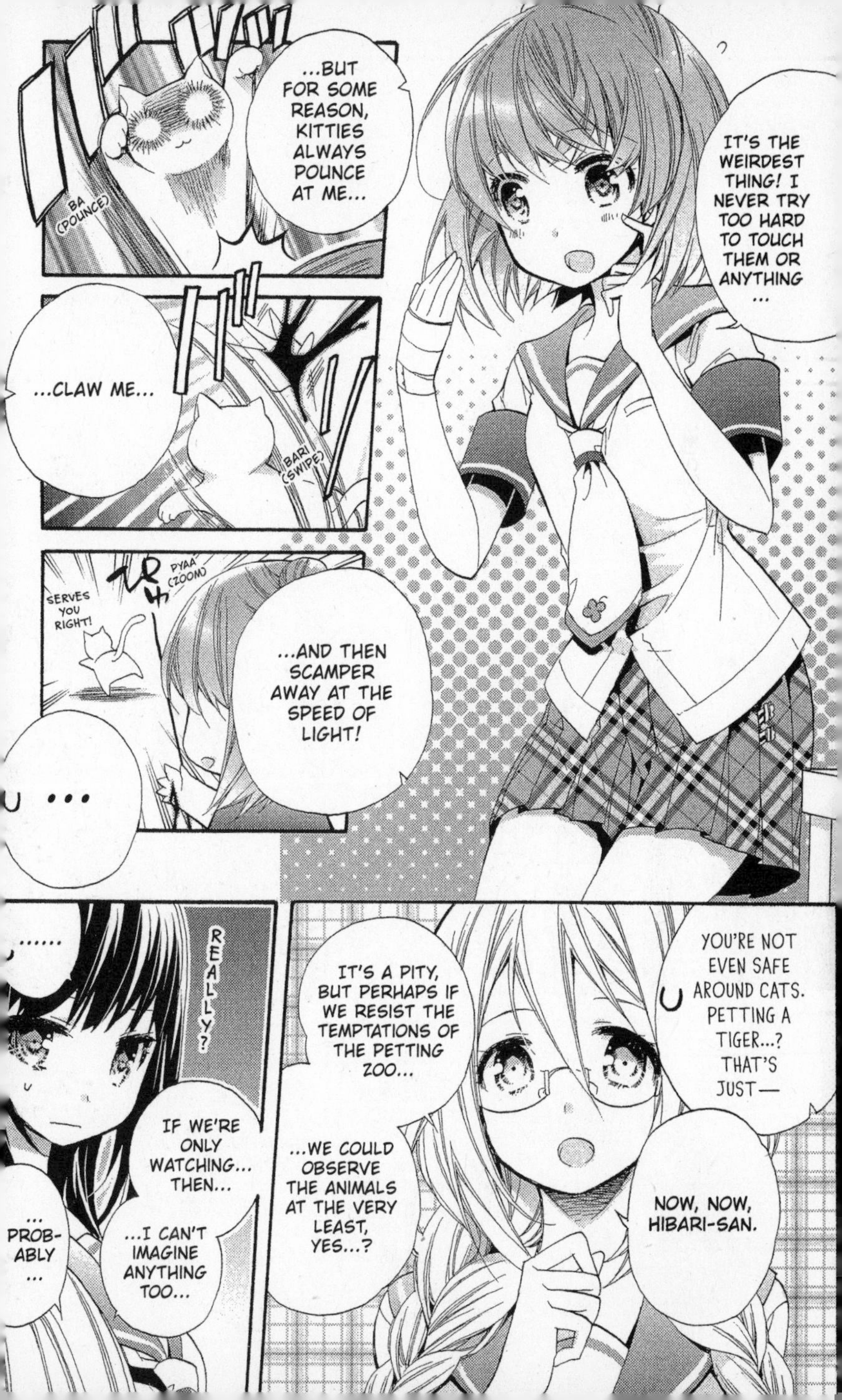
IT'S THE WEIRDEST THING! I NEVER TRY TOO HARD TO TOUCH THEM OR ANYTHING...
...BUT FOR SOME REASON, KITTIES ALWAYS POUNCE AT ME...
BA (POUNCE)
...CLAW ME...
BARI (SWIPE)
PYAA (ZOOM)
SERVES YOU RIGHT!
...AND THEN SCAMPER AWAY AT THE SPEED OF LIGHT!
...
YOU'RE NOT EVEN SAFE AROUND CATS. PETTING A TIGER...? THAT'S JUST—
NOW, NOW, HIBARI-SAN.
IT'S A PITY, BUT PERHAPS IF WE RESIST THE TEMPTATIONS OF THE PETTING ZOO...
...WE COULD OBSERVE THE ANIMALS AT THE VERY LEAST, YES...?
......
REALLY?
IF WE'RE ONLY WATCHING... THEN...
...I CAN'T IMAGINE ANYTHING TOO...
...PROBABLY...

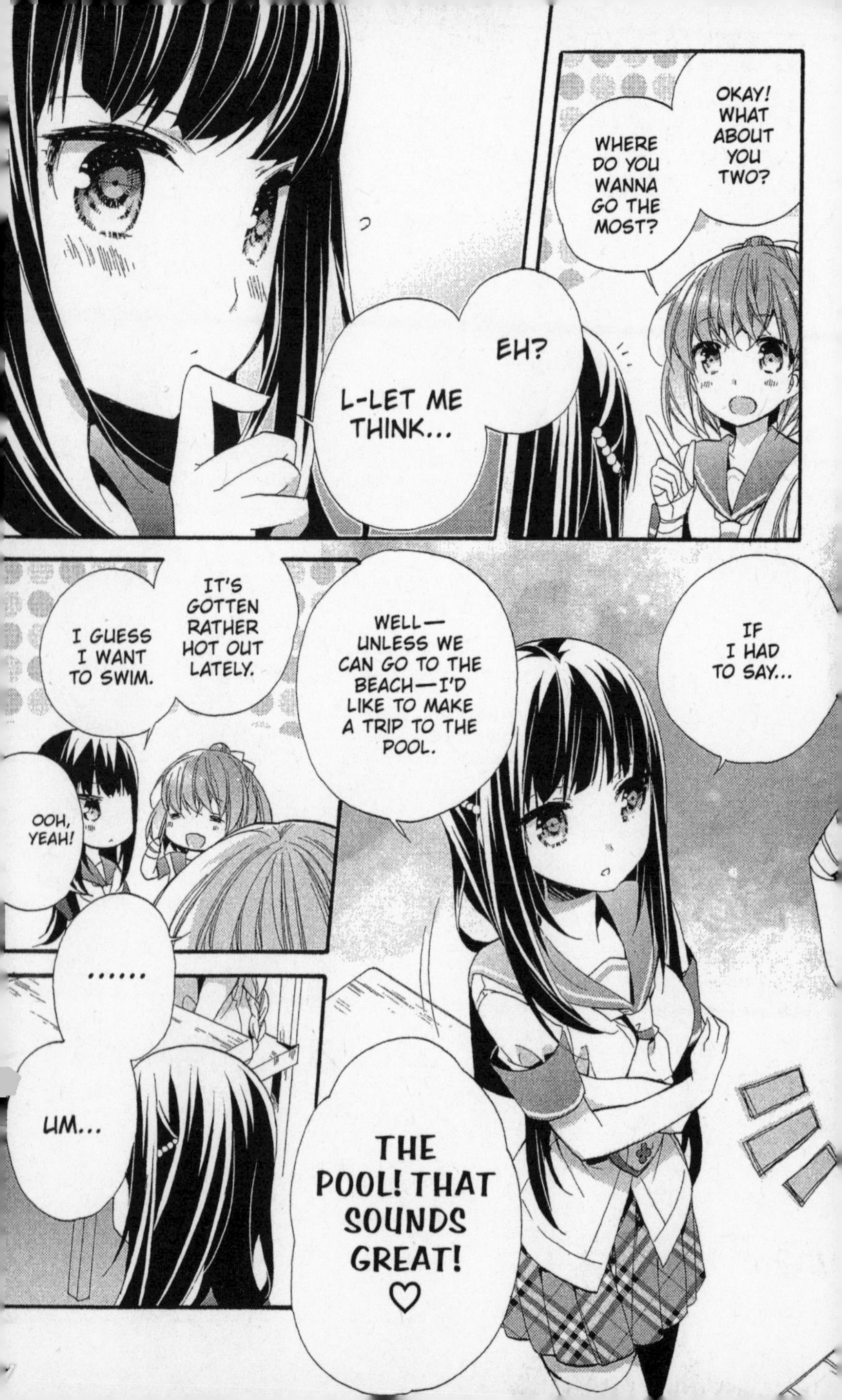
OKAY! WHAT ABOUT YOU TWO?
WHERE DO YOU WANNA GO THE MOST?
EH?
L-LET ME THINK...
IF I HAD TO SAY...
WELL—UNLESS WE CAN GO TO THE BEACH—I'D LIKE TO MAKE A TRIP TO THE POOL.
THE POOL! THAT SOUNDS GREAT! ♡
IT'S GOTTEN RATHER HOT OUT LATELY.
I GUESS I WANT TO SWIM.
OOH, YEAH!
......
UM...

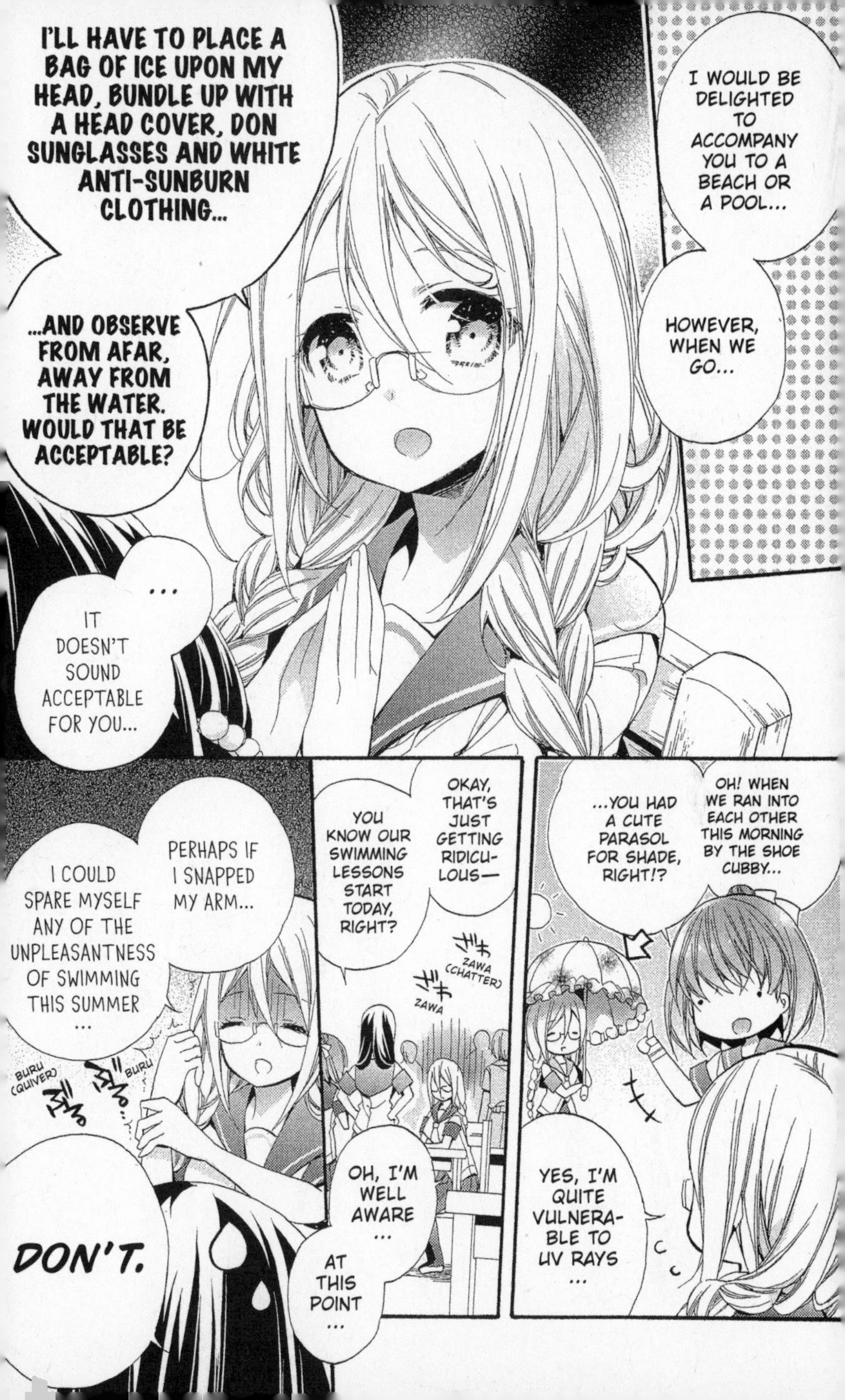

I WOULD BE DELIGHTED TO ACCOMPANY YOU TO A BEACH OR A POOL...
HOWEVER, WHEN WE GO...
I'LL HAVE TO PLACE A BAG OF ICE UPON MY HEAD, BUNDLE UP WITH A HEAD COVER, DON SUNGLASSES AND WHITE ANTI-SUNBURN CLOTHING...
...AND OBSERVE FROM AFAR, AWAY FROM THE WATER. WOULD THAT BE ACCEPTABLE?
...
IT DOESN'T SOUND ACCEPTABLE FOR YOU...
OH! WHEN WE RAN INTO EACH OTHER THIS MORNING BY THE SHOE CUBBY...
...YOU HAD A CUTE PARASOL FOR SHADE, RIGHT!?
YES, I'M QUITE VULNERA-BLE TO UV RAYS ...
OKAY, THAT'S JUST GETTING RIDICU-LOUS—
YOU KNOW OUR SWIMMING LESSONS START TODAY, RIGHT?
ZAWA (CHATTER)
ZAWA
OH, I'M WELL AWARE ...
AT THIS POINT ...
PERHAPS IF I SNAPPED MY ARM...
I COULD SPARE MYSELF ANY OF THE UNPLEASANTNESS OF SWIMMING THIS SUMMER ...
BURU
BURU (QUIVER)
DON'T.

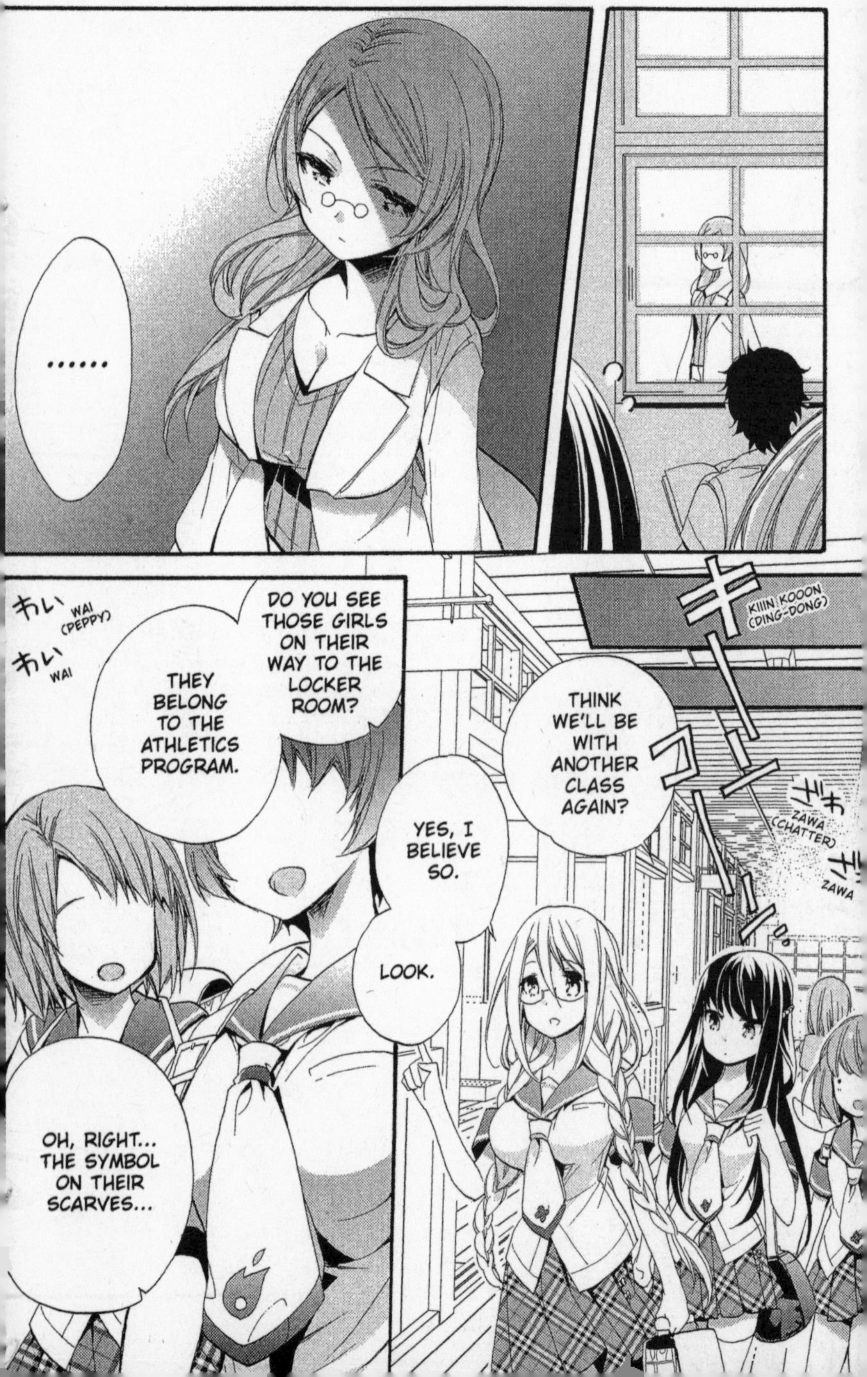
......
KIIIN KOOON (DING-DONG)
ZAWA (CHATTER)
ZAWA
THINK WE'LL BE WITH ANOTHER CLASS AGAIN?
YES, I BELIEVE SO.
LOOK.
DO YOU SEE THOSE GIRLS ON THEIR WAY TO THE LOCKER ROOM?
THEY BELONG TO THE ATHLETICS PROGRAM.
WAI (PEPPY)
WAI
OH, RIGHT... THE SYMBOL ON THEIR SCARVES...

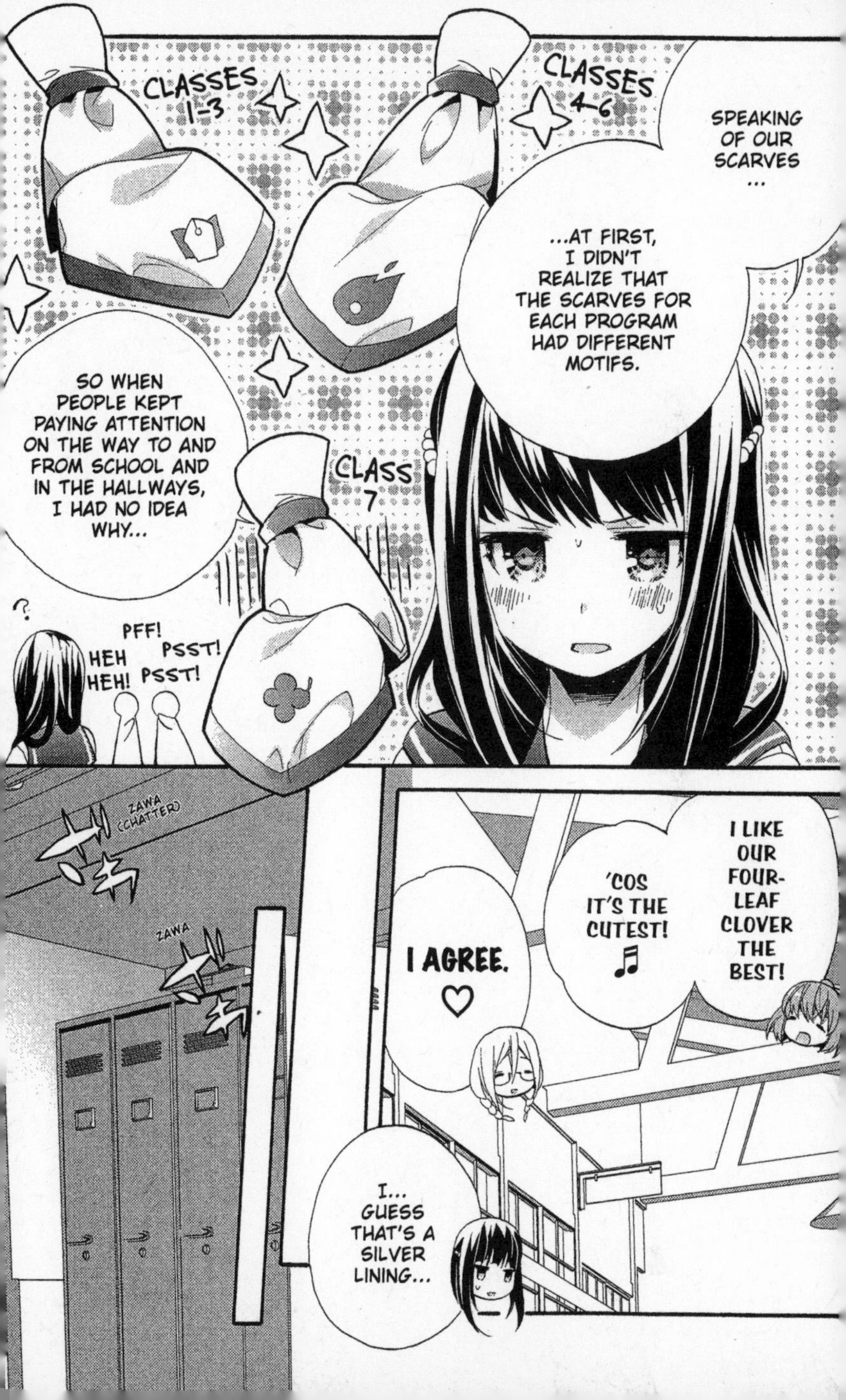
SPEAKING OF OUR SCARVES ...
...AT FIRST, I DIDN'T REALIZE THAT THE SCARVES FOR EACH PROGRAM HAD DIFFERENT MOTIFS.
CLASSES 4-6
CLASSES 1-3
CLASS 7
SO WHEN PEOPLE KEPT PAYING ATTENTION ON THE WAY TO AND FROM SCHOOL AND IN THE HALLWAYS, I HAD NO IDEA WHY...
PFF!
PSST! PSST!
HEH HEH!
I LIKE OUR FOUR-LEAF CLOVER THE BEST!
'COS IT'S THE CUTEST! ♬
I AGREE. ♡
I... GUESS THAT'S A SILVER LINING...
ZAWA (CHATTER)
ZAWA

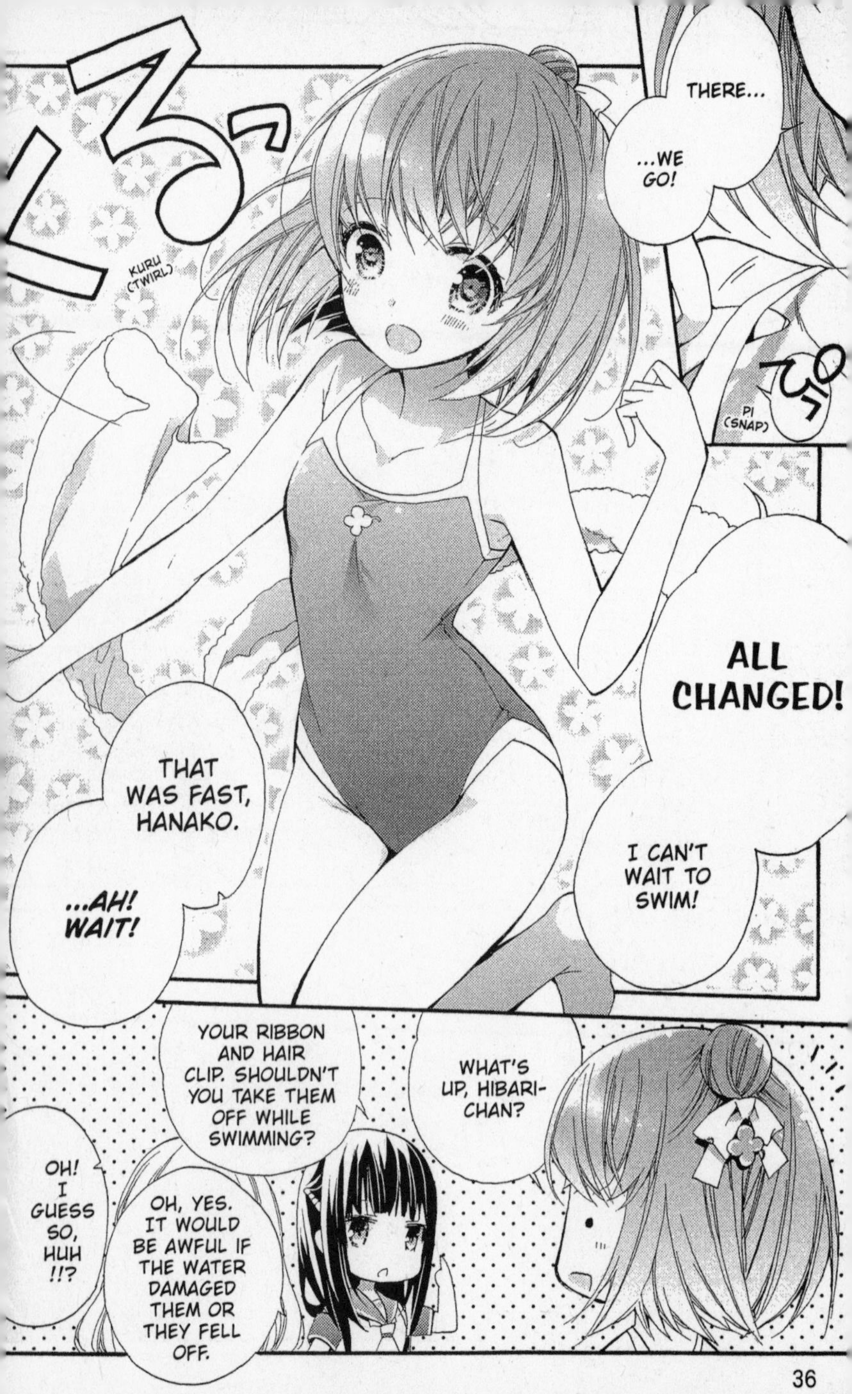
THERE...
...WE GO!
PI (SNAP)
KURU (TWIRL)
ALL CHANGED!
I CAN'T WAIT TO SWIM!
THAT WAS FAST, HANAKO.
...AH! WAIT!
WHAT'S UP, HIBARI-CHAN?
YOUR RIBBON AND HAIR CLIP. SHOULDN'T YOU TAKE THEM OFF WHILE SWIMMING?
OH, YES. IT WOULD BE AWFUL IF THE WATER DAMAGED THEM OR THEY FELL OFF.
OH! I GUESS SO, HUH!!?

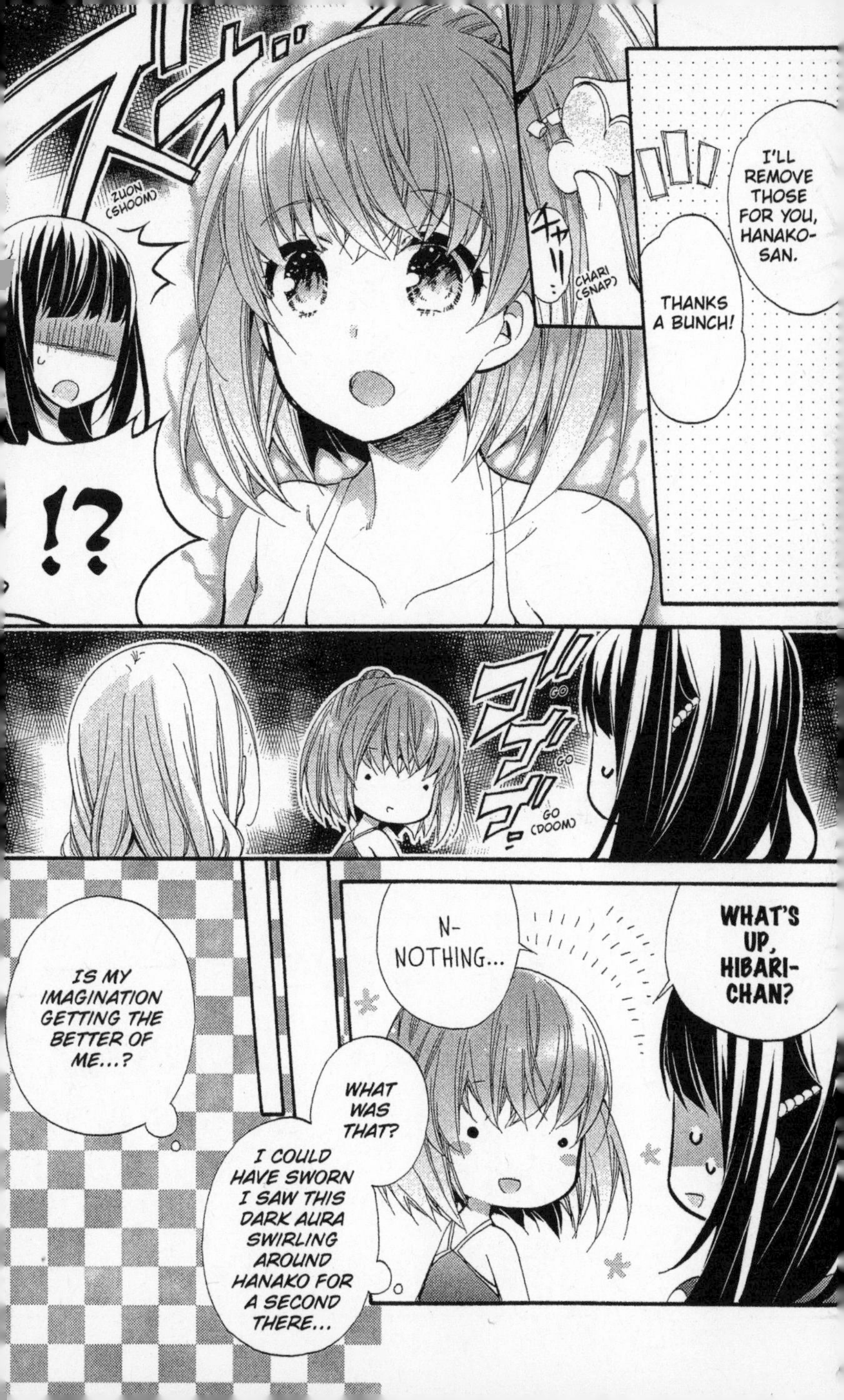
I'LL REMOVE THOSE FOR YOU, HANAKO-SAN.
CHARI (SNAP)
THANKS A BUNCH!
ZUON (SHOOM)
!?
GO
GO
GO (DOOM)
WHAT'S UP, HIBARI-CHAN?
N-NOTHING...
WHAT WAS THAT?
I COULD HAVE SWORN I SAW THIS DARK AURA SWIRLING AROUND HANAKO FOR A SECOND THERE...
IS MY IMAGINATION GETTING THE BETTER OF ME...?

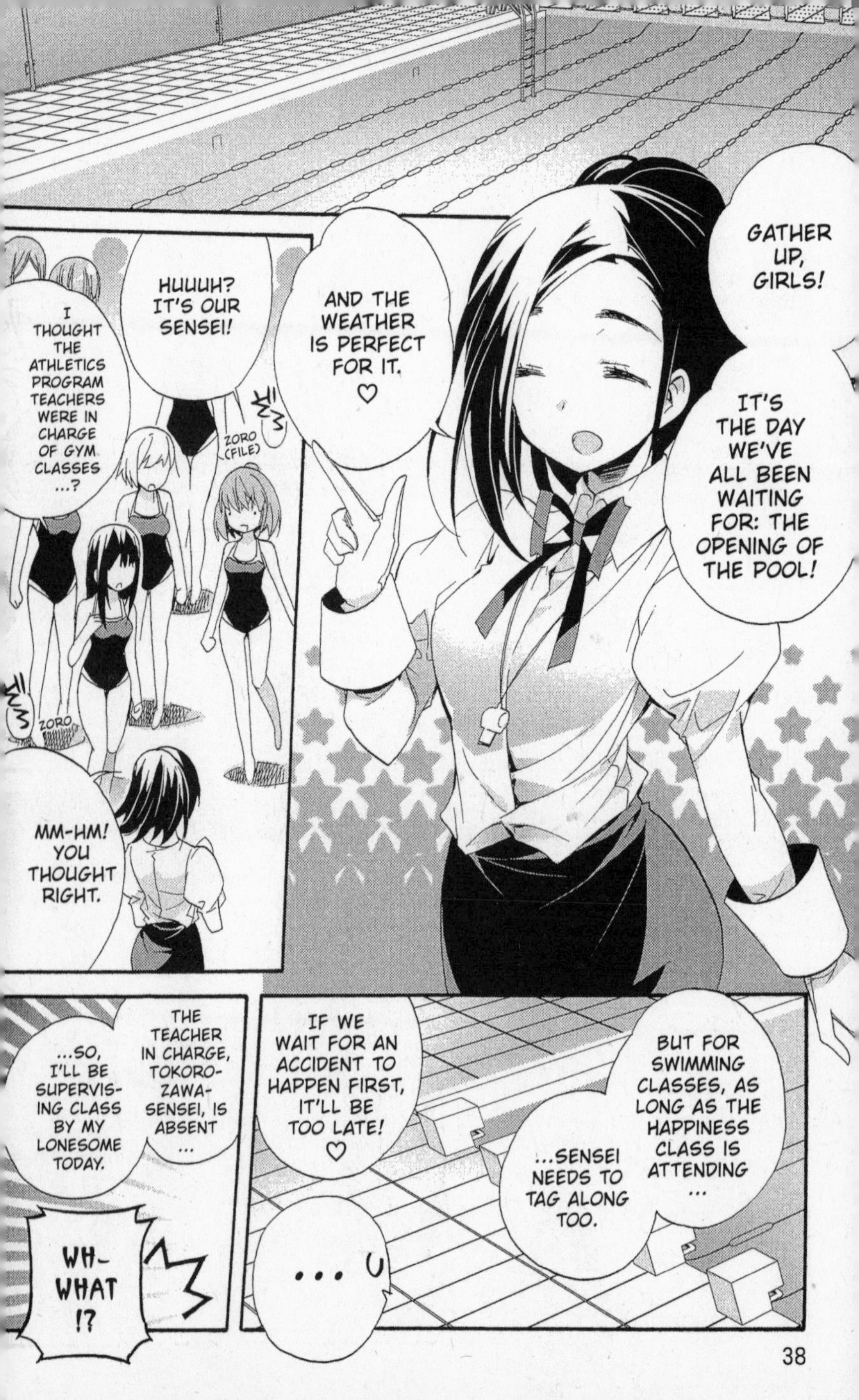
GATHER UP, GIRLS!
IT'S THE DAY WE'VE ALL BEEN WAITING FOR: THE OPENING OF THE POOL!
AND THE WEATHER IS PERFECT FOR IT. ♡
HUUUH? IT'S OUR SENSEI!
I THOUGHT THE ATHLETICS PROGRAM TEACHERS WERE IN CHARGE OF GYM CLASSES ...?
ZORO (FILE)
ZORO
MM-HM! YOU THOUGHT RIGHT.
BUT FOR SWIMMING CLASSES, AS LONG AS THE HAPPINESS CLASS IS ATTENDING ...
...SENSEI NEEDS TO TAG ALONG TOO.
IF WE WAIT FOR AN ACCIDENT TO HAPPEN FIRST, IT'LL BE TOO LATE! ♡
...
THE TEACHER IN CHARGE, TOKORO-ZAWA-SENSEI, IS ABSENT ...
...SO, I'LL BE SUPERVIS-ING CLASS BY MY LONESOME TODAY.
WH-WHAT !?

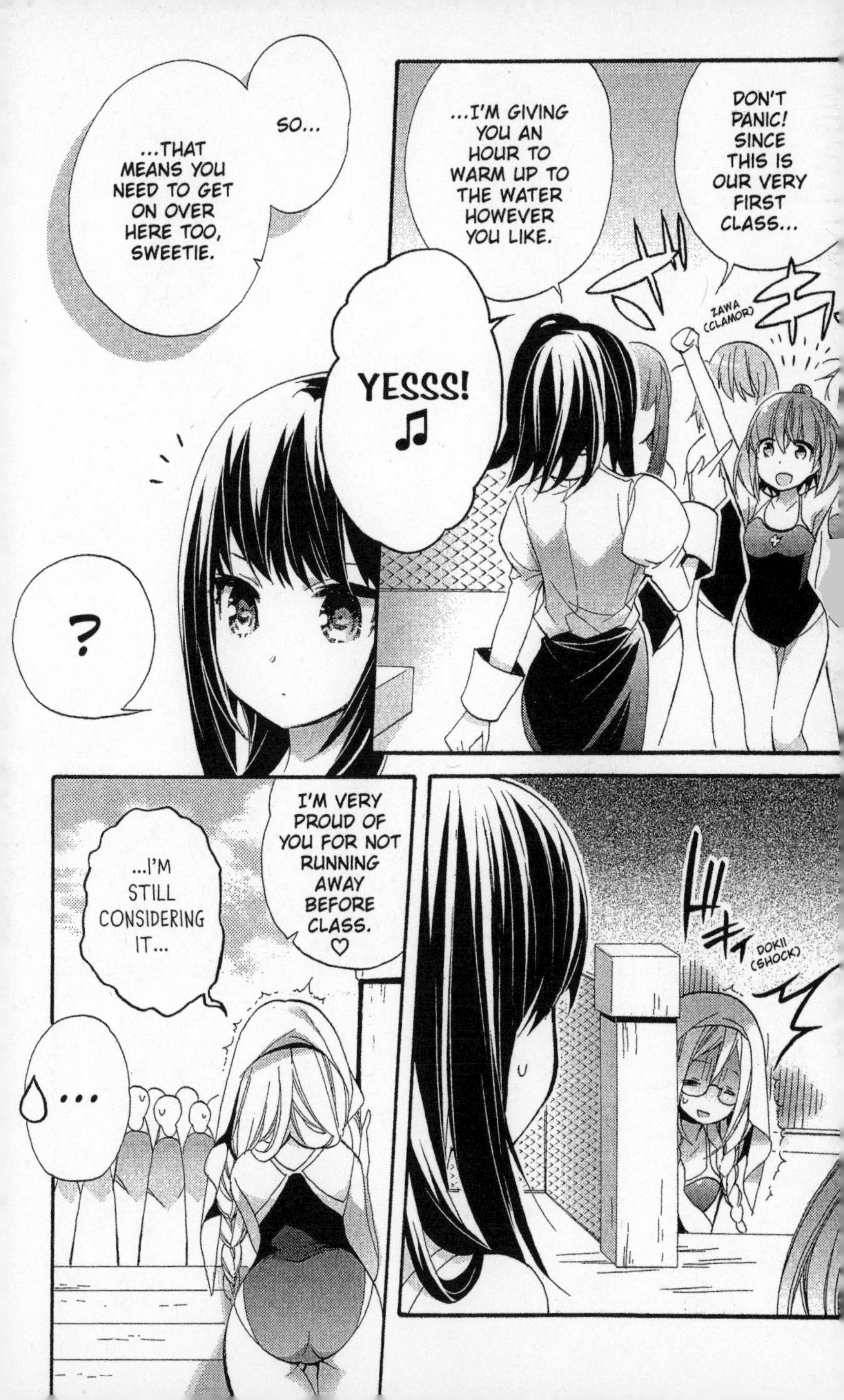
DON'T PANIC! SINCE THIS IS OUR VERY FIRST CLASS...
...I'M GIVING YOU AN HOUR TO WARM UP TO THE WATER HOWEVER YOU LIKE.
ZAWA (CLAMOR)
YESSS! ♫
SO...
...THAT MEANS YOU NEED TO GET ON OVER HERE TOO, SWEETIE.
?
DOKII (SHOCK)
I'M VERY PROUD OF YOU FOR NOT RUNNING AWAY BEFORE CLASS. ♡
...I'M STILL CONSIDERING IT...
...

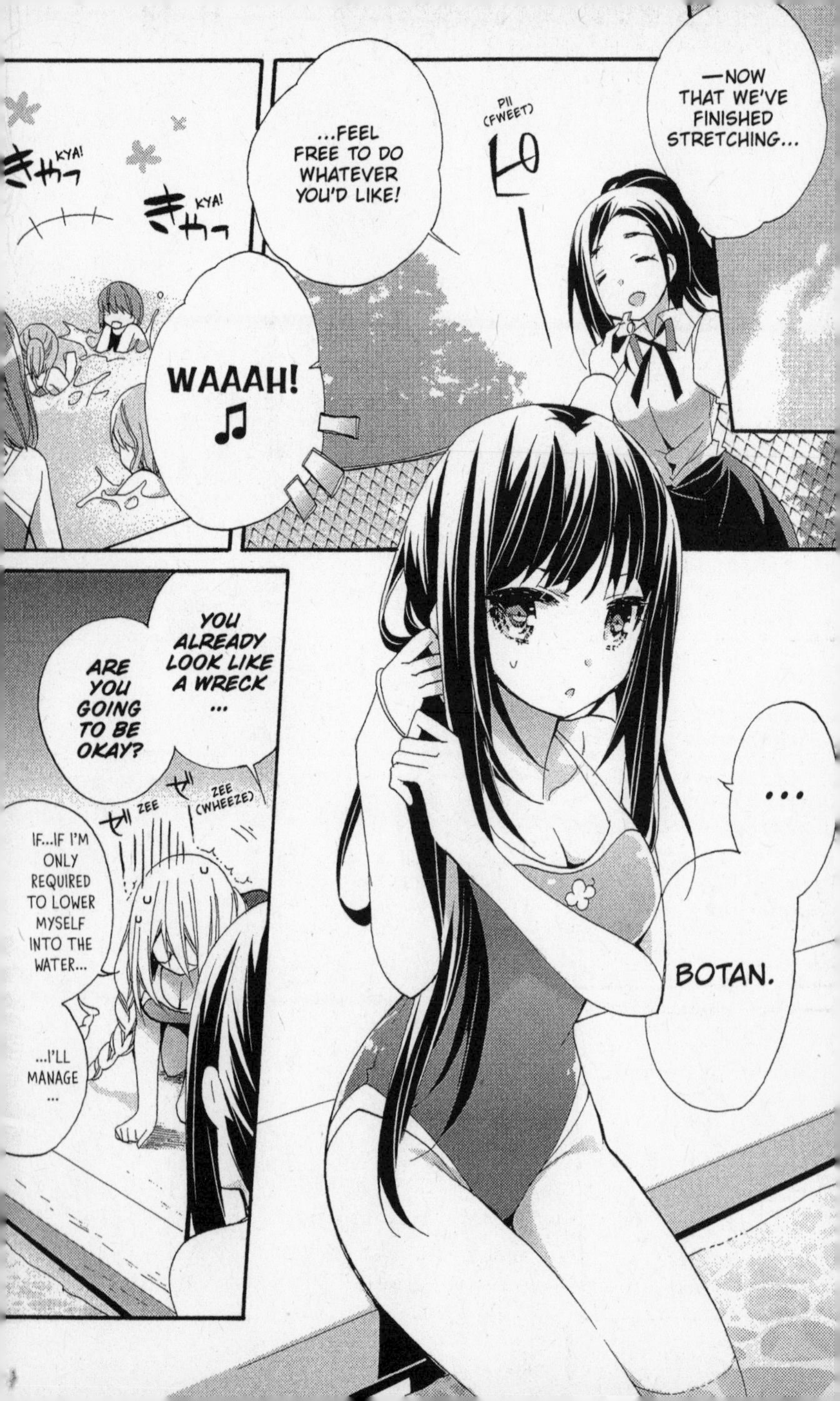
—NOW THAT WE'VE FINISHED STRETCHING...
PII (FWEET)
...FEEL FREE TO DO WHATEVER YOU'D LIKE!
KYA!
KYA!
WAAAH! ♫
...
BOTAN.
YOU ALREADY LOOK LIKE A WRECK ...
ARE YOU GOING TO BE OKAY?
ZEE (WHEEZE)
ZEE
IF...IF I'M ONLY REQUIRED TO LOWER MYSELF INTO THE WATER...
...I'LL MANAGE ...

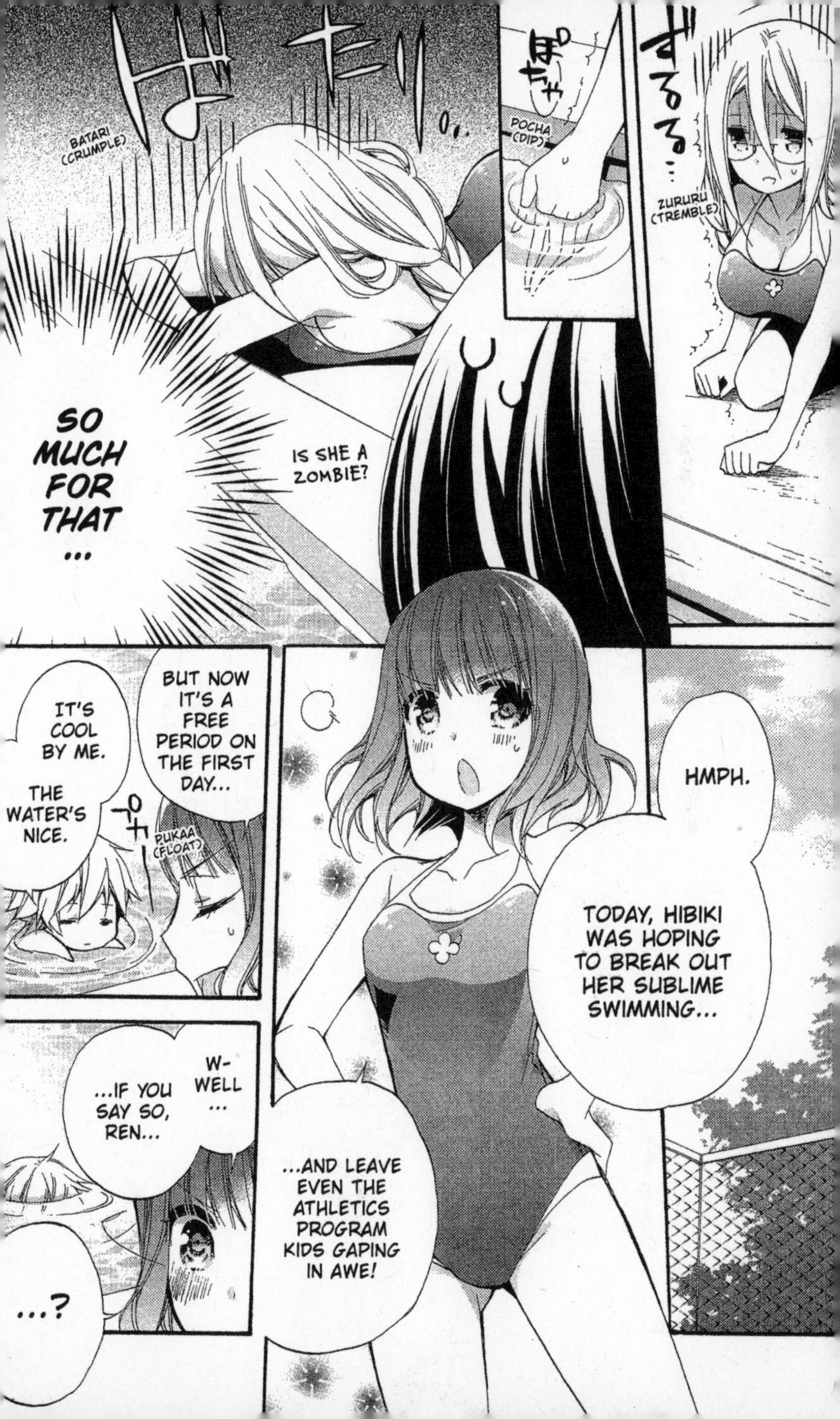
ずるる…
ZURURU (TREMBLE)
ぽちゃ
POCHA (DIP)
ばたり
BATARI (CRUMPLE)
SO MUCH FOR THAT...
IS SHE A ZOMBIE?
HMPH.
TODAY, HIBIKI WAS HOPING TO BREAK OUT HER SUBLIME SWIMMING...
...AND LEAVE EVEN THE ATHLETICS PROGRAM KIDS GAPING IN AWE!
BUT NOW IT'S A FREE PERIOD ON THE FIRST DAY...
IT'S COOL BY ME.
THE WATER'S NICE.
PUKAA (FLOAT)
W-WELL...
...IF YOU SAY SO, REN...
...?

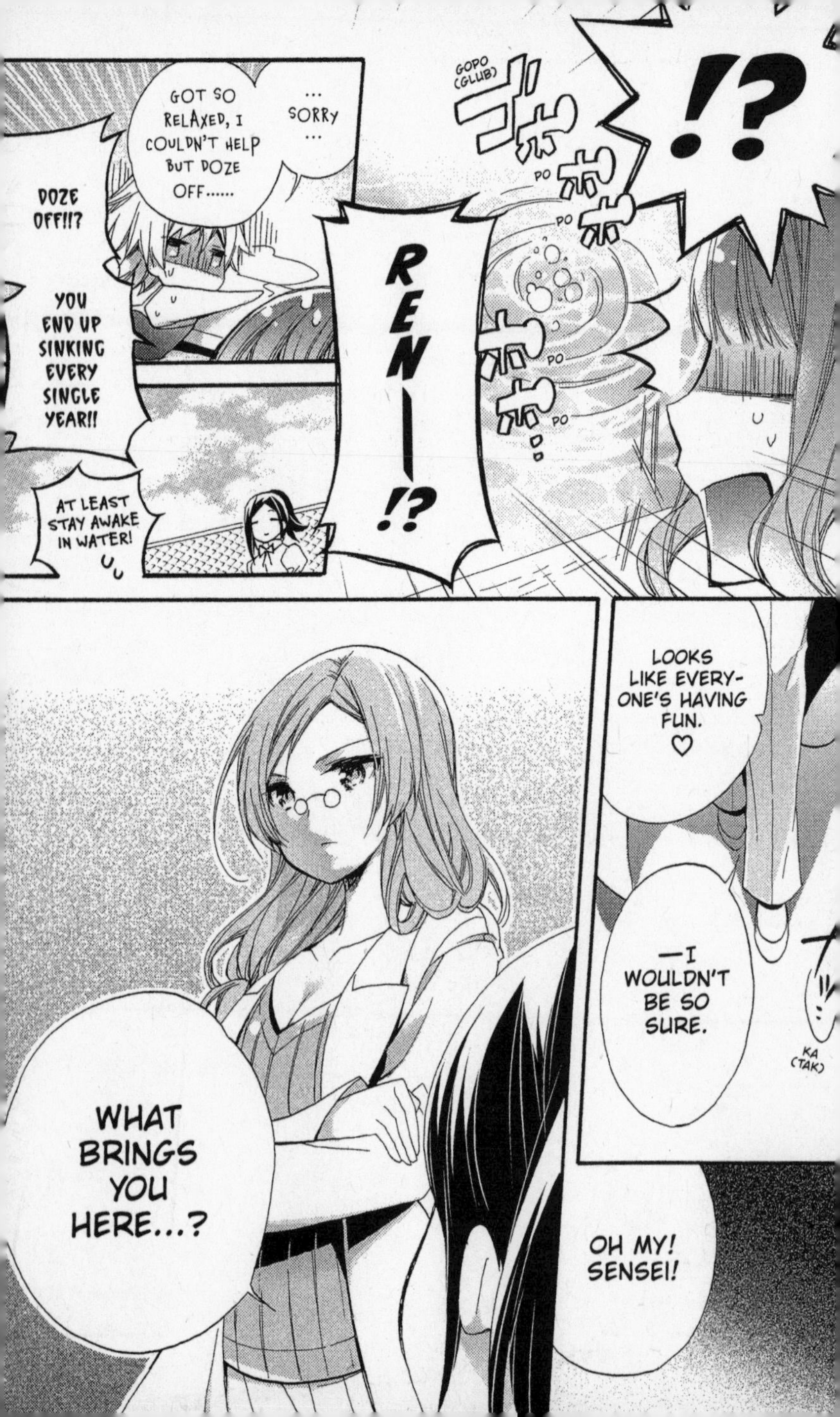
!?
GOPO (GLUB)
PO
PO
PO
PO
REN—!?
...SORRY...
GOT SO RELAXED, I COULDN'T HELP BUT DOZE OFF......
DOZE OFF!!?
YOU END UP SINKING EVERY SINGLE YEAR!!
AT LEAST STAY AWAKE IN WATER!
LOOKS LIKE EVERYONE'S HAVING FUN. ♡
KA (TAK)
—I WOULDN'T BE SO SURE.
OH MY! SENSEI!
WHAT BRINGS YOU HERE...?

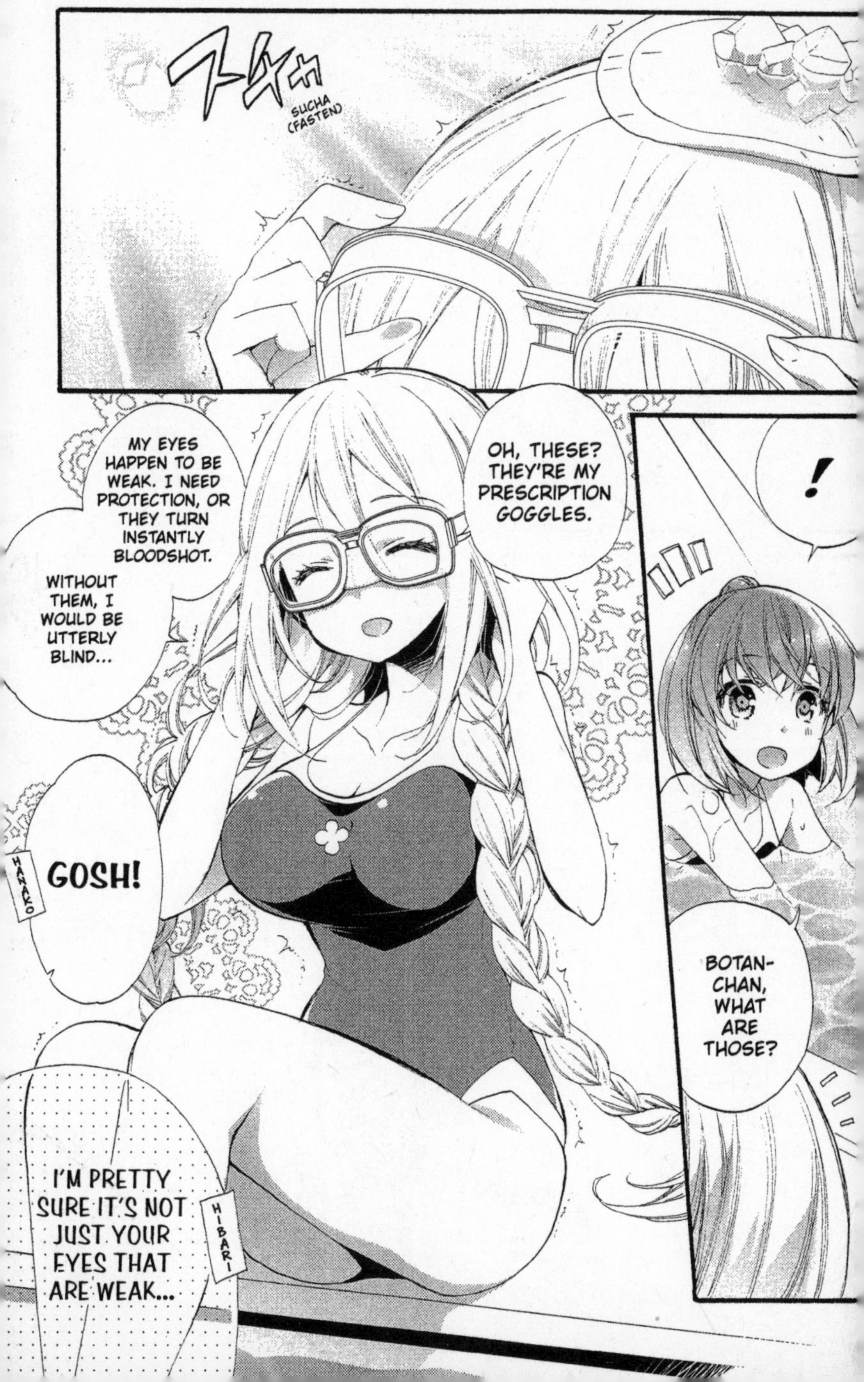
SUCHA (FASTEN)
!
BOTAN-CHAN, WHAT ARE THOSE?
OH, THESE? THEY'RE MY PRESCRIPTION GOGGLES.
MY EYES HAPPEN TO BE WEAK. I NEED PROTECTION, OR THEY TURN INSTANTLY BLOODSHOT.
WITHOUT THEM, I WOULD BE UTTERLY BLIND...
HANAKO
GOSH!
HIBARI
I'M PRETTY SURE IT'S NOT JUST YOUR EYES THAT ARE WEAK...

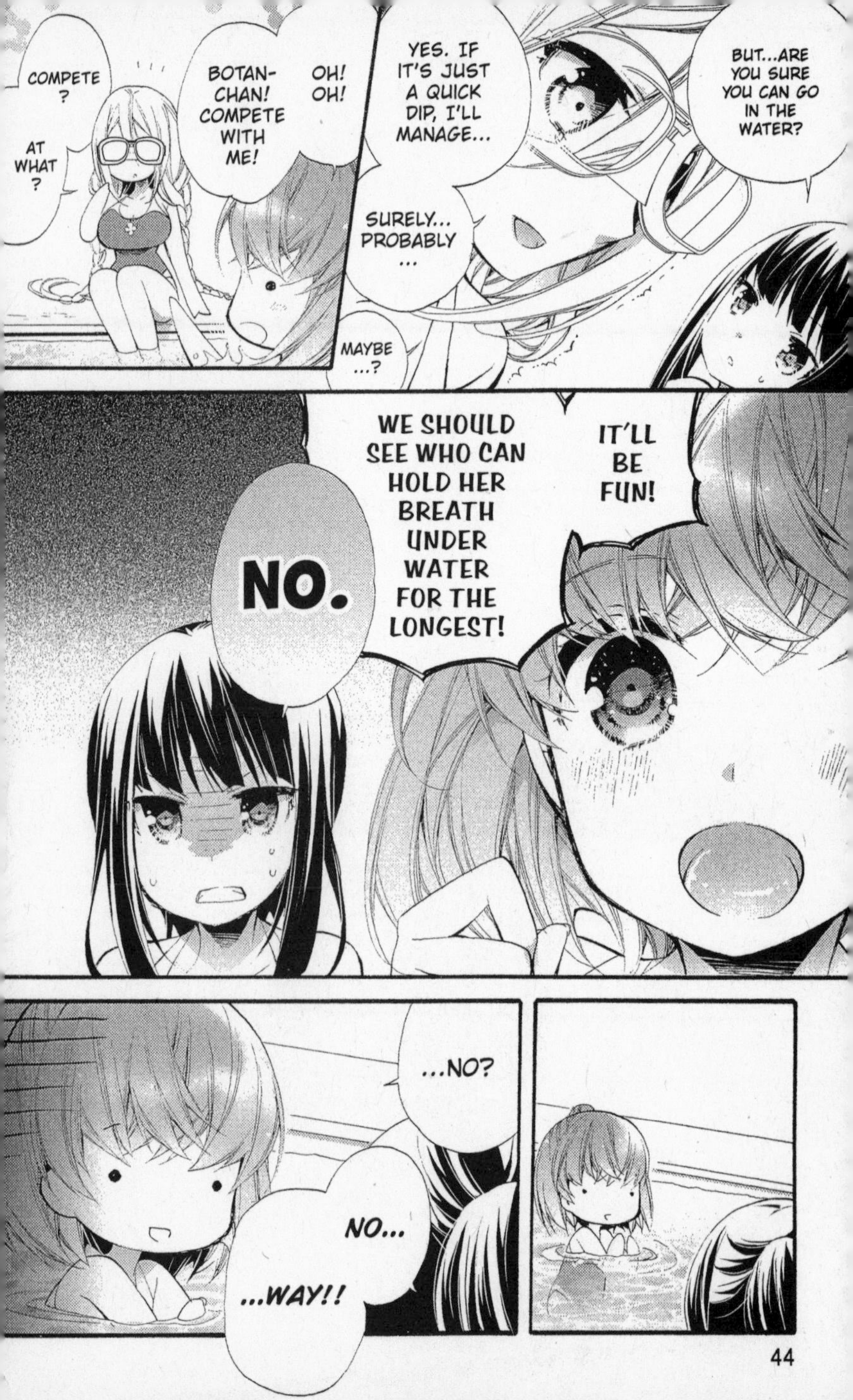
BUT...ARE YOU SURE YOU CAN GO IN THE WATER?
YES. IF IT'S JUST A QUICK DIP, I'LL MANAGE...
SURELY... PROBABLY ...
MAYBE ...?
OH! OH!
BOTAN-CHAN! COMPETE WITH ME!
COMPETE?
AT WHAT?
IT'LL BE FUN!
WE SHOULD SEE WHO CAN HOLD HER BREATH UNDER WATER FOR THE LONGEST!
NO.
...NO?
NO...
...WAY!!

Lucky. 17

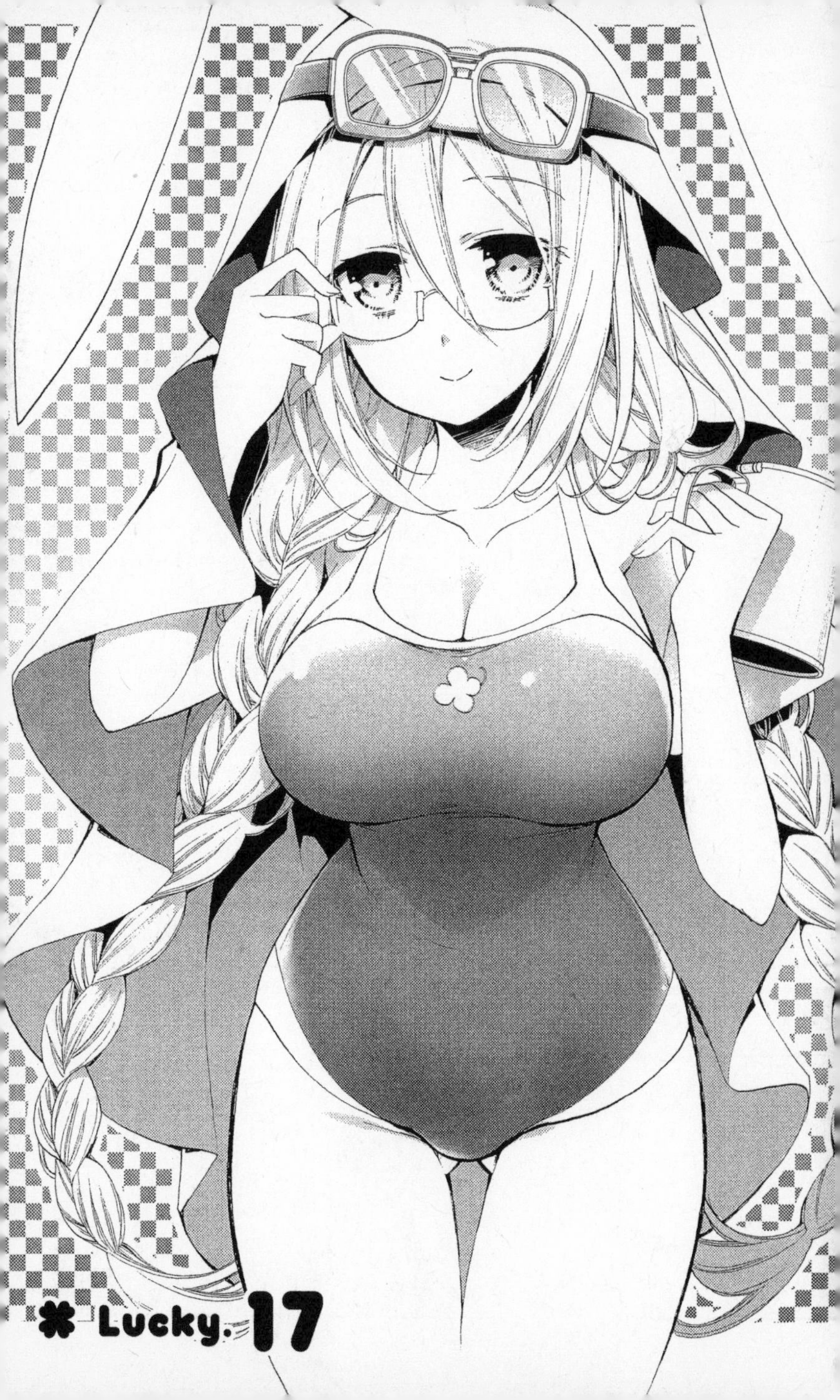

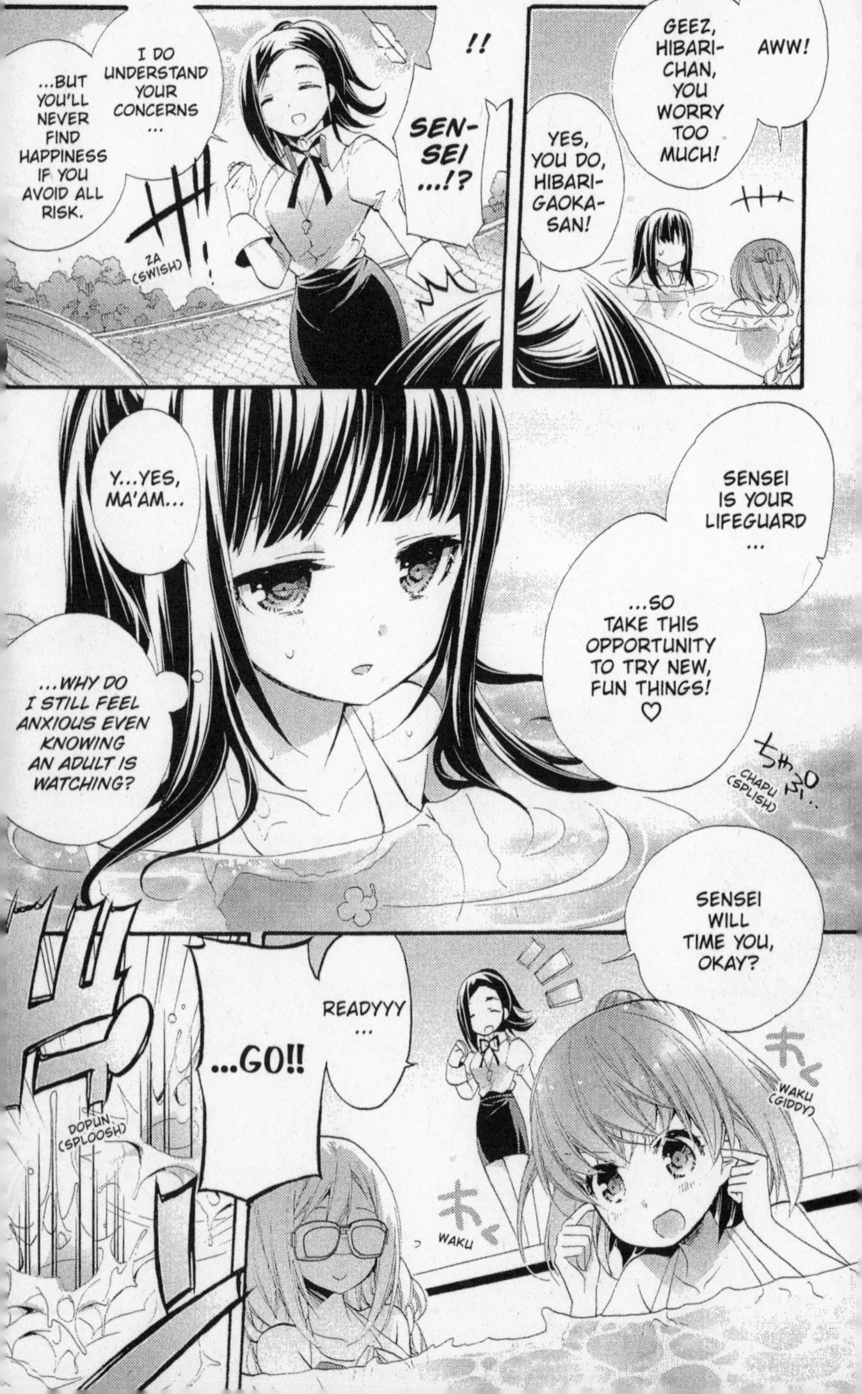
AWW!
GEEZ, HIBARI-CHAN, YOU WORRY TOO MUCH!
YES, YOU DO, HIBARI-GAOKA-SAN!
!!
SEN-SEI ...!?
I DO UNDERSTAND YOUR CONCERNS ...
...BUT YOU'LL NEVER FIND HAPPINESS IF YOU AVOID ALL RISK.
ZA (SWISH)
SENSEI IS YOUR LIFEGUARD ...
...SO TAKE THIS OPPORTUNITY TO TRY NEW, FUN THINGS! ♡
Y...YES, MA'AM...
CHAPU (SPLISH)
...WHY DO I STILL FEEL ANXIOUS EVEN KNOWING AN ADULT IS WATCHING?
SENSEI WILL TIME YOU, OKAY?
WAKU (GIDDY)
READYYY ...
WAKU
...GO!!
DOPUN (SPLOOSH)

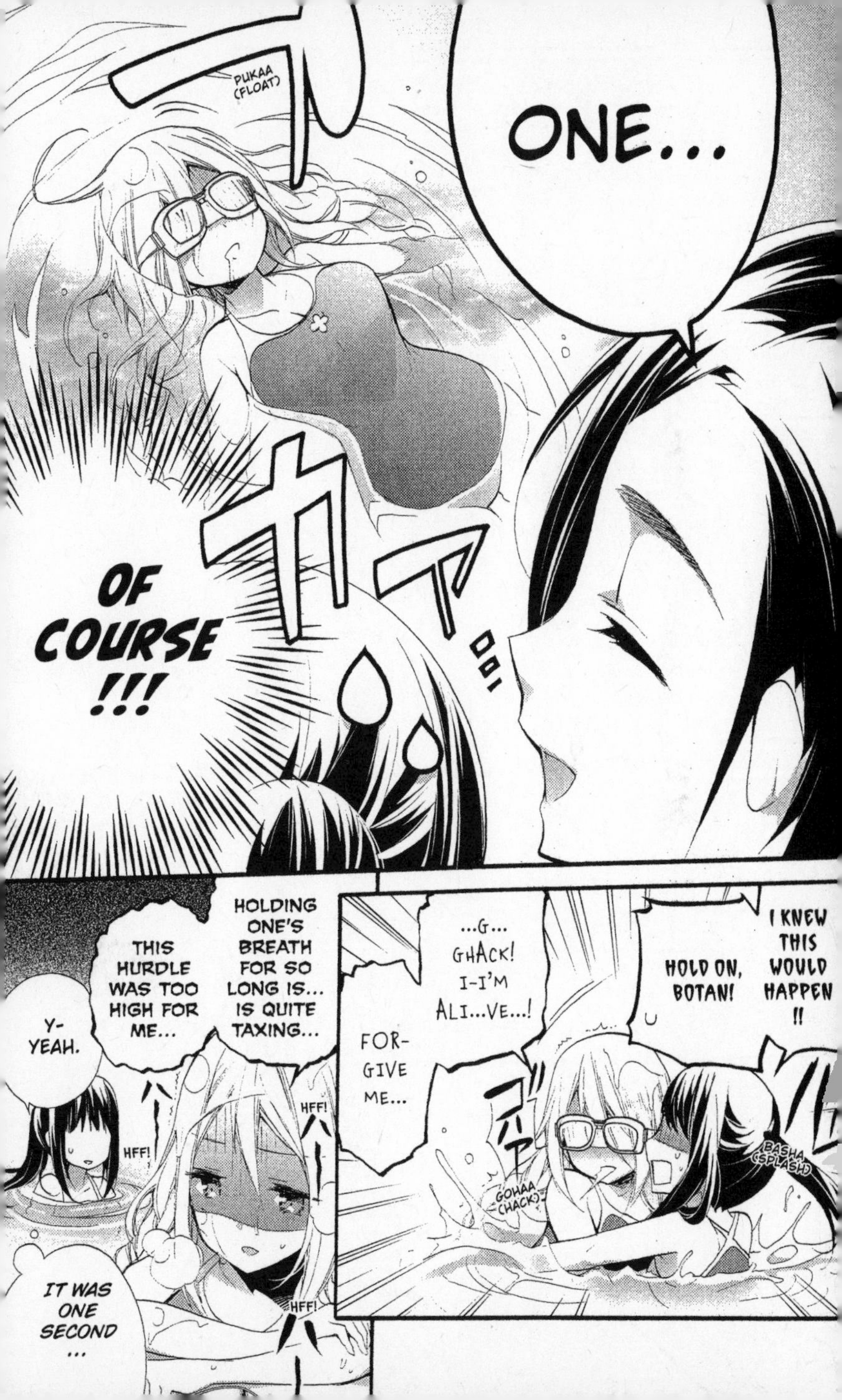
ONE...
PUKAA (FLOAT)
OF COURSE!!!
I KNEW THIS WOULD HAPPEN!!
HOLD ON, BOTAN!
...G... GHACK! I-I'M ALI...VE...!
FOR-GIVE ME...
BASHA (SPLASH)
GOHAA (HACK)
HOLDING ONE'S BREATH FOR SO LONG IS... IS QUITE TAXING...
THIS HURDLE WAS TOO HIGH FOR ME...
Y-YEAH.
HFF!
HFF!
HFF!
IT WAS ONE SECOND ...

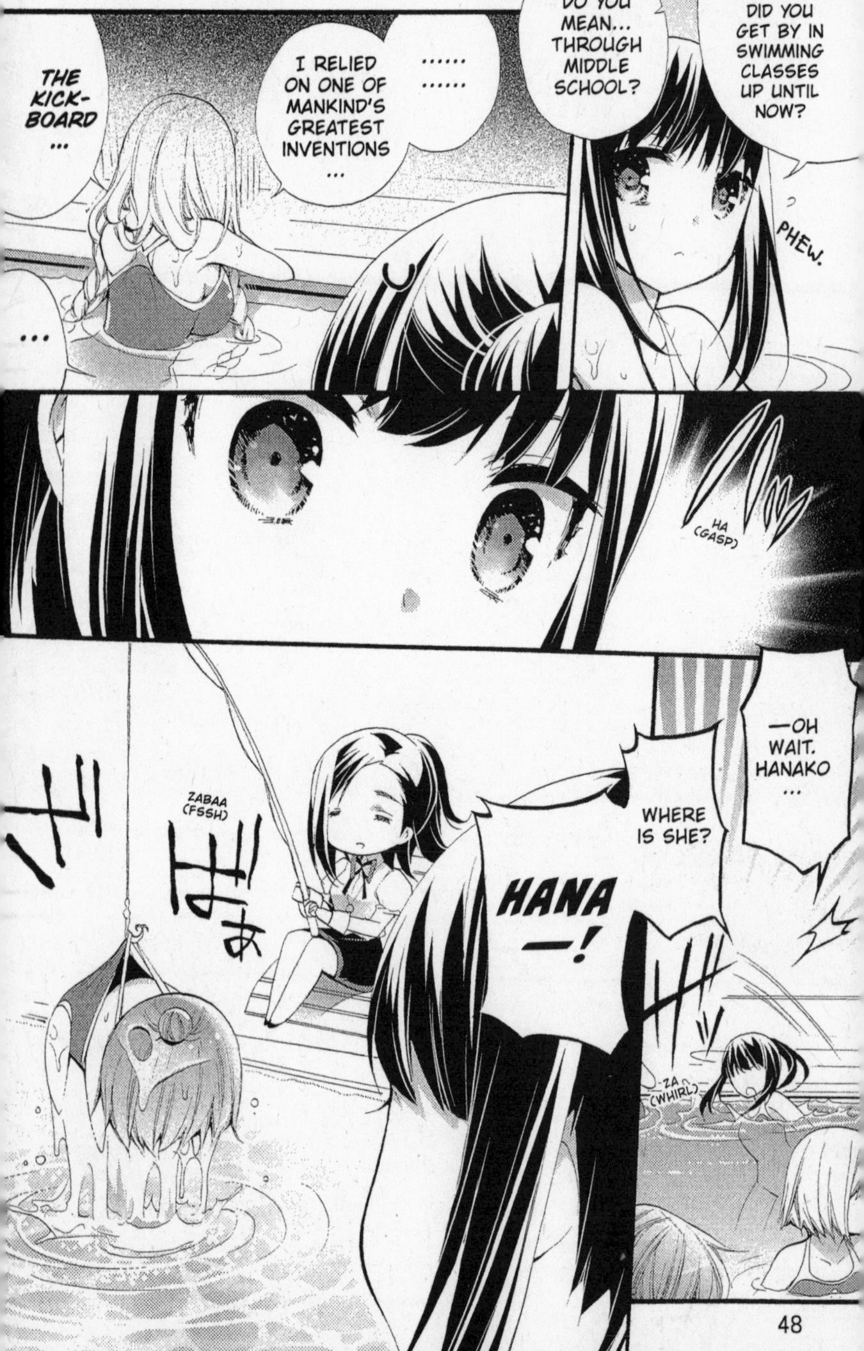
ERR...HOW DID YOU GET BY IN SWIMMING CLASSES UP UNTIL NOW?
PHEW.
DO YOU MEAN... THROUGH MIDDLE SCHOOL?
......
......
I RELIED ON ONE OF MANKIND'S GREATEST INVENTIONS ...
THE KICK-BOARD ...
...
HA (GASP)
—OH WAIT. HANAKO ...
WHERE IS SHE?
HANA—!
ZA (WHIRL)
ZABAA (FSSH)

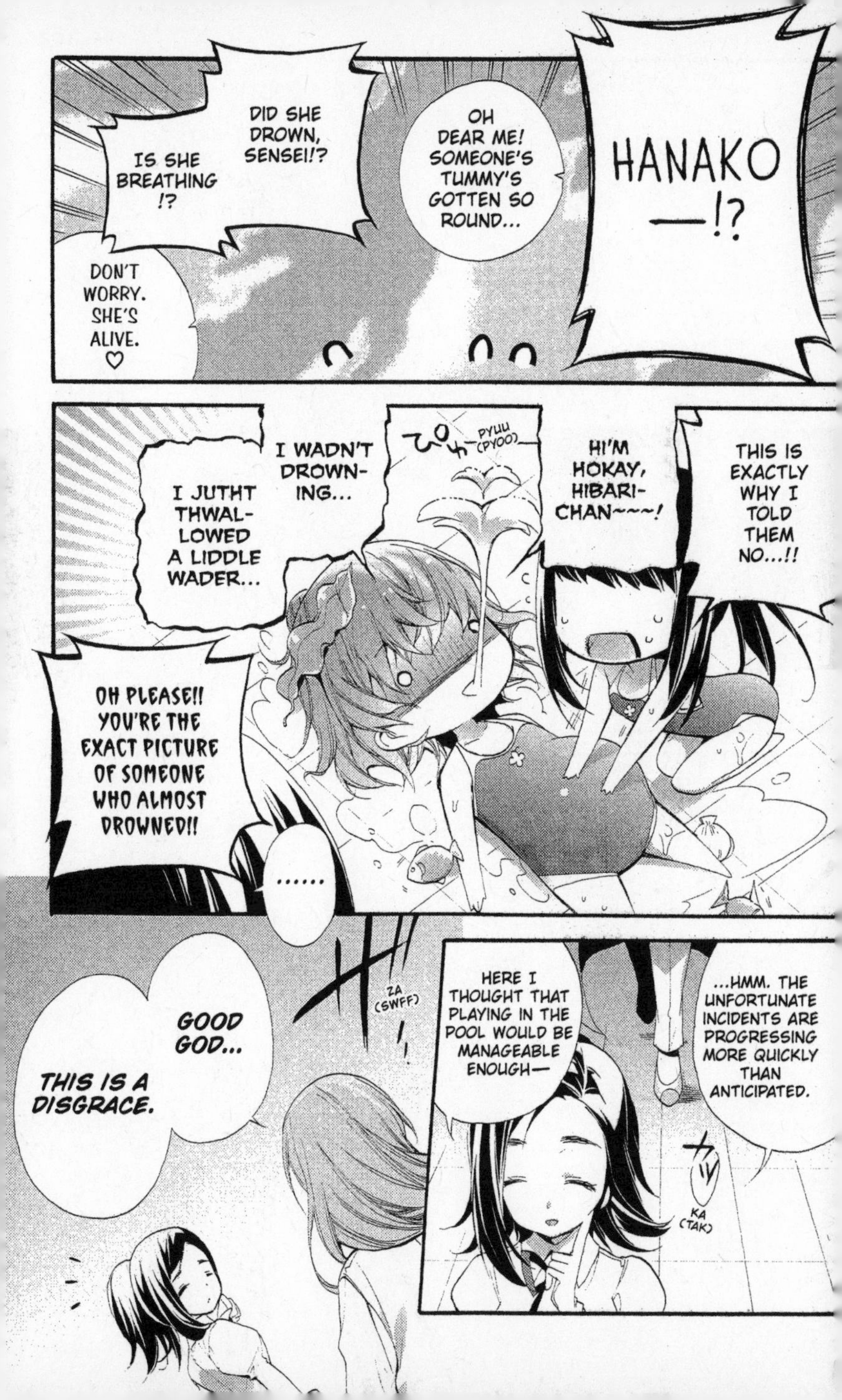
HANAKO—!?
OH DEAR ME! SOMEONE'S TUMMY'S GOTTEN SO ROUND...
DID SHE DROWN, SENSEI!?
IS SHE BREATHING!?
DON'T WORRY. SHE'S ALIVE. ♡
THIS IS EXACTLY WHY I TOLD THEM NO...!!
HI'M HOKAY, HIBARI-CHAN~~~!
PYUU (PYOO)
I WADN'T DROWNING...
I JUTHT THWALLOWED A LIDDLE WADER...
OH PLEASE!! YOU'RE THE EXACT PICTURE OF SOMEONE WHO ALMOST DROWNED!!
......
...HMM. THE UNFORTUNATE INCIDENTS ARE PROGRESSING MORE QUICKLY THAN ANTICIPATED.
KA (TAK)
HERE I THOUGHT THAT PLAYING IN THE POOL WOULD BE MANAGEABLE ENOUGH—
ZA (SWFF)
GOOD GOD...
THIS IS A DISGRACE.

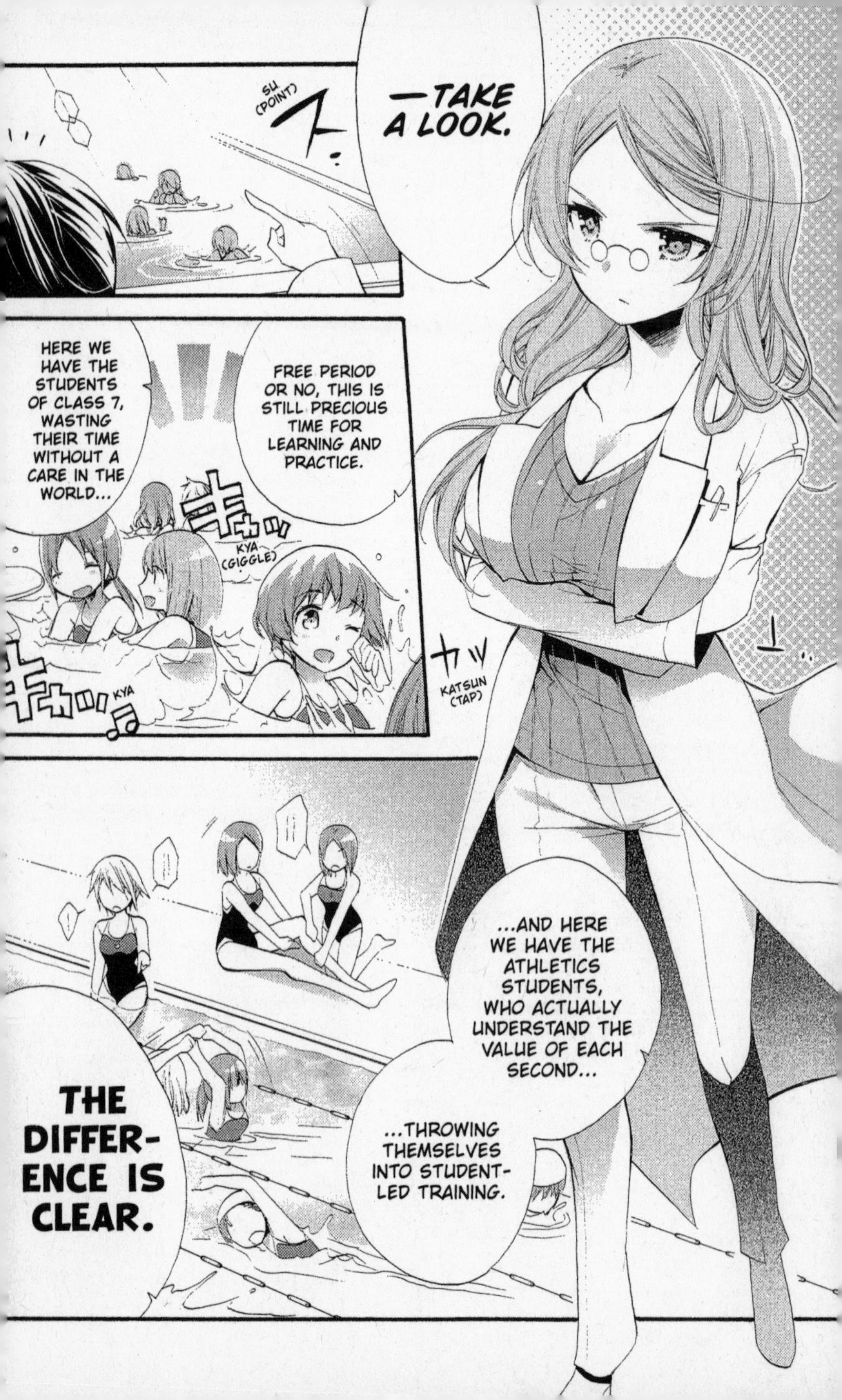
—TAKE A LOOK.
ス
SU (POINT)
FREE PERIOD OR NO, THIS IS STILL PRECIOUS TIME FOR LEARNING AND PRACTICE.
HERE WE HAVE THE STUDENTS OF CLASS 7, WASTING THEIR TIME WITHOUT A CARE IN THE WORLD...
キャッ
KYA (GIGGLE)
カツ
KATSUN (TAP)
キャッ♪
KYA
...AND HERE WE HAVE THE ATHLETICS STUDENTS, WHO ACTUALLY UNDERSTAND THE VALUE OF EACH SECOND...
...THROWING THEMSELVES INTO STUDENT-LED TRAINING.
THE DIFFERENCE IS CLEAR.

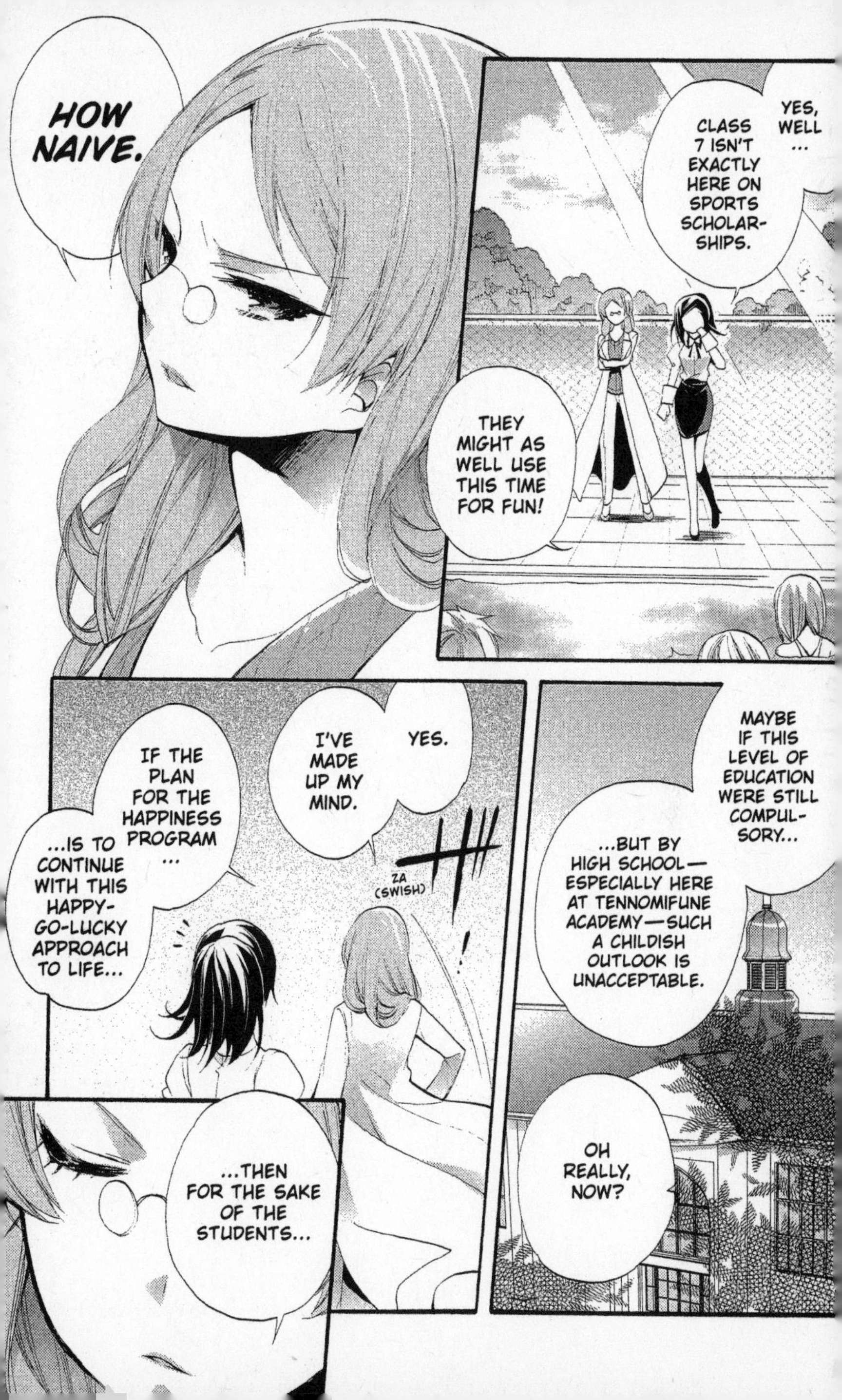
YES, WELL ...
CLASS 7 ISN'T EXACTLY HERE ON SPORTS SCHOLAR-SHIPS.
THEY MIGHT AS WELL USE THIS TIME FOR FUN!
HOW NAIVE.
MAYBE IF THIS LEVEL OF EDUCATION WERE STILL COMPUL-SORY...
...BUT BY HIGH SCHOOL—ESPECIALLY HERE AT TENNOMIFUNE ACADEMY—SUCH A CHILDISH OUTLOOK IS UNACCEPTABLE.
OH REALLY, NOW?
YES.
I'VE MADE UP MY MIND.
ZA (SWISH)
IF THE PLAN FOR THE HAPPINESS PROGRAM ...
...IS TO CONTINUE WITH THIS HAPPY-GO-LUCKY APPROACH TO LIFE...
...THEN FOR THE SAKE OF THE STUDENTS...

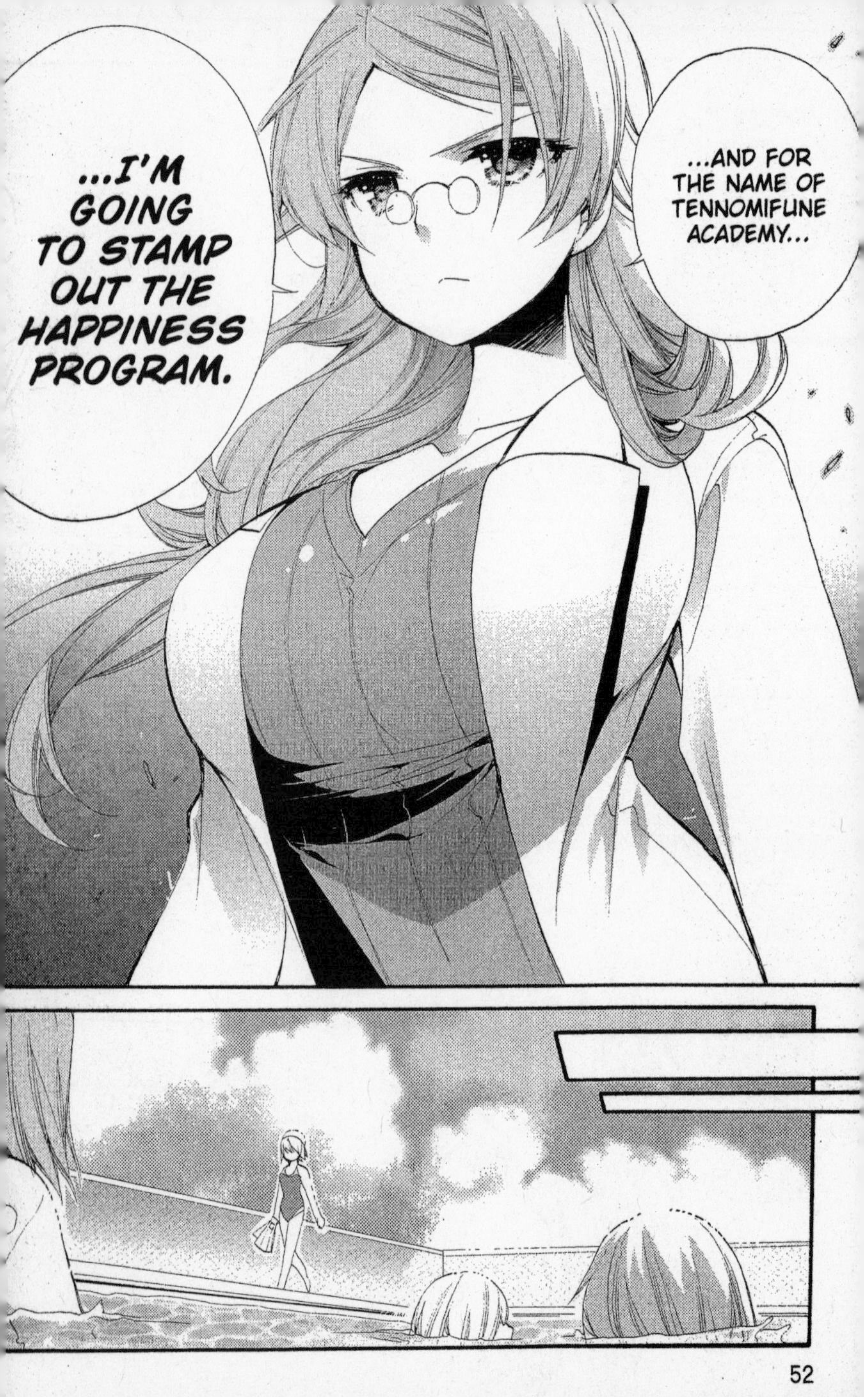
...AND FOR THE NAME OF TENNOMIFUNE ACADEMY...
...I'M GOING TO STAMP OUT THE HAPPINESS PROGRAM.

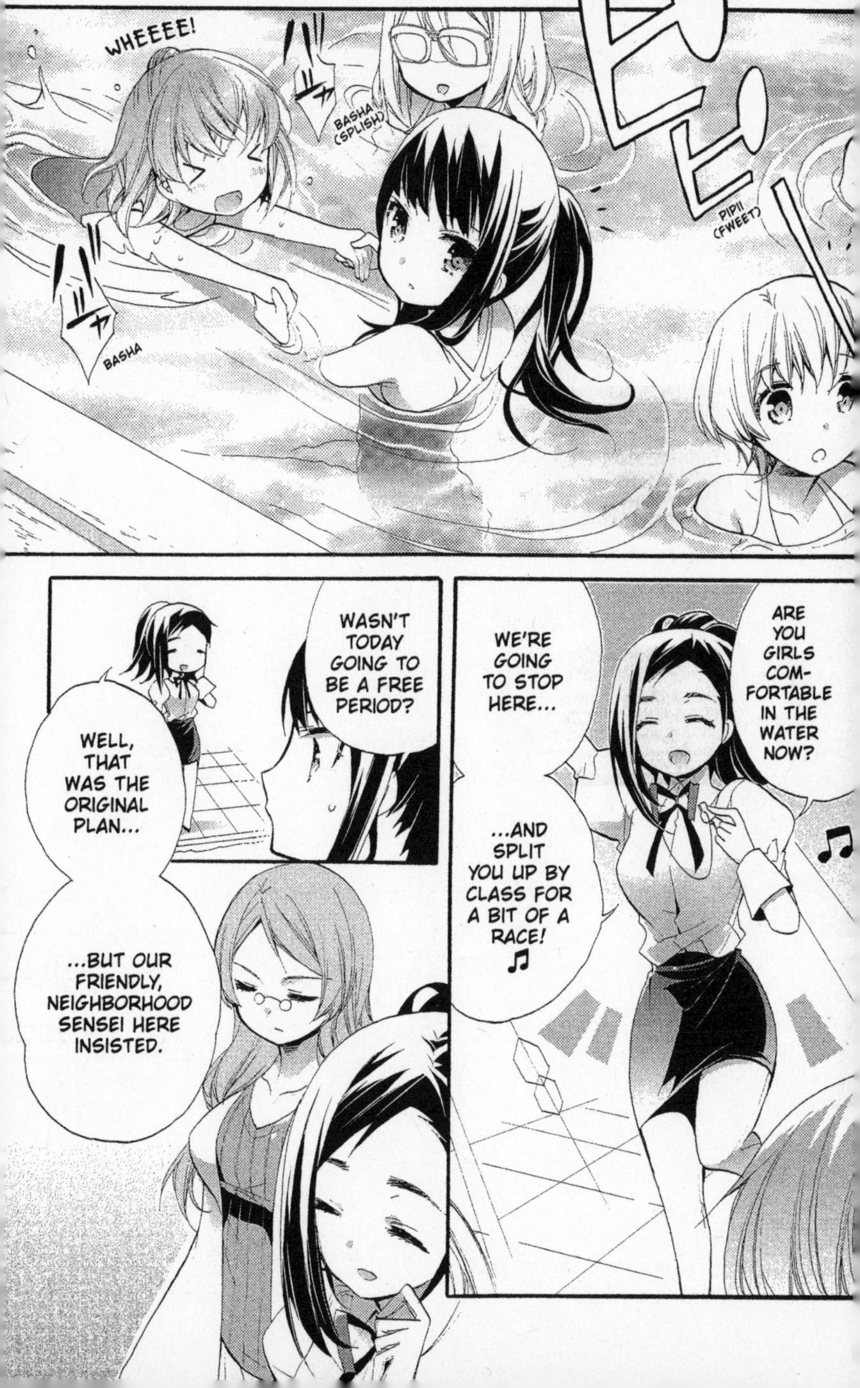
PIPII (FWEET)
BASHA (SPLISH)
WHEEEE!
BASHA
ARE YOU GIRLS COM-FORTABLE IN THE WATER NOW?
WE'RE GOING TO STOP HERE...
...AND SPLIT YOU UP BY CLASS FOR A BIT OF A RACE! ♫
WASN'T TODAY GOING TO BE A FREE PERIOD?
WELL, THAT WAS THE ORIGINAL PLAN...
...BUT OUR FRIENDLY, NEIGHBORHOOD SENSEI HERE INSISTED.

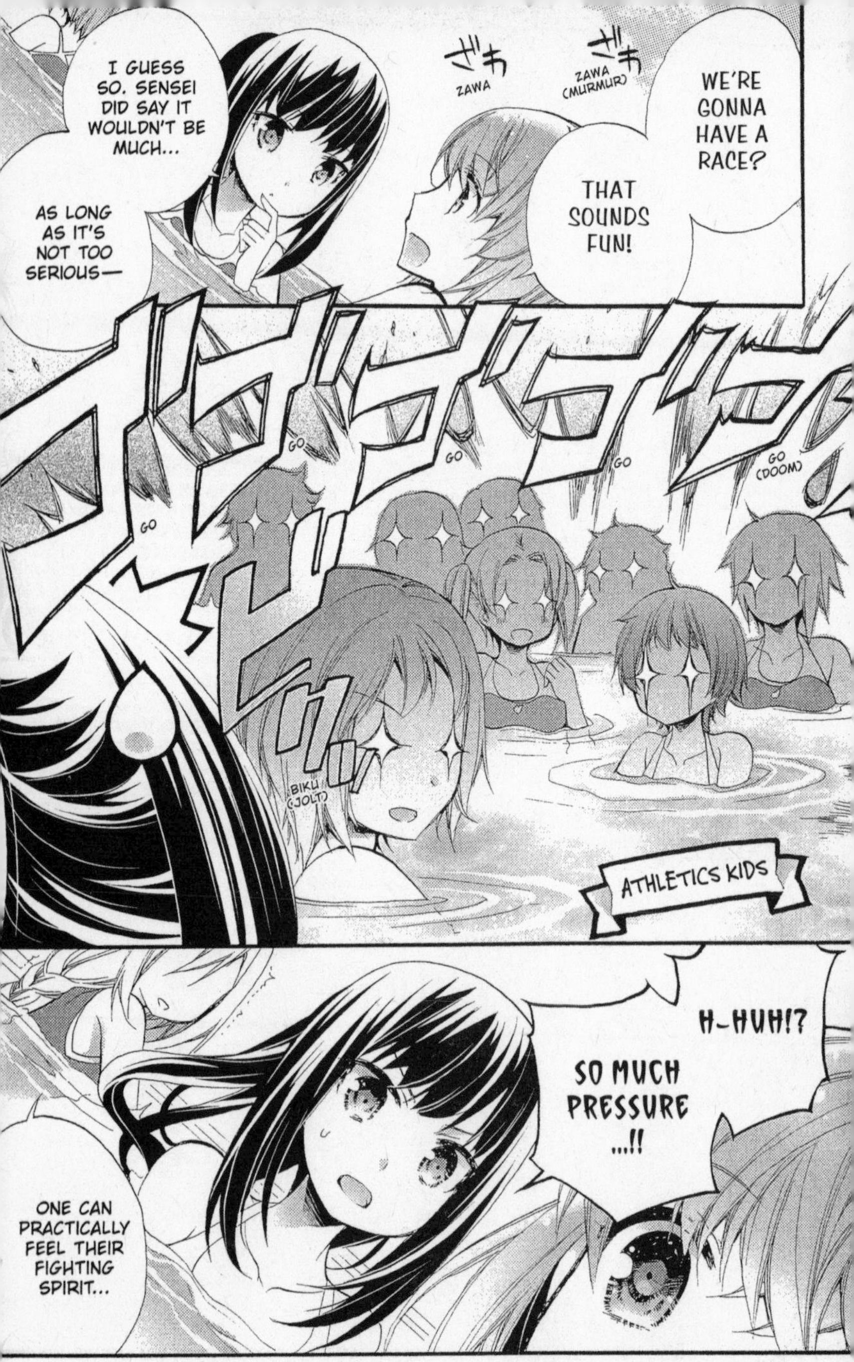
WE'RE GONNA HAVE A RACE?
THAT SOUNDS FUN!
ざわ
ZAWA (MURMUR)
ざわ
ZAWA
I GUESS SO. SENSEI DID SAY IT WOULDN'T BE MUCH...
AS LONG AS IT'S NOT TOO SERIOUS—
GO (DOOM)
GO
GO
GO
GO
BIKU (JOLT)
ATHLETICS KIDS
H-HUH!?
SO MUCH PRESSURE ...!!
ONE CAN PRACTICALLY FEEL THEIR FIGHTING SPIRIT...

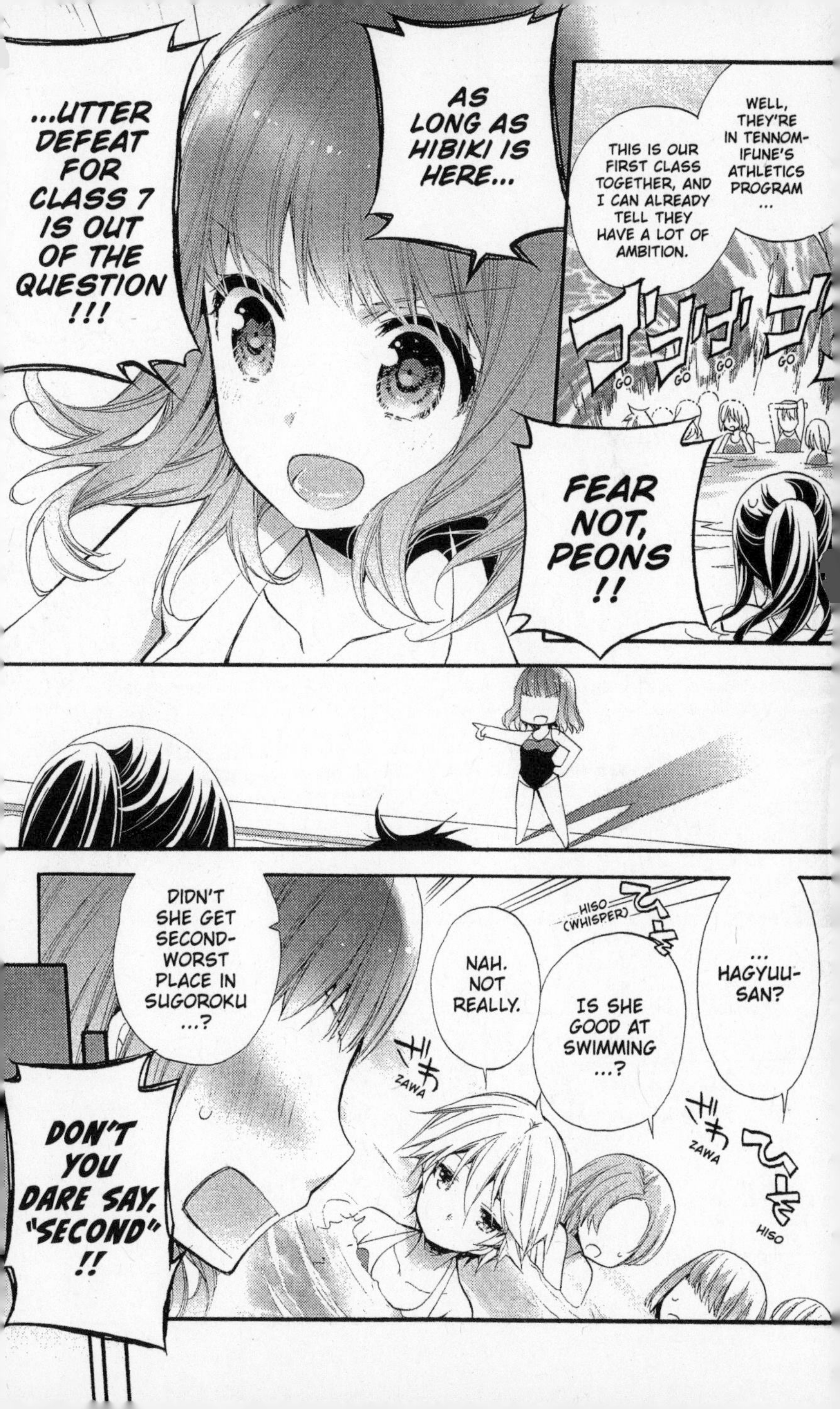
WELL, THEY'RE IN TENNOMIFUNE'S ATHLETICS PROGRAM...
THIS IS OUR FIRST CLASS TOGETHER, AND I CAN ALREADY TELL THEY HAVE A LOT OF AMBITION.
GO GO GO GO
FEAR NOT, PEONS!!
AS LONG AS HIBIKI IS HERE...
...UTTER DEFEAT FOR CLASS 7 IS OUT OF THE QUESTION!!!
...HAGYUU-SAN?
HISO (WHISPER)
IS SHE GOOD AT SWIMMING...?
NAH. NOT REALLY.
ZAWA
HISO
ZAWA
DIDN'T SHE GET SECOND-WORST PLACE IN SUGOROKU...?
DON'T YOU DARE SAY, "SECOND"!!

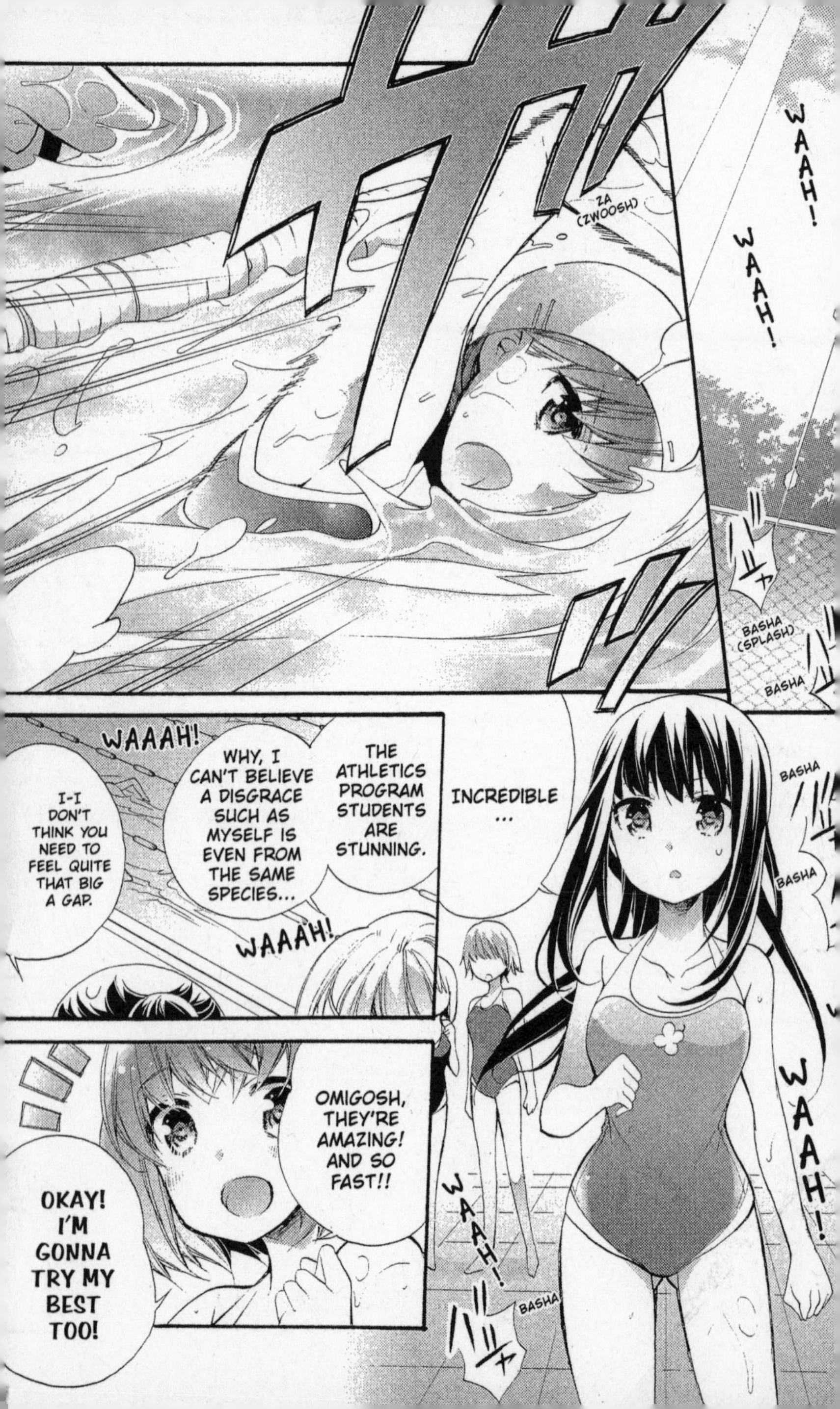
WAAH!
WAAH!
ZA (ZWOOSH)
BASHA (SPLASH)
BASHA
INCREDIBLE ...
BASHA
BASHA
WAAH!
WAAH!
BASHA
THE ATHLETICS PROGRAM STUDENTS ARE STUNNING.
WAAAH!
WHY, I CAN'T BELIEVE A DISGRACE SUCH AS MYSELF IS EVEN FROM THE SAME SPECIES...
I-I DON'T THINK YOU NEED TO FEEL QUITE THAT BIG A GAP.
WAAAH!
OMIGOSH, THEY'RE AMAZING! AND SO FAST!!
OKAY! I'M GONNA TRY MY BEST TOO!

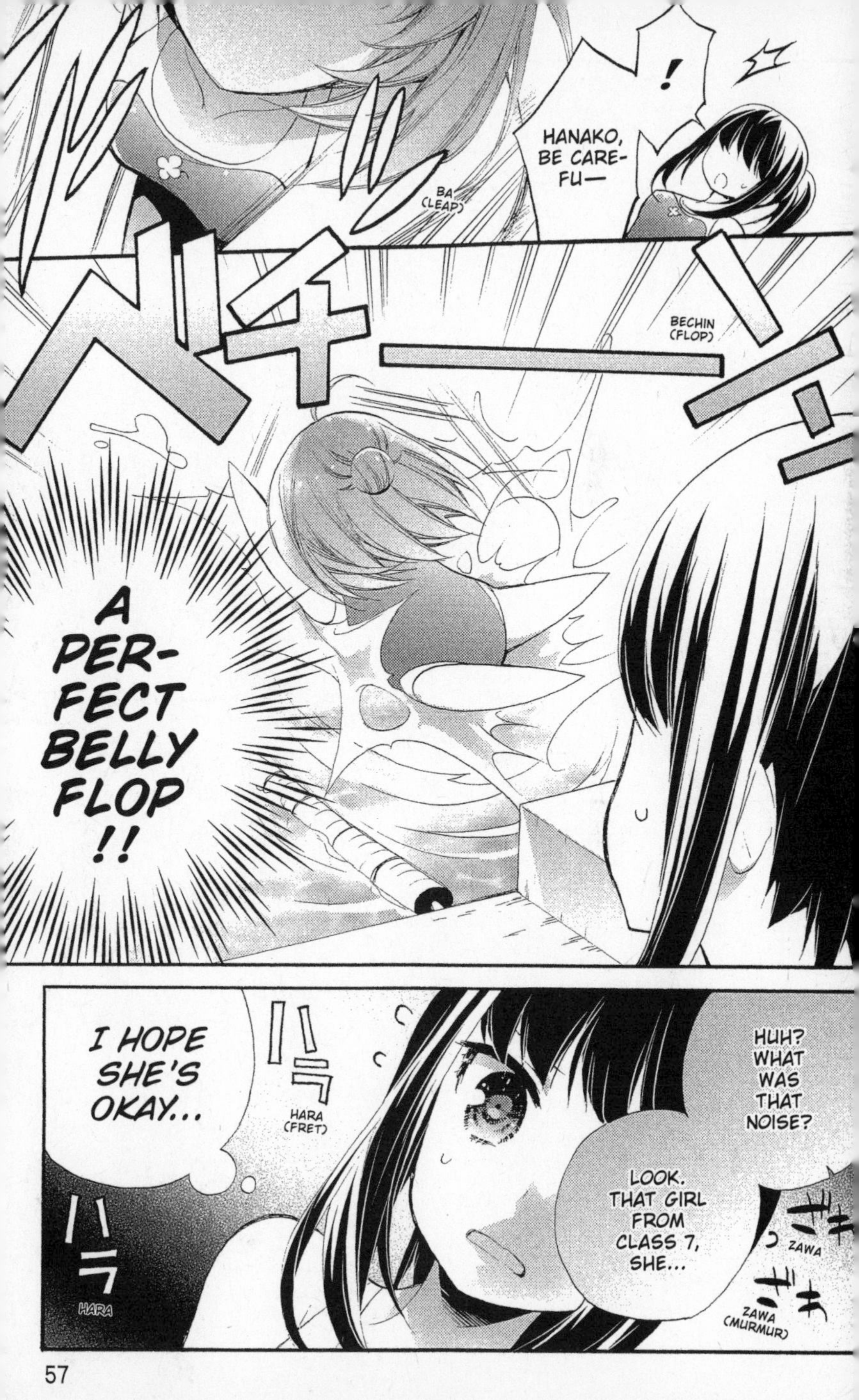
!
HANAKO, BE CARE-FU—
BA (LEAP)
BECHIN (FLOP)
A PER-FECT BELLY FLOP!!
HUH? WHAT WAS THAT NOISE?
ZAWA
LOOK. THAT GIRL FROM CLASS 7, SHE...
ZAWA (MURMUR)
HARA (FRET)
I HOPE SHE'S OKAY...
HARA

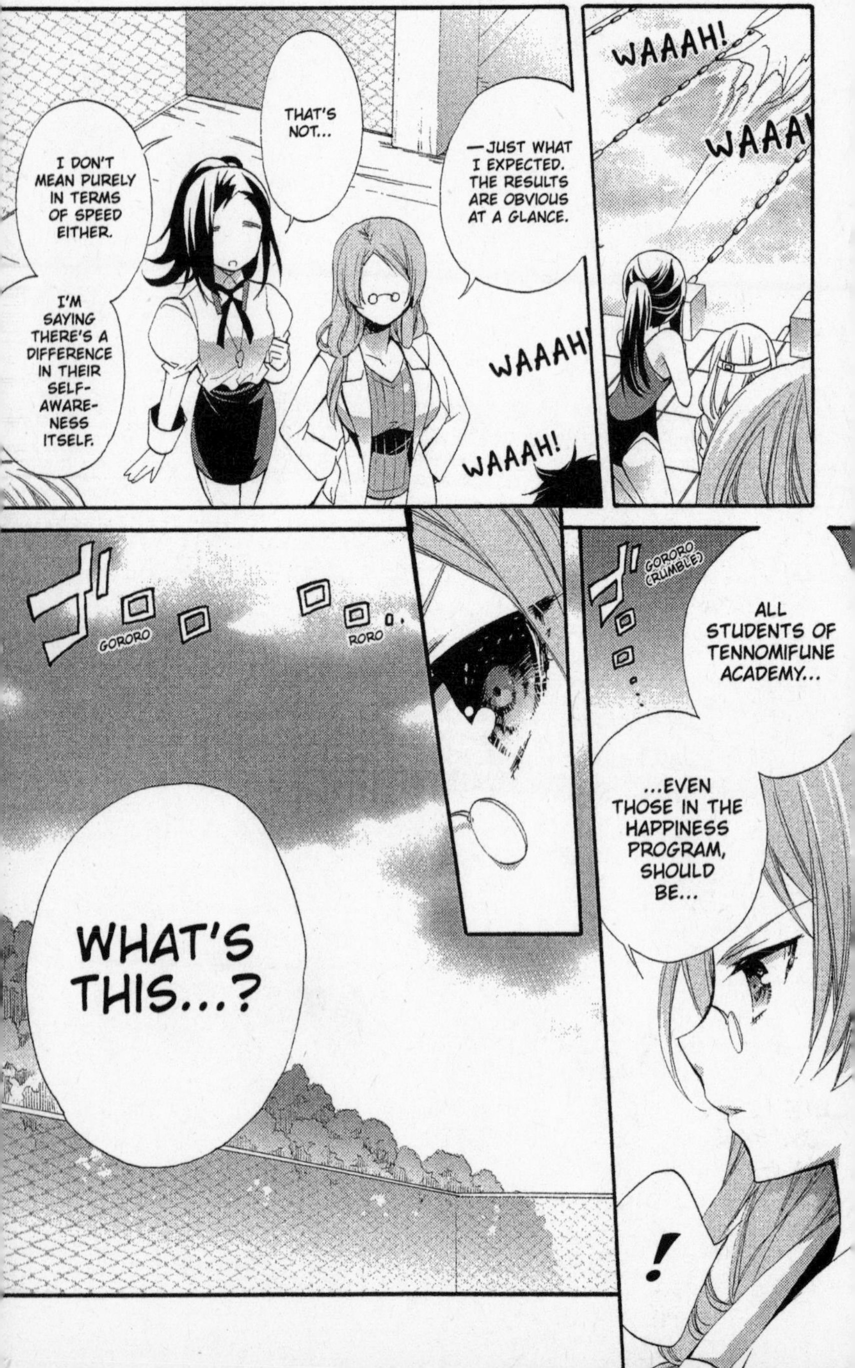
WAAAH!
WAAA
—JUST WHAT I EXPECTED. THE RESULTS ARE OBVIOUS AT A GLANCE.
WAAAH!
WAAAH!
THAT'S NOT...
I DON'T MEAN PURELY IN TERMS OF SPEED EITHER.
I'M SAYING THERE'S A DIFFERENCE IN THEIR SELF-AWARENESS ITSELF.
GORORO (RUMBLE)
ALL STUDENTS OF TENNOMIFUNE ACADEMY...
...EVEN THOSE IN THE HAPPINESS PROGRAM, SHOULD BE...
!
GORORO
RORO
WHAT'S THIS...?

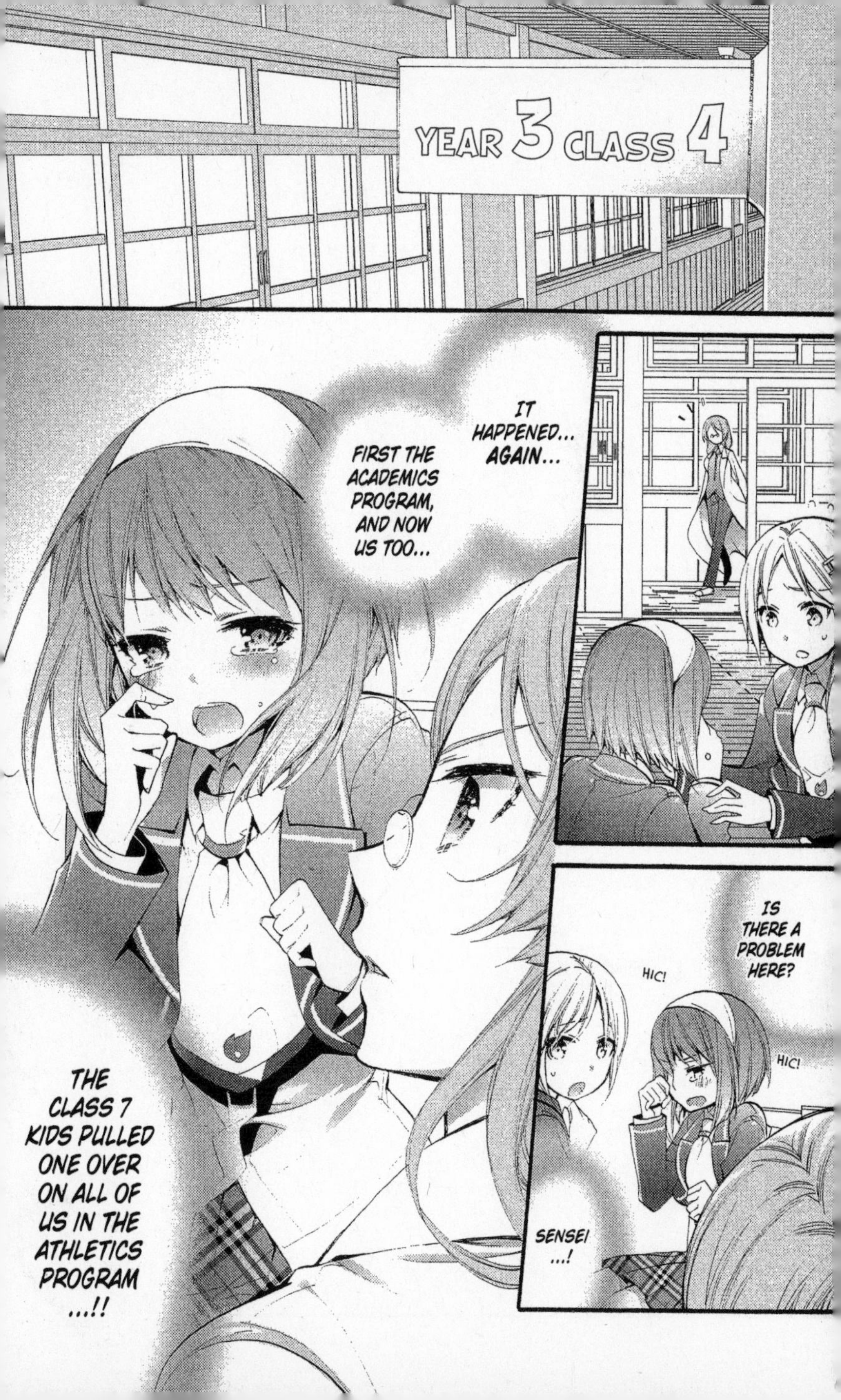

YEAR 3 CLASS 4
IT HAPPENED... AGAIN...
FIRST THE ACADEMICS PROGRAM, AND NOW US TOO...
THE CLASS 7 KIDS PULLED ONE OVER ON ALL OF US IN THE ATHLETICS PROGRAM ...!!
IS THERE A PROBLEM HERE?
HIC!
HIC!
SENSEI ...!

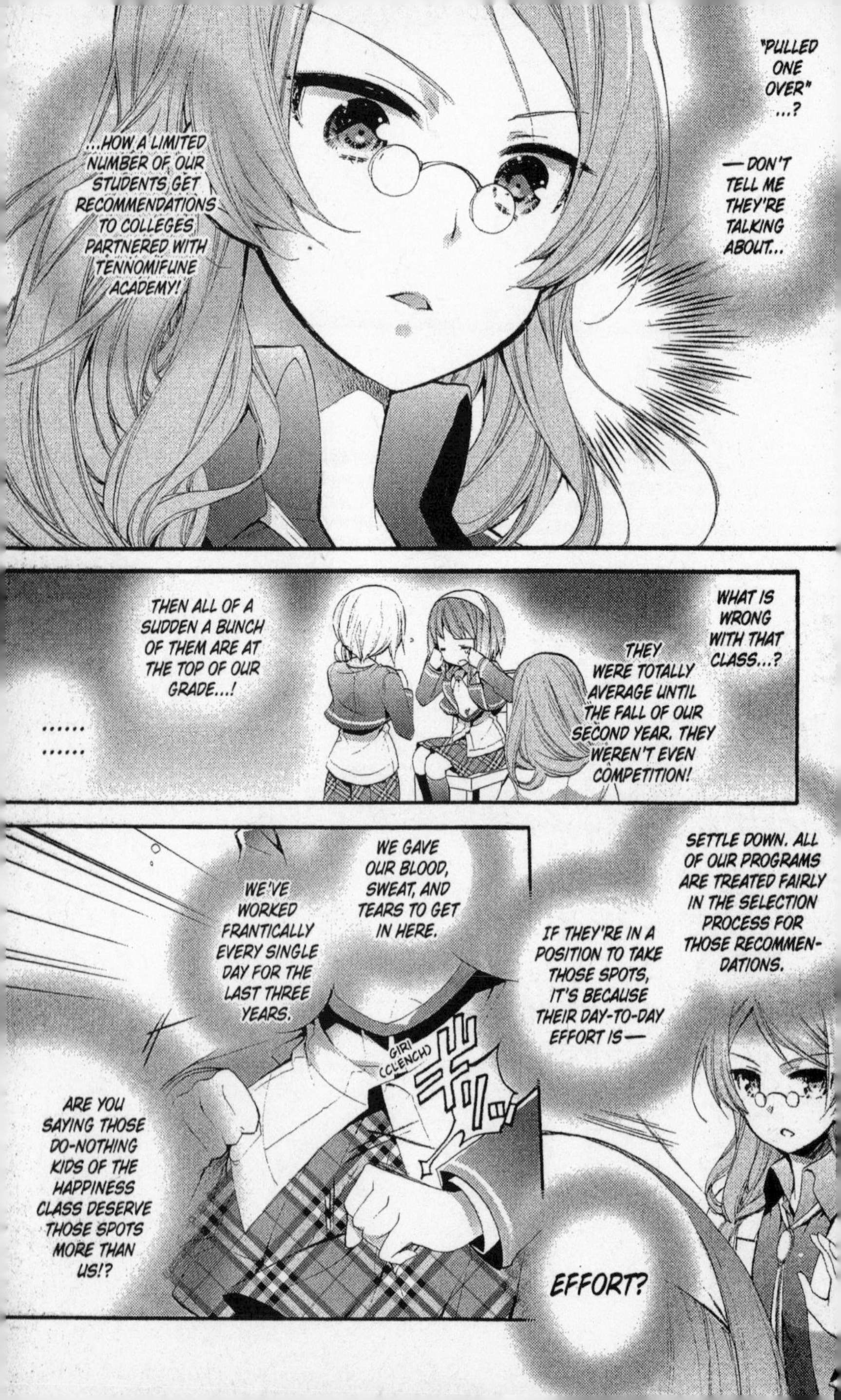
"PULLED ONE OVER" ...?
—DON'T TELL ME THEY'RE TALKING ABOUT...
...HOW A LIMITED NUMBER OF OUR STUDENTS GET RECOMMENDATIONS TO COLLEGES PARTNERED WITH TENNOMIFUNE ACADEMY!
WHAT IS WRONG WITH THAT CLASS...?
THEY WERE TOTALLY AVERAGE UNTIL THE FALL OF OUR SECOND YEAR. THEY WEREN'T EVEN COMPETITION!
THEN ALL OF A SUDDEN A BUNCH OF THEM ARE AT THE TOP OF OUR GRADE...!
....
SETTLE DOWN. ALL OF OUR PROGRAMS ARE TREATED FAIRLY IN THE SELECTION PROCESS FOR THOSE RECOMMEN-DATIONS.
IF THEY'RE IN A POSITION TO TAKE THOSE SPOTS, IT'S BECAUSE THEIR DAY-TO-DAY EFFORT IS—
EFFORT?
WE GAVE OUR BLOOD, SWEAT, AND TEARS TO GET IN HERE.
WE'VE WORKED FRANTICALLY EVERY SINGLE DAY FOR THE LAST THREE YEARS.
GIRI (CLENCH)
ARE YOU SAYING THOSE DO-NOTHING KIDS OF THE HAPPINESS CLASS DESERVE THOSE SPOTS MORE THAN US!?

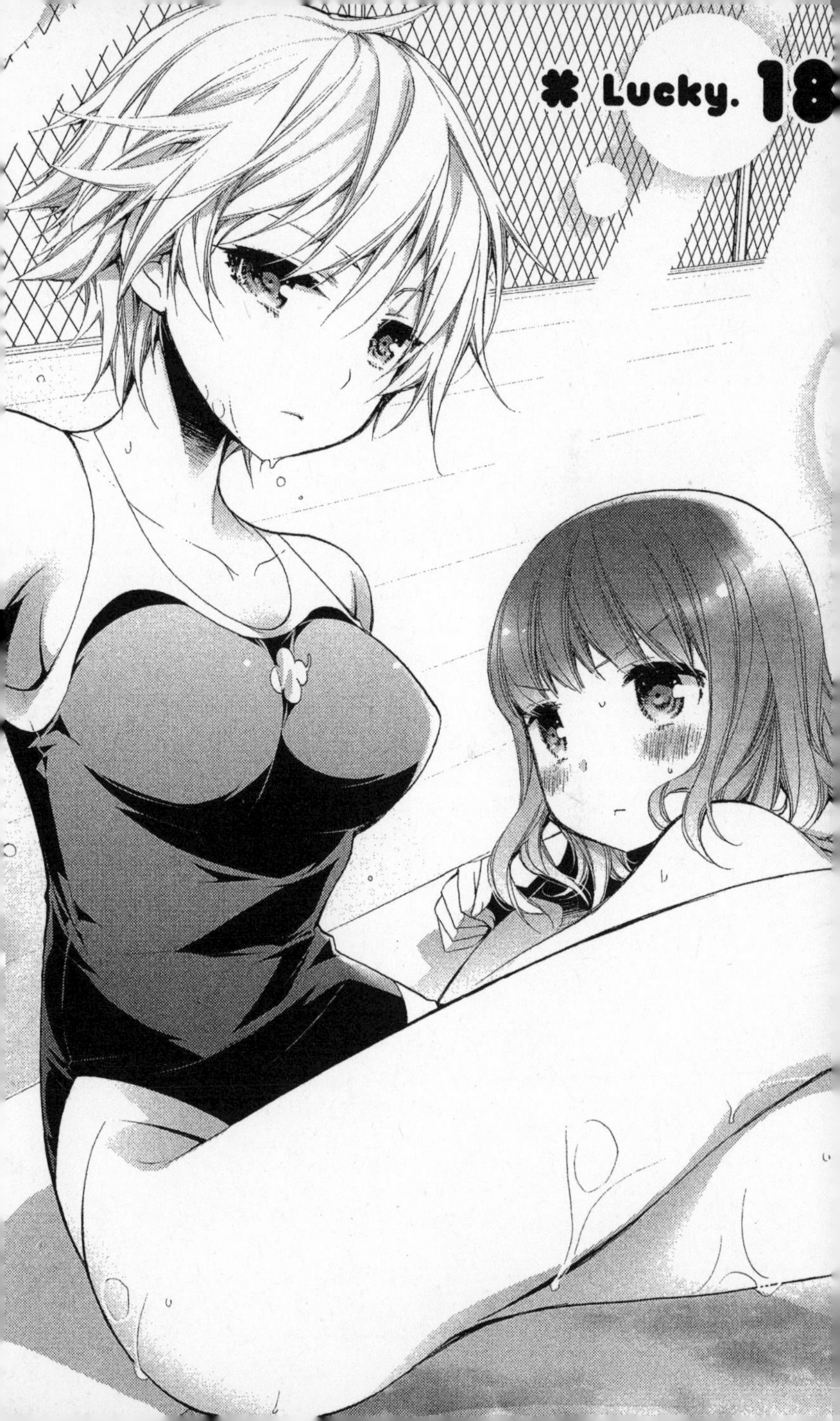
Lucky. 18

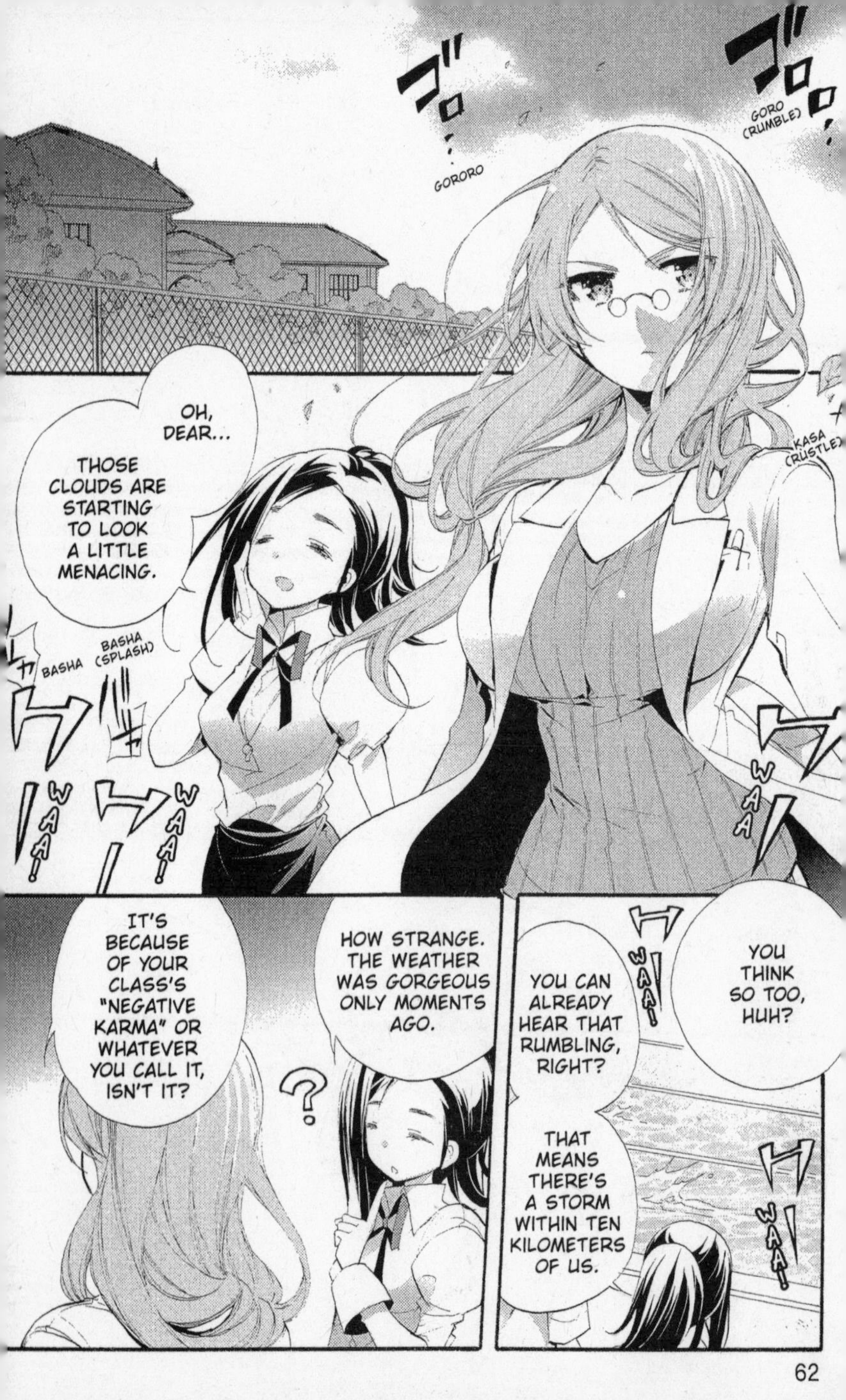
GORO (RUMBLE)
GORORO
KASA (RUSTLE)
OH, DEAR... THOSE CLOUDS ARE STARTING TO LOOK A LITTLE MENACING.
WAAA!
BASHA (SPLASH)
BASHA
WAAA!
WAAA!
YOU THINK SO TOO, HUH?
WAAA!
YOU CAN ALREADY HEAR THAT RUMBLING, RIGHT?
THAT MEANS THERE'S A STORM WITHIN TEN KILOMETERS OF US.
WAAA!
HOW STRANGE. THE WEATHER WAS GORGEOUS ONLY MOMENTS AGO.
?
IT'S BECAUSE OF YOUR CLASS'S "NEGATIVE KARMA" OR WHATEVER YOU CALL IT, ISN'T IT?

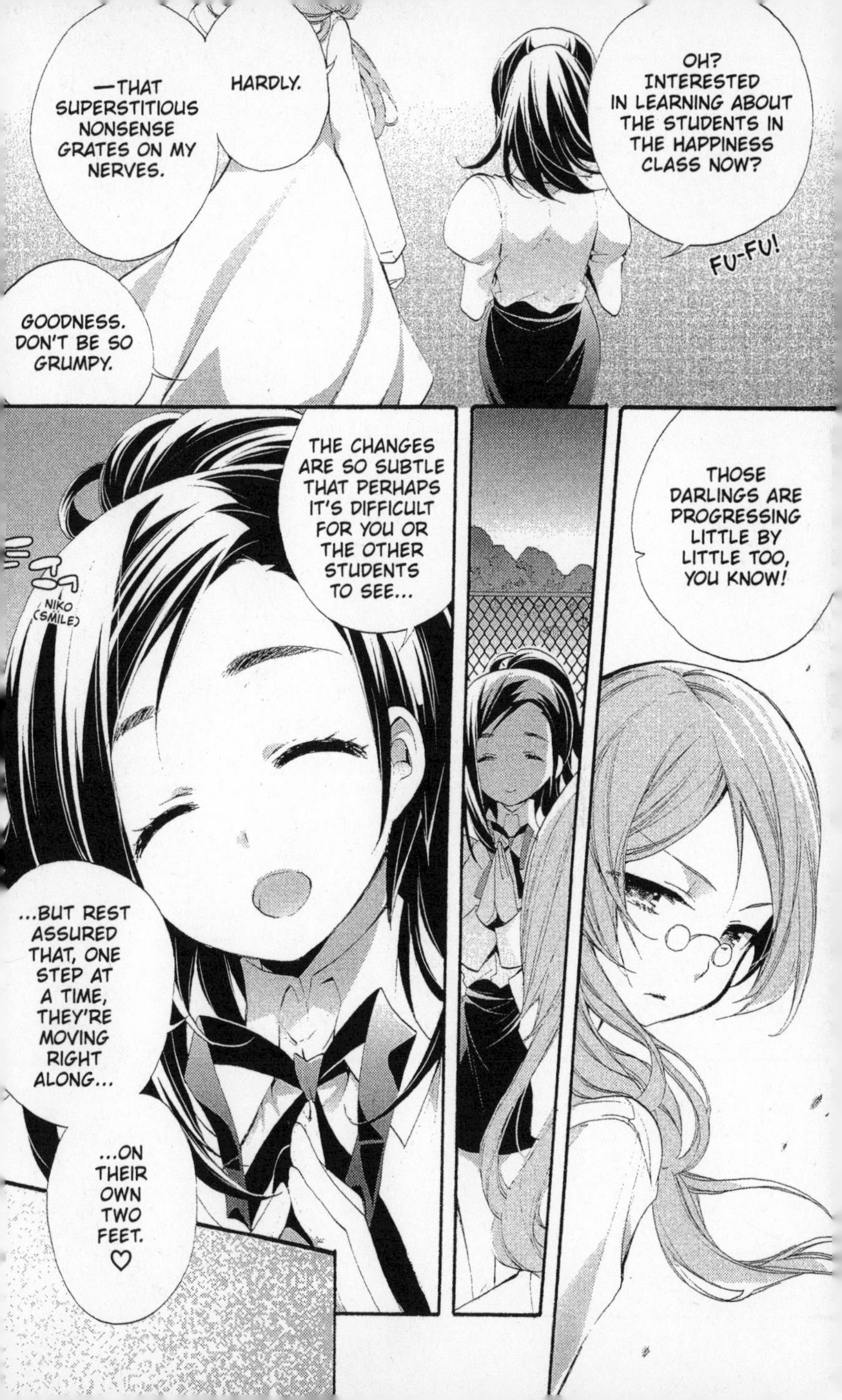
OH? INTERESTED IN LEARNING ABOUT THE STUDENTS IN THE HAPPINESS CLASS NOW?
FU-FU!
HARDLY.
—THAT SUPERSTITIOUS NONSENSE GRATES ON MY NERVES.
GOODNESS. DON'T BE SO GRUMPY.
THOSE DARLINGS ARE PROGRESSING LITTLE BY LITTLE TOO, YOU KNOW!
THE CHANGES ARE SO SUBTLE THAT PERHAPS IT'S DIFFICULT FOR YOU OR THE OTHER STUDENTS TO SEE...
NIKO (SMILE)
...BUT REST ASSURED THAT, ONE STEP AT A TIME, THEY'RE MOVING RIGHT ALONG...
...ON THEIR OWN TWO FEET. ♡

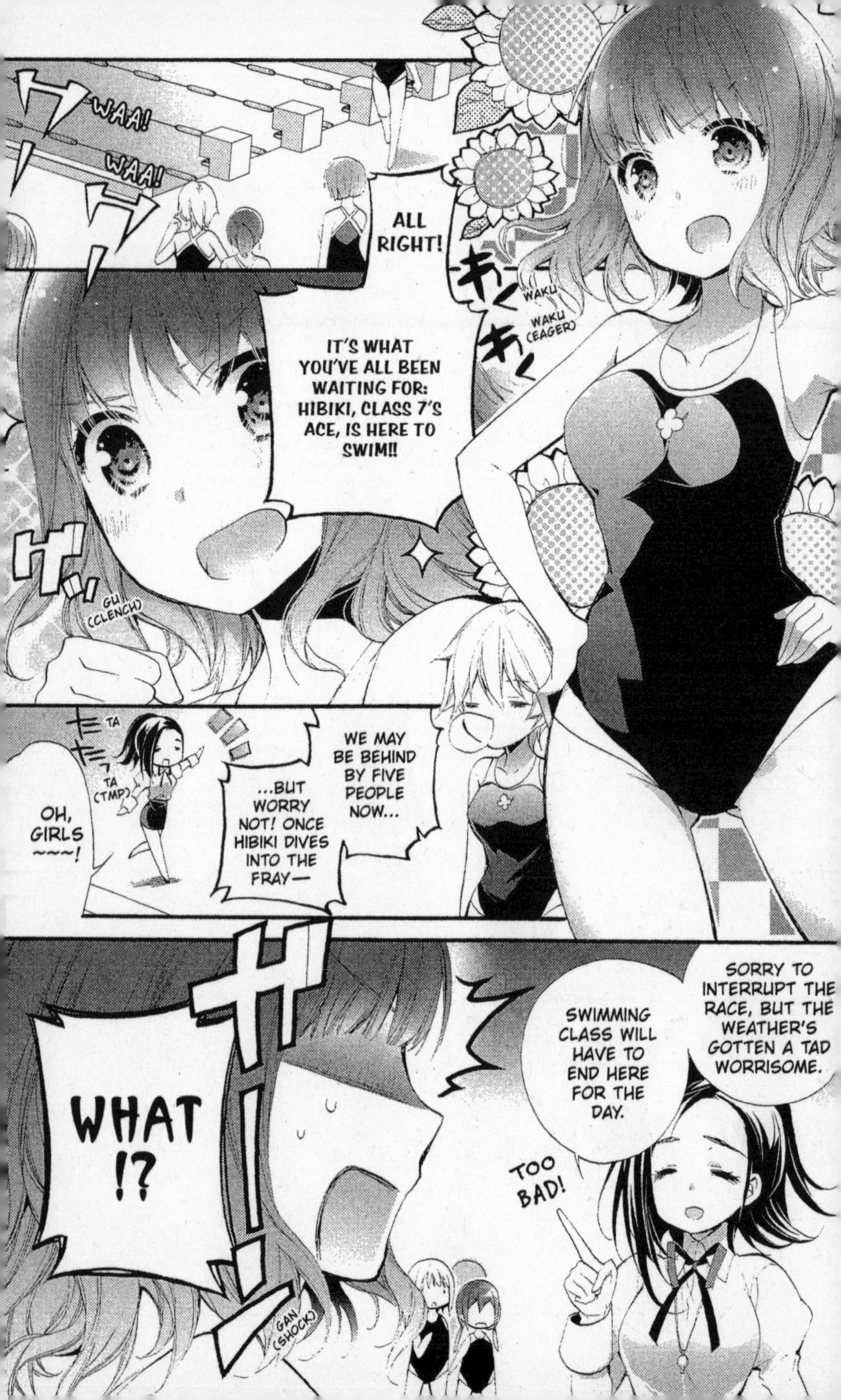

WAKU
WAKU (EAGER)
WAA!
WAA!
ALL RIGHT!
IT'S WHAT YOU'VE ALL BEEN WAITING FOR: HIBIKI, CLASS 7'S ACE, IS HERE TO SWIM!!
GU (CLENCH)
WE MAY BE BEHIND BY FIVE PEOPLE NOW...
...BUT WORRY NOT! ONCE HIBIKI DIVES INTO THE FRAY—
TA
TA (TMP)
OH, GIRLS ~~~!
SORRY TO INTERRUPT THE RACE, BUT THE WEATHER'S GOTTEN A TAD WORRISOME.
SWIMMING CLASS WILL HAVE TO END HERE FOR THE DAY.
TOO BAD!
GAN (SHOCK)
WHAT !?

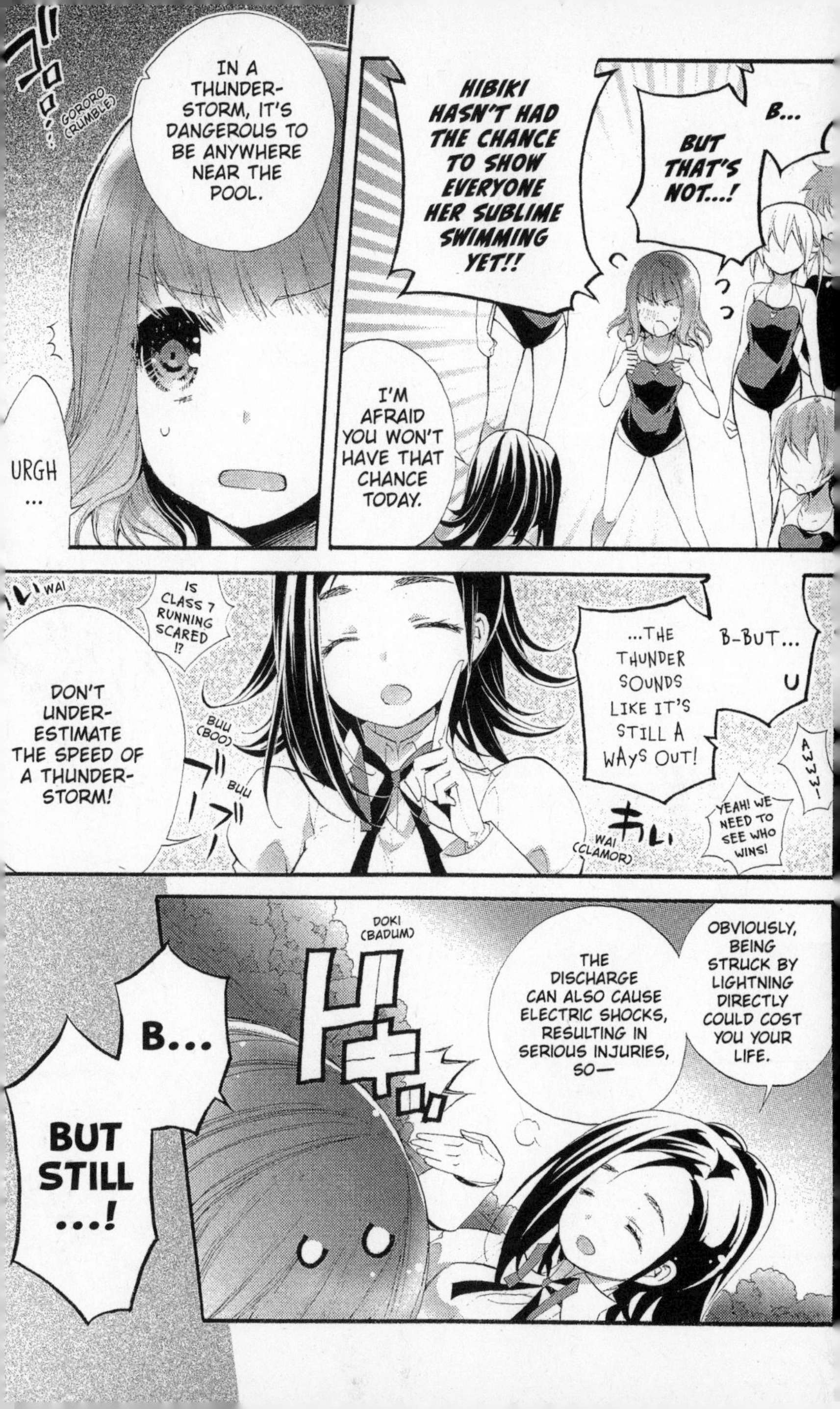
B...
BUT THAT'S NOT...!
HIBIKI HASN'T HAD THE CHANCE TO SHOW EVERYONE HER SUBLIME SWIMMING YET!!
I'M AFRAID YOU WON'T HAVE THAT CHANCE TODAY.
GORORO (RUMBLE)
IN A THUNDER-STORM, IT'S DANGEROUS TO BE ANYWHERE NEAR THE POOL.
URGH ...
B-BUT...
...THE THUNDER SOUNDS LIKE IT'S STILL A WAYS OUT!
AWWW!
YEAH! WE NEED TO SEE WHO WINS!
WAI (CLAMOR)
IS CLASS 7 RUNNING SCARED!?
WAI
BUU (BOO)
BUU
DON'T UNDER-ESTIMATE THE SPEED OF A THUNDER-STORM!
OBVIOUSLY, BEING STRUCK BY LIGHTNING DIRECTLY COULD COST YOU YOUR LIFE.
THE DISCHARGE CAN ALSO CAUSE ELECTRIC SHOCKS, RESULTING IN SERIOUS INJURIES, SO—
DOKI (BADUM)
B... BUT STILL ...!

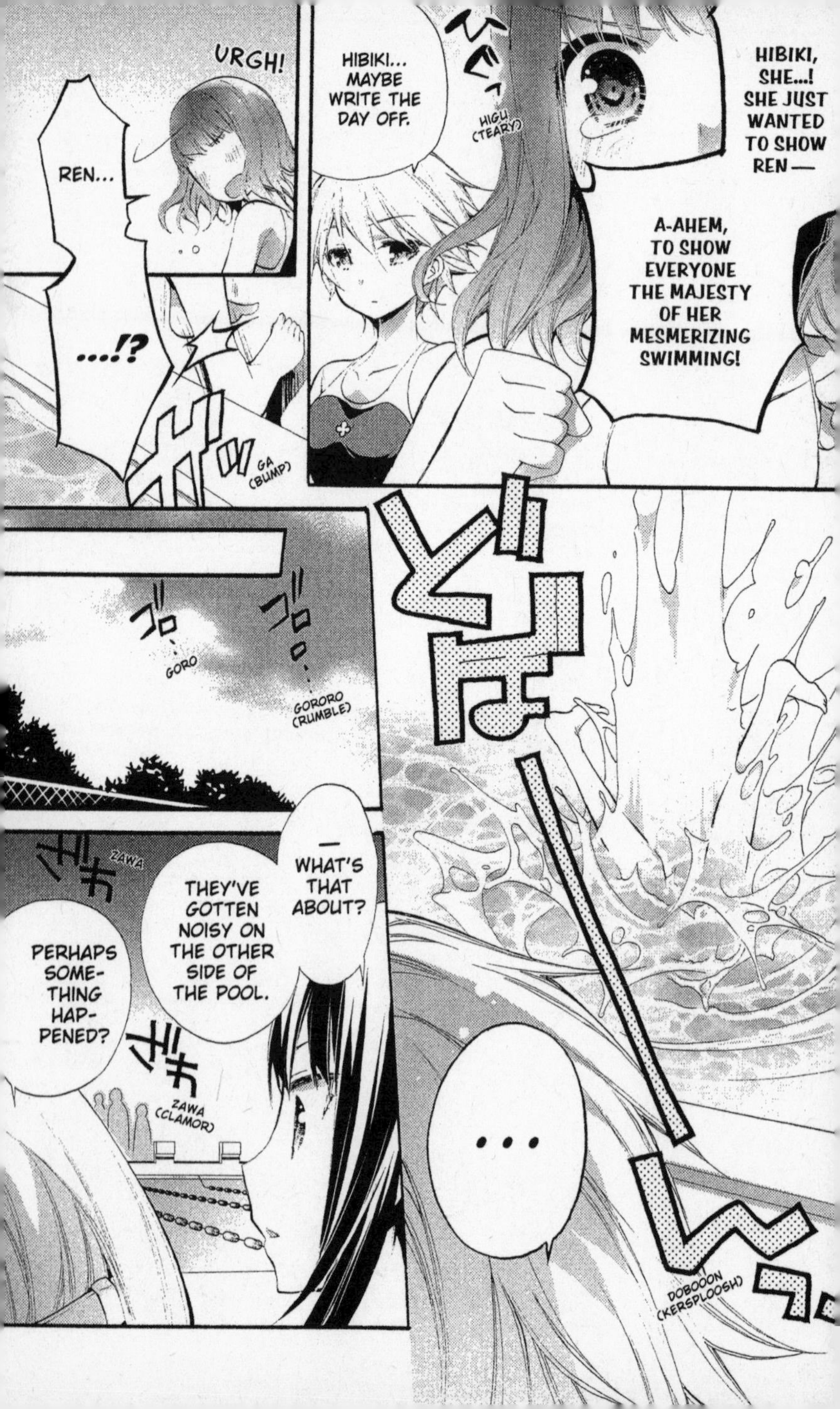
HIBIKI, SHE...! SHE JUST WANTED TO SHOW REN —
A-AHEM, TO SHOW EVERYONE THE MAJESTY OF HER MESMERIZING SWIMMING!
HIGU (TEARY)
HIBIKI... MAYBE WRITE THE DAY OFF.
URGH!
REN...
...!?
GA (BUMP)
DOBOOON (KERSPLOOSH)
...
GORO
GORORO (RUMBLE)
— WHAT'S THAT ABOUT?
THEY'VE GOTTEN NOISY ON THE OTHER SIDE OF THE POOL.
ZAWA
PERHAPS SOME-THING HAP-PENED?
ZAWA (CLAMOR)

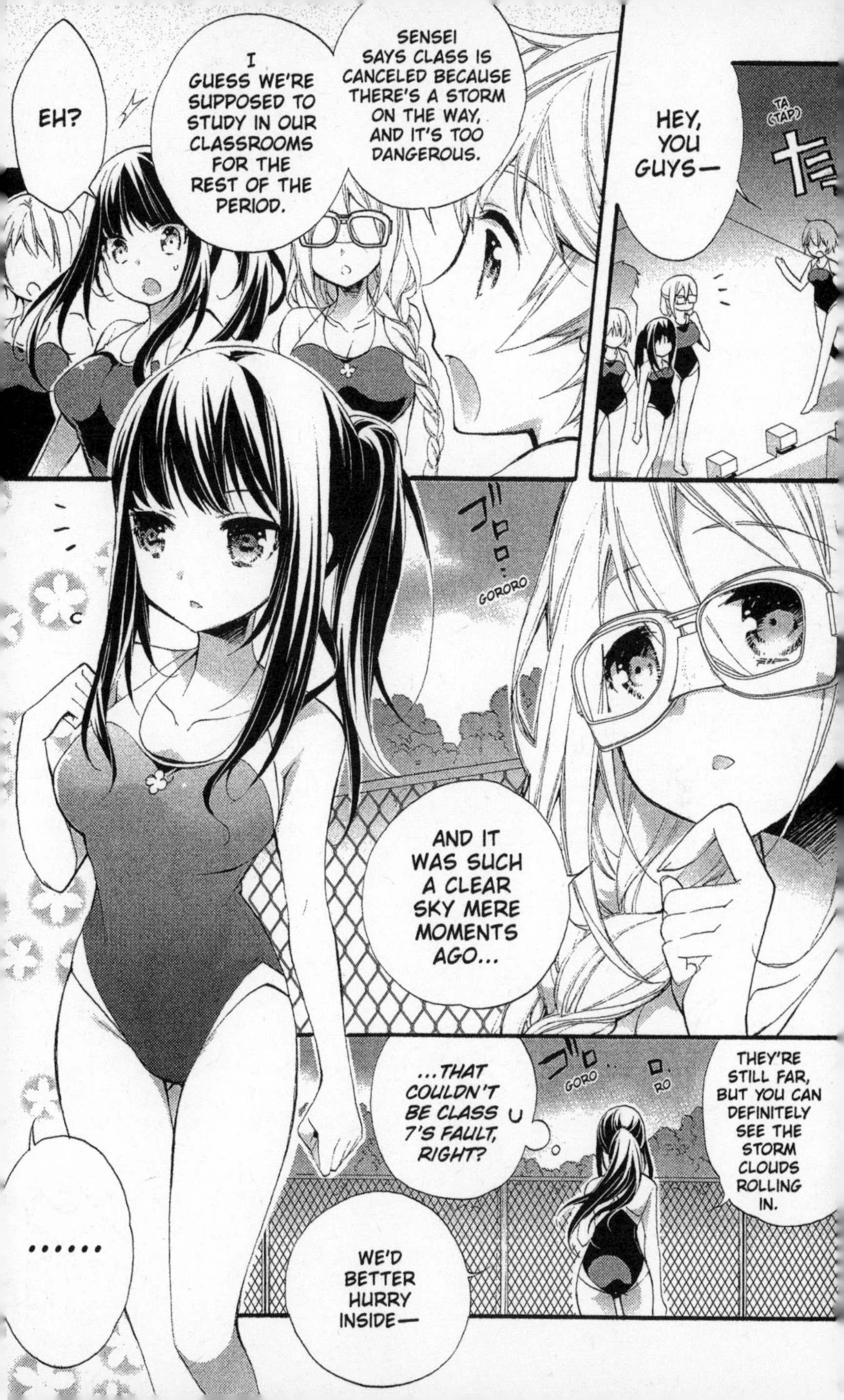
HEY, YOU GUYS—
TA (TAP)
SENSEI SAYS CLASS IS CANCELED BECAUSE THERE'S A STORM ON THE WAY, AND IT'S TOO DANGEROUS.
I GUESS WE'RE SUPPOSED TO STUDY IN OUR CLASSROOMS FOR THE REST OF THE PERIOD.
EH?
GORORO
AND IT WAS SUCH A CLEAR SKY MERE MOMENTS AGO...
THEY'RE STILL FAR, BUT YOU CAN DEFINITELY SEE THE STORM CLOUDS ROLLING IN.
GORO
RO
...THAT COULDN'T BE CLASS 7'S FAULT, RIGHT?
WE'D BETTER HURRY INSIDE—
......

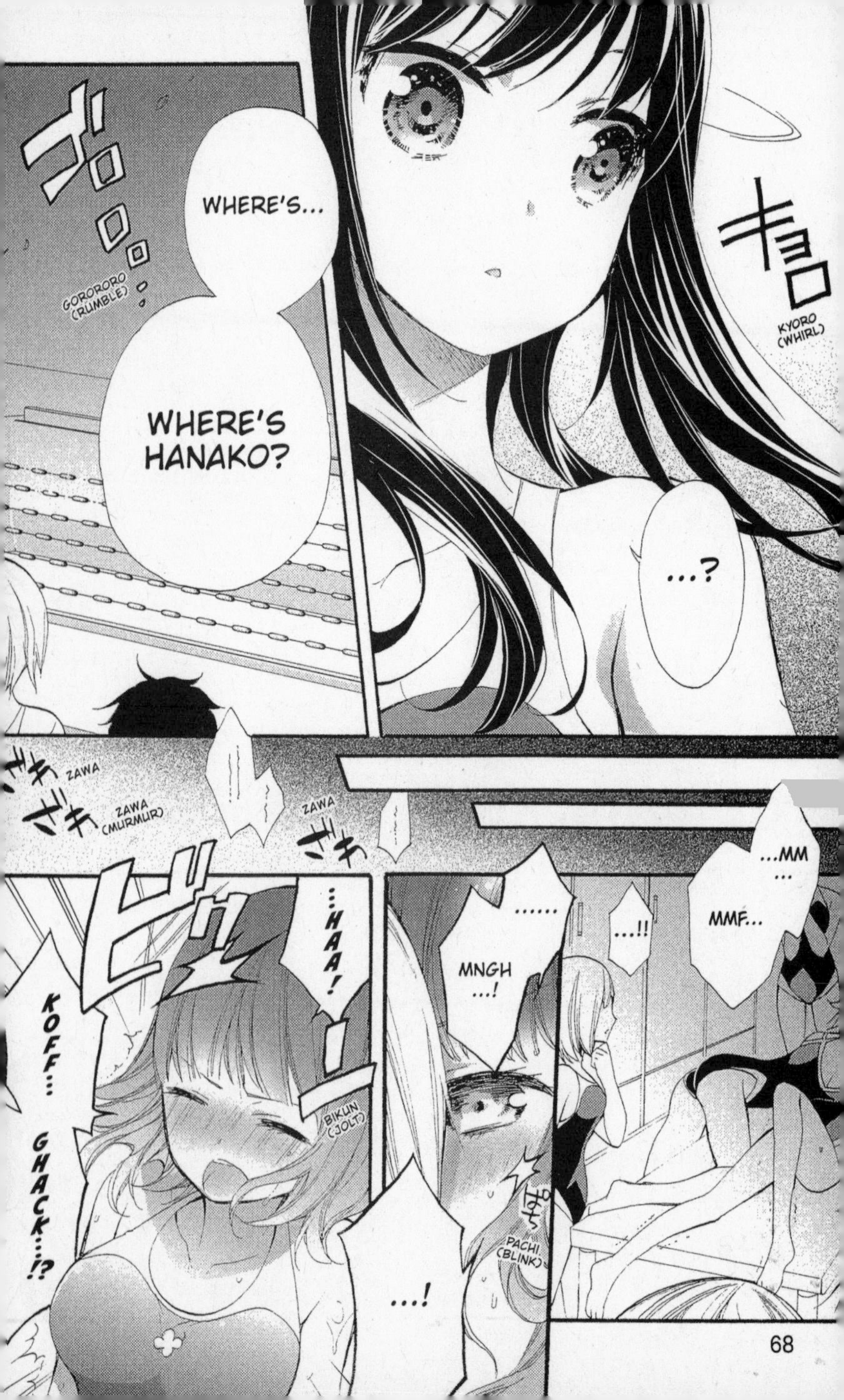
KYORO (WHIRL)
WHERE'S...
WHERE'S HANAKO?
...?
GORORORO (RUMBLE)
ZAWA
ZAWA
ZAWA (MURMUR)
...MM ...
MMF...
...!!
......
MNGH ...!
PACHI (BLINK)
...!
...HAA!
BIKUN (JOLT)
KOFF... GHACK...!?

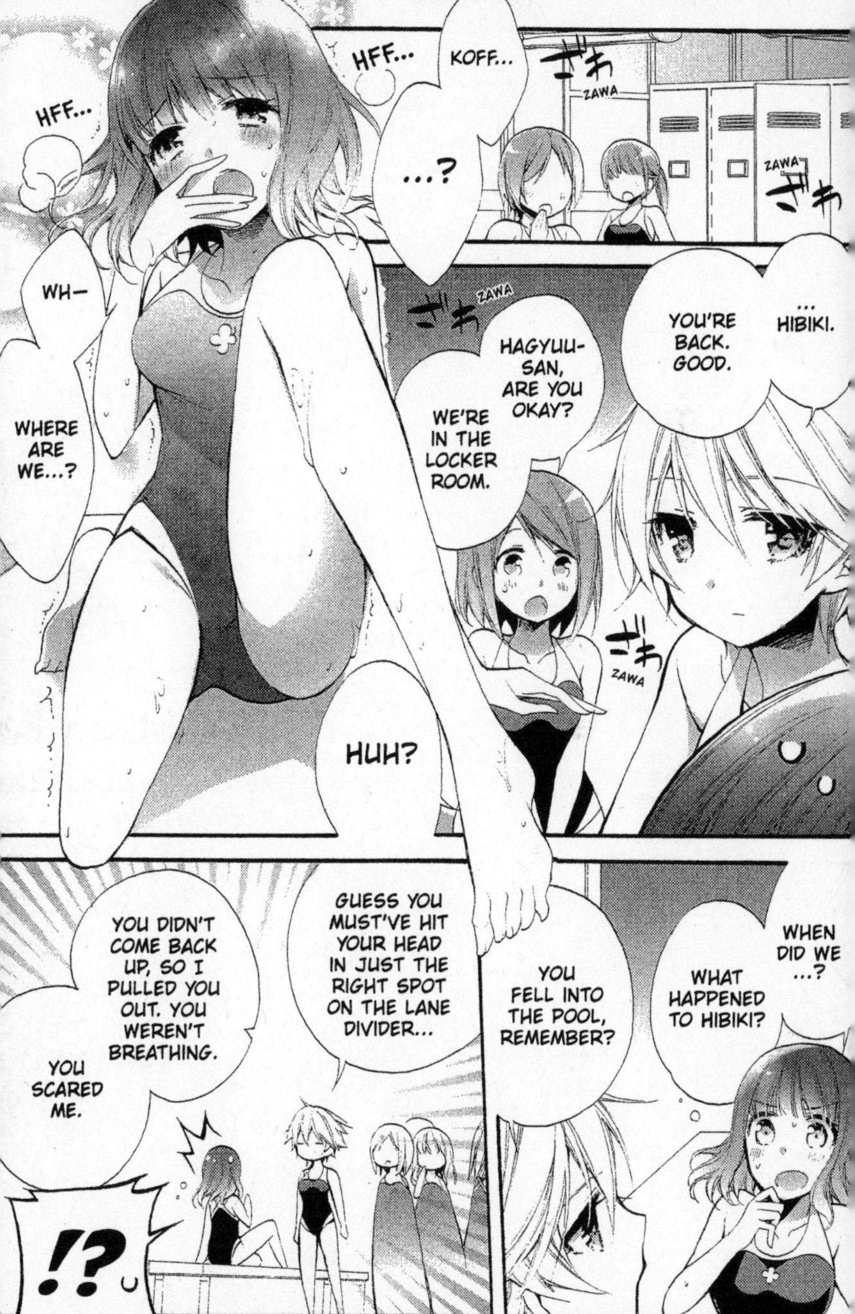
KOFF...
HFF...
ざわ
ZAWA
ZAWA
ざわ
...?
HFF...
WH–
WHERE ARE WE...?
ざわ
ZAWA
... HIBIKI.
YOU'RE BACK. GOOD.
HAGYUU-SAN, ARE YOU OKAY?
WE'RE IN THE LOCKER ROOM.
ざわ
ZAWA
HUH?
WHEN DID WE ...?
WHAT HAPPENED TO HIBIKI?
YOU FELL INTO THE POOL, REMEMBER?
GUESS YOU MUST'VE HIT YOUR HEAD IN JUST THE RIGHT SPOT ON THE LANE DIVIDER...
YOU DIDN'T COME BACK UP, SO I PULLED YOU OUT. YOU WEREN'T BREATHING.
YOU SCARED ME.
!?

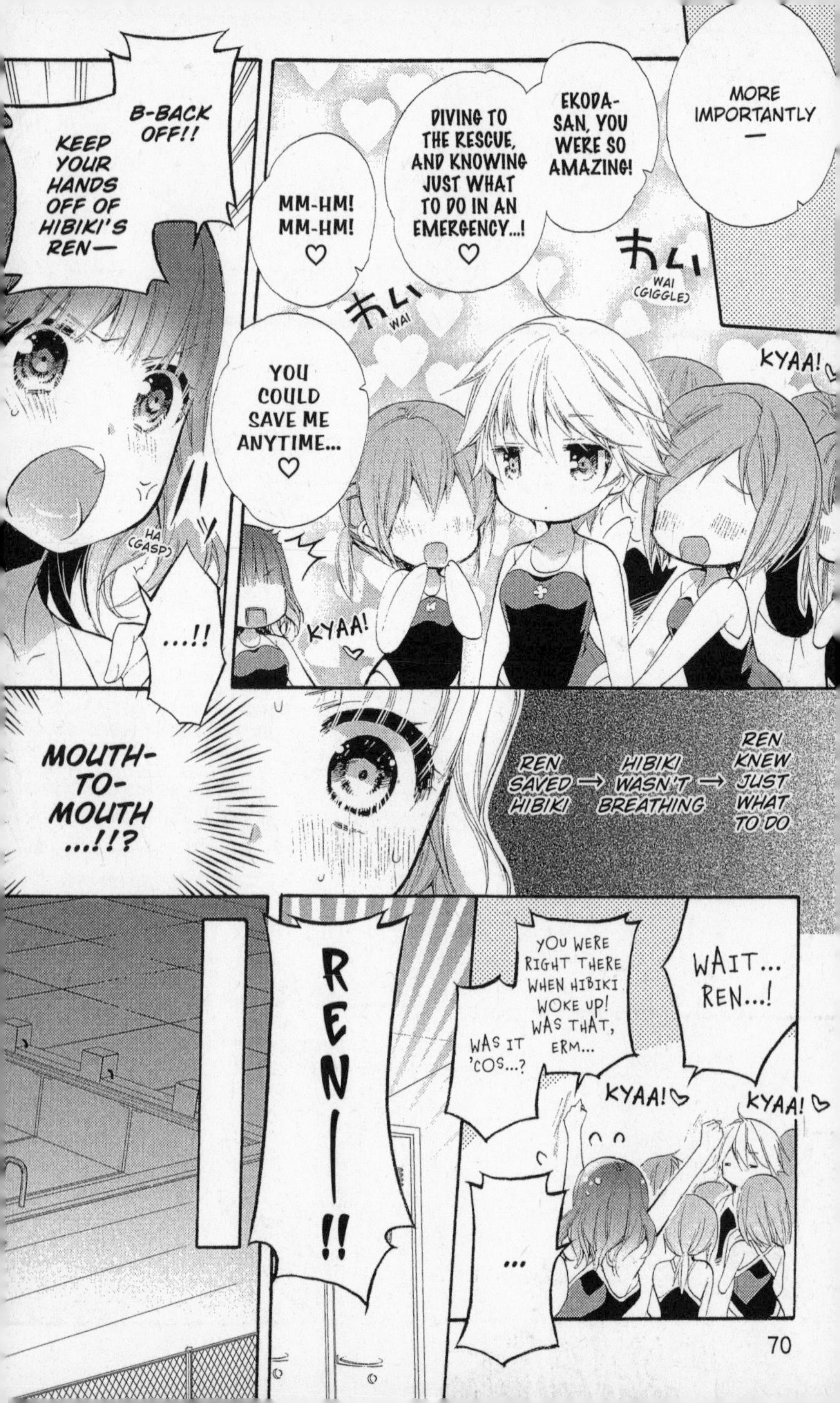
MORE IMPORTANTLY—
EKODA-SAN, YOU WERE SO AMAZING!
DIVING TO THE RESCUE, AND KNOWING JUST WHAT TO DO IN AN EMERGENCY...! ♡
MM-HM! MM-HM! ♡
わい
WAI (GIGGLE)
わい
WAI
YOU COULD SAVE ME ANYTIME... ♡
KYAA! ♡
KYAA! ♡
B-BACK OFF!!
KEEP YOUR HANDS OFF OF HIBIKI'S REN—
HA (GASP)
...!!
REN SAVED HIBIKI → HIBIKI WASN'T BREATHING → REN KNEW JUST WHAT TO DO
MOUTH-TO-MOUTH ...!!?
WAIT... REN...!
YOU WERE RIGHT THERE WHEN HIBIKI WOKE UP! WAS THAT, ERM...
WAS IT 'COS...?
KYAA! ♡
KYAA! ♡
...
REN—!!

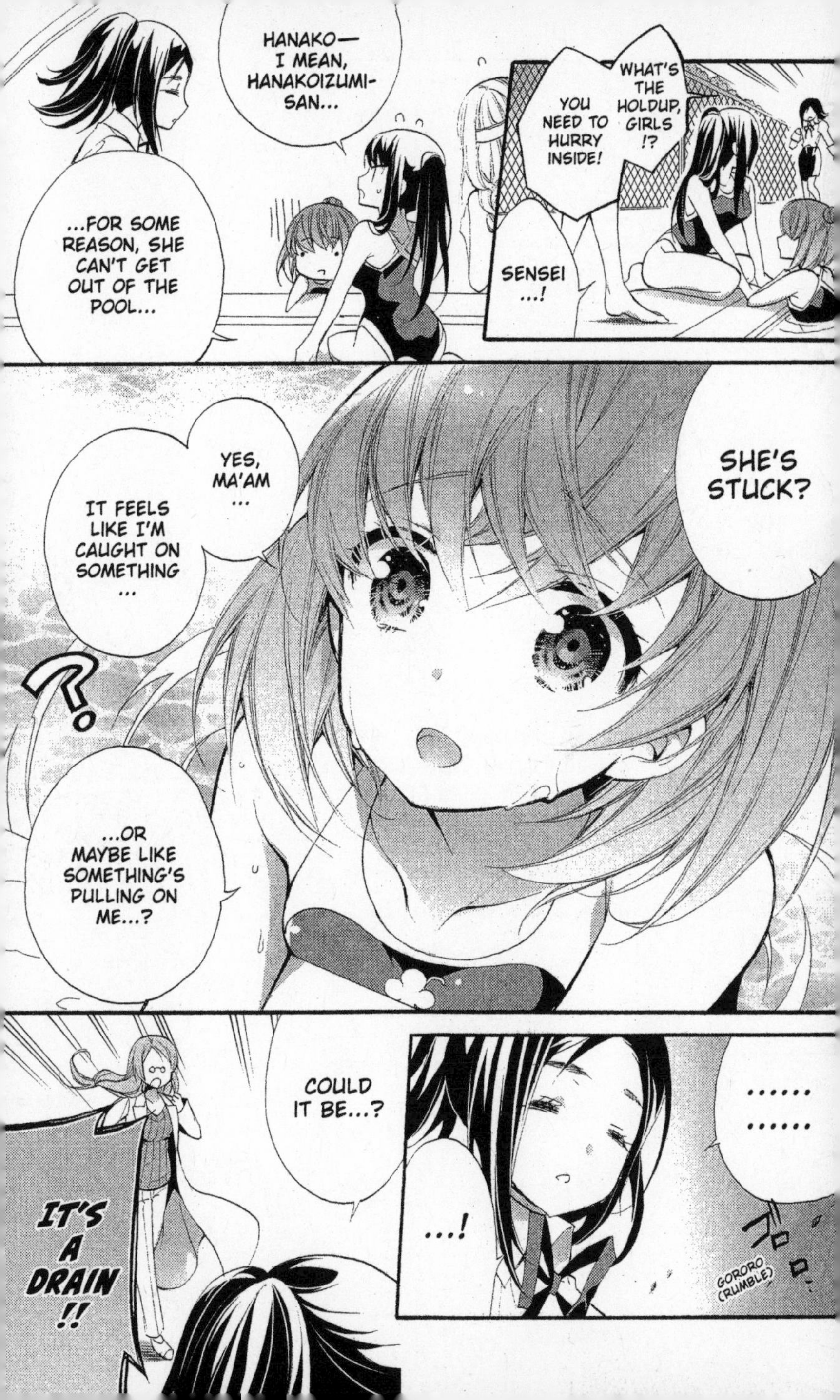
WHAT'S THE HOLDUP, GIRLS!?
YOU NEED TO HURRY INSIDE!
SENSEI...!
HANAKO— I MEAN, HANAKOIZUMI-SAN...
...FOR SOME REASON, SHE CAN'T GET OUT OF THE POOL...
SHE'S STUCK?
YES, MA'AM...
IT FEELS LIKE I'M CAUGHT ON SOMETHING...
?
...OR MAYBE LIKE SOMETHING'S PULLING ON ME...?
......
......
...!
GORORO (RUMBLE)
COULD IT BE...?
IT'S A DRAIN!!

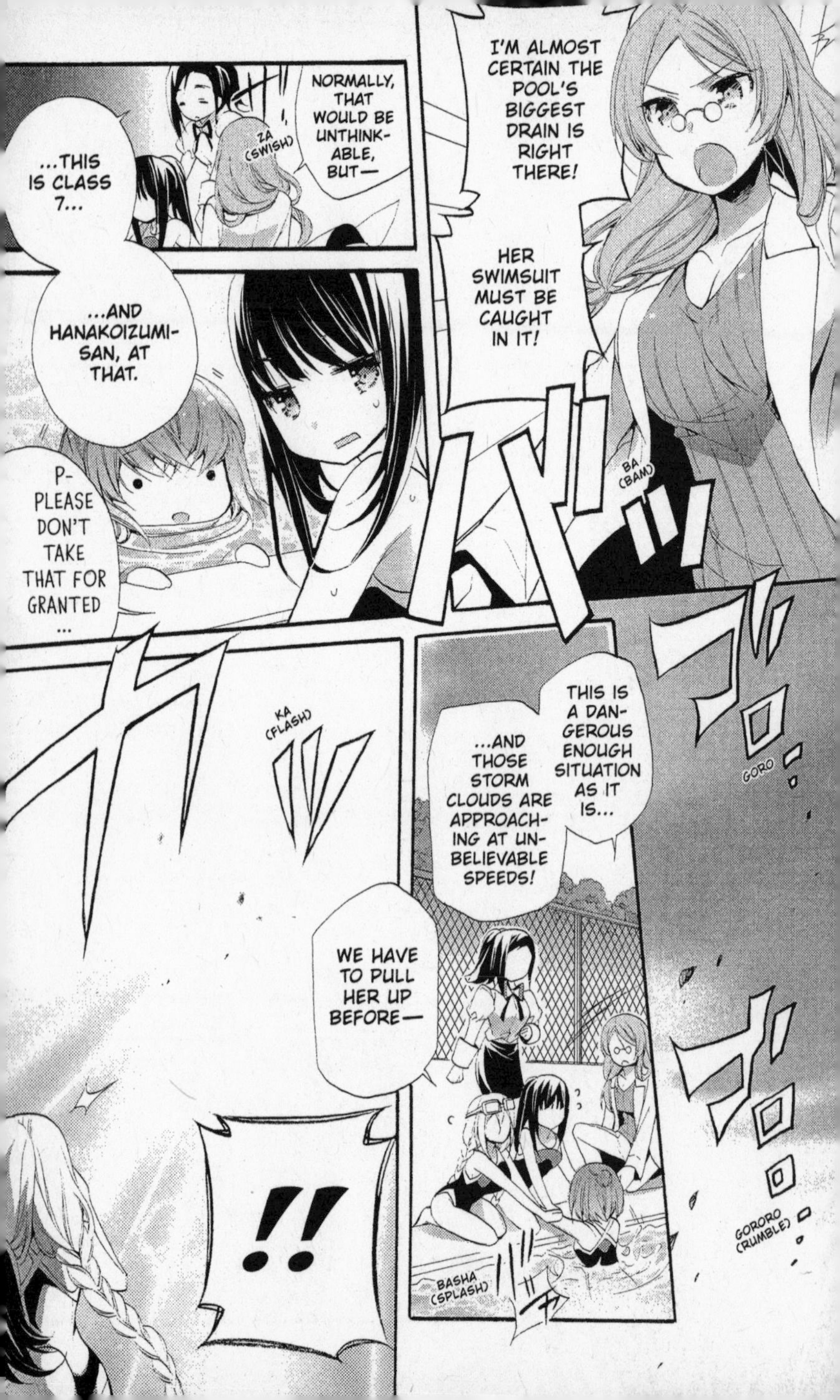
I'M ALMOST CERTAIN THE POOL'S BIGGEST DRAIN IS RIGHT THERE!
HER SWIMSUIT MUST BE CAUGHT IN IT!
BA (BAM)
NORMALLY, THAT WOULD BE UNTHINK-ABLE, BUT—
ZA (SWISH)
...THIS IS CLASS 7...
...AND HANAKOIZUMI-SAN, AT THAT.
P-PLEASE DON'T TAKE THAT FOR GRANTED ...
GORO
THIS IS A DAN-GEROUS ENOUGH SITUATION AS IT IS...
...AND THOSE STORM CLOUDS ARE APPROACH-ING AT UN-BELIEVABLE SPEEDS!
WE HAVE TO PULL HER UP BEFORE—
GORORO (RUMBLE)
BASHA (SPLASH)
KA (FLASH)
!!

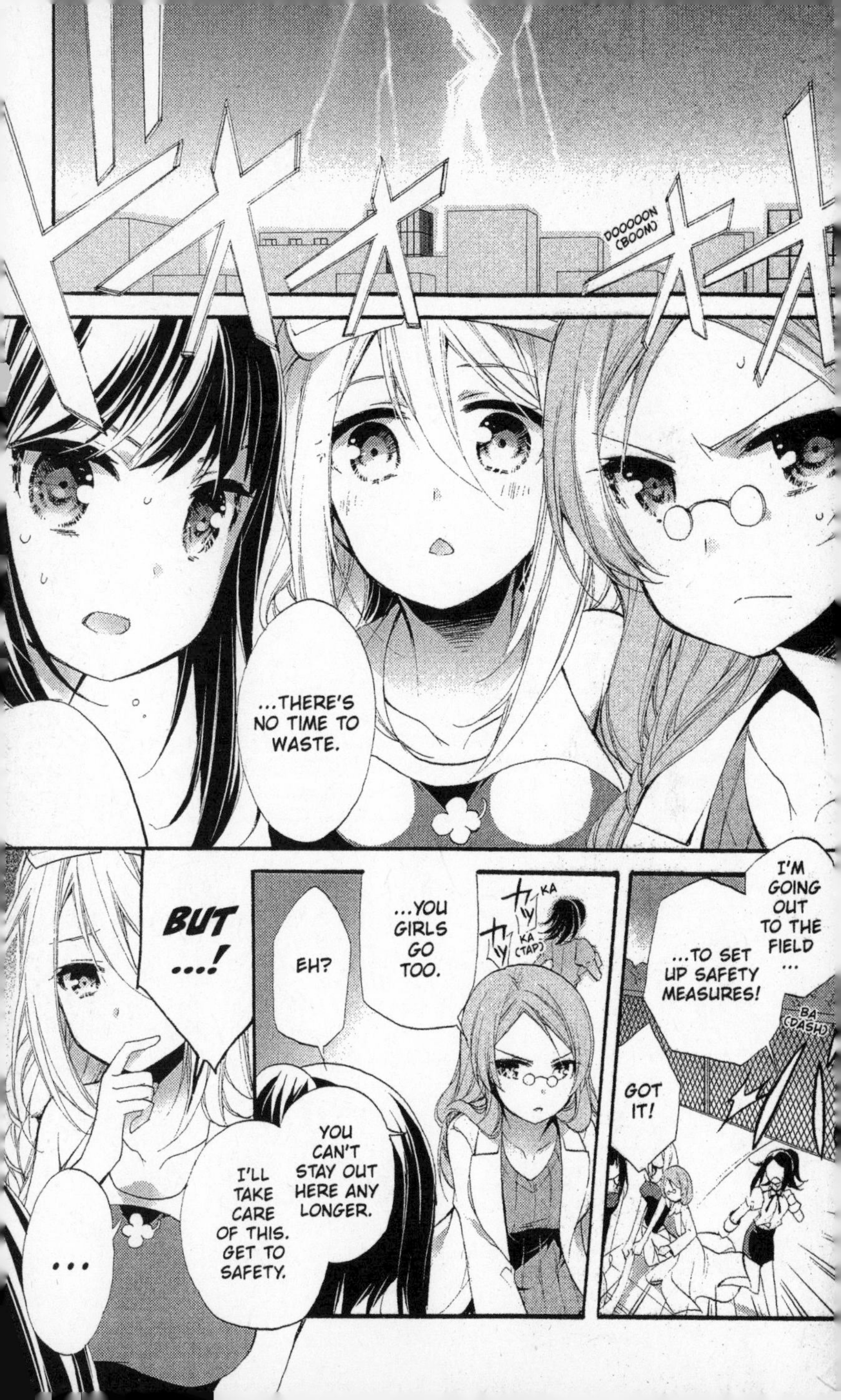
DOOOOON (BOOM)
...THERE'S NO TIME TO WASTE.
I'M GOING OUT TO THE FIELD ...
...TO SET UP SAFETY MEASURES!
BA (DASH)
GOT IT!
KA KA (TAP)
...YOU GIRLS GO TOO.
EH?
YOU CAN'T STAY OUT HERE ANY LONGER.
I'LL TAKE CARE OF THIS. GET TO SAFETY.
BUT ...!
...

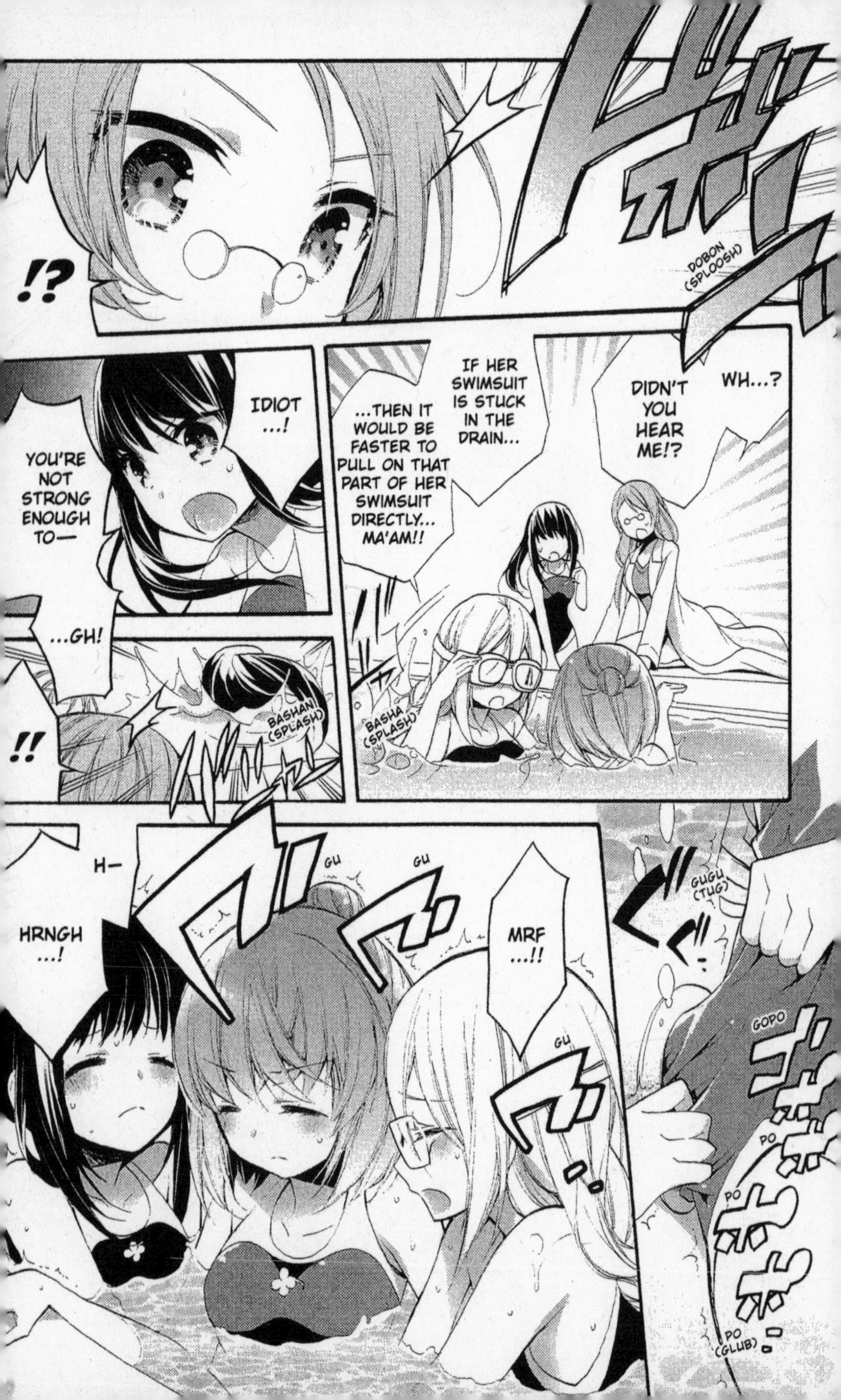
DOBON (SPLOOSH)
!?
WH...?
DIDN'T YOU HEAR ME!?
IF HER SWIMSUIT IS STUCK IN THE DRAIN...
...THEN IT WOULD BE FASTER TO PULL ON THAT PART OF HER SWIMSUIT DIRECTLY... MA'AM!!
BASHA (SPLASH)
IDIOT ...!
YOU'RE NOT STRONG ENOUGH TO—
...GH!
BASHAN (SPLASH)
!!
GUGU (TUG)
GOPO
PO
PO
PO (GLUB)
MRF ...!!
GU
GU
GU
H—
HRNGH ...!

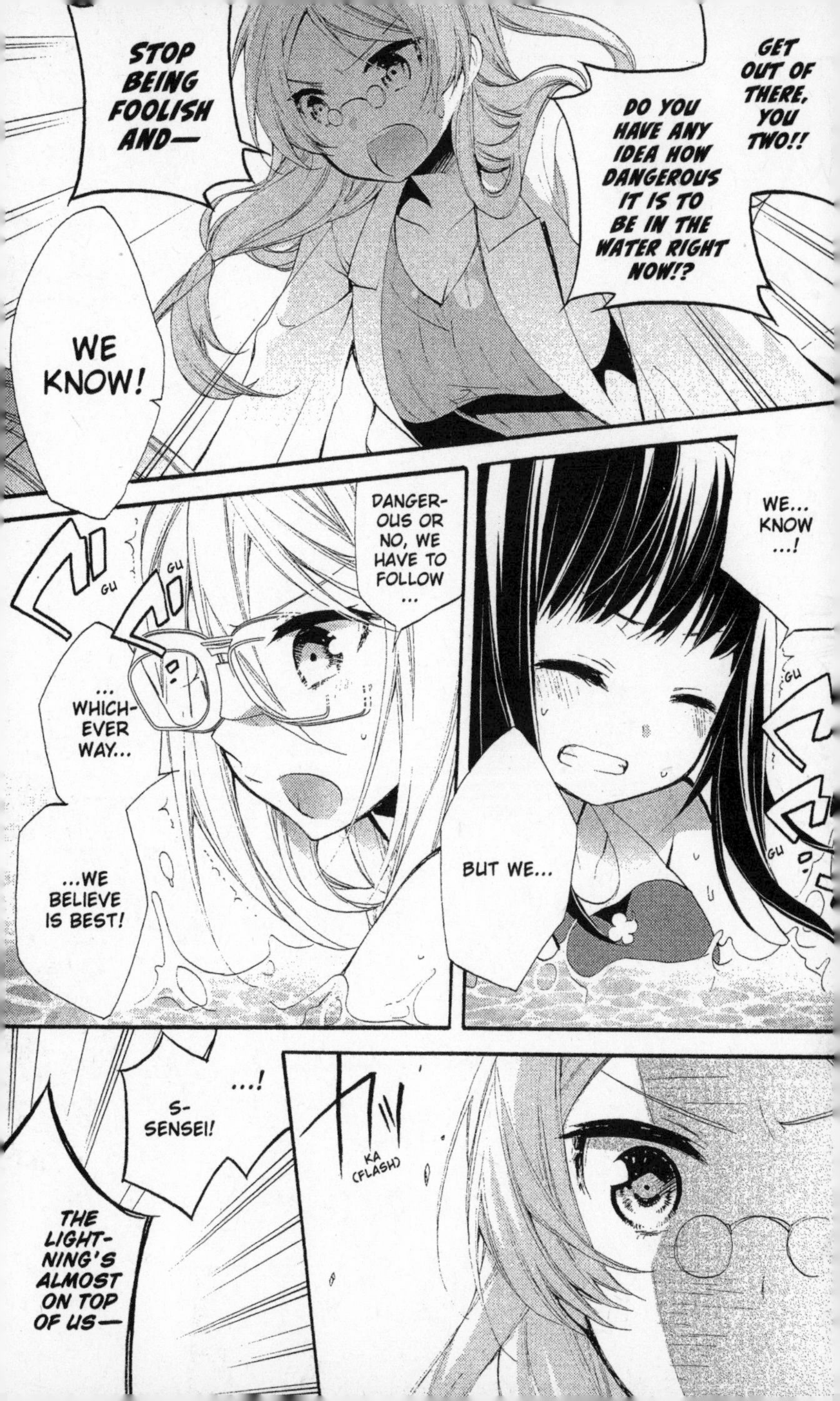

GET OUT OF THERE, YOU TWO!!
DO YOU HAVE ANY IDEA HOW DANGEROUS IT IS TO BE IN THE WATER RIGHT NOW!?
STOP BEING FOOLISH AND—
WE KNOW!
WE... KNOW ...!
GU
GU
BUT WE...
DANGER-OUS OR NO, WE HAVE TO FOLLOW ...
... WHICH-EVER WAY...
...WE BELIEVE IS BEST!
GU
GU
KA (FLASH)
...!
S-SENSEI!
THE LIGHT-NING'S ALMOST ON TOP OF US—

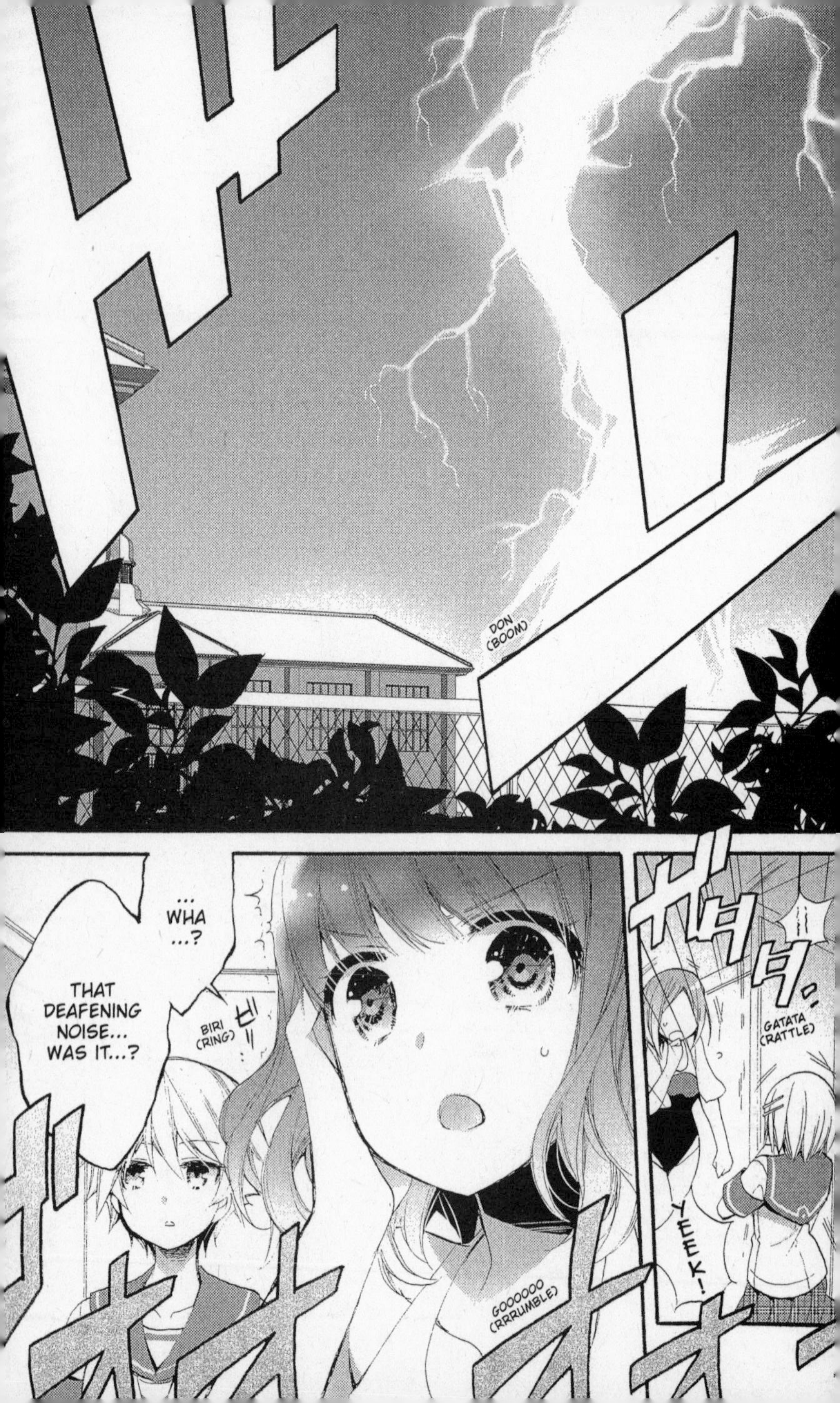
DON
(BOOM)
GATATA
(RATTLE)
YEEEK!
... WHA ...?
THAT DEAFENING NOISE... WAS IT...?
BIRI
(RING)
GOOOOOO
(RRRUMBLE)

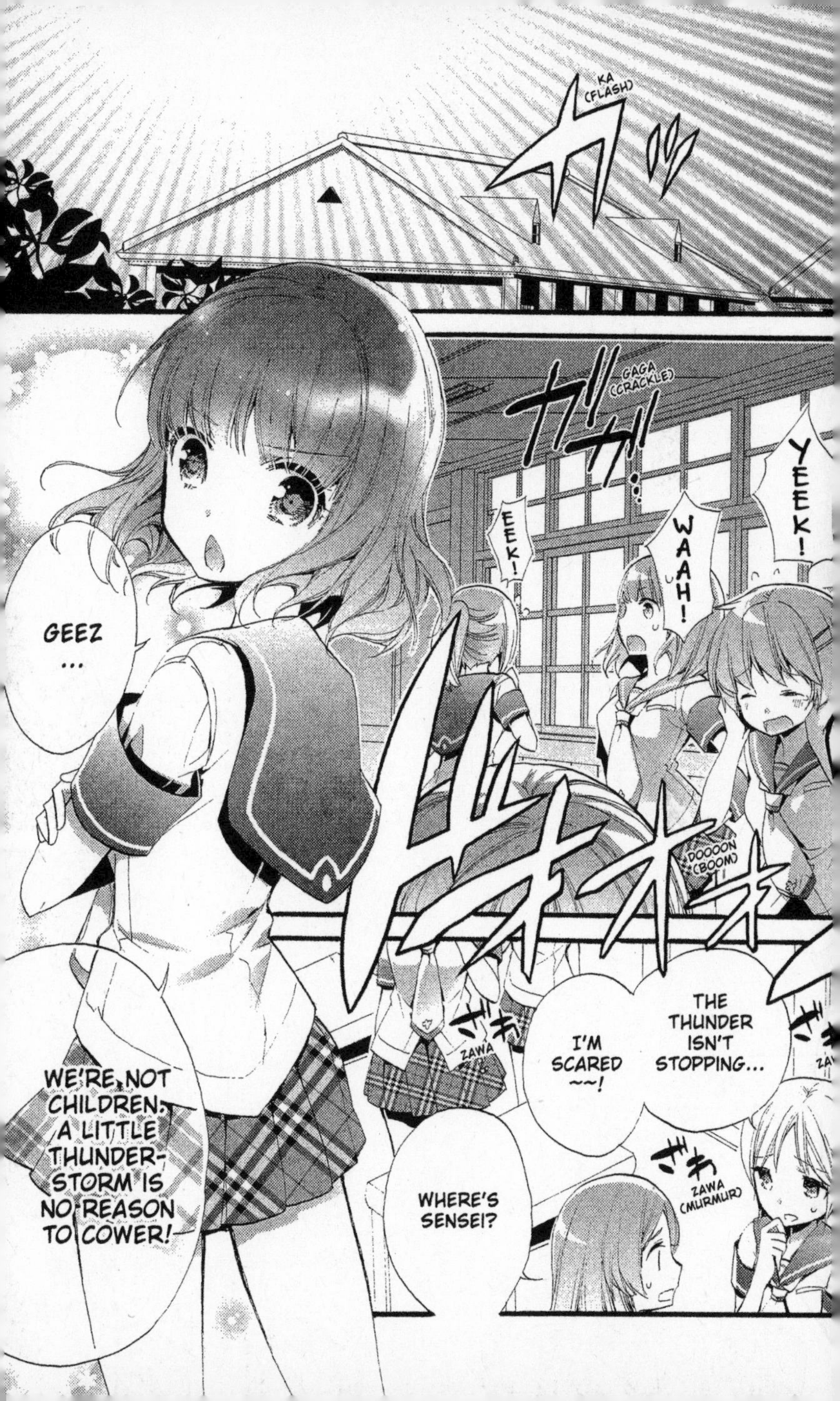
KA (FLASH)
GAGA (CRACKLE)
YEEK!
WAAH!
EEK!
GEEZ ...
DOOOON (BOOM)
THE THUNDER ISN'T STOPPING...
I'M SCARED ~~!
ZAWA
ZAWA (MURMUR)
WHERE'S SENSEI?
WE'RE NOT CHILDREN. A LITTLE THUNDER-STORM IS NO REASON TO COWER!

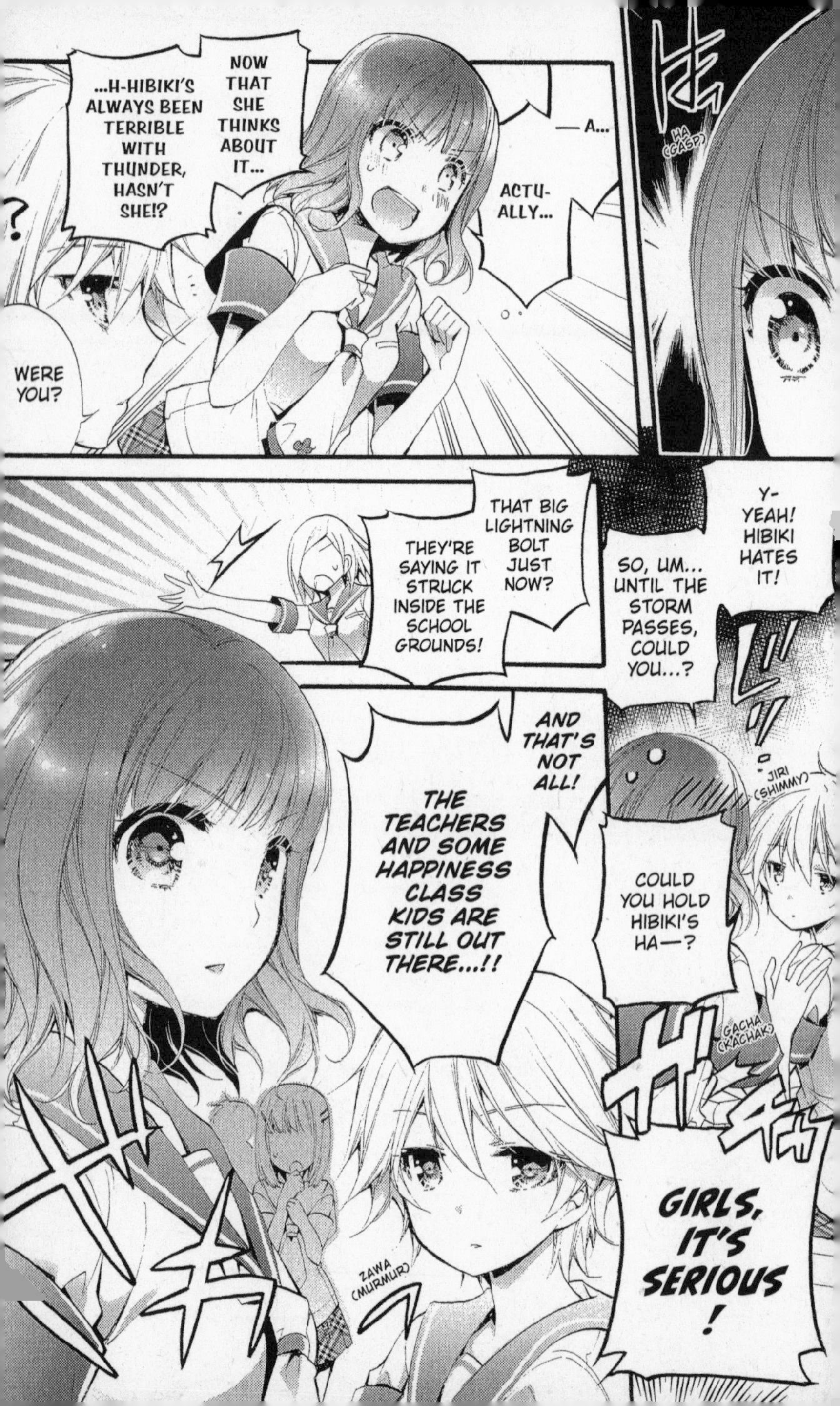
HA (GASP)
—A...
ACTU-ALLY...
NOW THAT SHE THINKS ABOUT IT...
...H-HIBIKI'S ALWAYS BEEN TERRIBLE WITH THUNDER, HASN'T SHE!?
?
WERE YOU?
Y-YEAH! HIBIKI HATES IT!
SO, UM... UNTIL THE STORM PASSES, COULD YOU...?
JIRI (SHIMMY)
COULD YOU HOLD HIBIKI'S HA—?
GACHA (KACHAK)
GIRLS, IT'S SERIOUS!
THAT BIG LIGHTNING BOLT JUST NOW?
THEY'RE SAYING IT STRUCK INSIDE THE SCHOOL GROUNDS!
AND THAT'S NOT ALL!
THE TEACHERS AND SOME HAPPINESS CLASS KIDS ARE STILL OUT THERE...!!
ZAWA (MURMUR)

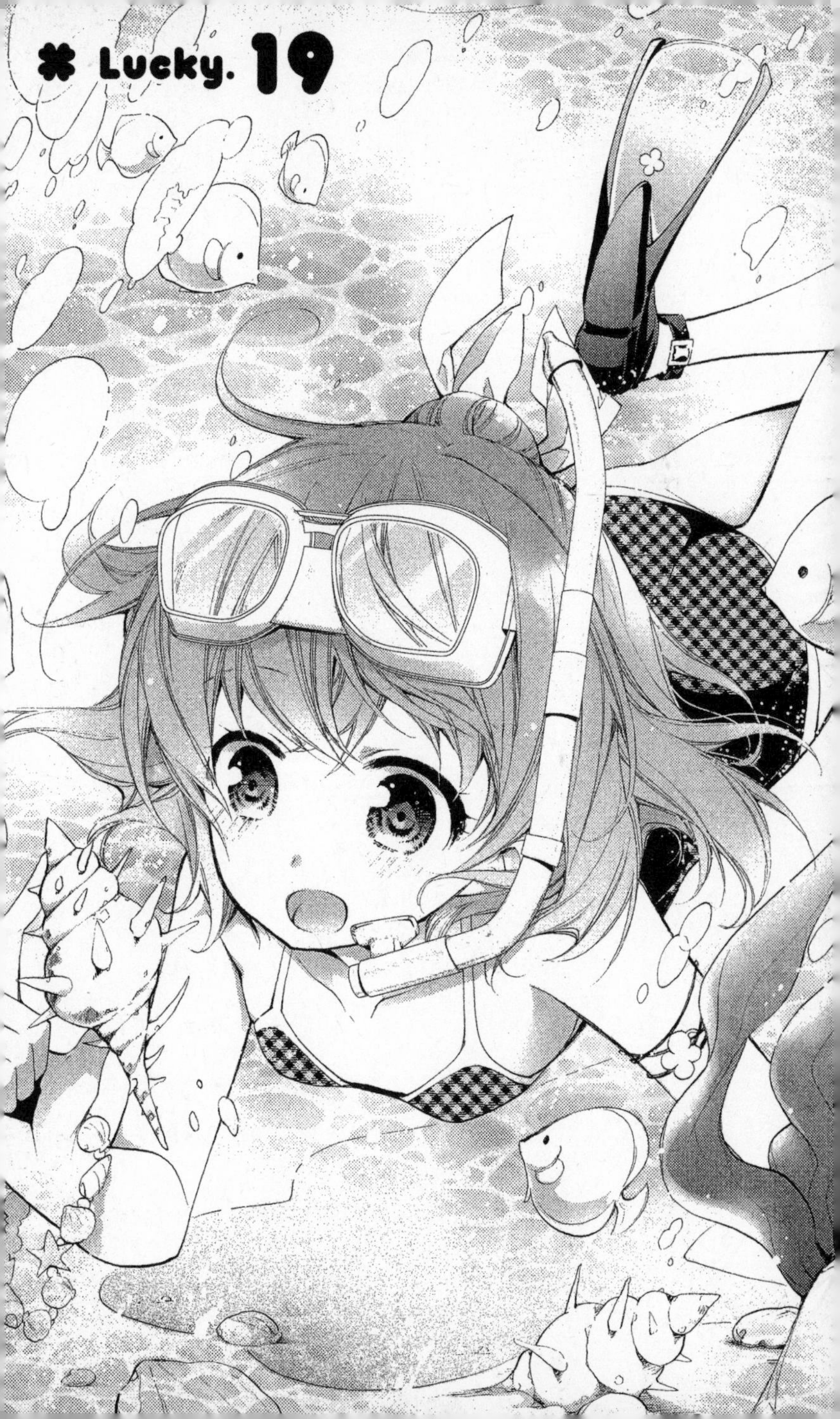
Lucky. 19

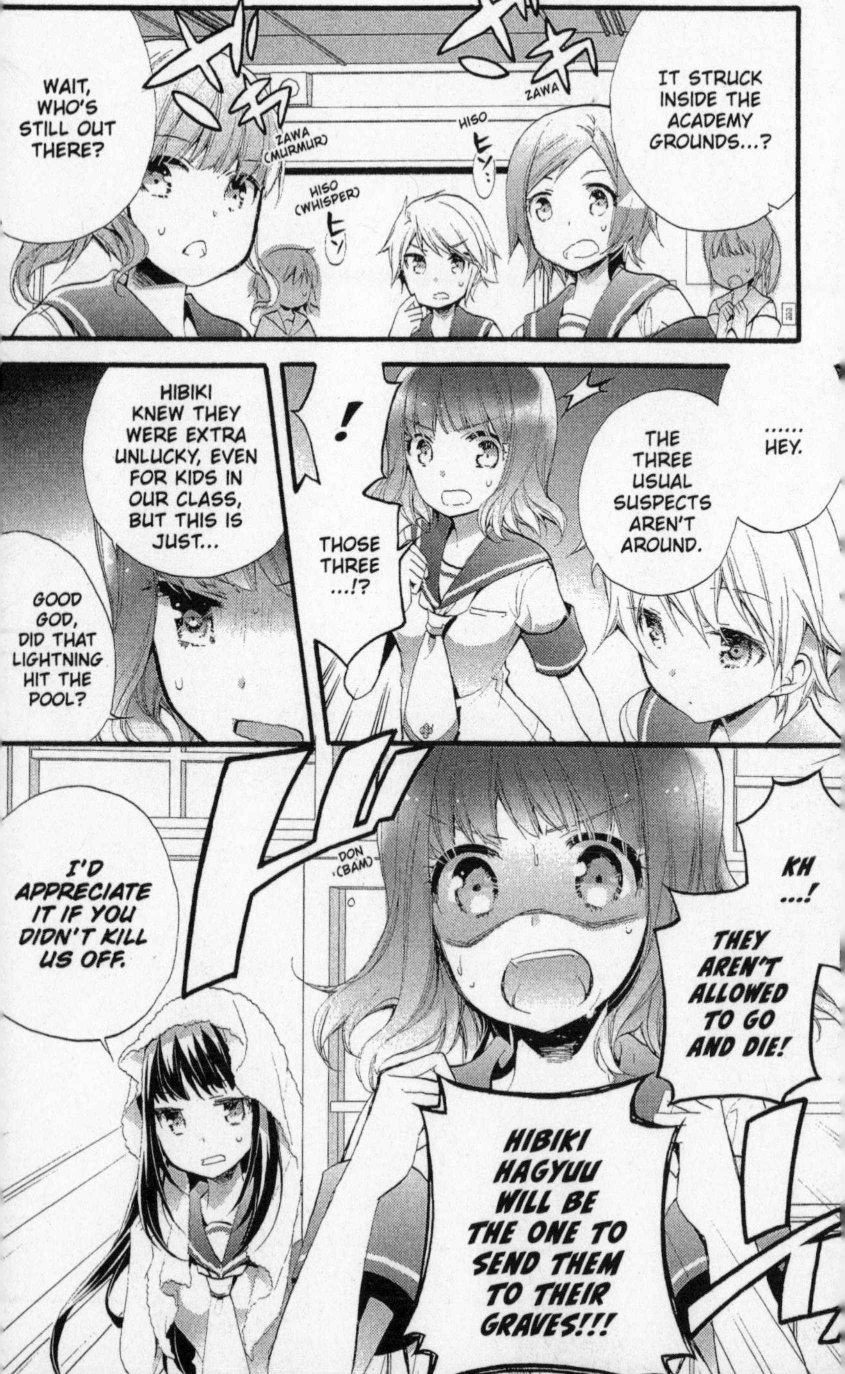
IT STRUCK INSIDE THE ACADEMY GROUNDS...?
ZAWA
HISO
HISO (WHISPER)
ZAWA (MURMUR)
WAIT, WHO'S STILL OUT THERE?
...... HEY.
THE THREE USUAL SUSPECTS AREN'T AROUND.
THOSE THREE ...!?
HIBIKI KNEW THEY WERE EXTRA UNLUCKY, EVEN FOR KIDS IN OUR CLASS, BUT THIS IS JUST...
GOOD GOD, DID THAT LIGHTNING HIT THE POOL?
KH ...!
THEY AREN'T ALLOWED TO GO AND DIE!
HIBIKI HAGYUU WILL BE THE ONE TO SEND THEM TO THEIR GRAVES!!!
DON (BAM)
I'D APPRECIATE IT IF YOU DIDN'T KILL US OFF.

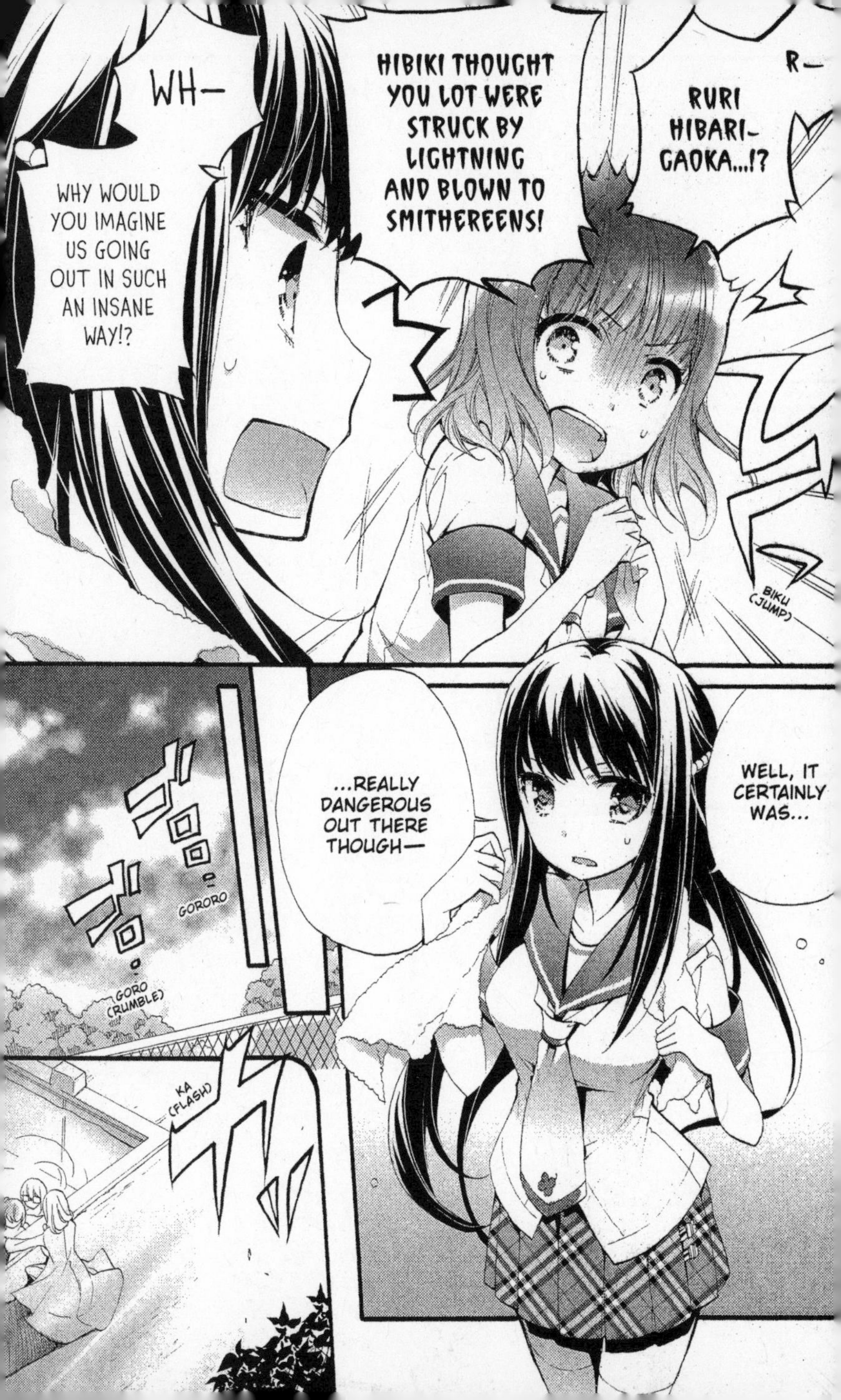
R—
RURI HIBARI-GAOKA...!?
HIBIKI THOUGHT YOU LOT WERE STRUCK BY LIGHTNING AND BLOWN TO SMITHEREENS!
WH—
WHY WOULD YOU IMAGINE US GOING OUT IN SUCH AN INSANE WAY!?
BIKU (JUMP)
WELL, IT CERTAINLY WAS...
...REALLY DANGEROUS OUT THERE THOUGH—
GORORO
GORO (RUMBLE)
KA (FLASH)

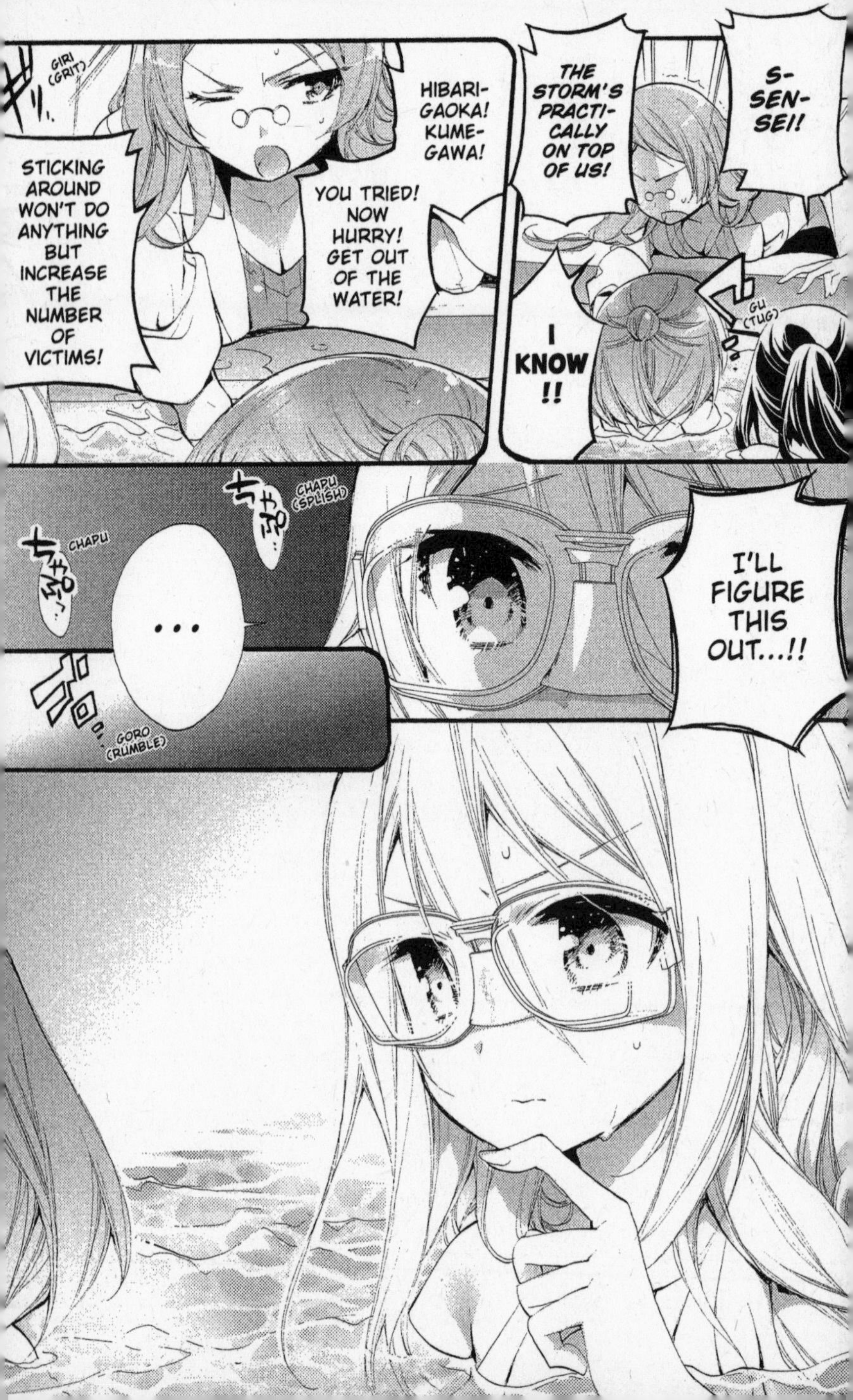

S-SEN-SEI!!
THE STORM'S PRACTI-CALLY ON TOP OF US!
GU (TUG)
I KNOW!!
GIRI (GRIT)
HIBARI-GAOKA! KUME-GAWA!
YOU TRIED! NOW HURRY! GET OUT OF THE WATER!
STICKING AROUND WON'T DO ANYTHING BUT INCREASE THE NUMBER OF VICTIMS!
I'LL FIGURE THIS OUT...!!
CHAPU (SPLISH)
CHAPU
...
GORO (RUMBLE)

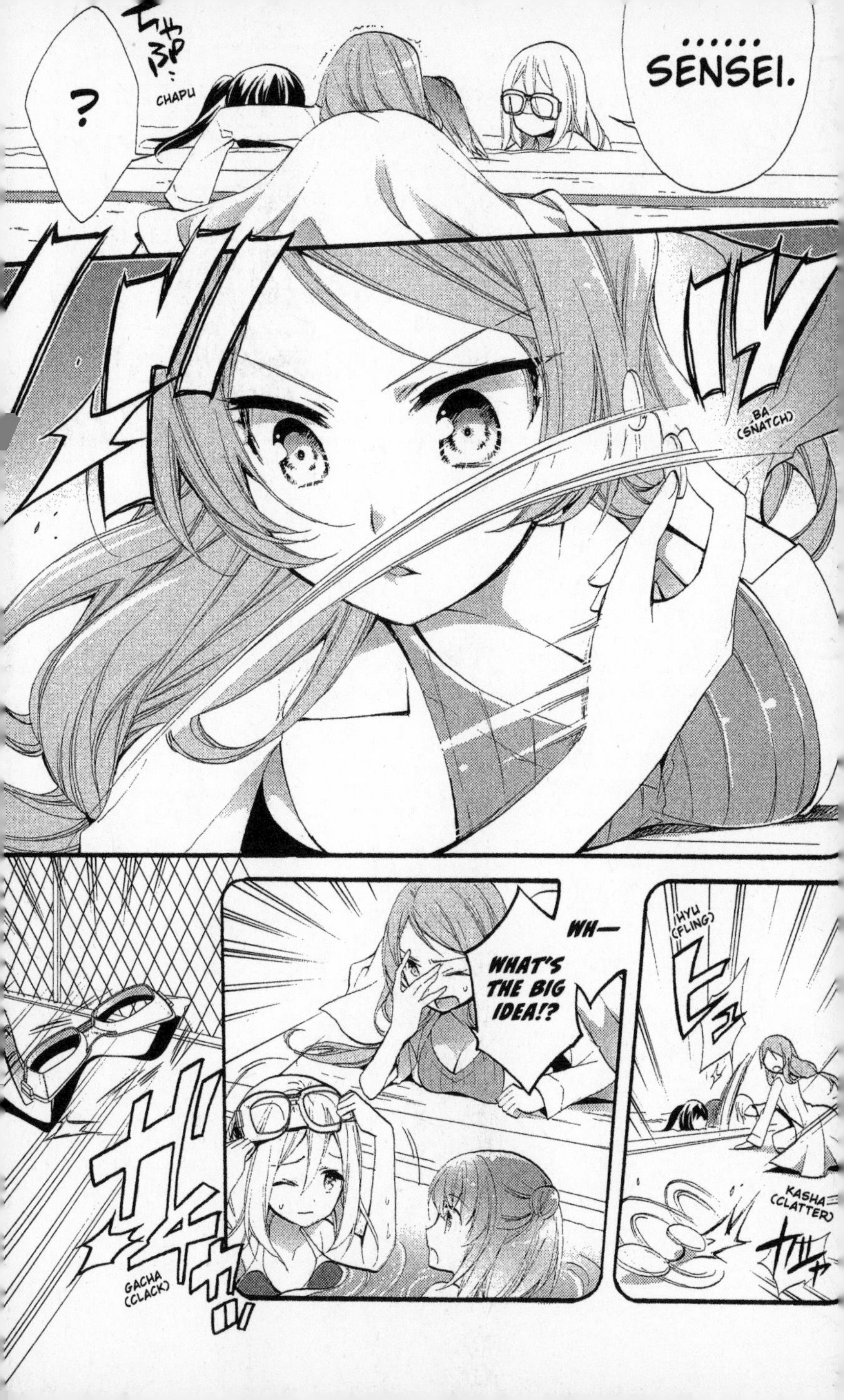

......
SENSEI.
?
CHAPU
BA (SNATCH)
HYU (FLING)
KASHA (CLATTER)
WH—
WHAT'S THE BIG IDEA!?
GACHA (CLACK)

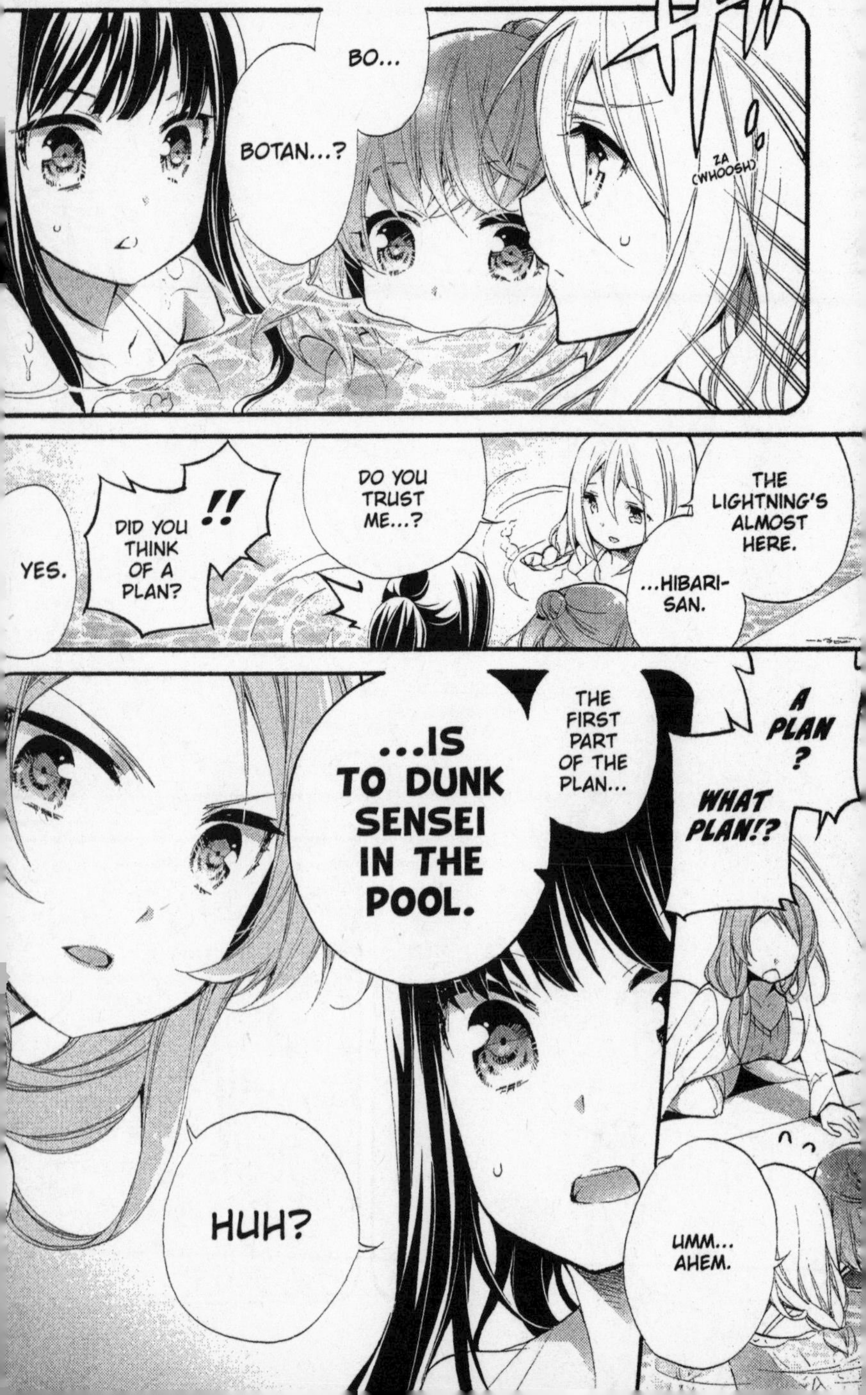
ZA (WHOOSH)
BO...
BOTAN...?
THE LIGHTNING'S ALMOST HERE.
...HIBARI-SAN.
DO YOU TRUST ME...?
!!
DID YOU THINK OF A PLAN?
YES.
A PLAN?
WHAT PLAN!?
UMM... AHEM.
THE FIRST PART OF THE PLAN...
...IS TO DUNK SENSEI IN THE POOL.
HUH?

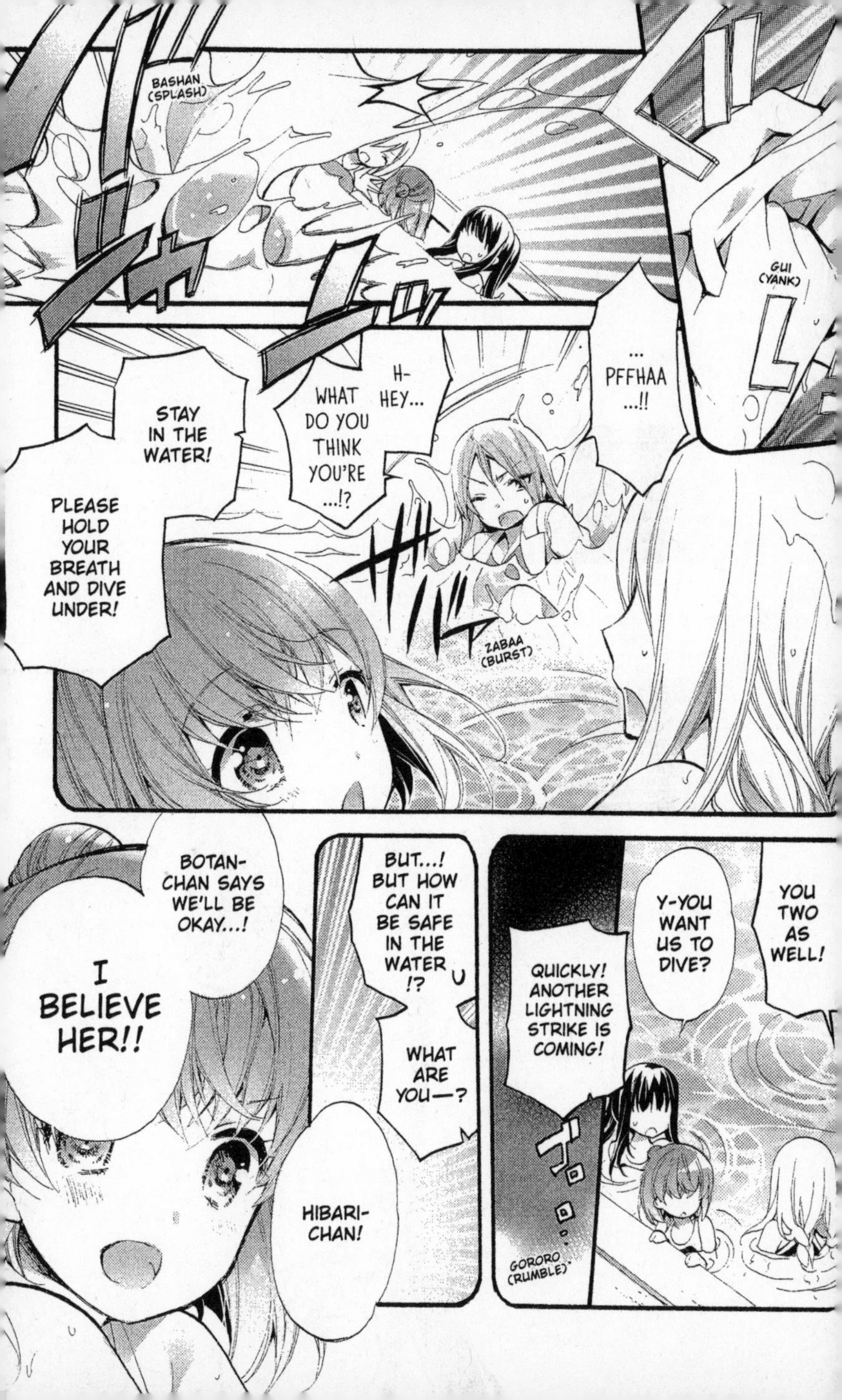
GUI (YANK)
BASHAN (SPLASH)
...PFFHAA...!!
H-HEY...
WHAT DO YOU THINK YOU'RE ...!?
ZABAA (BURST)
STAY IN THE WATER!
PLEASE HOLD YOUR BREATH AND DIVE UNDER!
YOU TWO AS WELL!
Y-YOU WANT US TO DIVE?
QUICKLY! ANOTHER LIGHTNING STRIKE IS COMING!
GORORO (RUMBLE)
BUT...! BUT HOW CAN IT BE SAFE IN THE WATER!?
WHAT ARE YOU—?
HIBARI-CHAN!
BOTAN-CHAN SAYS WE'LL BE OKAY...!
I BELIEVE HER!!

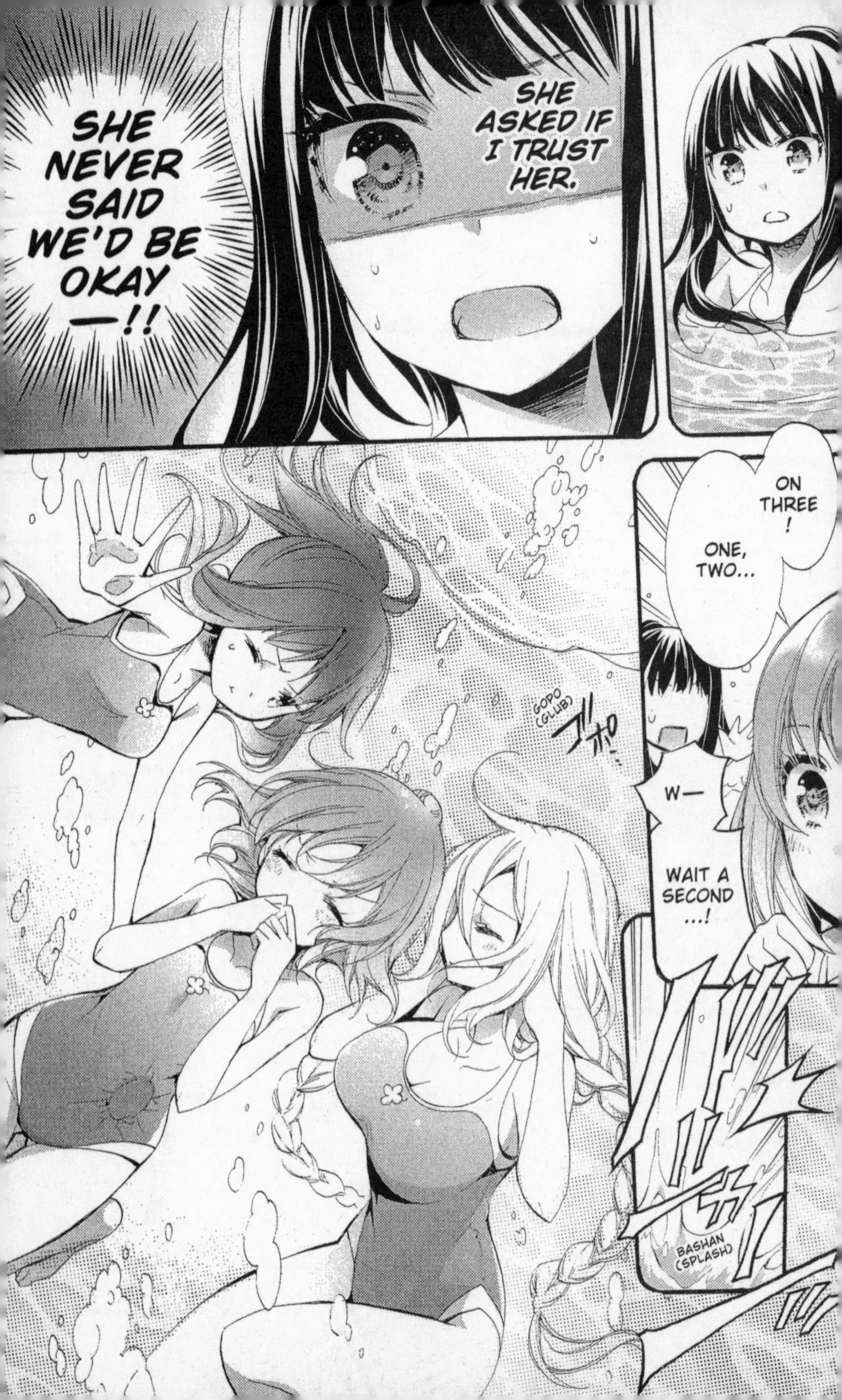
SHE ASKED IF I TRUST HER.
SHE NEVER SAID WE'D BE OKAY—!!
ON THREE!
ONE, TWO...
W—
WAIT A SECOND...!
BASHAN (SPLASH)
GOPO (GLUB)

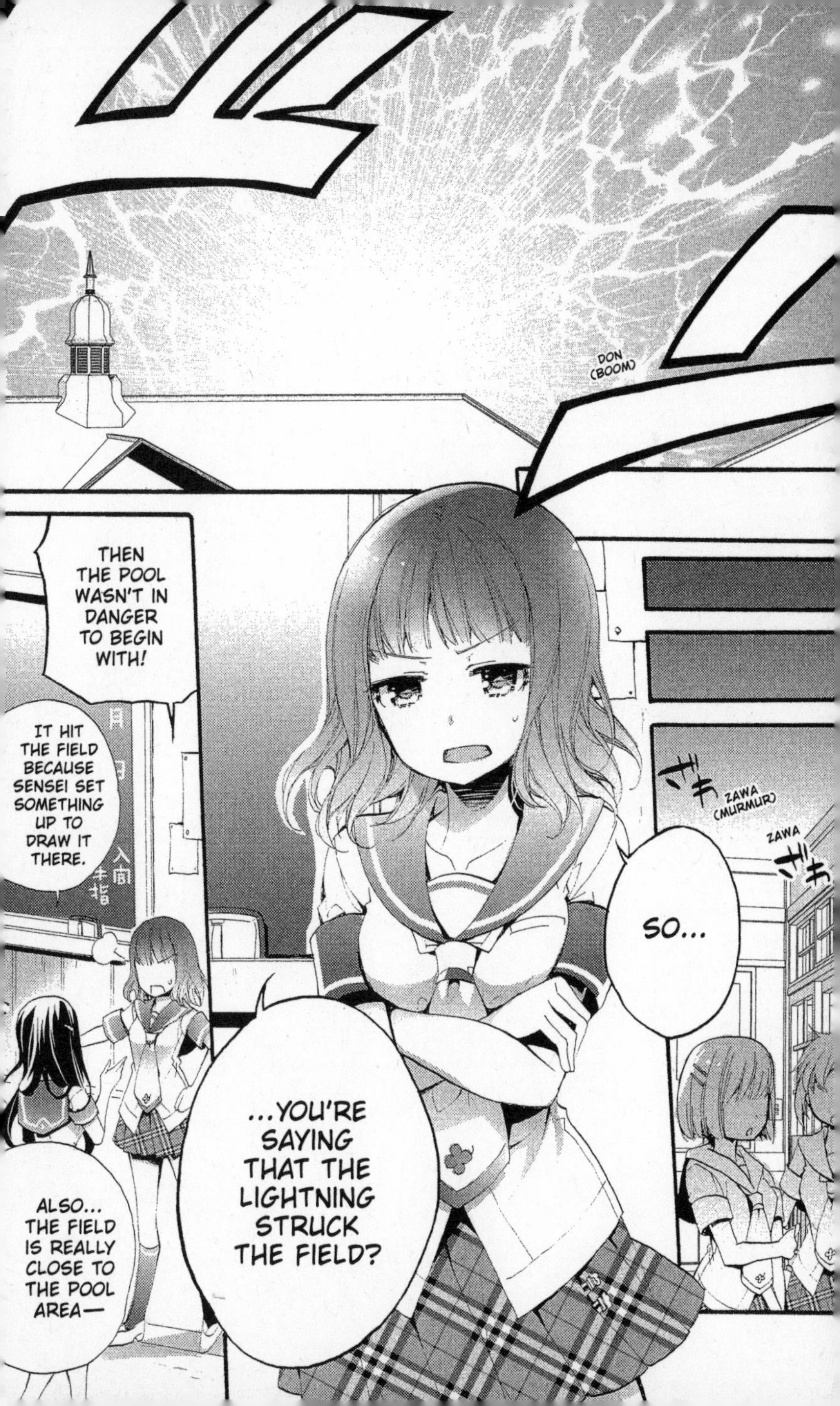
DON (BOOM)
ざわ
ZAWA (MURMUR)
ZAWA
ざわ
SO...
...YOU'RE SAYING THAT THE LIGHTNING STRUCK THE FIELD?
THEN THE POOL WASN'T IN DANGER TO BEGIN WITH!
IT HIT THE FIELD BECAUSE SENSEI SET SOMETHING UP TO DRAW IT THERE.
ALSO... THE FIELD IS REALLY CLOSE TO THE POOL AREA—

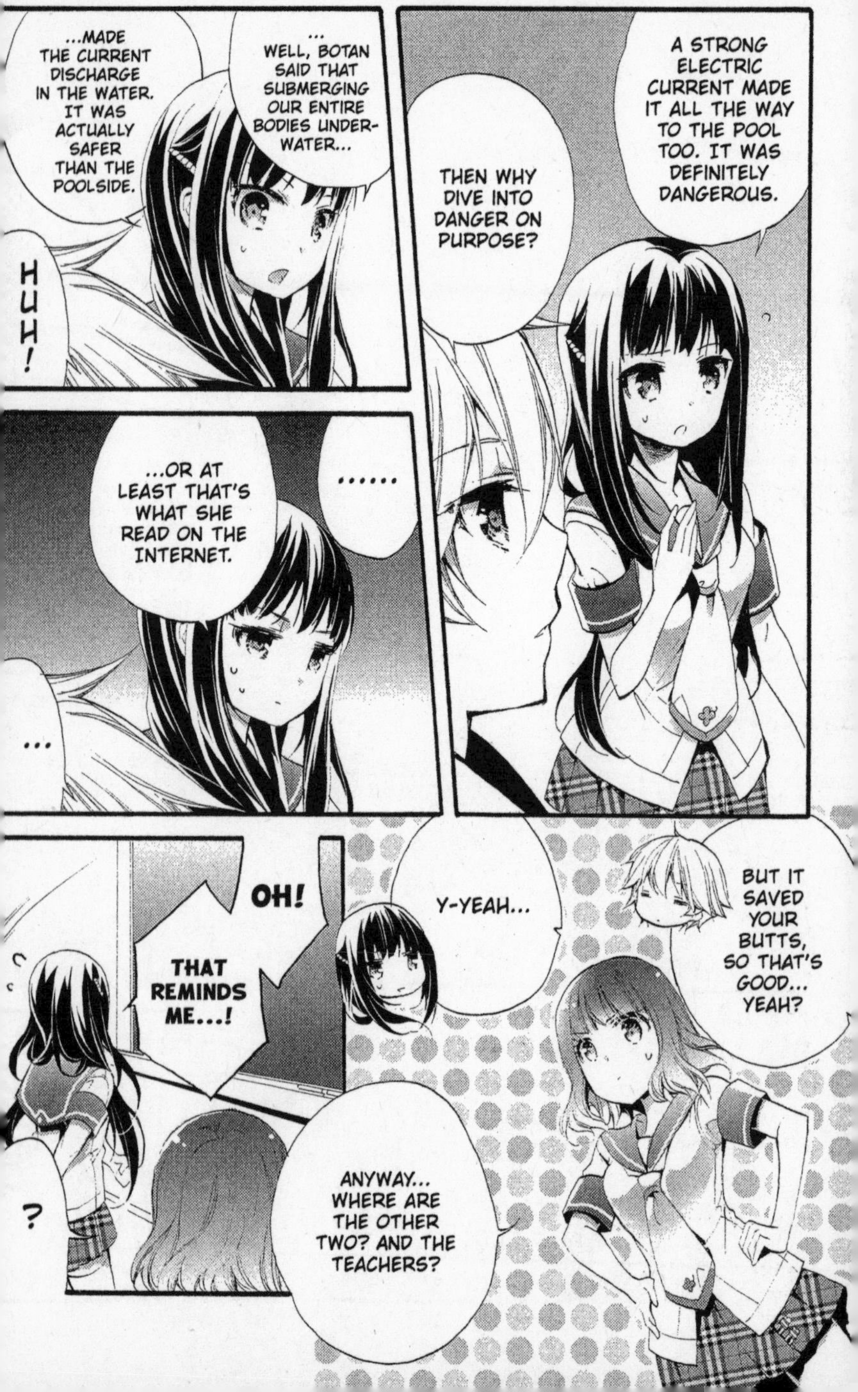
A STRONG ELECTRIC CURRENT MADE IT ALL THE WAY TO THE POOL TOO. IT WAS DEFINITELY DANGEROUS.
THEN WHY DIVE INTO DANGER ON PURPOSE?
... WELL, BOTAN SAID THAT SUBMERGING OUR ENTIRE BODIES UNDER-WATER...
...MADE THE CURRENT DISCHARGE IN THE WATER. IT WAS ACTUALLY SAFER THAN THE POOLSIDE.
HUH!
......
...OR AT LEAST THAT'S WHAT SHE READ ON THE INTERNET.
...
BUT IT SAVED YOUR BUTTS, SO THAT'S GOOD... YEAH?
Y-YEAH...
ANYWAY... WHERE ARE THE OTHER TWO? AND THE TEACHERS?
OH!
THAT REMINDS ME...!
?

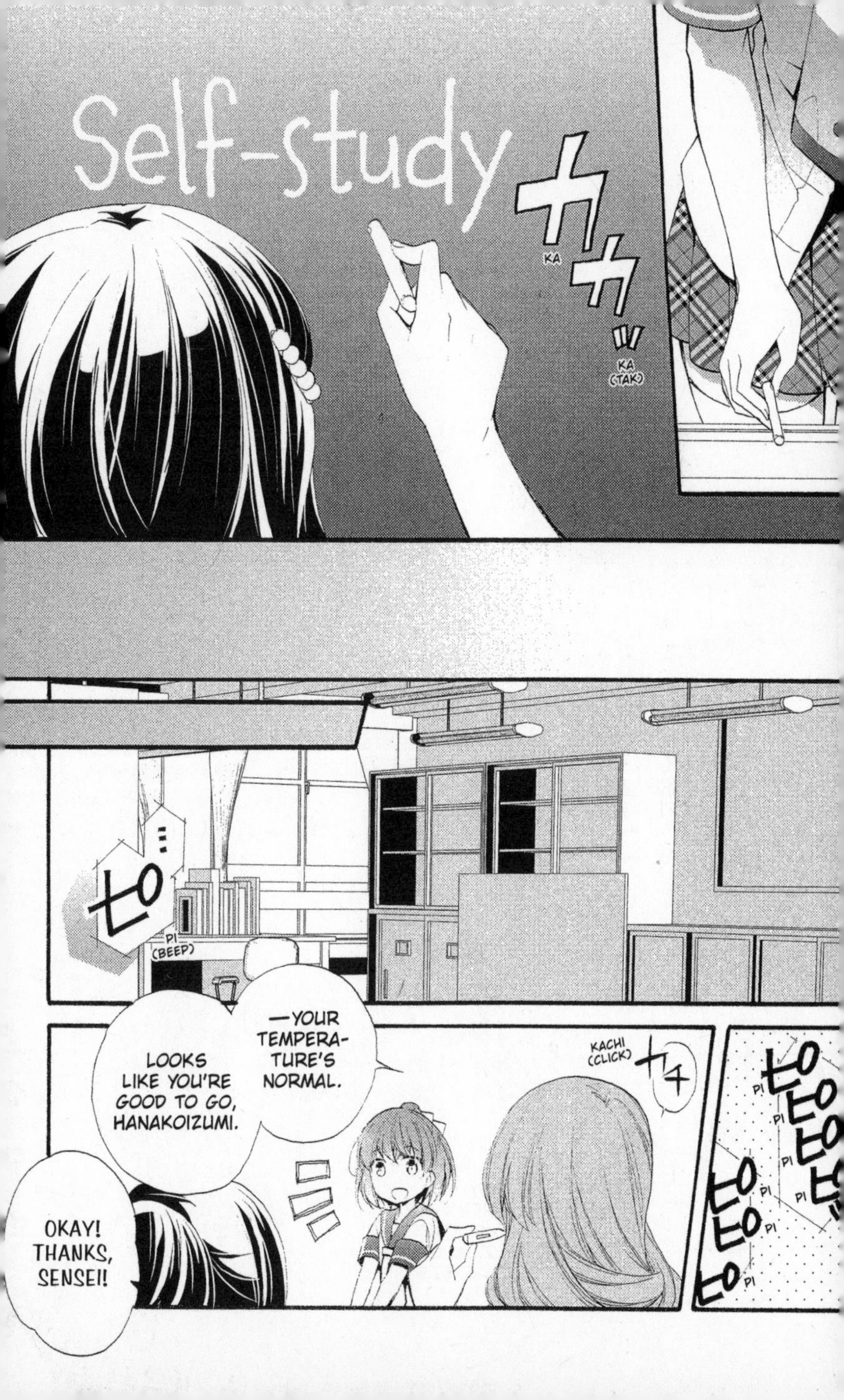
Self-study
KA
KA (TAK)
PI (BEEP)
PI
PI
PI
PI
PI
PI
KACHI (CLICK)
—YOUR TEMPERA-TURE'S NORMAL.
LOOKS LIKE YOU'RE GOOD TO GO, HANAKOIZUMI.
OKAY! THANKS, SENSEI!

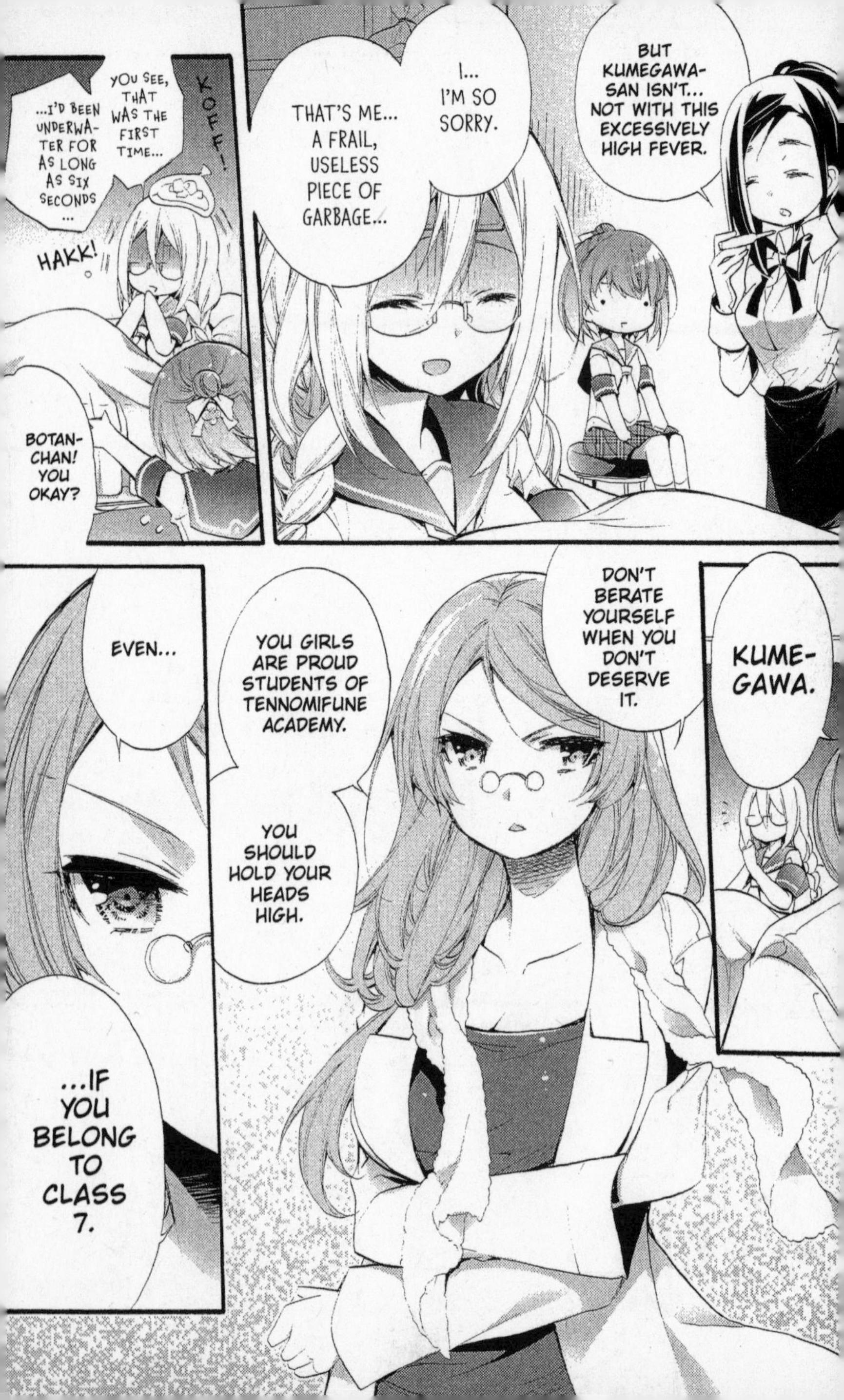
BUT KUMEGAWA-SAN ISN'T... NOT WITH THIS EXCESSIVELY HIGH FEVER.
I... I'M SO SORRY.
THAT'S ME... A FRAIL, USELESS PIECE OF GARBAGE...
YOU SEE, THAT WAS THE FIRST TIME...
...I'D BEEN UNDERWATER FOR AS LONG AS SIX SECONDS ...
KOFF!
HAKK!
BOTAN-CHAN! YOU OKAY?
KUME-GAWA.
DON'T BERATE YOURSELF WHEN YOU DON'T DESERVE IT.
YOU GIRLS ARE PROUD STUDENTS OF TENNOMIFUNE ACADEMY.
YOU SHOULD HOLD YOUR HEADS HIGH.
EVEN...
...IF YOU BELONG TO CLASS 7.

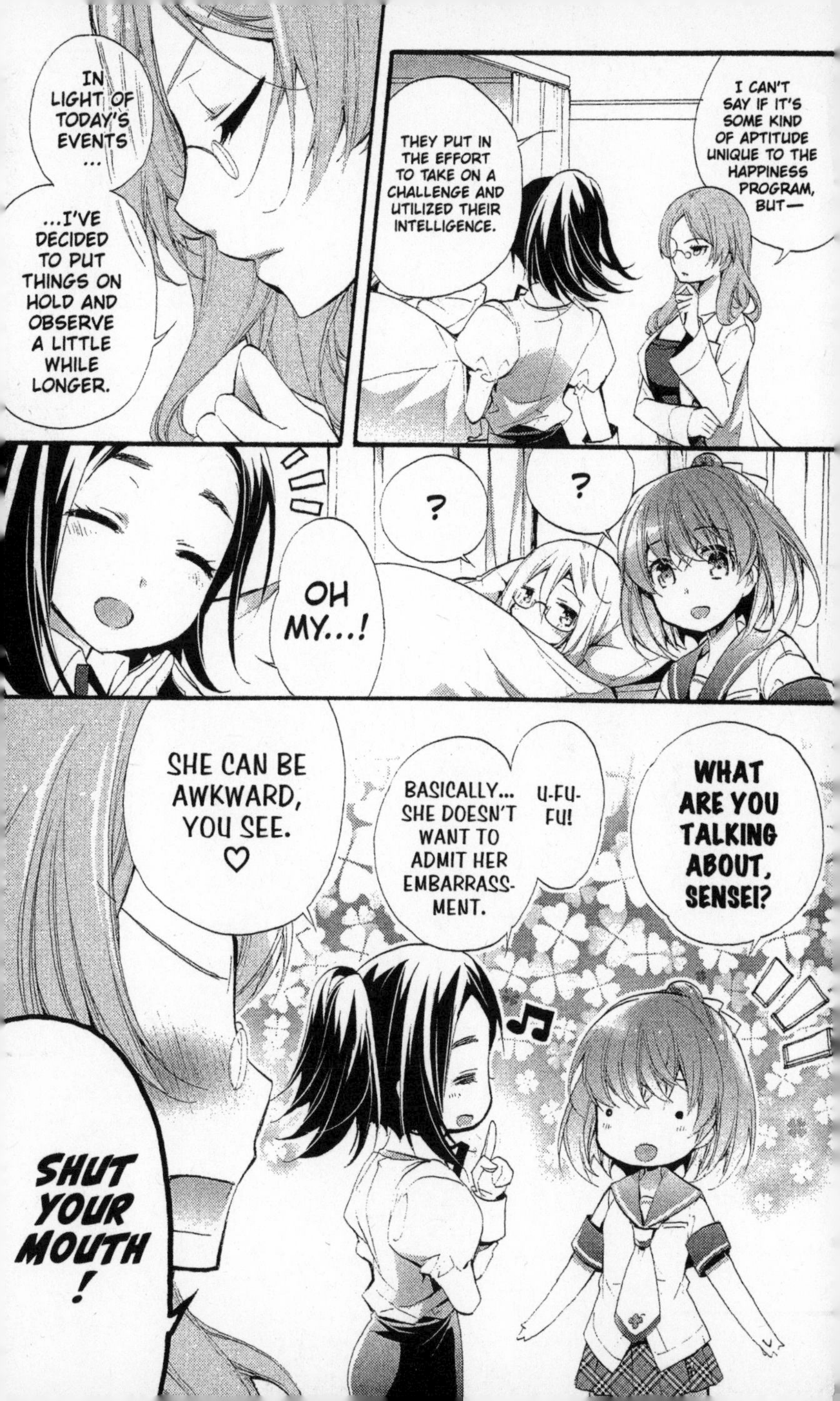
I CAN'T SAY IF IT'S SOME KIND OF APTITUDE UNIQUE TO THE HAPPINESS PROGRAM, BUT—
THEY PUT IN THE EFFORT TO TAKE ON A CHALLENGE AND UTILIZED THEIR INTELLIGENCE.
IN LIGHT OF TODAY'S EVENTS...
...I'VE DECIDED TO PUT THINGS ON HOLD AND OBSERVE A LITTLE WHILE LONGER.
?
?
OH MY...!
WHAT ARE YOU TALKING ABOUT, SENSEI?
U-FU-FU!
BASICALLY... SHE DOESN'T WANT TO ADMIT HER EMBARRASS-MENT.
SHE CAN BE AWKWARD, YOU SEE. ♡
SHUT YOUR MOUTH!

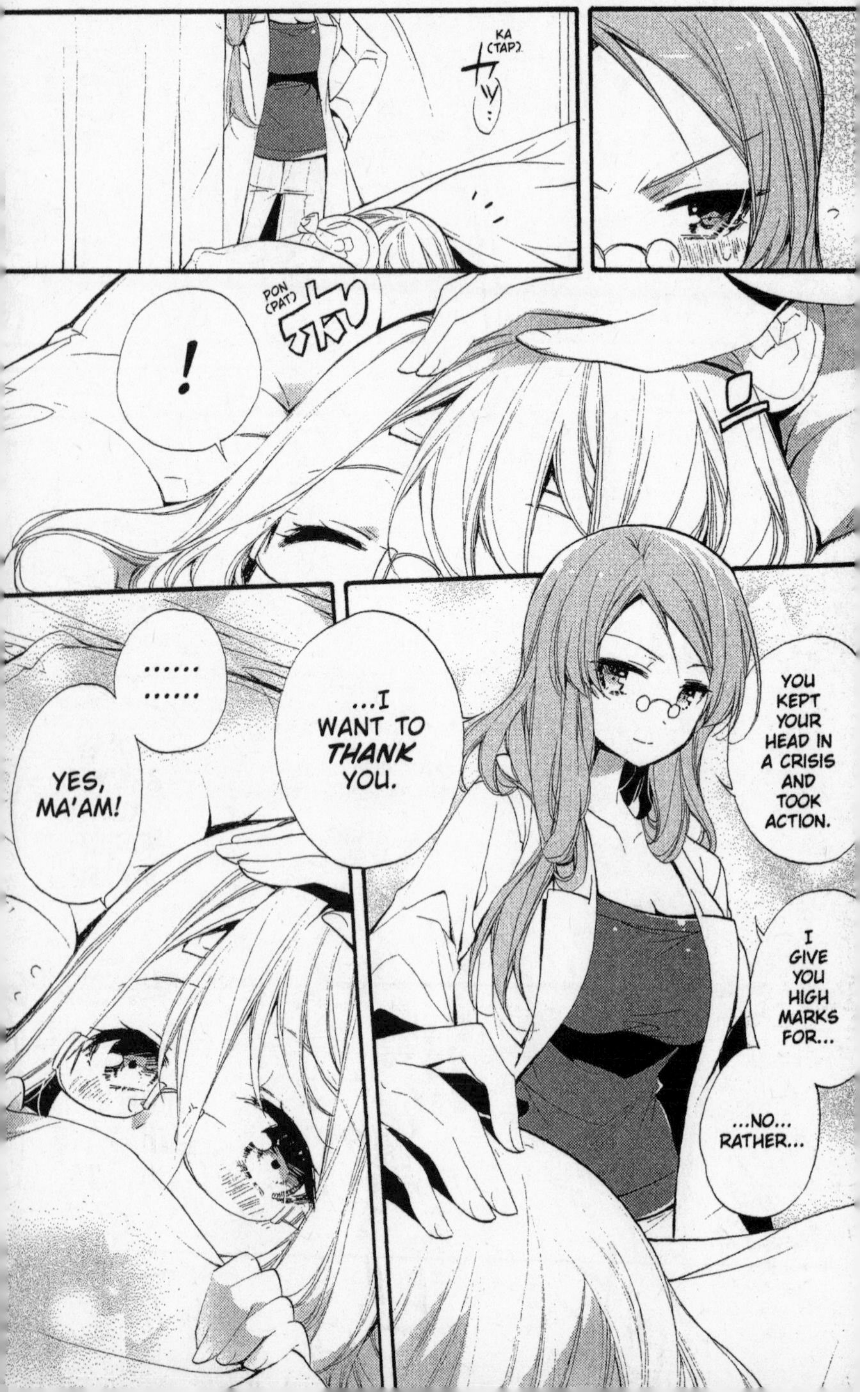
KA (TAP)
カッ
PON (PAT)
ポン
!
YOU KEPT YOUR HEAD IN A CRISIS AND TOOK ACTION.
I GIVE YOU HIGH MARKS FOR...
...NO... RATHER...
...I WANT TO THANK YOU.
....
YES, MA'AM!

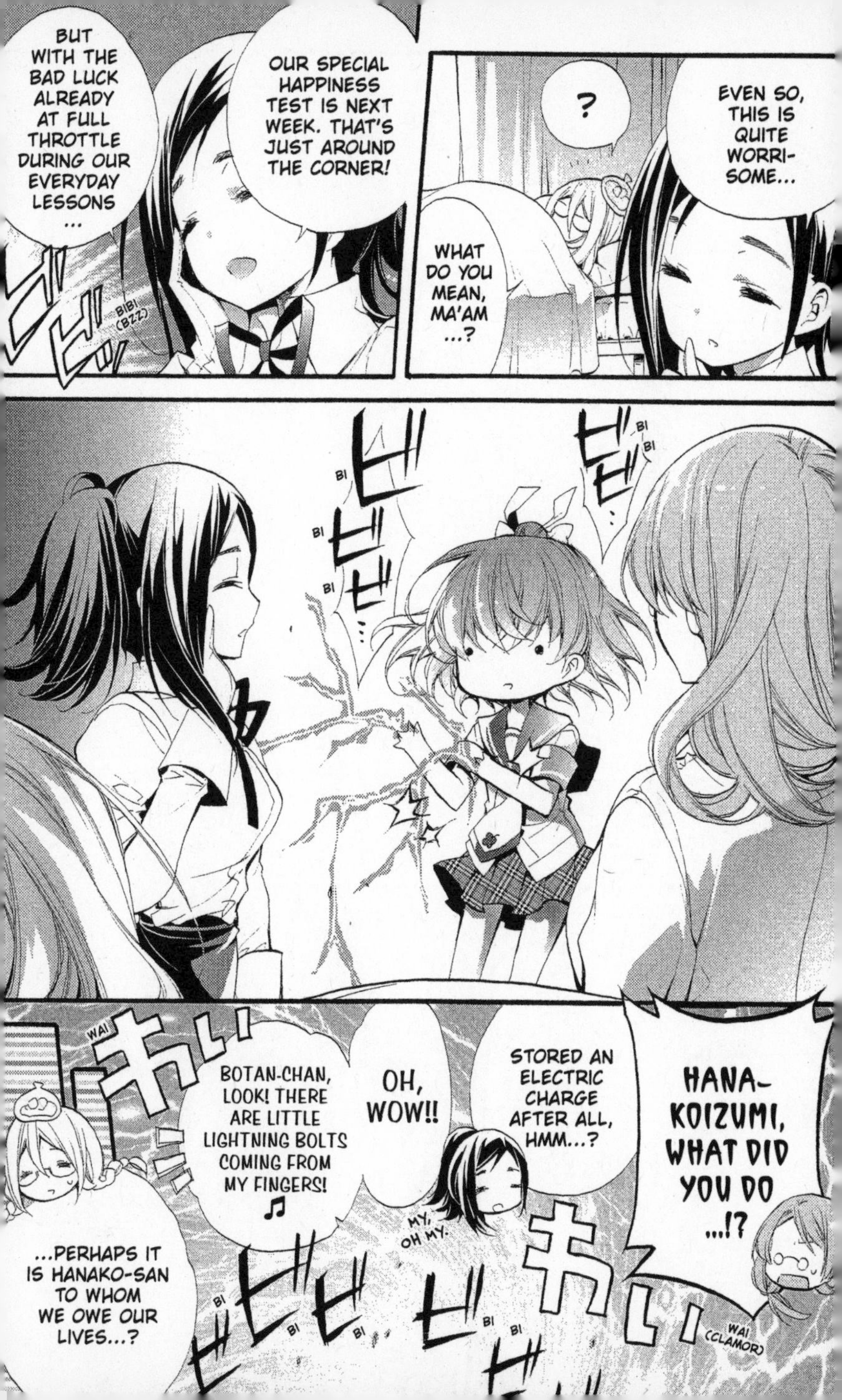
EVEN SO, THIS IS QUITE WORRI-SOME...
?
WHAT DO YOU MEAN, MA'AM ...?
OUR SPECIAL HAPPINESS TEST IS NEXT WEEK. THAT'S JUST AROUND THE CORNER!
BUT WITH THE BAD LUCK ALREADY AT FULL THROTTLE DURING OUR EVERYDAY LESSONS ...
BIBI (BZZ)
BI
BI
BI
BI
BI
HANA-KOIZUMI, WHAT DID YOU DO ...!?
STORED AN ELECTRIC CHARGE AFTER ALL, HMM...?
OH, WOW!!
BOTAN-CHAN, LOOK! THERE ARE LITTLE LIGHTNING BOLTS COMING FROM MY FINGERS! ♫
WAI
MY, OH MY.
WAI (CLAMOR)
BI
BI
BI
BI
BI
...PERHAPS IT IS HANAKO-SAN TO WHOM WE OWE OUR LIVES...?

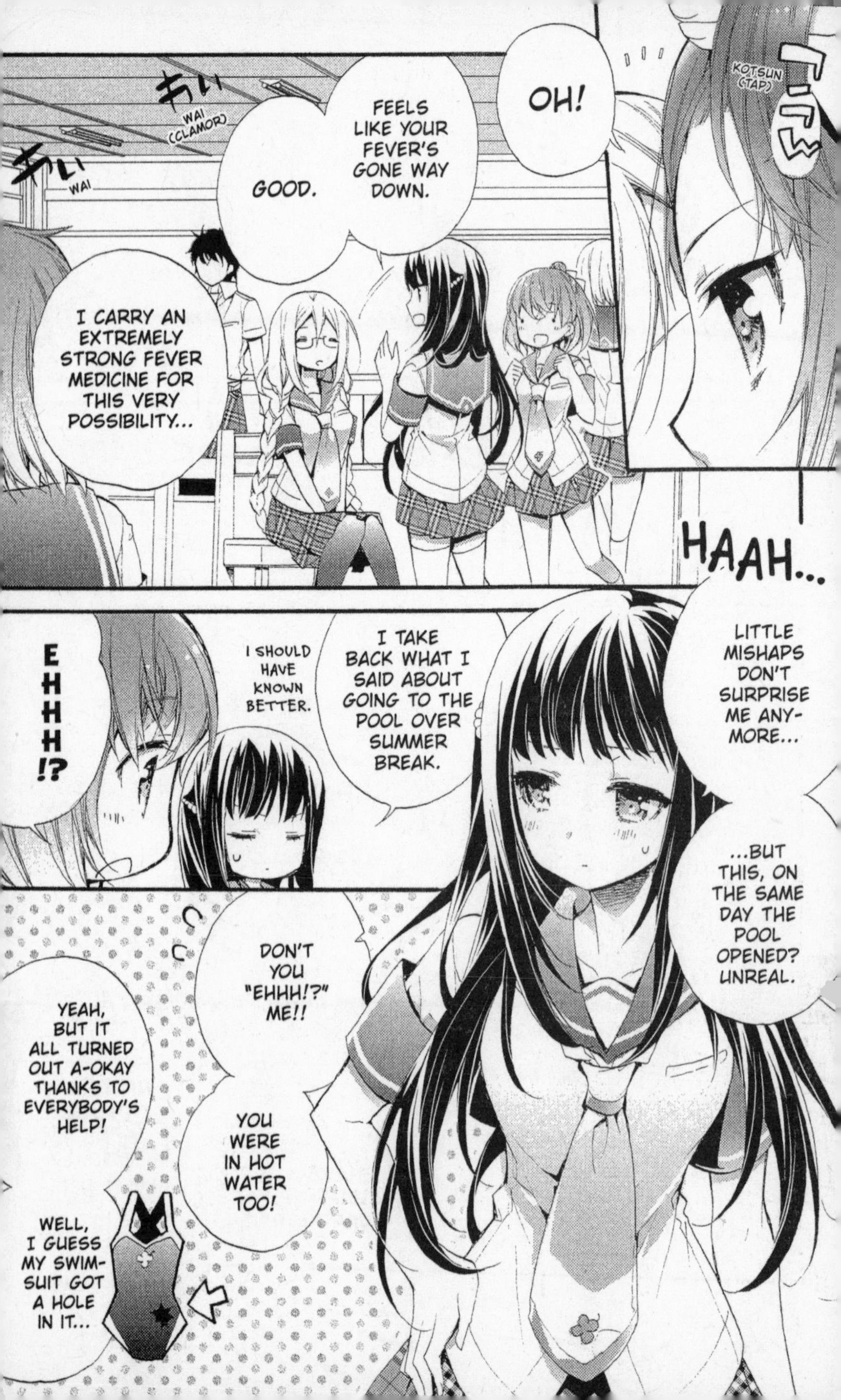
KOTSUN (TAP)
OH!
FEELS LIKE YOUR FEVER'S GONE WAY DOWN.
GOOD.
WAI (CLAMOR)
WAI
I CARRY AN EXTREMELY STRONG FEVER MEDICINE FOR THIS VERY POSSIBILITY...
HAAH...
LITTLE MISHAPS DON'T SURPRISE ME ANY-MORE...
...BUT THIS, ON THE SAME DAY THE POOL OPENED? UNREAL.
I TAKE BACK WHAT I SAID ABOUT GOING TO THE POOL OVER SUMMER BREAK.
I SHOULD HAVE KNOWN BETTER.
EHHHH!?
DON'T YOU "EHHH!?" ME!!
YEAH, BUT IT ALL TURNED OUT A-OKAY THANKS TO EVERYBODY'S HELP!
YOU WERE IN HOT WATER TOO!
WELL, I GUESS MY SWIM-SUIT GOT A HOLE IN IT...

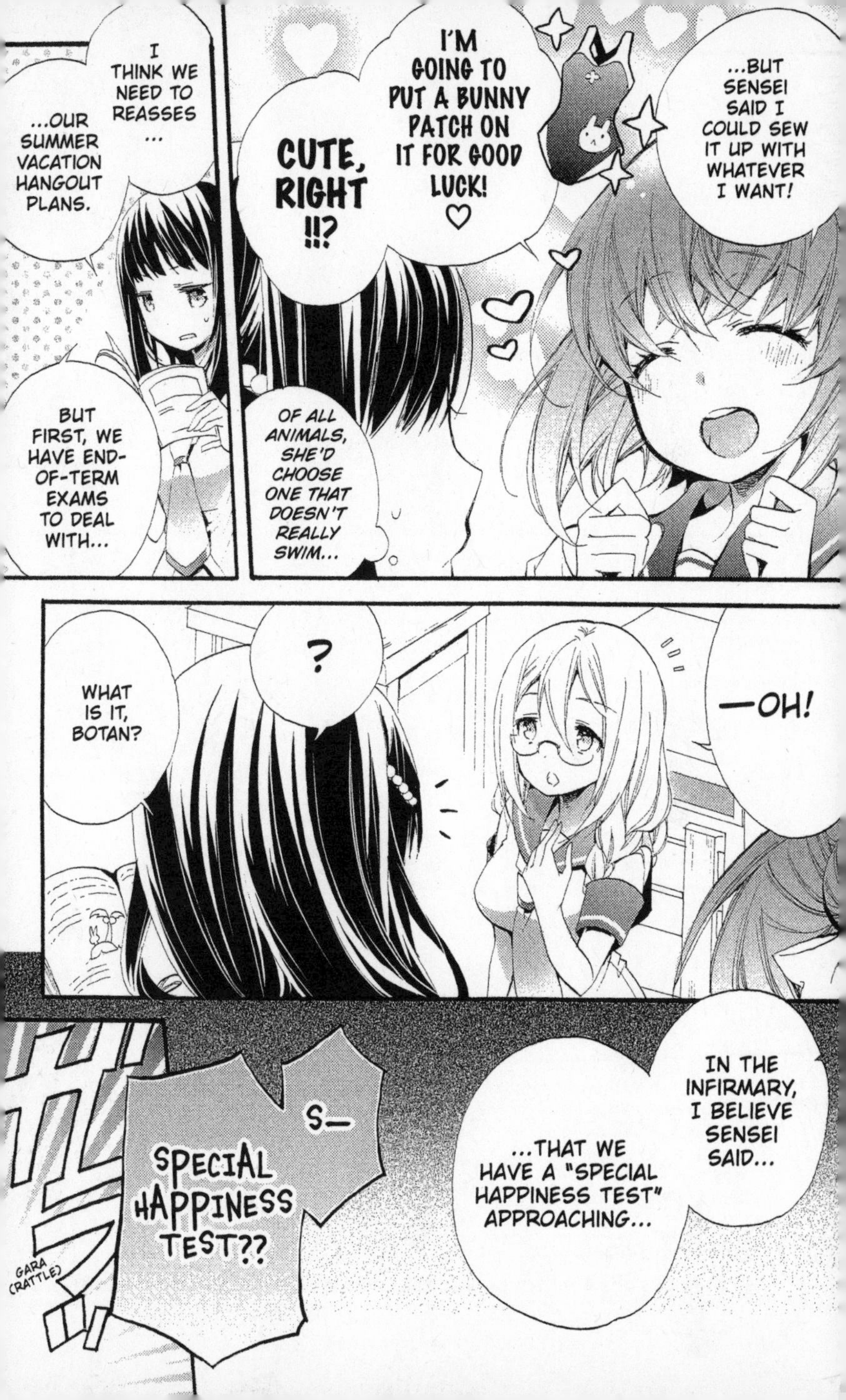
...BUT SENSEI SAID I COULD SEW IT UP WITH WHATEVER I WANT!
I'M GOING TO PUT A BUNNY PATCH ON IT FOR GOOD LUCK! ♡
CUTE, RIGHT!!?
OF ALL ANIMALS, SHE'D CHOOSE ONE THAT DOESN'T REALLY SWIM...
I THINK WE NEED TO REASSES...
...OUR SUMMER VACATION HANGOUT PLANS.
BUT FIRST, WE HAVE END-OF-TERM EXAMS TO DEAL WITH...
—OH!
?
WHAT IS IT, BOTAN?
IN THE INFIRMARY, I BELIEVE SENSEI SAID...
...THAT WE HAVE A "SPECIAL HAPPINESS TEST" APPROACHING...
S—
SPECIAL HAPPINESS TEST??
GARA (RATTLE)

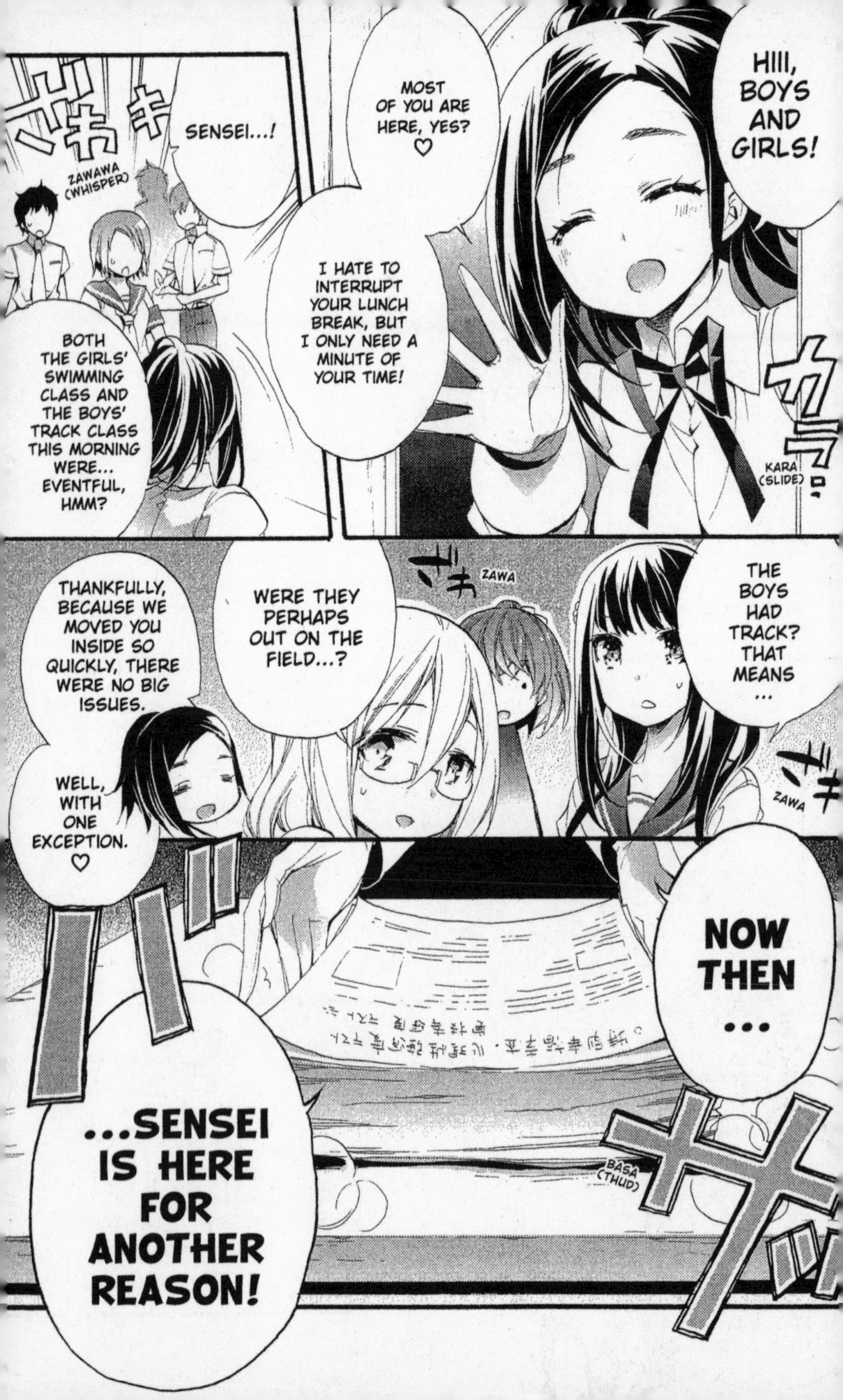
HIII, BOYS AND GIRLS!
KARA (SLIDE)
MOST OF YOU ARE HERE, YES? ♡
I HATE TO INTERRUPT YOUR LUNCH BREAK, BUT I ONLY NEED A MINUTE OF YOUR TIME!
SENSEI...!
ZAWAWA (WHISPER)
BOTH THE GIRLS' SWIMMING CLASS AND THE BOYS' TRACK CLASS THIS MORNING WERE... EVENTFUL, HMM?
THE BOYS HAD TRACK? THAT MEANS ...
ZAWA
ZAWA
WERE THEY PERHAPS OUT ON THE FIELD...?
THANKFULLY, BECAUSE WE MOVED YOU INSIDE SO QUICKLY, THERE WERE NO BIG ISSUES.
WELL, WITH ONE EXCEPTION. ♡
NOW THEN ...
BASA (THUD)
...SENSEI IS HERE FOR ANOTHER REASON!

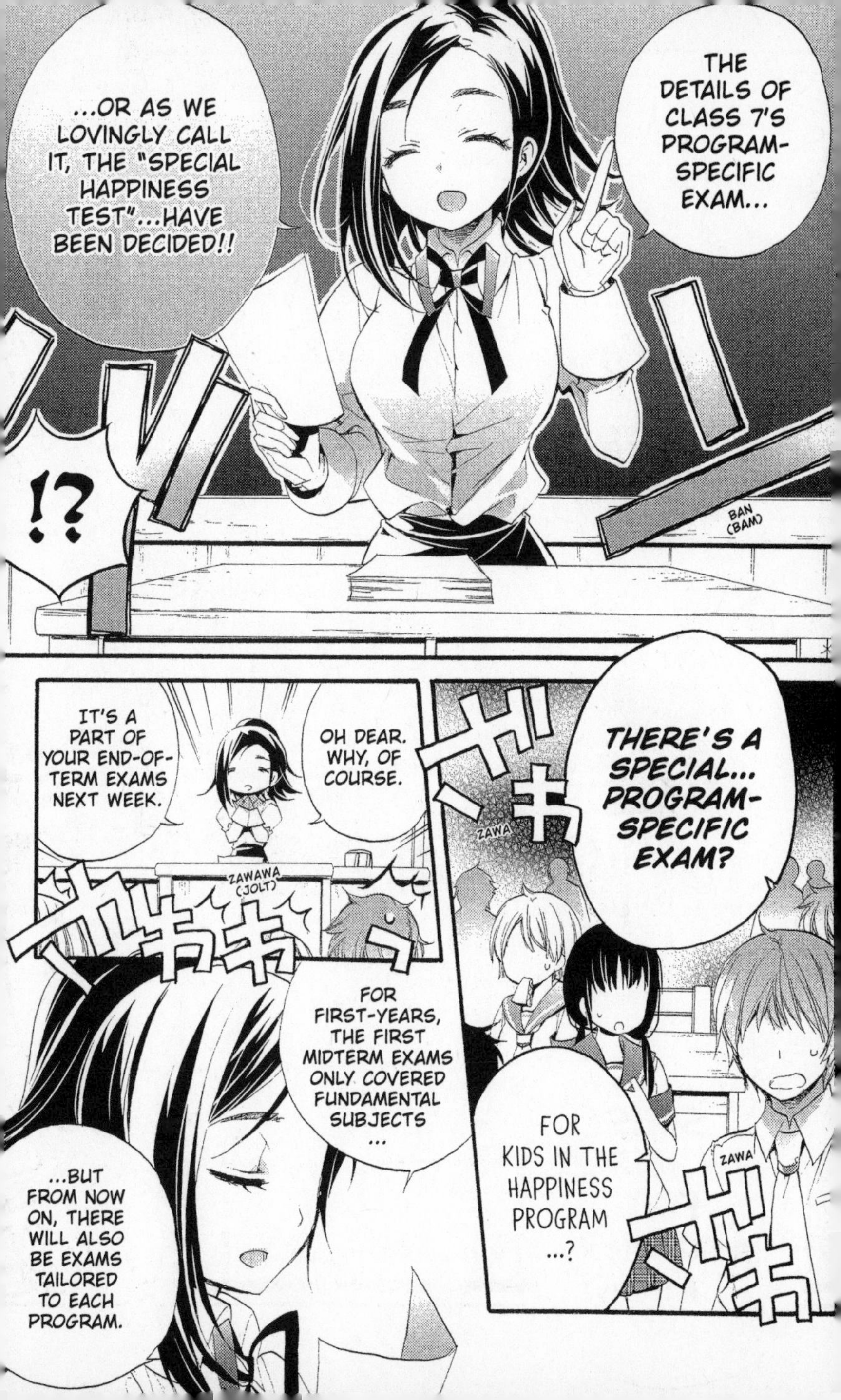
THE DETAILS OF CLASS 7'S PROGRAM-SPECIFIC EXAM...
...OR AS WE LOVINGLY CALL IT, THE "SPECIAL HAPPINESS TEST"...HAVE BEEN DECIDED!!
BAN (BAM)
!?
THERE'S A SPECIAL... PROGRAM-SPECIFIC EXAM?
ZAWA
FOR KIDS IN THE HAPPINESS PROGRAM ...?
ZAWA
OH DEAR. WHY, OF COURSE.
IT'S A PART OF YOUR END-OF-TERM EXAMS NEXT WEEK.
ZAWAWA (JOLT)
FOR FIRST-YEARS, THE FIRST MIDTERM EXAMS ONLY COVERED FUNDAMENTAL SUBJECTS ...
...BUT FROM NOW ON, THERE WILL ALSO BE EXAMS TAILORED TO EACH PROGRAM.

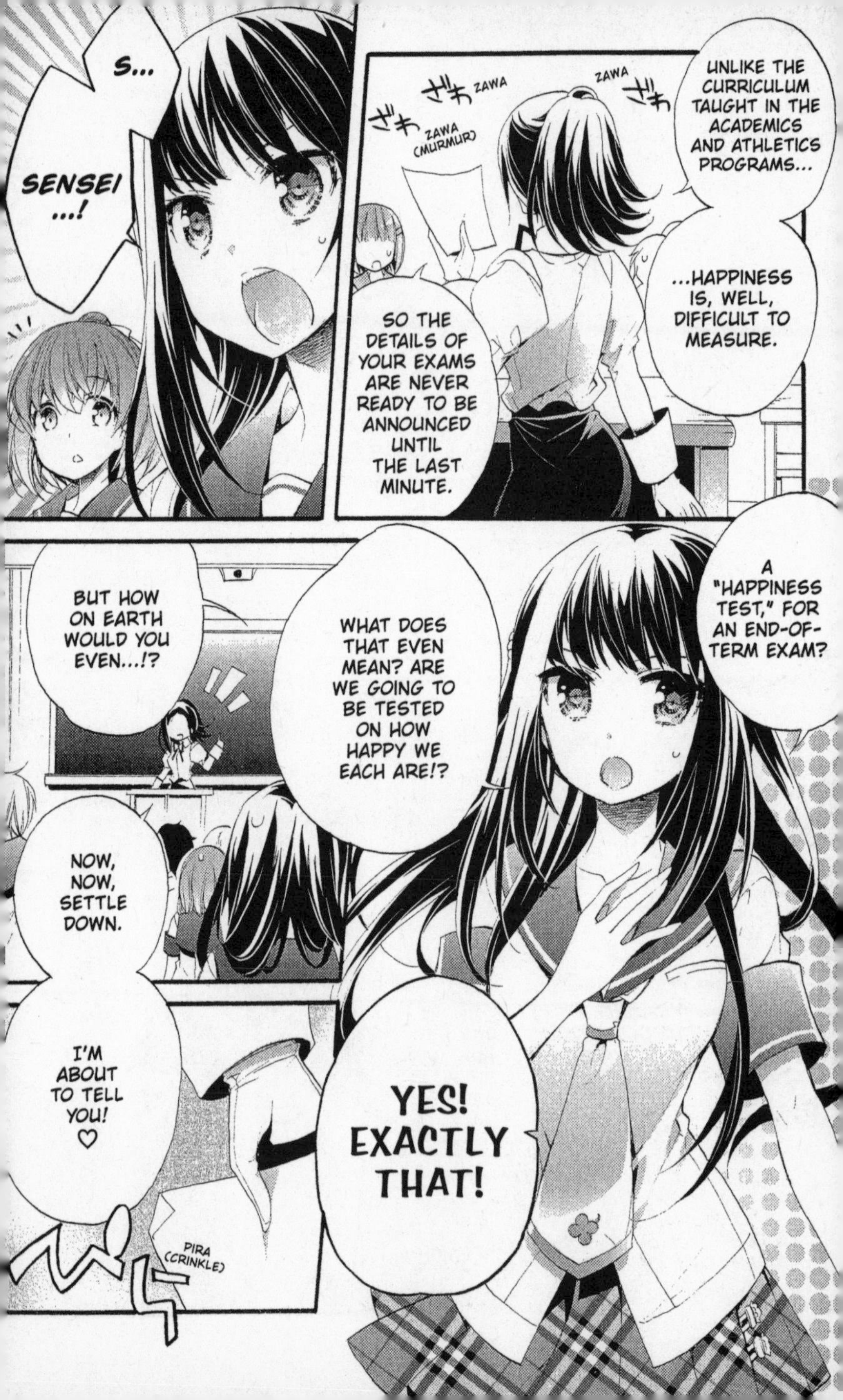
UNLIKE THE CURRICULUM TAUGHT IN THE ACADEMICS AND ATHLETICS PROGRAMS...
ZAWA
ZAWA
ZAWA (MURMUR)
...HAPPINESS IS, WELL, DIFFICULT TO MEASURE.
SO THE DETAILS OF YOUR EXAMS ARE NEVER READY TO BE ANNOUNCED UNTIL THE LAST MINUTE.
S...
SENSEI ...!
A "HAPPINESS TEST," FOR AN END-OF-TERM EXAM?
WHAT DOES THAT EVEN MEAN? ARE WE GOING TO BE TESTED ON HOW HAPPY WE EACH ARE!?
YES! EXACTLY THAT!
BUT HOW ON EARTH WOULD YOU EVEN...!?
NOW, NOW, SETTLE DOWN.
I'M ABOUT TO TELL YOU! ♡
PIRA (CRINKLE)

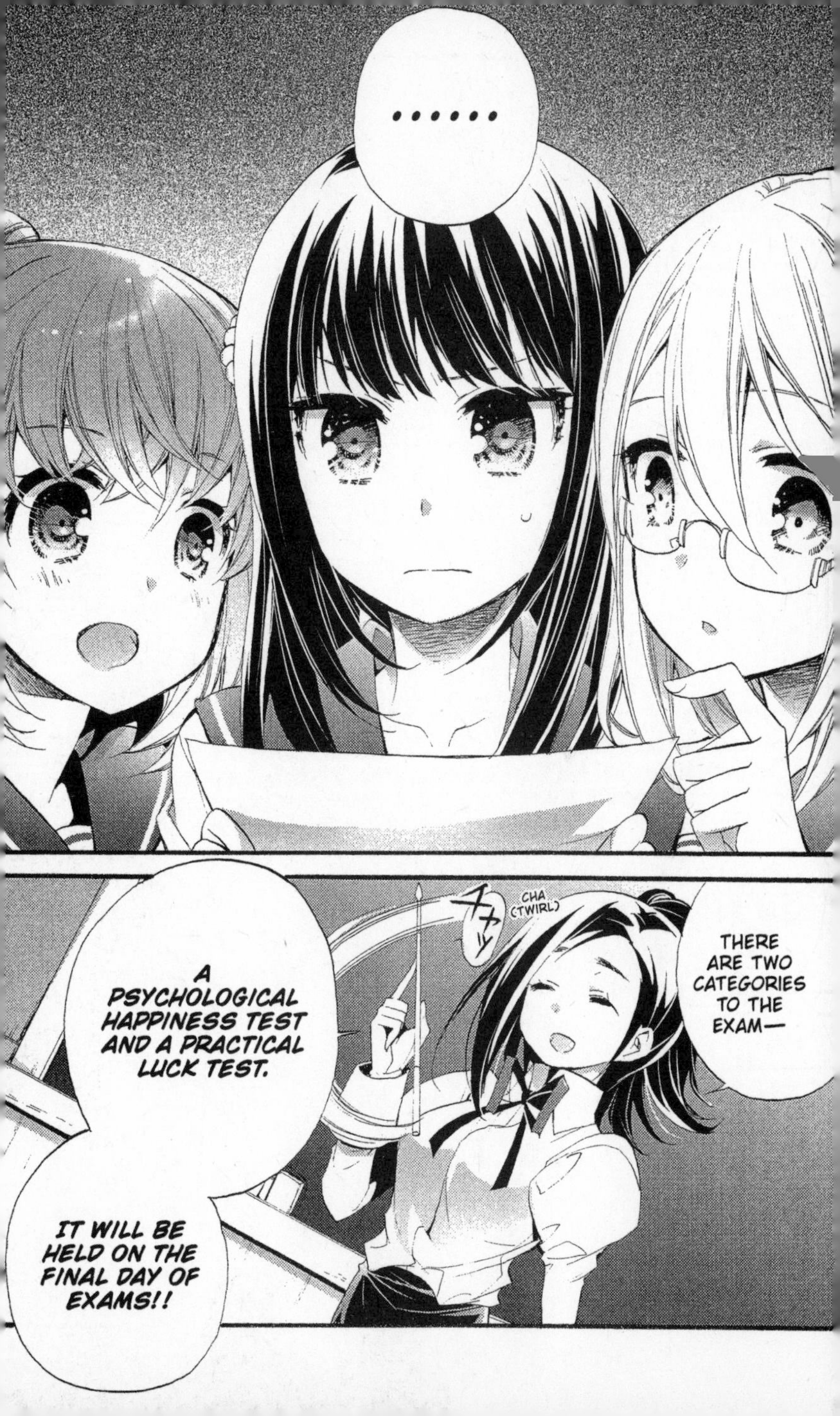
......
THERE ARE TWO CATEGORIES TO THE EXAM—
CHA (TWIRL)
A PSYCHOLOGICAL HAPPINESS TEST AND A PRACTICAL LUCK TEST.
IT WILL BE HELD ON THE FINAL DAY OF EXAMS!!

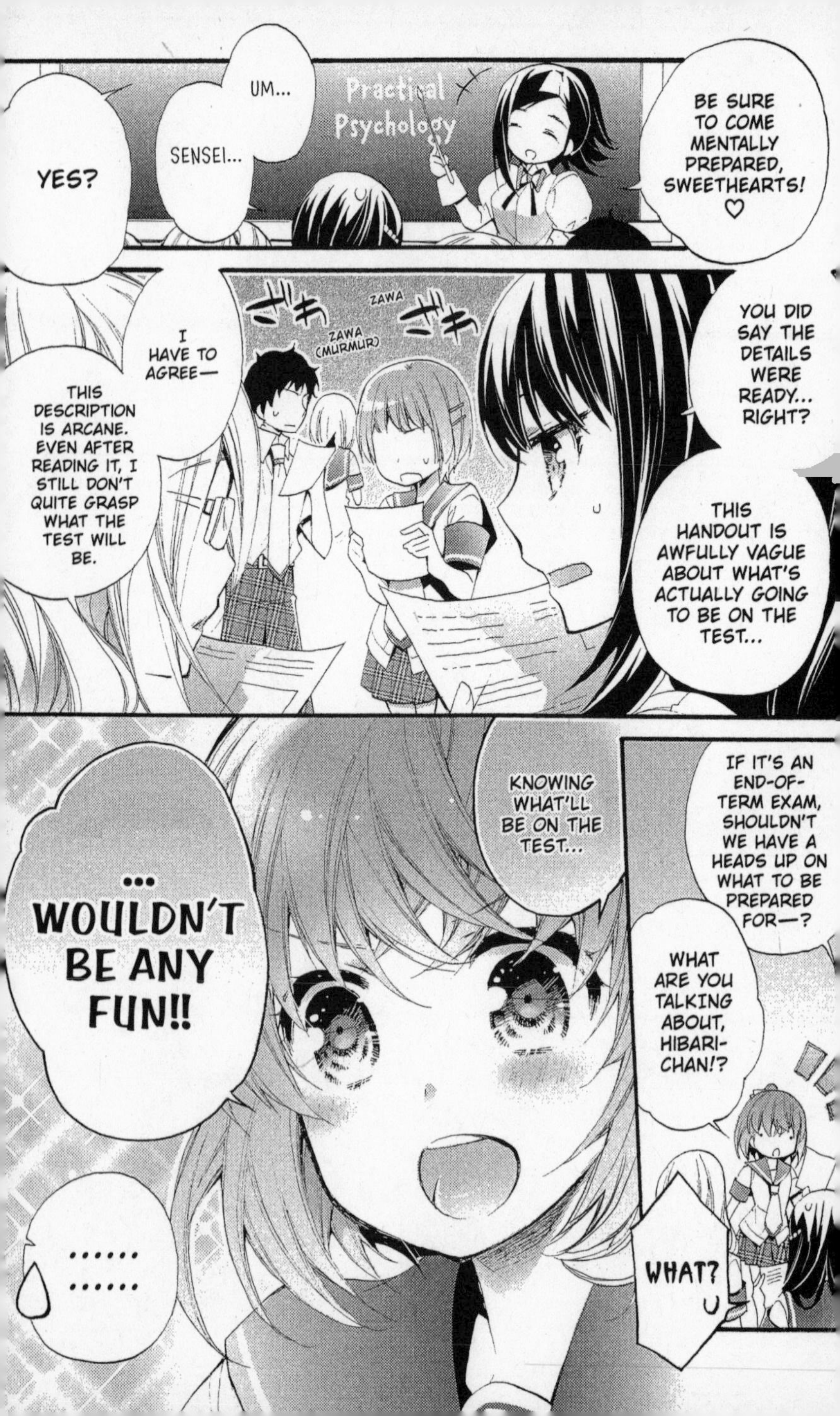
BE SURE TO COME MENTALLY PREPARED, SWEETHEARTS! ♡
Practical Psychology
UM...
SENSEI...
YES?
YOU DID SAY THE DETAILS WERE READY... RIGHT?
THIS HANDOUT IS AWFULLY VAGUE ABOUT WHAT'S ACTUALLY GOING TO BE ON THE TEST...
ZAWA
ZAWA (MURMUR)
I HAVE TO AGREE—
THIS DESCRIPTION IS ARCANE. EVEN AFTER READING IT, I STILL DON'T QUITE GRASP WHAT THE TEST WILL BE.
IF IT'S AN END-OF-TERM EXAM, SHOULDN'T WE HAVE A HEADS UP ON WHAT TO BE PREPARED FOR—?
WHAT ARE YOU TALKING ABOUT, HIBARI-CHAN!?
WHAT?
KNOWING WHAT'LL BE ON THE TEST...
...WOULDN'T BE ANY FUN!!
....

Anne Happy

unhappy go lucky!

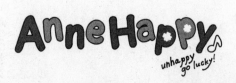

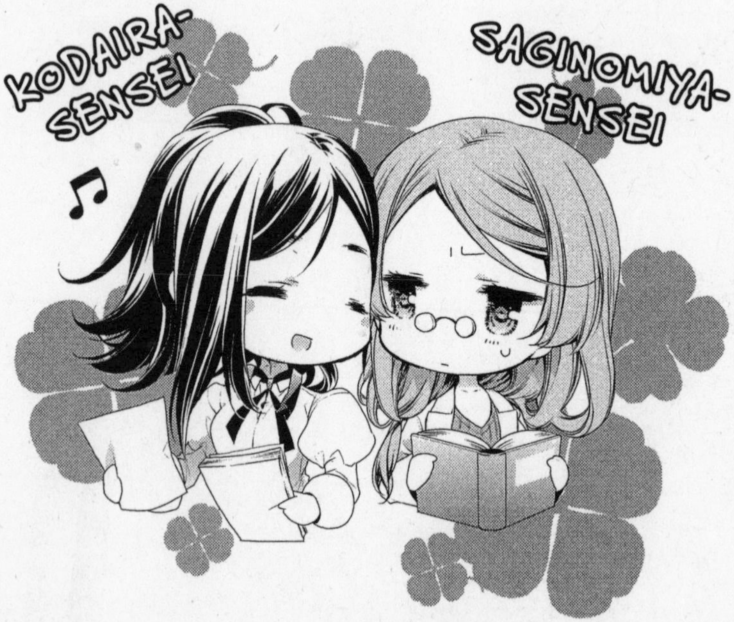
KODAIRA-SENSEI
SAGINOMIYA-SENSEI

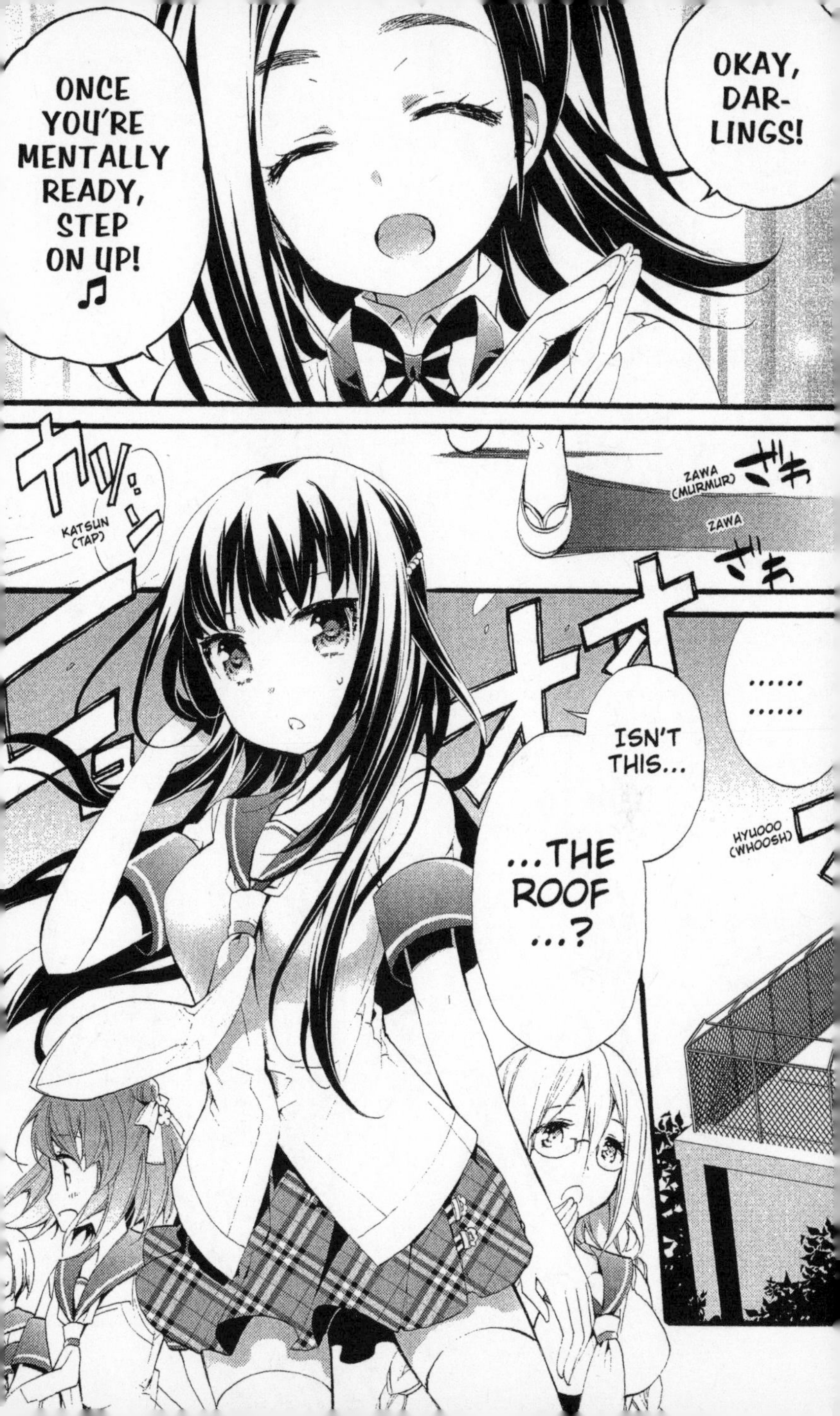
OKAY, DARLINGS!
ONCE YOU'RE MENTALLY READY, STEP ON UP! ♫
ZAWA (MURMUR)
ZAWA
KATSUN (TAP)
......
......
ISN'T THIS...
...THE ROOF ...?
HYUOOO (WHOOSH)

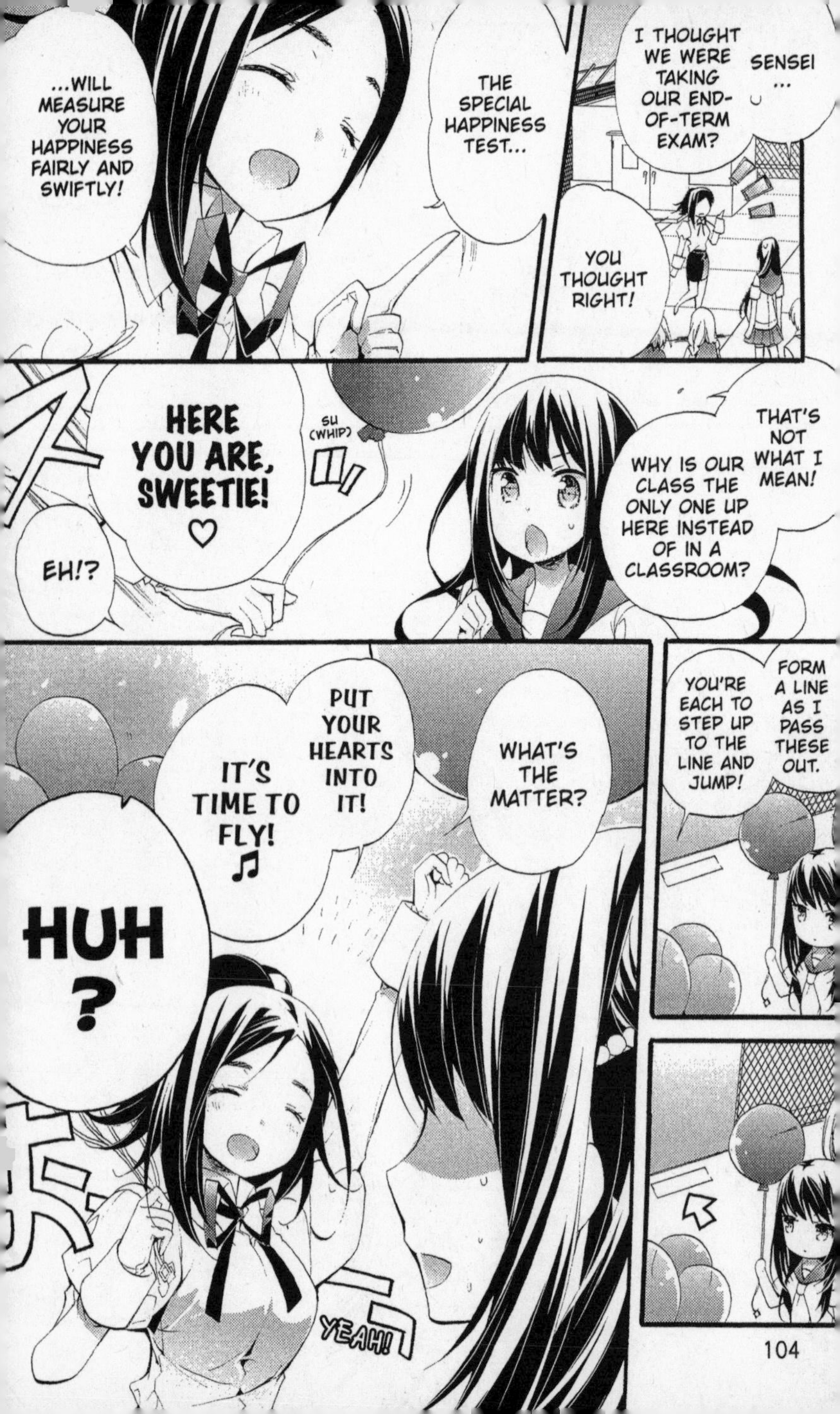
SENSEI ...
I THOUGHT WE WERE TAKING OUR END-OF-TERM EXAM?
YOU THOUGHT RIGHT!
THE SPECIAL HAPPINESS TEST...
...WILL MEASURE YOUR HAPPINESS FAIRLY AND SWIFTLY!
THAT'S NOT WHAT I MEAN!
WHY IS OUR CLASS THE ONLY ONE UP HERE INSTEAD OF IN A CLASSROOM?
SU (WHIP)
HERE YOU ARE, SWEETIE! ♡
EH!?
FORM A LINE AS I PASS THESE OUT.
YOU'RE EACH TO STEP UP TO THE LINE AND JUMP!
WHAT'S THE MATTER?
PUT YOUR HEARTS INTO IT!
IT'S TIME TO FLY! ♫
HUH?
YEAH!

✤ Lucky. 20

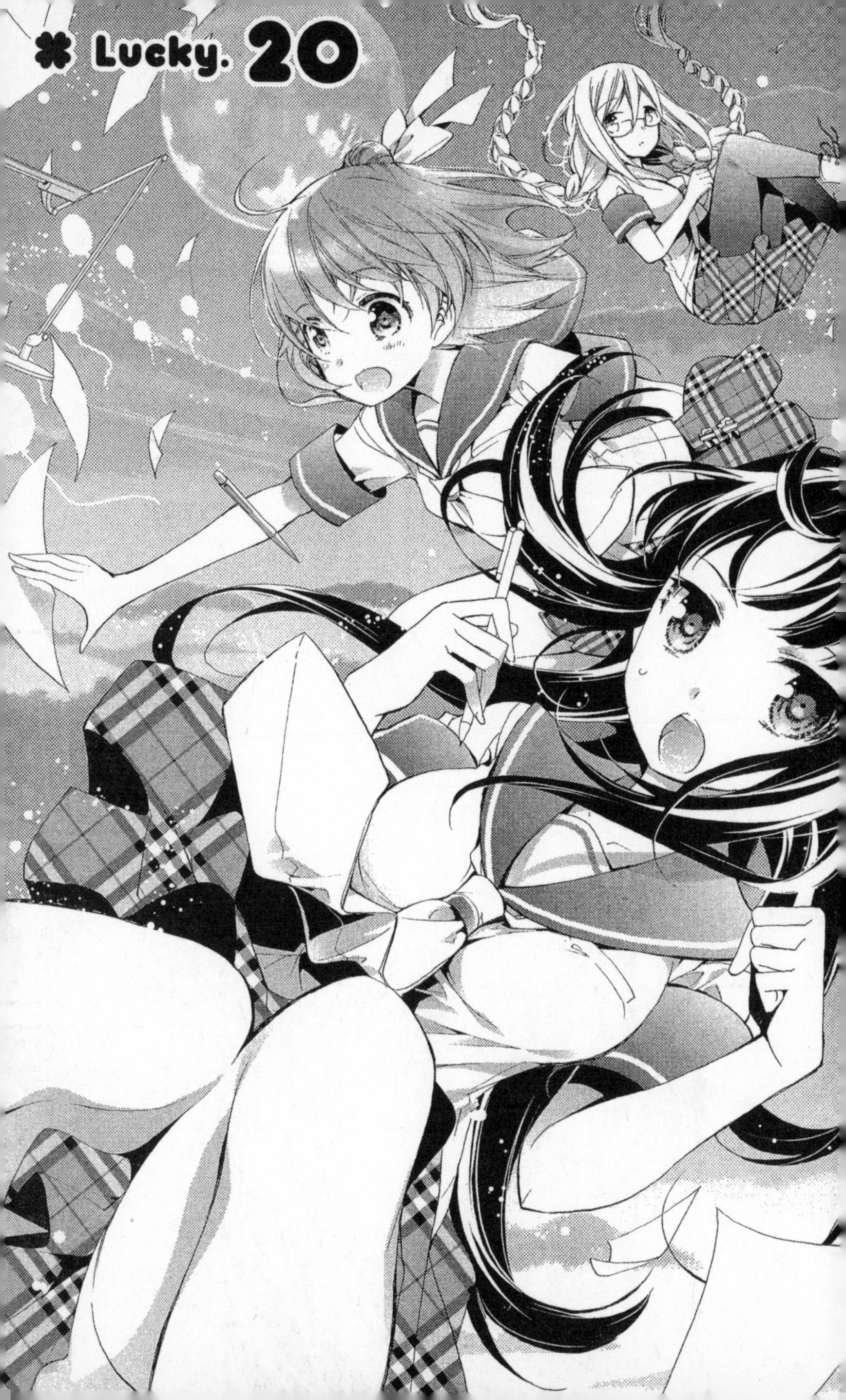

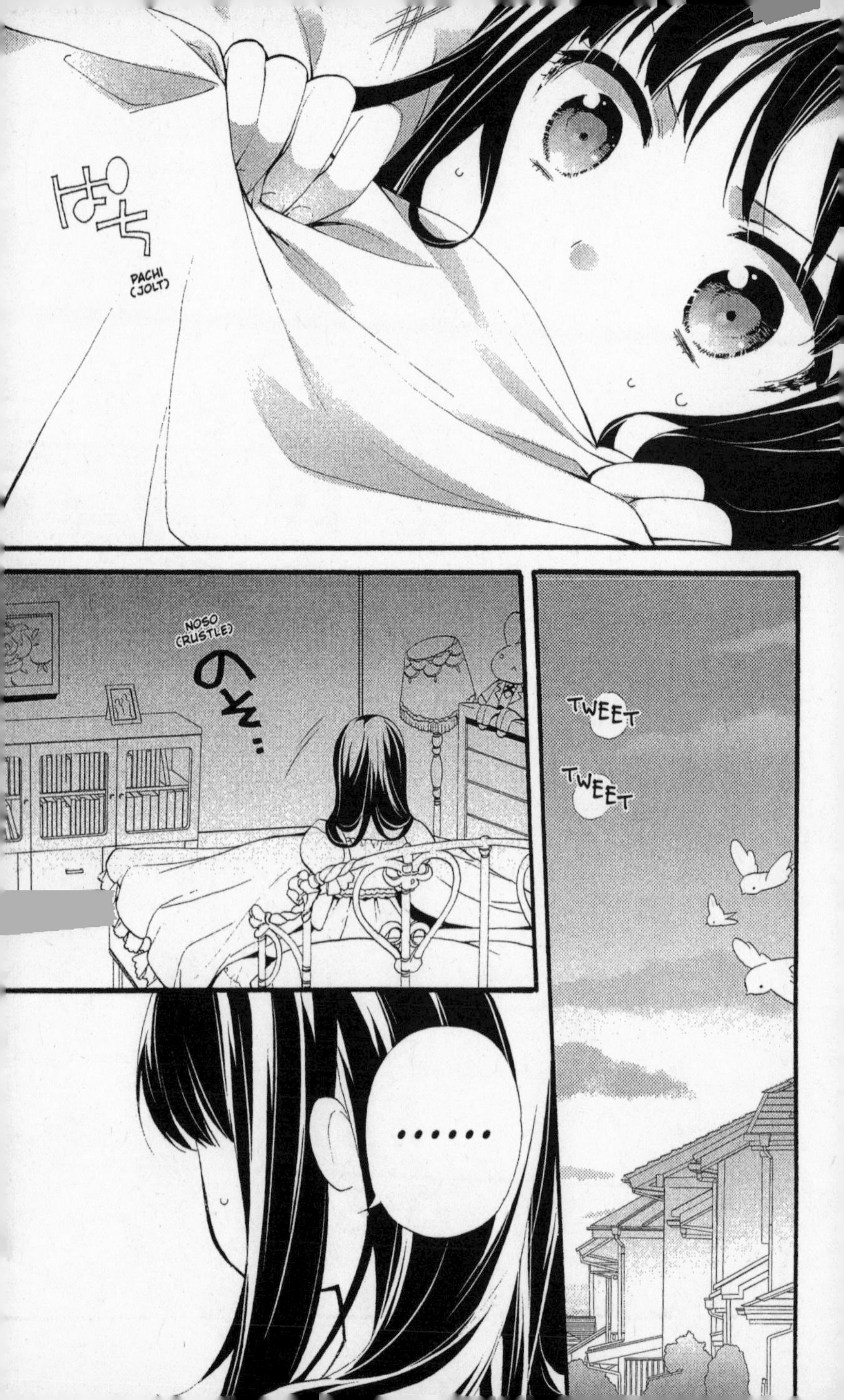
はっ
PACHI (JOLT)
TWEET
TWEET
のそ…
NOSO (RUSTLE)
......

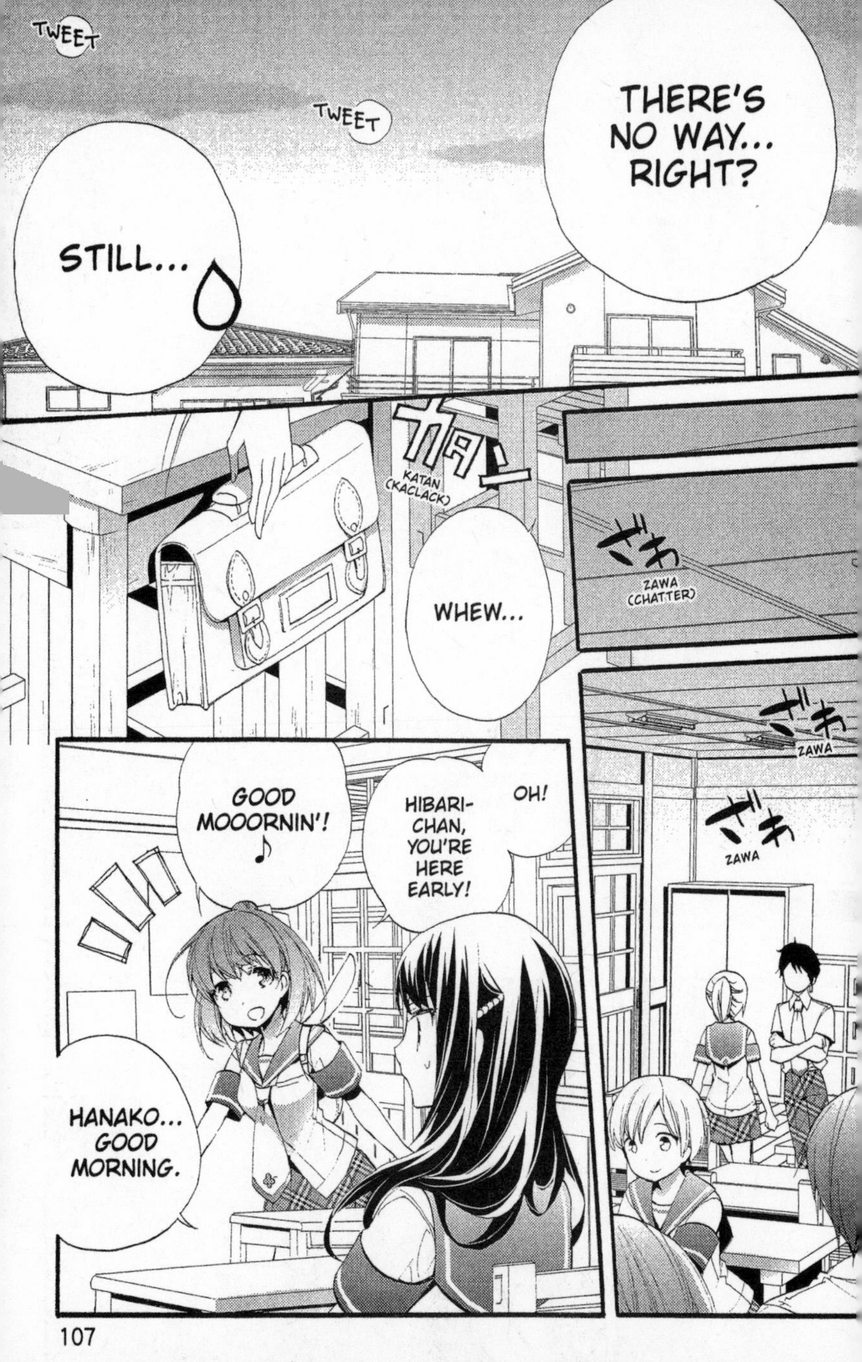
THERE'S NO WAY... RIGHT?
TWEET
TWEET
STILL...
ZAWA (CHATTER)
ZAWA
ZAWA
KATAN (KACLACK)
WHEW...
OH!
HIBARI-CHAN, YOU'RE HERE EARLY!
GOOD MOOORNIN'! ♪
HANAKO... GOOD MORNING.

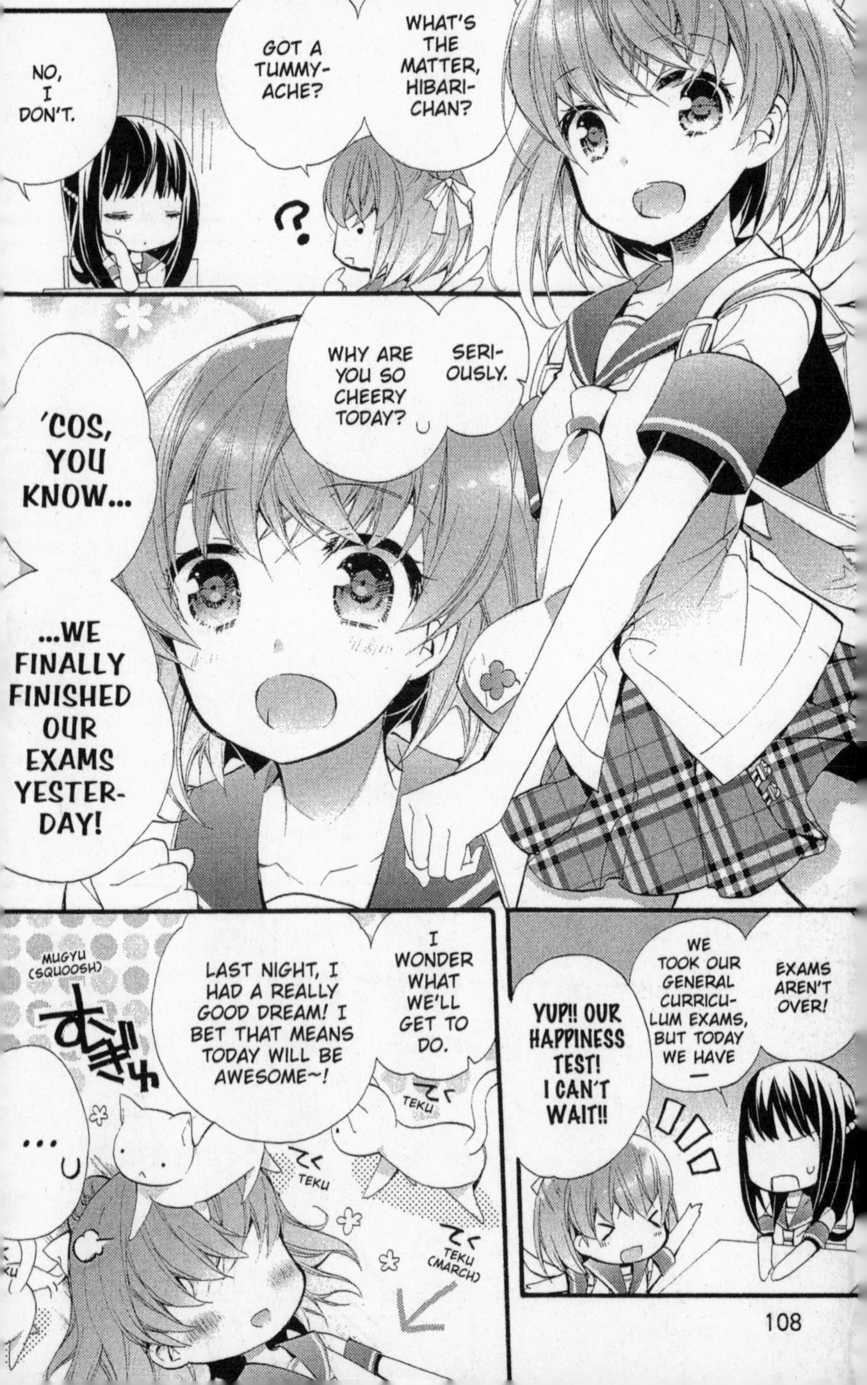
WHAT'S THE MATTER, HIBARI-CHAN?
GOT A TUMMY-ACHE?
NO, I DON'T.
SERIOUSLY.
WHY ARE YOU SO CHEERY TODAY?
'COS, YOU KNOW...
...WE FINALLY FINISHED OUR EXAMS YESTERDAY!
EXAMS AREN'T OVER!
WE TOOK OUR GENERAL CURRICULUM EXAMS, BUT TODAY WE HAVE—
YUP!! OUR HAPPINESS TEST! I CAN'T WAIT!!
I WONDER WHAT WE'LL GET TO DO.
LAST NIGHT, I HAD A REALLY GOOD DREAM! I BET THAT MEANS TODAY WILL BE AWESOME~!
TEKU
TEKU
TEKU (MARCH)
MUGYU (SQUOOSH)
...

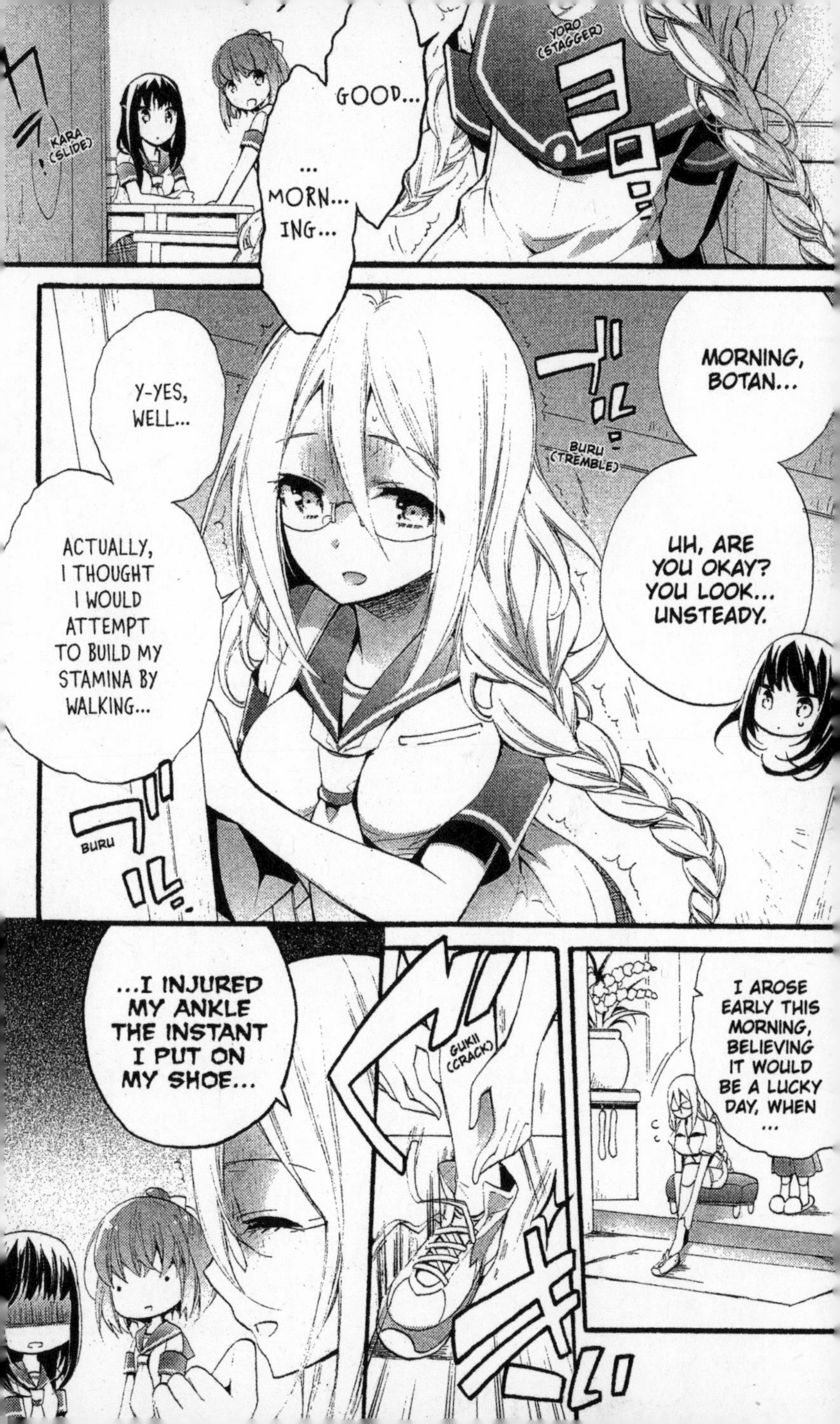
YORO (STAGGER)
GOOD...
... MORN... ING...
KARA (SLIDE)
MORNING, BOTAN...
BURU (TREMBLE)
UH, ARE YOU OKAY? YOU LOOK... UNSTEADY.
Y-YES, WELL...
ACTUALLY, I THOUGHT I WOULD ATTEMPT TO BUILD MY STAMINA BY WALKING...
BURU
I AROSE EARLY THIS MORNING, BELIEVING IT WOULD BE A LUCKY DAY, WHEN ...
GUKII (CRACK)
...I INJURED MY ANKLE THE INSTANT I PUT ON MY SHOE...

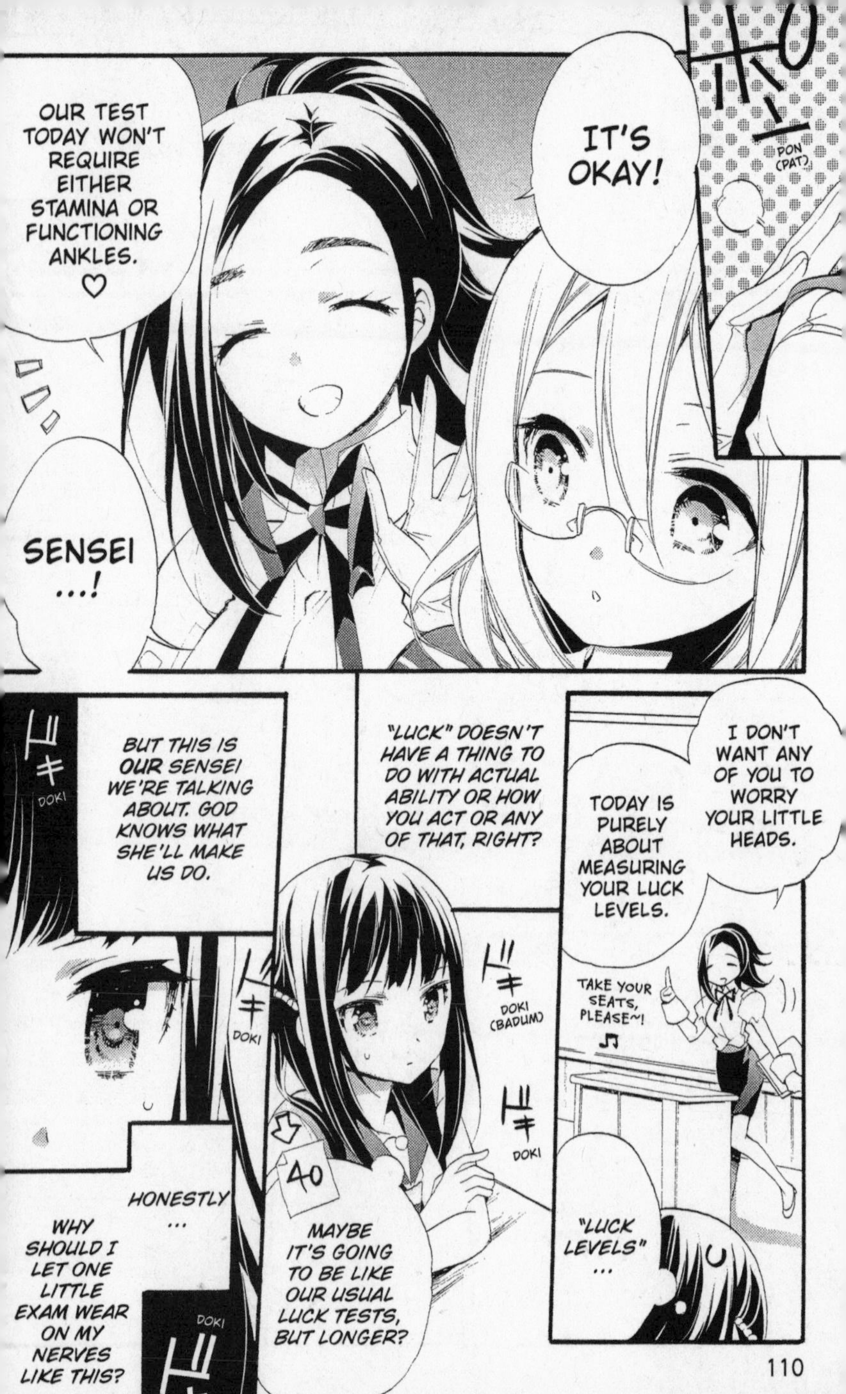
IT'S OKAY!
PON (PAT)
OUR TEST TODAY WON'T REQUIRE EITHER STAMINA OR FUNCTIONING ANKLES. ♡
SENSEI ...!
I DON'T WANT ANY OF YOU TO WORRY YOUR LITTLE HEADS.
TODAY IS PURELY ABOUT MEASURING YOUR LUCK LEVELS.
TAKE YOUR SEATS, PLEASE~! ♫
"LUCK LEVELS" ...
"LUCK" DOESN'T HAVE A THING TO DO WITH ACTUAL ABILITY OR HOW YOU ACT OR ANY OF THAT, RIGHT?
DOKI (BADUM)
DOKI
DOKI
40
MAYBE IT'S GOING TO BE LIKE OUR USUAL LUCK TESTS, BUT LONGER?
DOKI
BUT THIS IS OUR SENSEI WE'RE TALKING ABOUT. GOD KNOWS WHAT SHE'LL MAKE US DO.
HONESTLY ...
WHY SHOULD I LET ONE LITTLE EXAM WEAR ON MY NERVES LIKE THIS?
DOKI

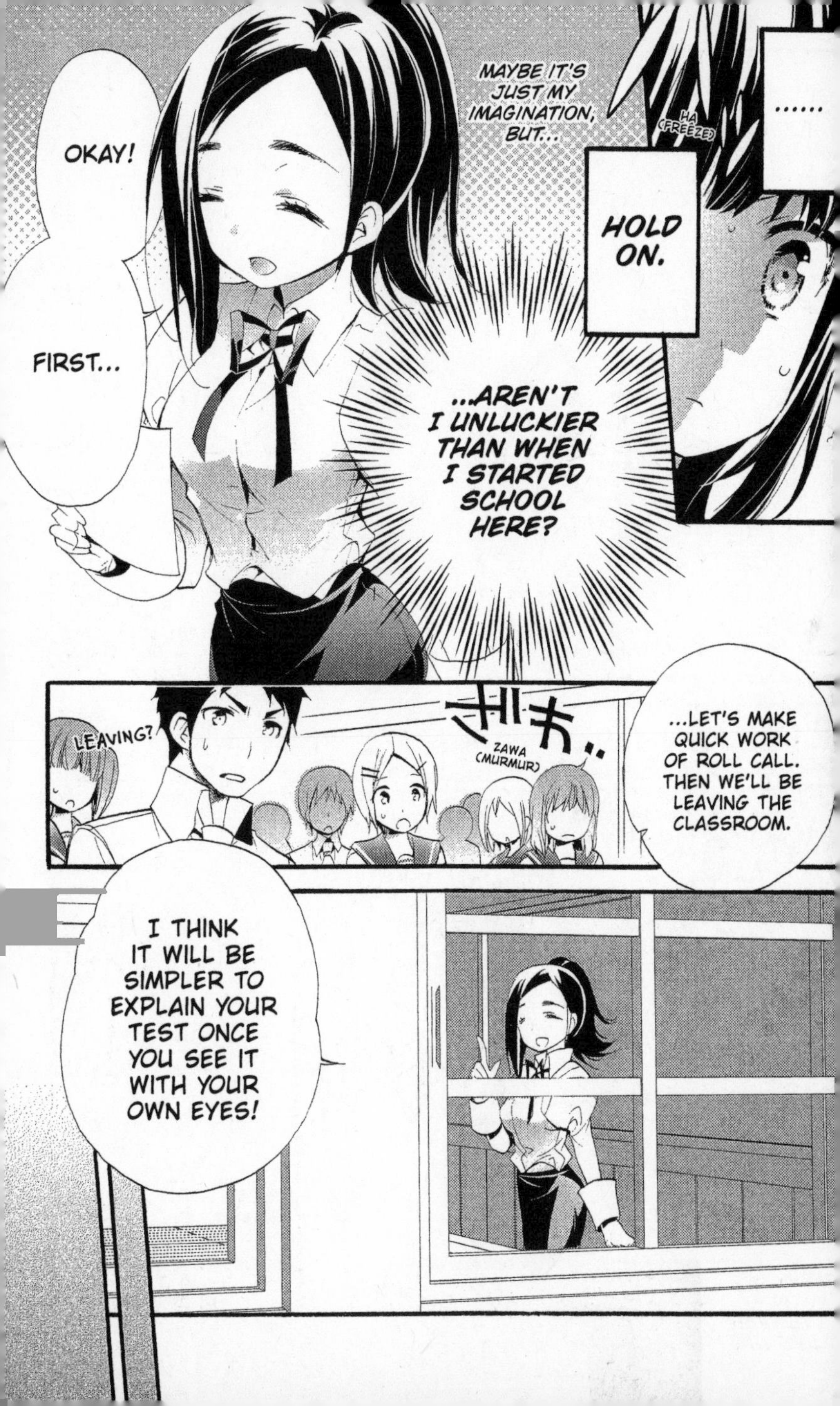
......
HA (FREEZE)
HOLD ON.
MAYBE IT'S JUST MY IMAGINATION, BUT...
...AREN'T I UNLUCKIER THAN WHEN I STARTED SCHOOL HERE?
OKAY!
FIRST...
...LET'S MAKE QUICK WORK OF ROLL CALL. THEN WE'LL BE LEAVING THE CLASSROOM.
ZAWA (MURMUR)
LEAVING?
I THINK IT WILL BE SIMPLER TO EXPLAIN YOUR TEST ONCE YOU SEE IT WITH YOUR OWN EYES!

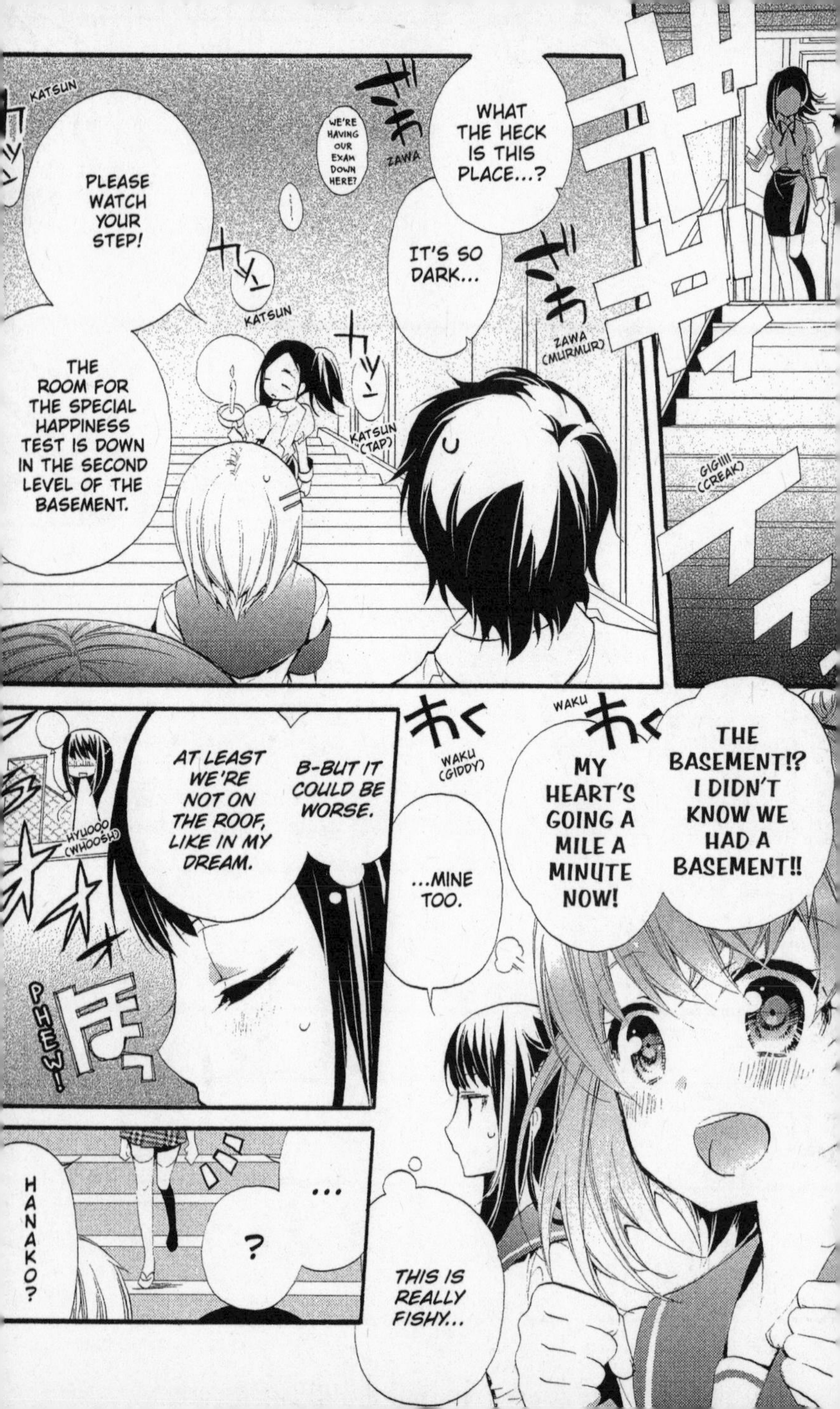
GIGIII (CREAK)
WHAT THE HECK IS THIS PLACE...?
ZAWA
WE'RE HAVING OUR EXAM DOWN HERE?
...!
IT'S SO DARK...
ZAWA (MURMUR)
KATSUN
PLEASE WATCH YOUR STEP!
KATSUN
KATSUN (TAP)
THE ROOM FOR THE SPECIAL HAPPINESS TEST IS DOWN IN THE SECOND LEVEL OF THE BASEMENT.
THE BASEMENT!? I DIDN'T KNOW WE HAD A BASEMENT!!
WAKU
WAKU (GIDDY)
MY HEART'S GOING A MILE A MINUTE NOW!
...MINE TOO.
THIS IS REALLY FISHY...
B-BUT IT COULD BE WORSE.
AT LEAST WE'RE NOT ON THE ROOF, LIKE IN MY DREAM.
HYUOOO (WHOOSH)
PHEW!
...
?
HANAKO?

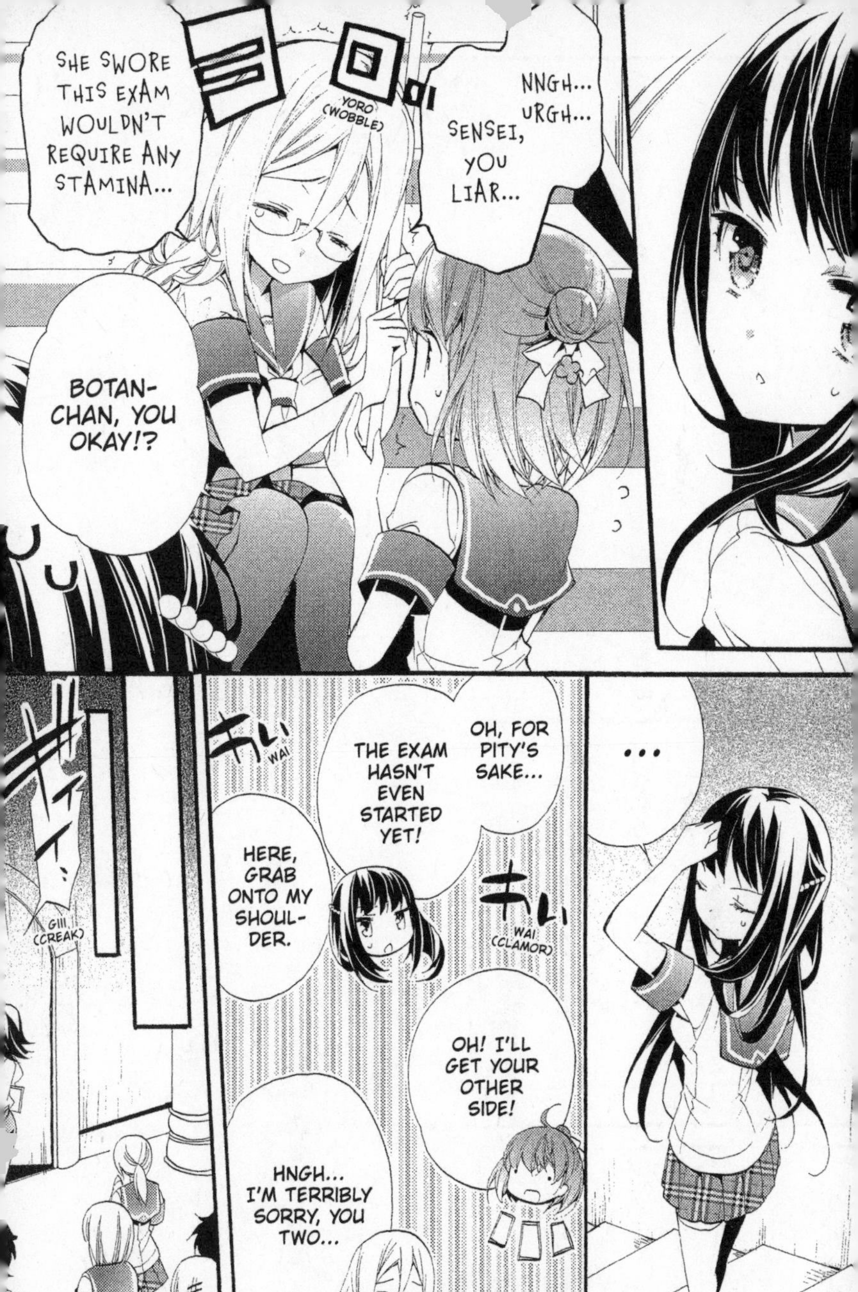
NNGH... URGH... SENSEI, YOU LIAR...
YORO (WOBBLE)
SHE SWORE THIS EXAM WOULDN'T REQUIRE ANY STAMINA...
BOTAN-CHAN, YOU OKAY!?
...
OH, FOR PITY'S SAKE...
THE EXAM HASN'T EVEN STARTED YET!
WAI
HERE, GRAB ONTO MY SHOULDER.
WAI (CLAMOR)
OH! I'LL GET YOUR OTHER SIDE!
HNGH... I'M TERRIBLY SORRY, YOU TWO...
GIII (CREAK)

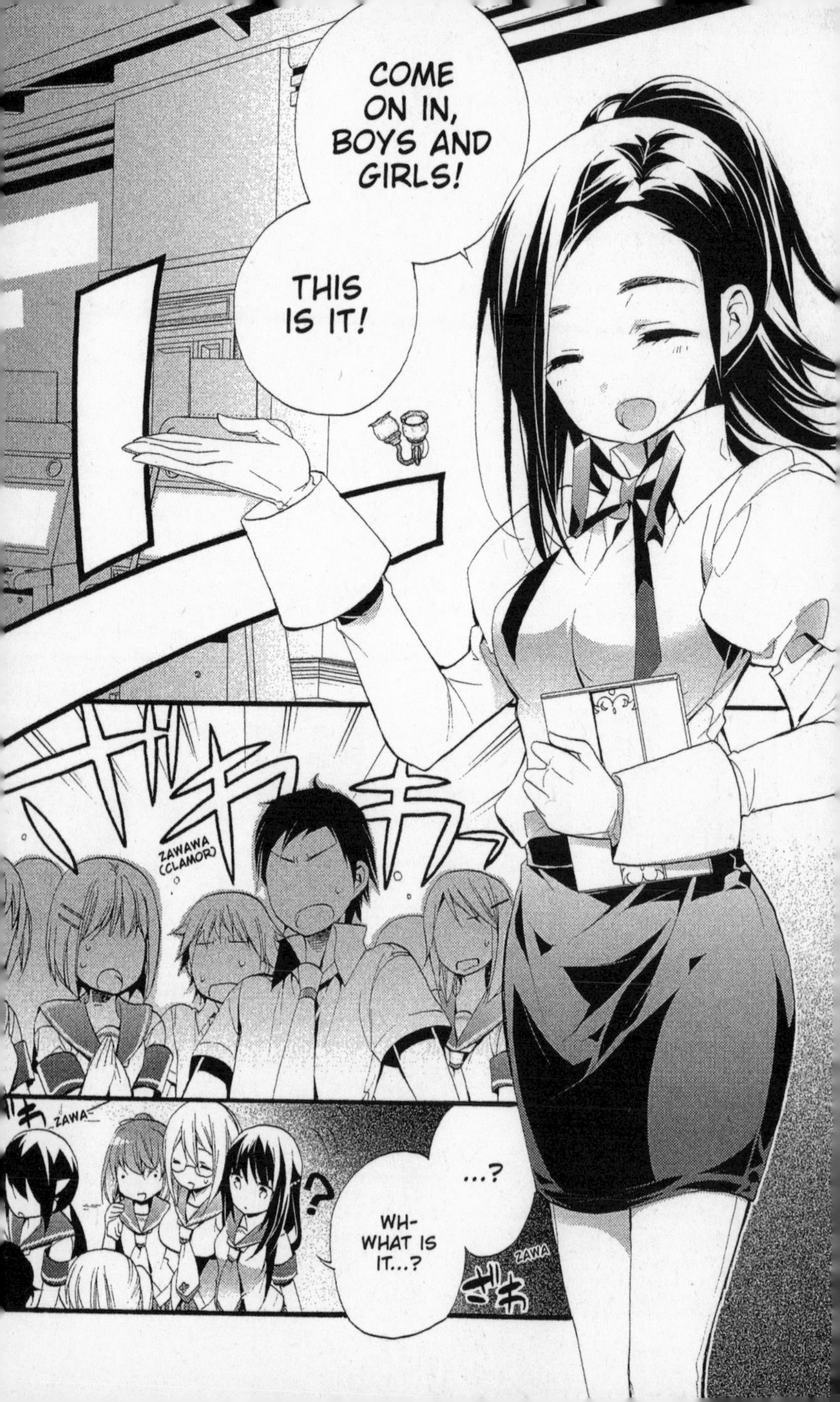
COME ON IN, BOYS AND GIRLS!
THIS IS IT!
ZAWAWA (CLAMOR)
ZAWA
...?
WH- WHAT IS IT...?
ZAWA
ZAWA

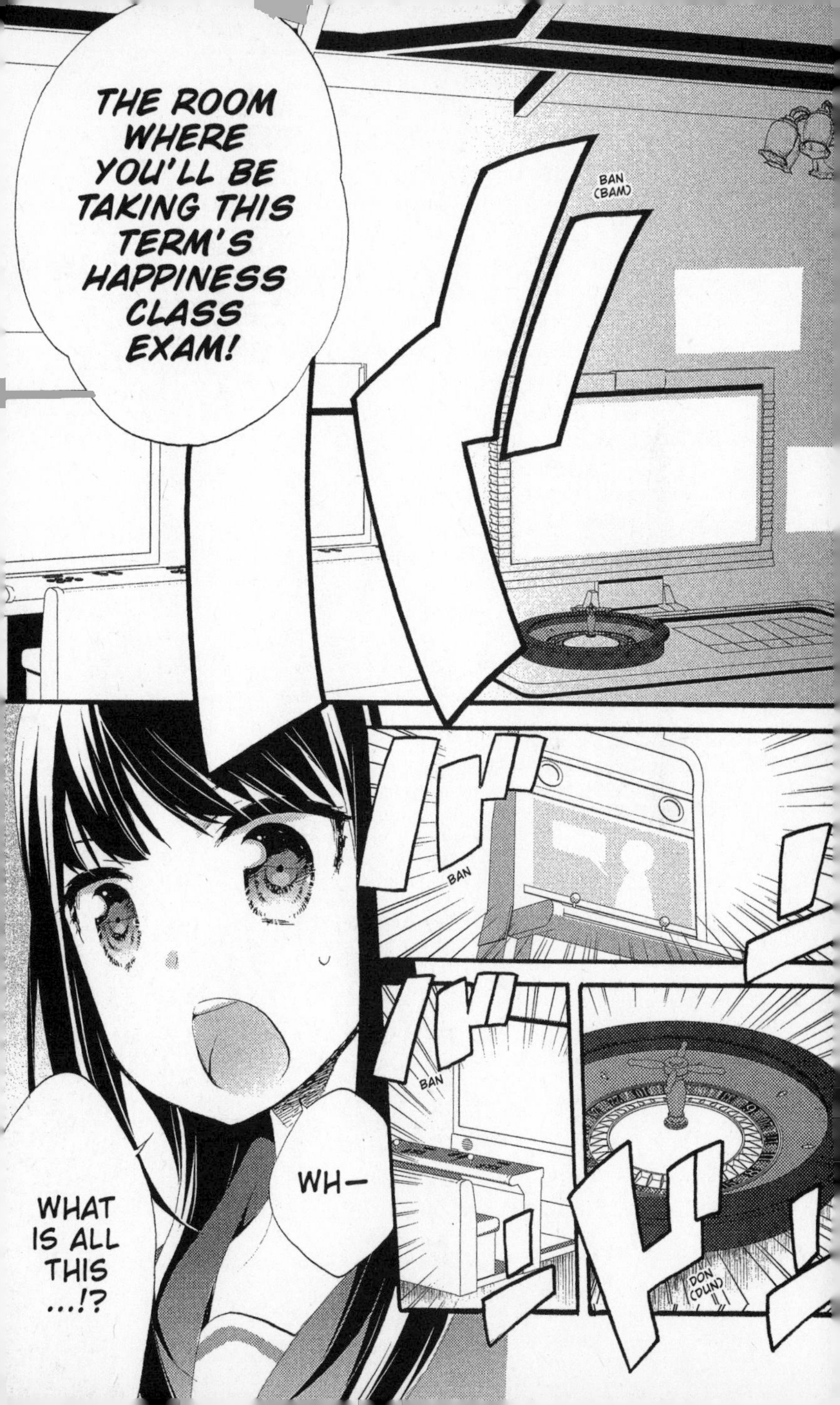
THE ROOM WHERE YOU'LL BE TAKING THIS TERM'S HAPPINESS CLASS EXAM!
BAN (BAM)
BAN
BAN
DON (DUN)
WH—
WHAT IS ALL THIS ...!?

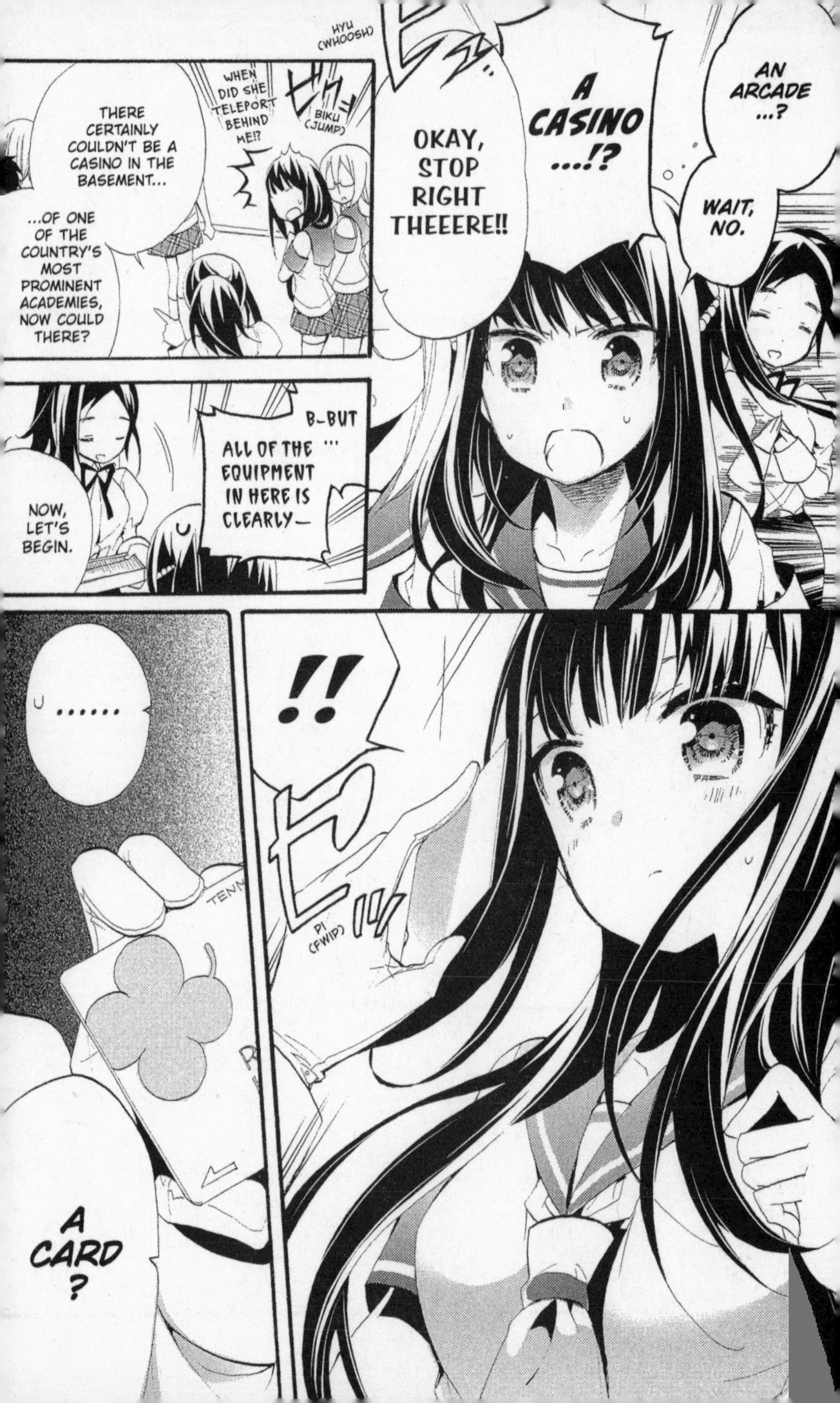
AN ARCADE ...?
WAIT, NO.
A CASINO ...!?
HYU (WHOOSH)
OKAY, STOP RIGHT THEEERE!!
BIKU (JUMP)
WHEN DID SHE TELEPORT BEHIND ME!?
THERE CERTAINLY COULDN'T BE A CASINO IN THE BASEMENT...
...OF ONE OF THE COUNTRY'S MOST PROMINENT ACADEMIES, NOW COULD THERE?
B-BUT ...
ALL OF THE EQUIPMENT IN HERE IS CLEARLY—
NOW, LET'S BEGIN.
!!
PI (FWIP)
......
A CARD ?

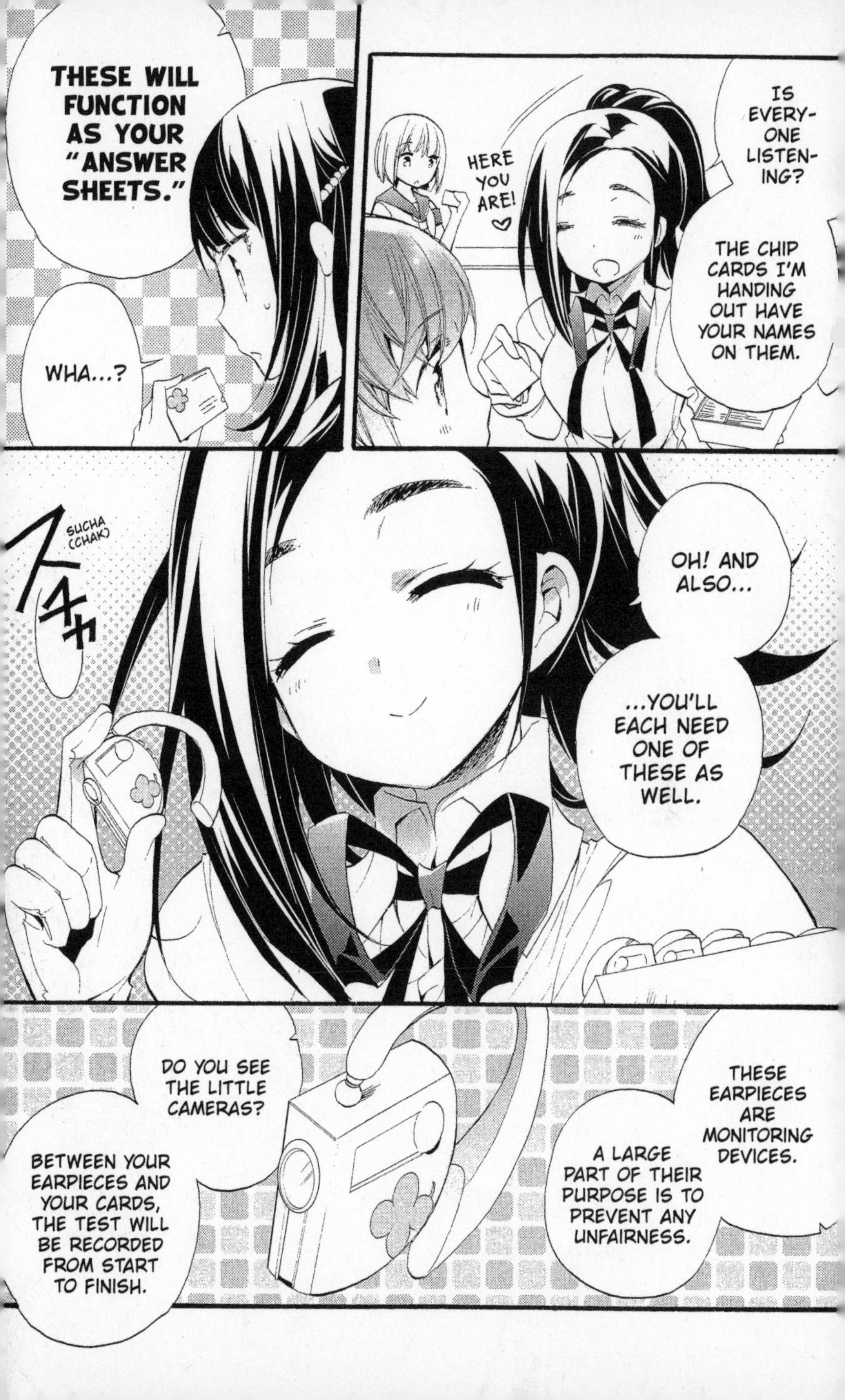
IS EVERYONE LISTENING?
THE CHIP CARDS I'M HANDING OUT HAVE YOUR NAMES ON THEM.
HERE YOU ARE! ♥
THESE WILL FUNCTION AS YOUR "ANSWER SHEETS."
WHA...?
OH! AND ALSO...
...YOU'LL EACH NEED ONE OF THESE AS WELL.
SUCHA (CHAK)
THESE EARPIECES ARE MONITORING DEVICES.
A LARGE PART OF THEIR PURPOSE IS TO PREVENT ANY UNFAIRNESS.
DO YOU SEE THE LITTLE CAMERAS?
BETWEEN YOUR EARPIECES AND YOUR CARDS, THE TEST WILL BE RECORDED FROM START TO FINISH.

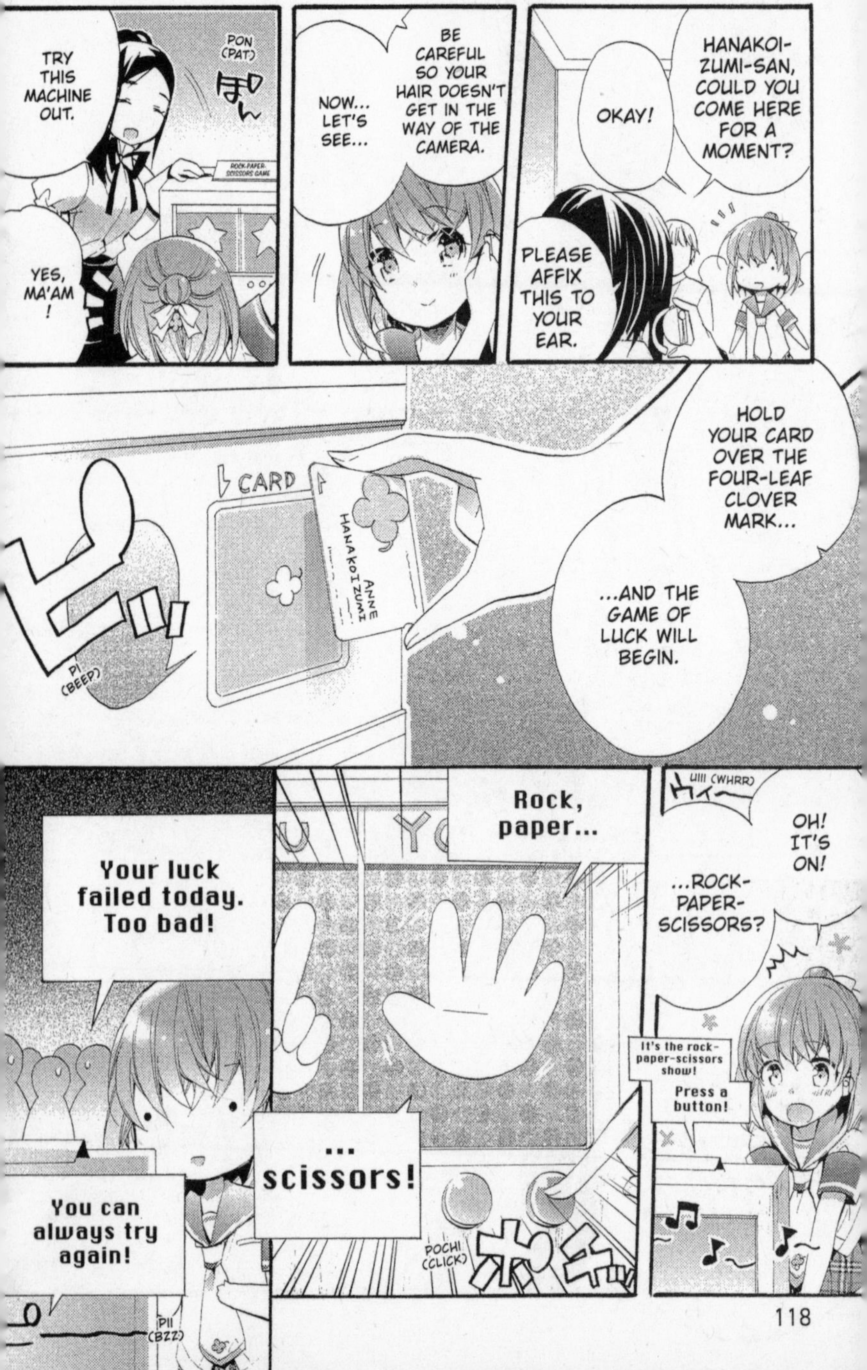
HANAKOIZUMI-SAN, COULD YOU COME HERE FOR A MOMENT?
OKAY!
PLEASE AFFIX THIS TO YOUR EAR.
BE CAREFUL SO YOUR HAIR DOESN'T GET IN THE WAY OF THE CAMERA.
NOW... LET'S SEE...
PON (PAT)
TRY THIS MACHINE OUT.
ROCK-PAPER-SCISSORS GAME
YES, MA'AM!
HOLD YOUR CARD OVER THE FOUR-LEAF CLOVER MARK...
...AND THE GAME OF LUCK WILL BEGIN.
CARD
ANNE HANAKOIZUMI
PI (BEEP)
UIII (WHRR)
OH! IT'S ON!
...ROCK-PAPER-SCISSORS?
It's the rock-paper-scissors show!
Press a button!
Rock, paper...
...scissors!
POCHI (CLICK)
Your luck failed today. Too bad!
You can always try again!
PII (BZZ)

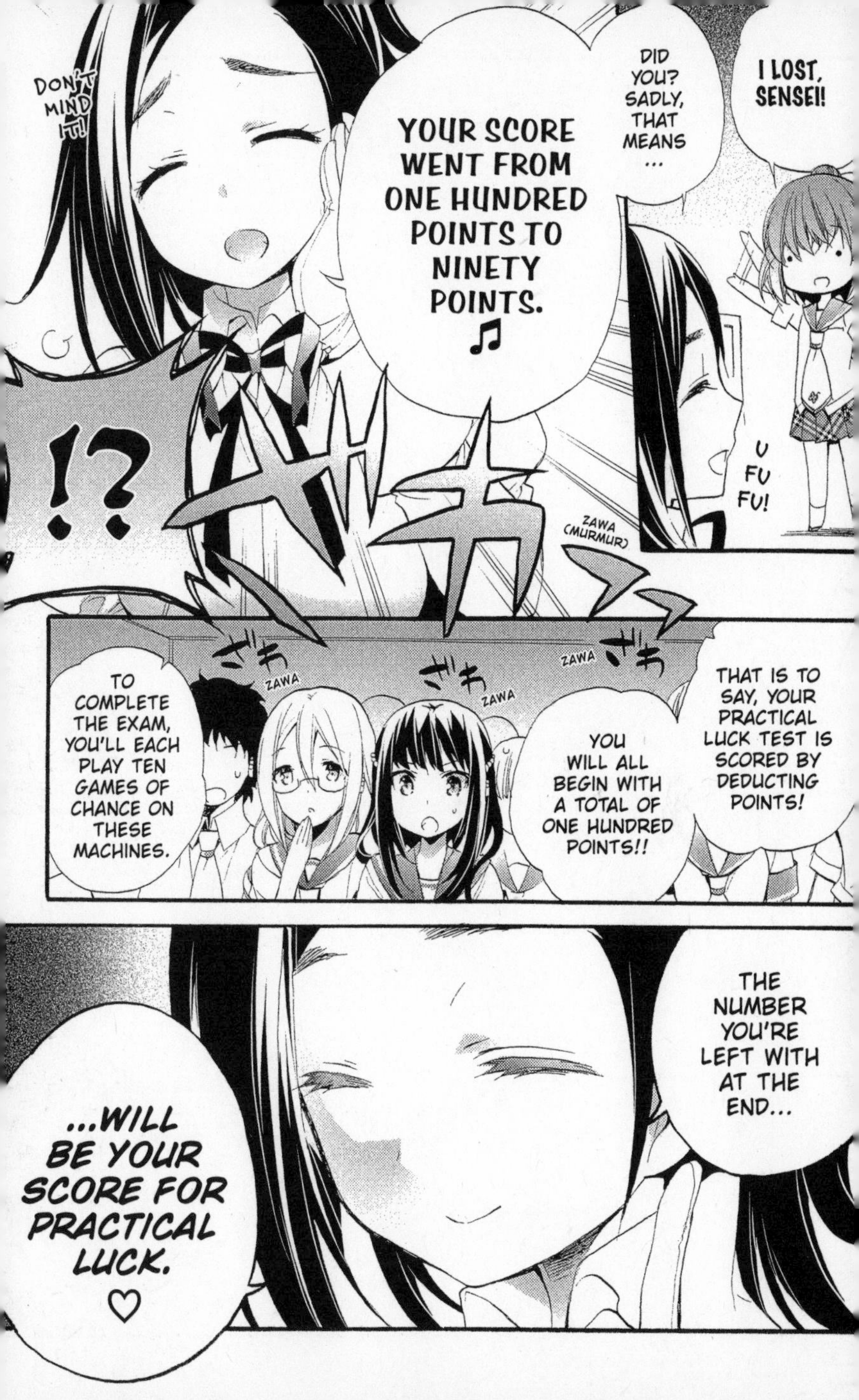
I LOST, SENSEI!
DID YOU? SADLY, THAT MEANS ...
U FU FU!
YOUR SCORE WENT FROM ONE HUNDRED POINTS TO NINETY POINTS. ♫
DON'T MIND IT!
!?
ZAWA (MURMUR)
ZAWA
ZAWA
ZAWA
THAT IS TO SAY, YOUR PRACTICAL LUCK TEST IS SCORED BY DEDUCTING POINTS!
YOU WILL ALL BEGIN WITH A TOTAL OF ONE HUNDRED POINTS!!
TO COMPLETE THE EXAM, YOU'LL EACH PLAY TEN GAMES OF CHANCE ON THESE MACHINES.
THE NUMBER YOU'RE LEFT WITH AT THE END...
...WILL BE YOUR SCORE FOR PRACTICAL LUCK. ♡

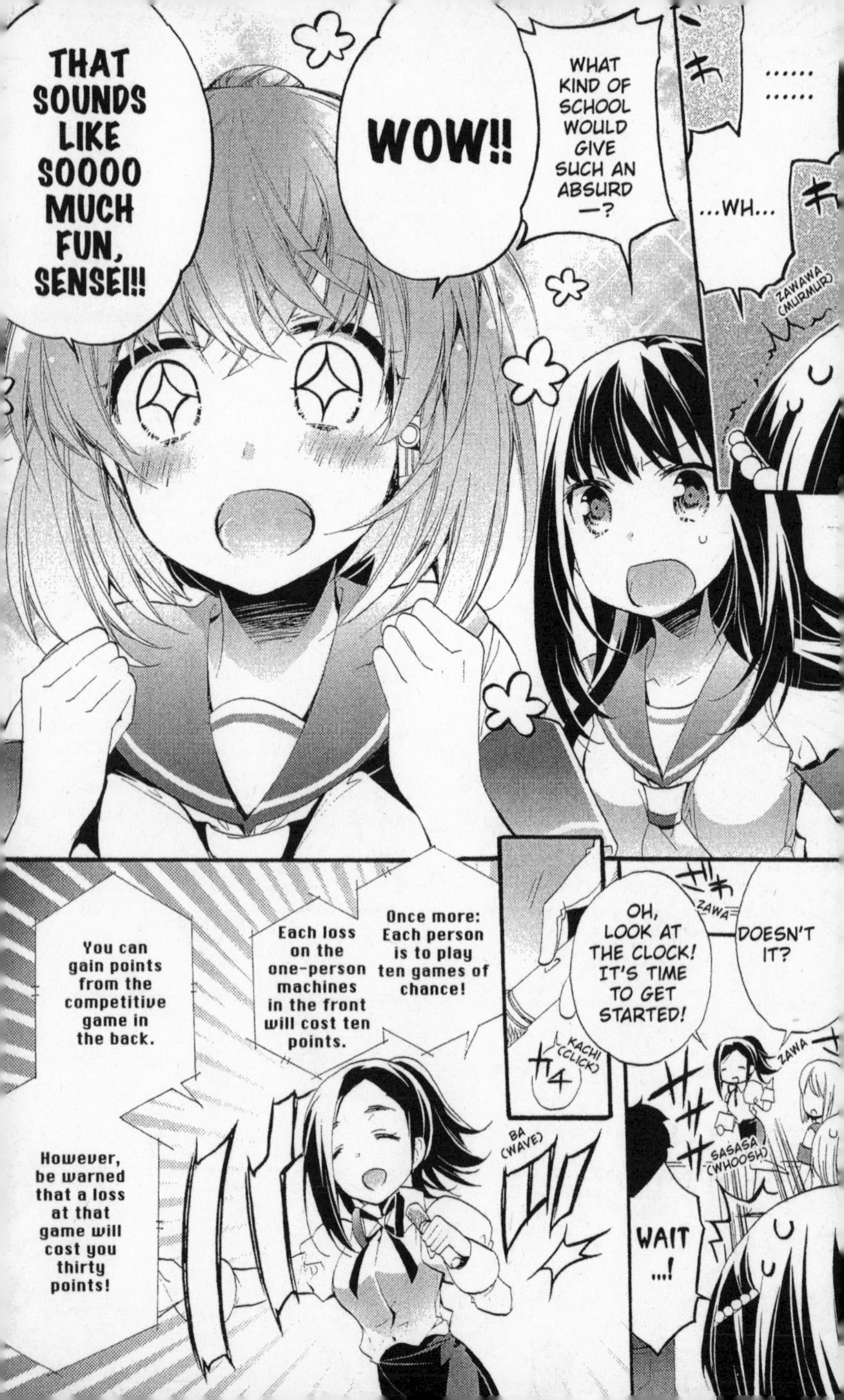
......
......
...WH...
ZAWAWA (MURMUR)
WHAT KIND OF SCHOOL WOULD GIVE SUCH AN ABSURD —?
WOW!!
THAT SOUNDS LIKE SOOOO MUCH FUN, SENSEI!!!
DOESN'T IT?
ZAWA
OH, LOOK AT THE CLOCK! IT'S TIME TO GET STARTED!
KACHI (CLICK)
ZAWA
SASASA (WHOOSH)
WAIT ...!
Once more: Each person is to play ten games of chance!
Each loss on the one-person machines in the front will cost ten points.
You can gain points from the competitive game in the back.
BA (WAVE)
However, be warned that a loss at that game will cost you thirty points!

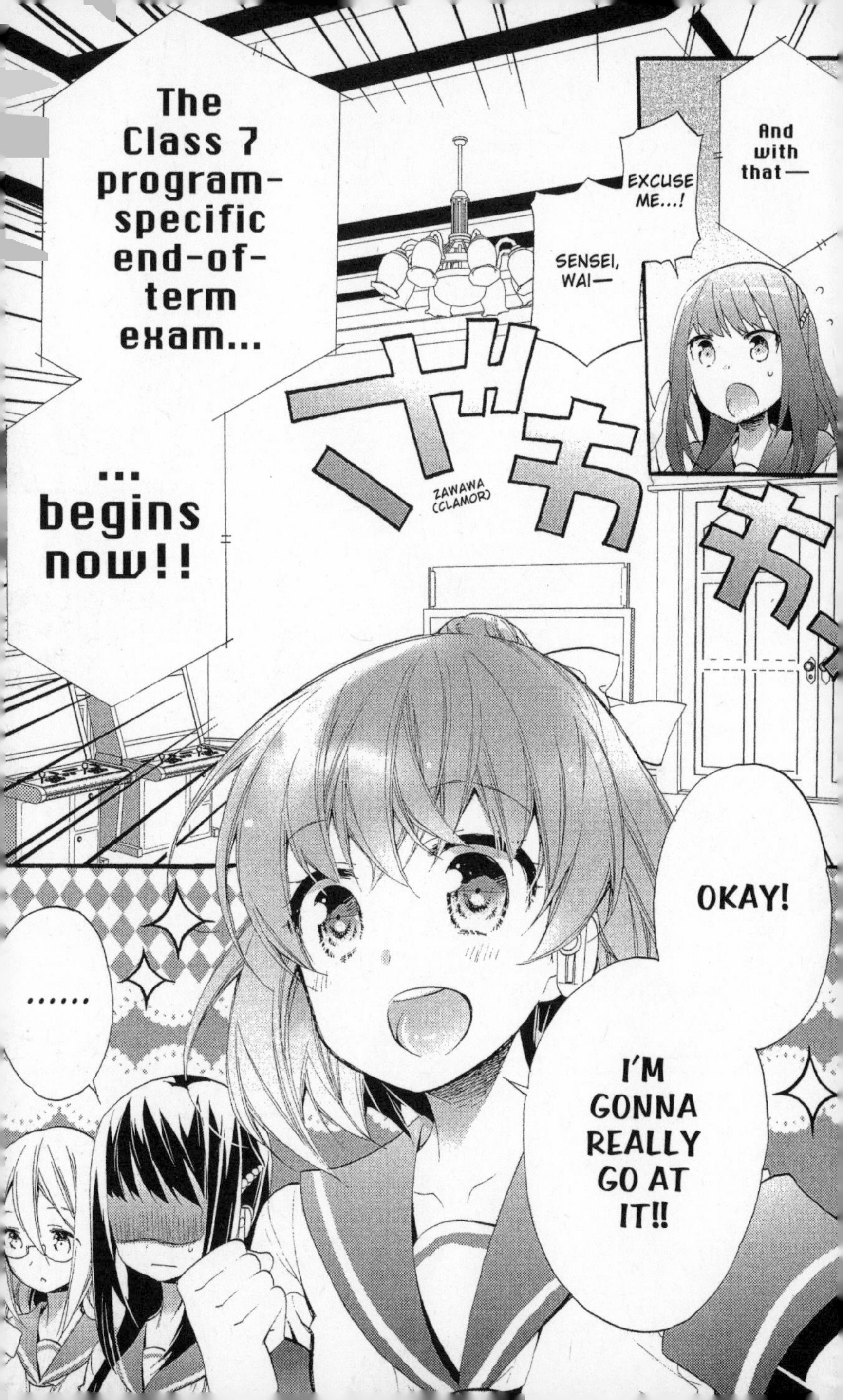

And with that—
The Class 7 program-specific end-of-term exam...
... begins now!!
EXCUSE ME...!
SENSEI, WAI—
ZAWAWA (CLAMOR)
OKAY!
I'M GONNA REALLY GO AT IT!!
......

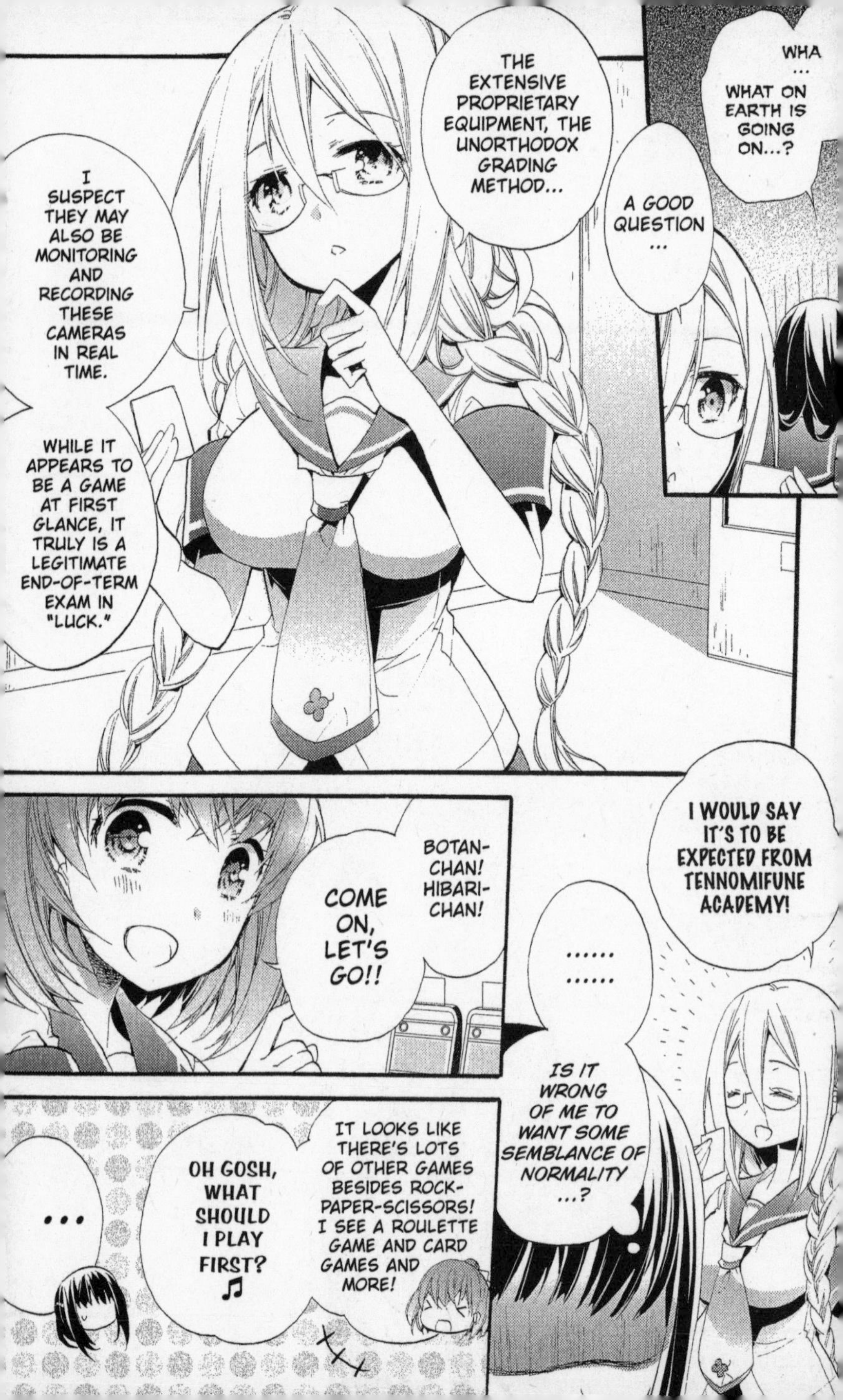

WHA ...
WHAT ON EARTH IS GOING ON...?
A GOOD QUESTION ...
THE EXTENSIVE PROPRIETARY EQUIPMENT, THE UNORTHODOX GRADING METHOD...
I SUSPECT THEY MAY ALSO BE MONITORING AND RECORDING THESE CAMERAS IN REAL TIME.
WHILE IT APPEARS TO BE A GAME AT FIRST GLANCE, IT TRULY IS A LEGITIMATE END-OF-TERM EXAM IN "LUCK."
I WOULD SAY IT'S TO BE EXPECTED FROM TENNOMIFUNE ACADEMY!
....
IS IT WRONG OF ME TO WANT SOME SEMBLANCE OF NORMALITY ...?
BOTAN-CHAN! HIBARI-CHAN!
COME ON, LET'S GO!!
IT LOOKS LIKE THERE'S LOTS OF OTHER GAMES BESIDES ROCK-PAPER-SCISSORS! I SEE A ROULETTE GAME AND CARD GAMES AND MORE!
OH GOSH, WHAT SHOULD I PLAY FIRST? ♫
...

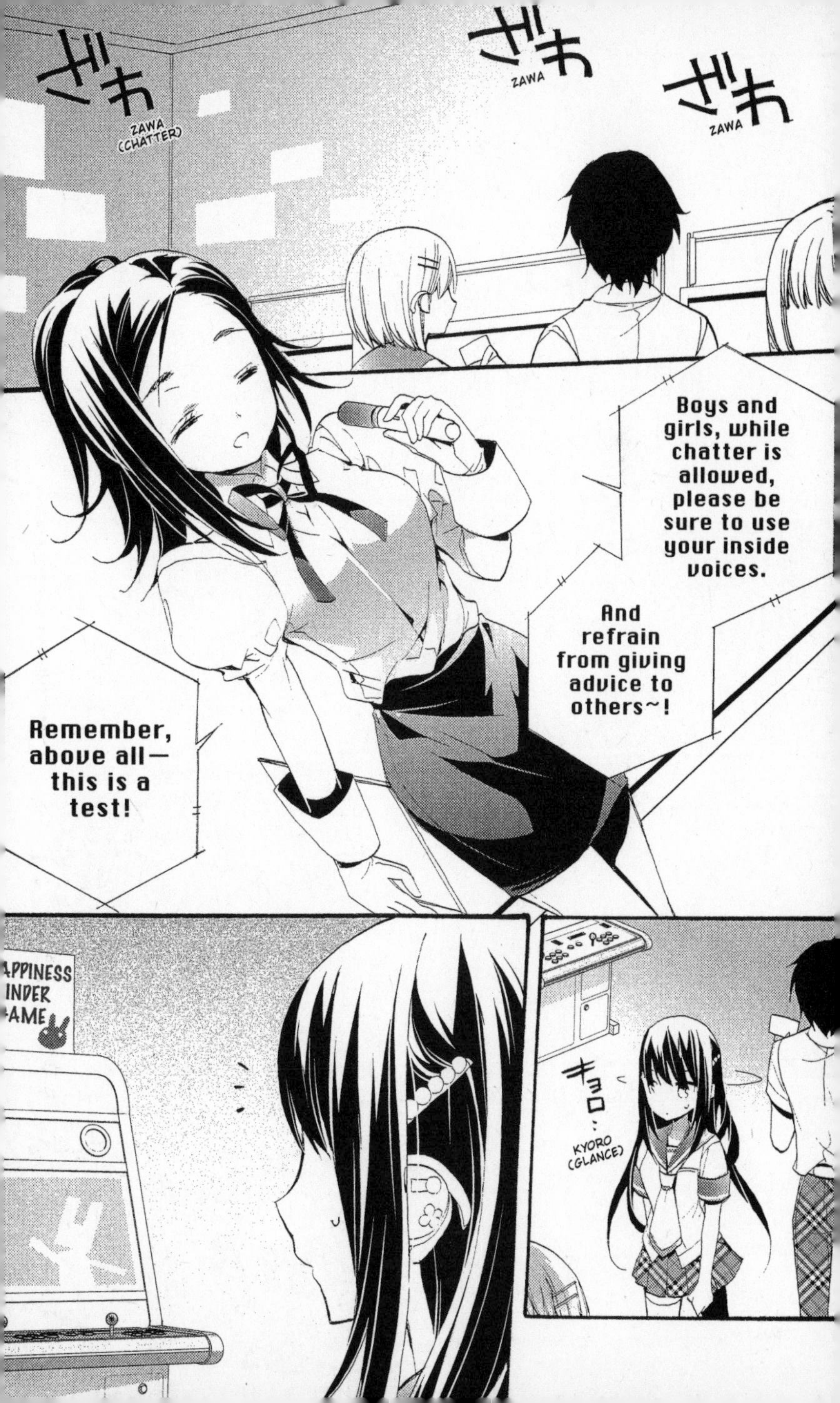
ざわ
ZAWA
ざわ
ZAWA
ざわ
ZAWA (CHATTER)
Boys and girls, while chatter is allowed, please be sure to use your inside voices.
And refrain from giving advice to others~!
Remember, above all—this is a test!
キョロ
KYORO (GLANCE)

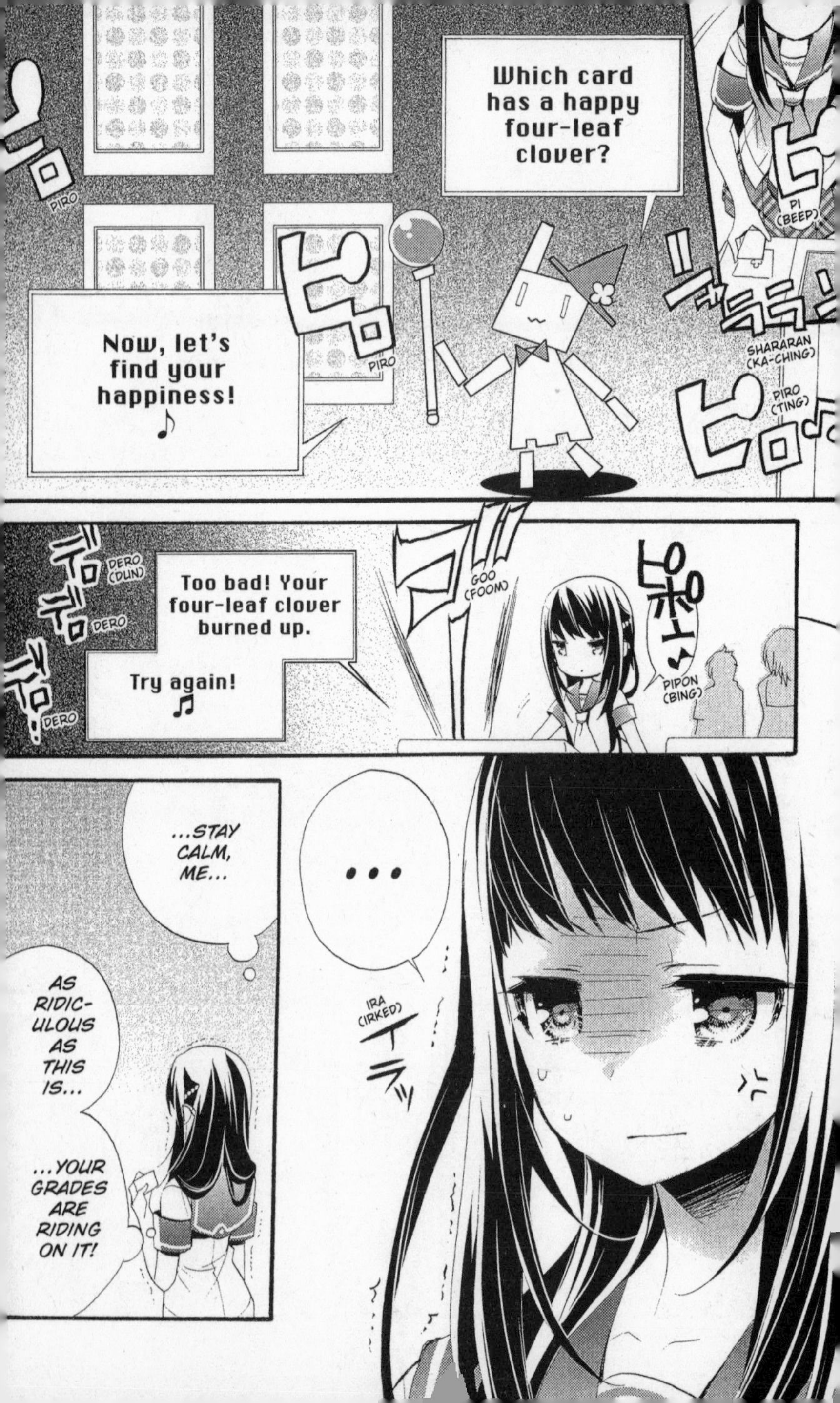
PI (BEEP)
SHARARAN (KA-CHING)
PIRO (TING)
Which card has a happy four-leaf clover?
PIRO
Now, let's find your happiness! ♪
PIRO
PIPON (BING)
GOO (FOOM)
Too bad! Your four-leaf clover burned up.
Try again! ♫
DERO (DUN)
DERO
DERO
IRA (IRKED)
...
...STAY CALM, ME...
AS RIDIC-ULOUS AS THIS IS...
...YOUR GRADES ARE RIDING ON IT!

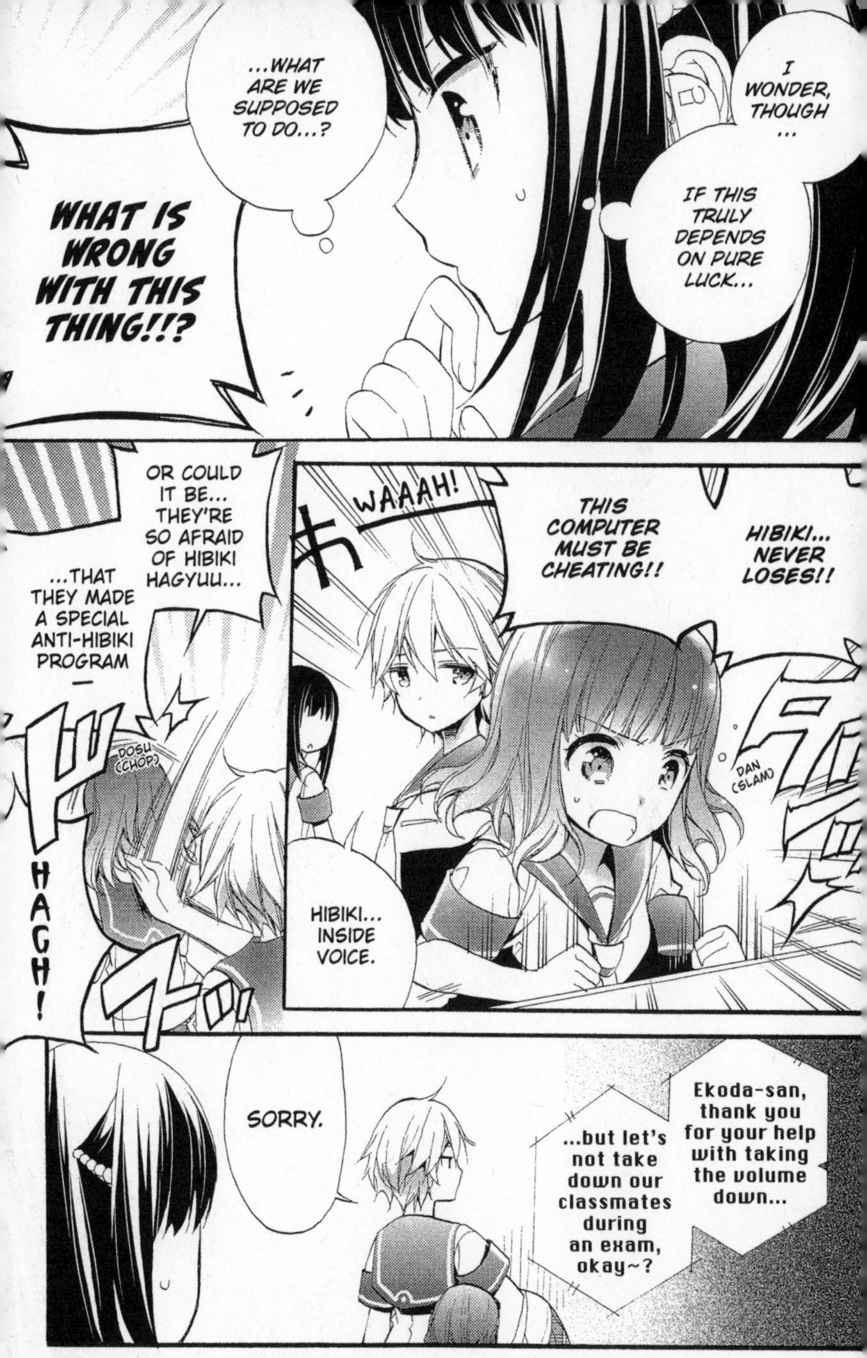
I WONDER, THOUGH...
IF THIS TRULY DEPENDS ON PURE LUCK...
...WHAT ARE WE SUPPOSED TO DO...?
WHAT IS WRONG WITH THIS THING!!?
HIBIKI... NEVER LOSES!!
THIS COMPUTER MUST BE CHEATING!!
WAAAH!
DAN (SLAM)
HIBIKI... INSIDE VOICE.
OR COULD IT BE... THEY'RE SO AFRAID OF HIBIKI HAGYUU...
...THAT THEY MADE A SPECIAL ANTI-HIBIKI PROGRAM —
DOSU (CHOP)
HAGH!
Ekoda-san, thank you for your help with taking the volume down...
...but let's not take down our classmates during an exam, okay~?
SORRY.

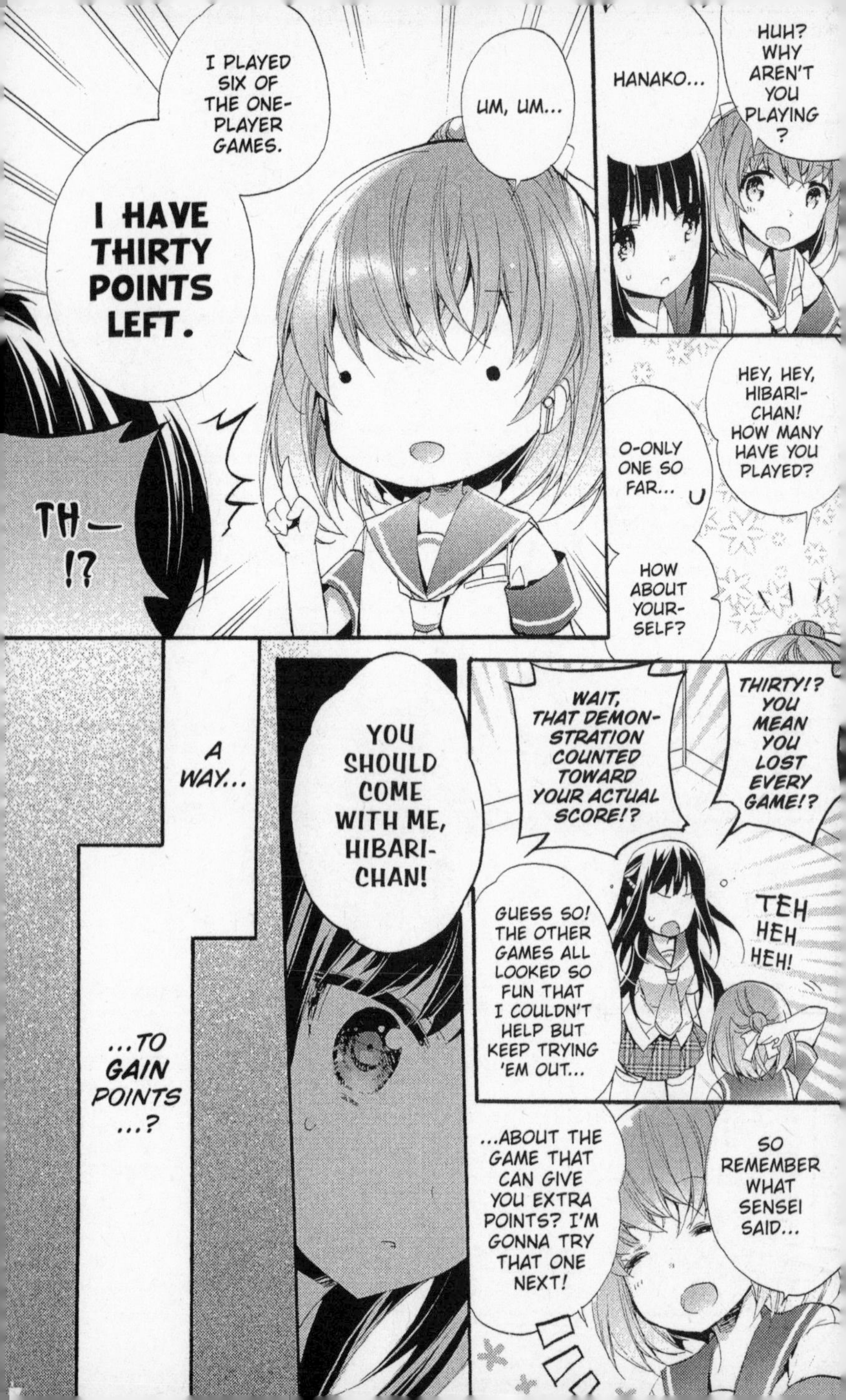
HUH? WHY AREN'T YOU PLAYING?
HANAKO...
HEY, HEY, HIBARI-CHAN! HOW MANY HAVE YOU PLAYED?
O-ONLY ONE SO FAR...
HOW ABOUT YOURSELF?
UM, UM...
I PLAYED SIX OF THE ONE-PLAYER GAMES.
I HAVE THIRTY POINTS LEFT.
TH— !?
THIRTY!? YOU MEAN YOU LOST EVERY GAME!?
WAIT, THAT DEMONSTRATION COUNTED TOWARD YOUR ACTUAL SCORE!?
TEH HEH HEH!
GUESS SO! THE OTHER GAMES ALL LOOKED SO FUN THAT I COULDN'T HELP BUT KEEP TRYING 'EM OUT...
SO REMEMBER WHAT SENSEI SAID...
...ABOUT THE GAME THAT CAN GIVE YOU EXTRA POINTS? I'M GONNA TRY THAT ONE NEXT!
YOU SHOULD COME WITH ME, HIBARI-CHAN!
A WAY...
...TO GAIN POINTS...?

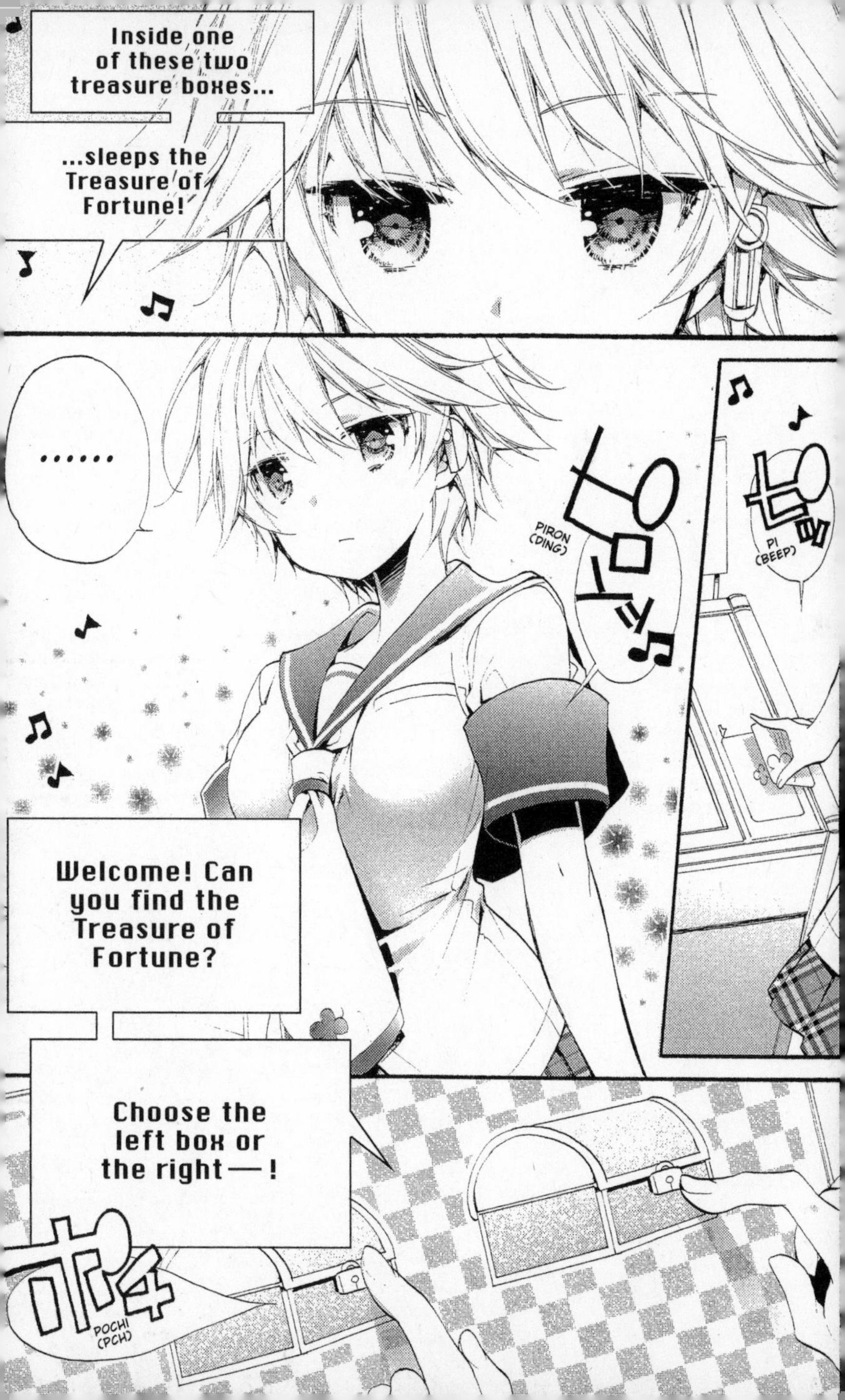

Inside one of these two treasure boxes...
...sleeps the Treasure of Fortune!
PI (BEEP)
PIRON (DING)
......
Welcome! Can you find the Treasure of Fortune?
Choose the left box or the right—!
POCHI (PCH)

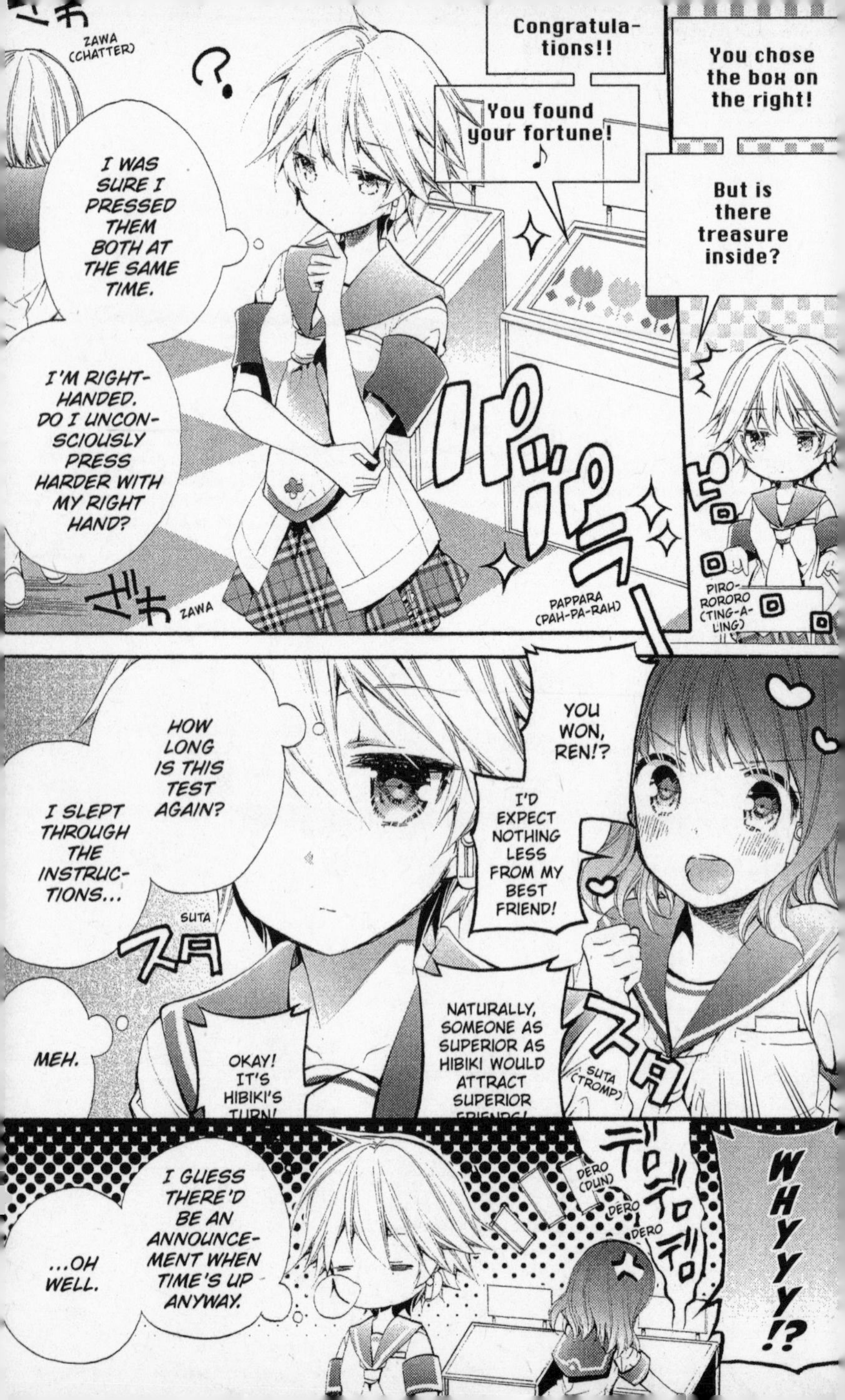

Congratula-tions!!
You chose the box on the right!
You found your fortune! ♪
But is there treasure inside?
PIRO-ROROROO (TING-A-LING)
PAPPARA (PAH-PA-RAH)
?
ZAWA (CHATTER)
I WAS SURE I PRESSED THEM BOTH AT THE SAME TIME.
I'M RIGHT-HANDED. DO I UNCON-SCIOUSLY PRESS HARDER WITH MY RIGHT HAND?
ZAWA
YOU WON, REN!?
I'D EXPECT NOTHING LESS FROM MY BEST FRIEND!
NATURALLY, SOMEONE AS SUPERIOR AS HIBIKI WOULD ATTRACT SUPERIOR
SUTA (TROMP)
OKAY! IT'S HIBIKI'S
HOW LONG IS THIS TEST AGAIN?
I SLEPT THROUGH THE INSTRUC-TIONS...
SUTA
MEH.
WHYYY!?
DERO (DUN) DERO DERO
I GUESS THERE'D BE AN ANNOUNCE-MENT WHEN TIME'S UP ANYWAY.
...OH WELL.

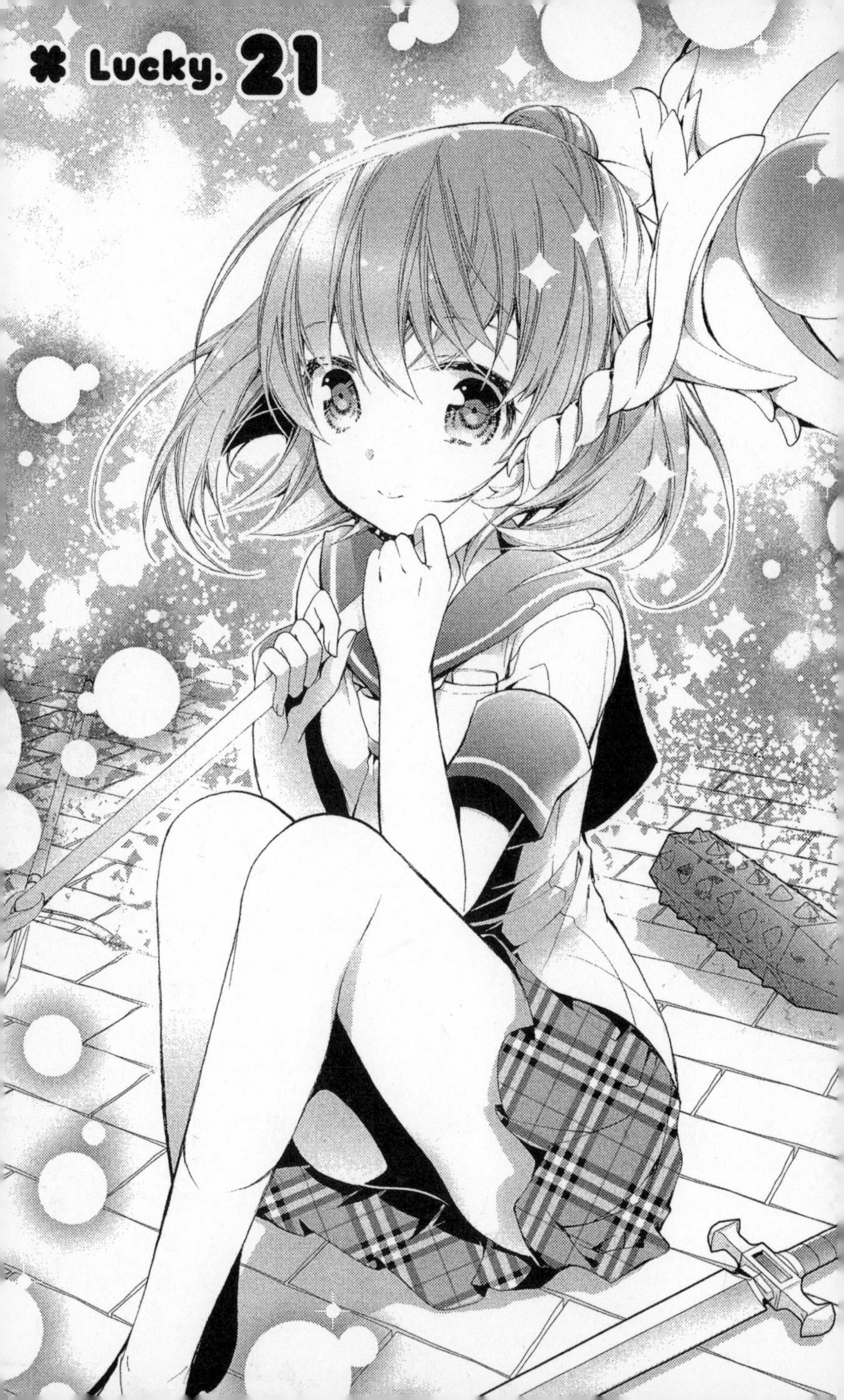
Lucky. 21

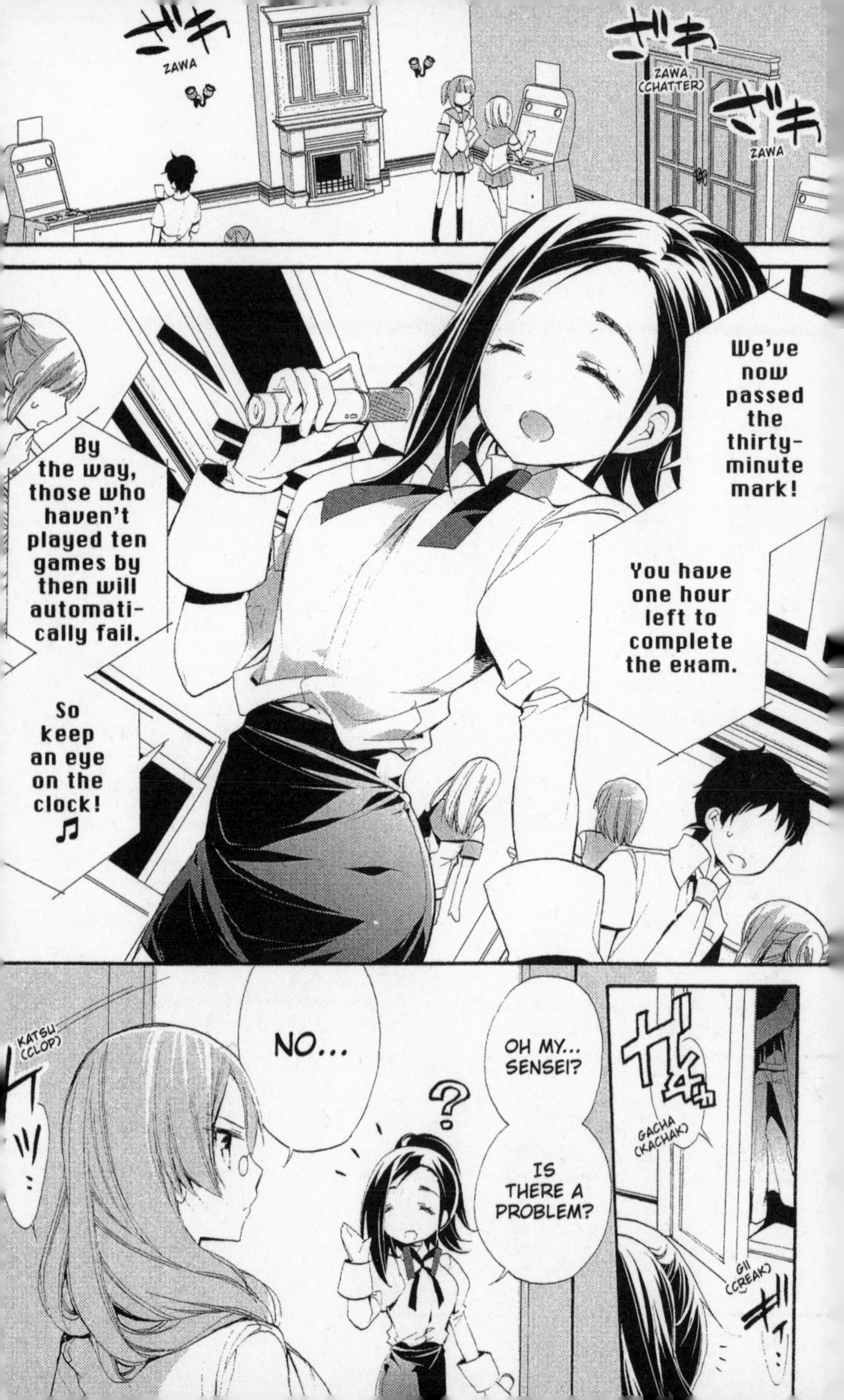
ZAWA (CHATTER)
ZAWA
ZAWA
We've now passed the thirty-minute mark!
You have one hour left to complete the exam.
By the way, those who haven't played ten games by then will automatically fail.
So keep an eye on the clock! ♫
GACHA (KACHAK)
GII (CREAK)
OH MY... SENSEI?
IS THERE A PROBLEM?
?
NO...
KATSU (CLOP)

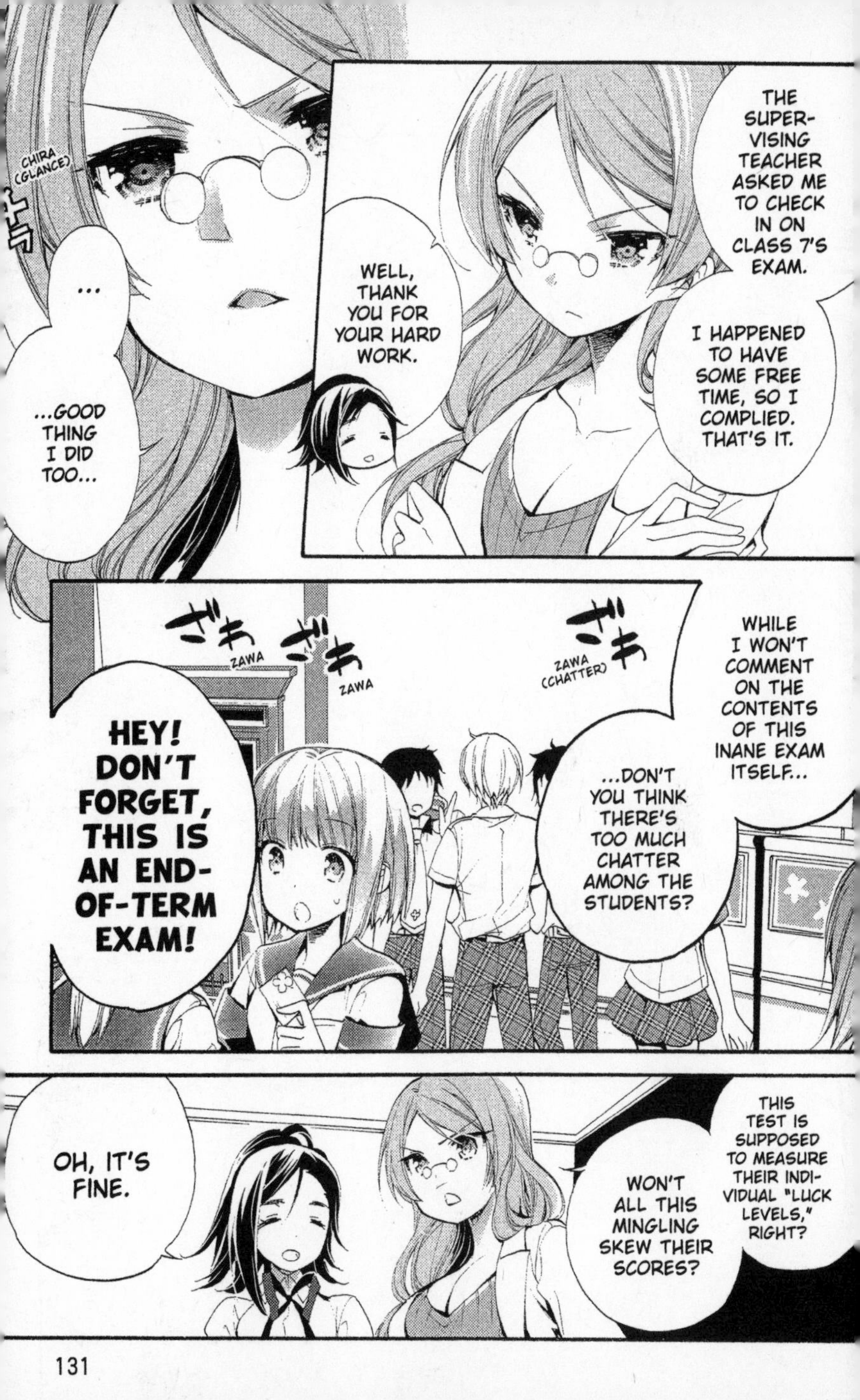
THE SUPER-VISING TEACHER ASKED ME TO CHECK IN ON CLASS 7'S EXAM.
I HAPPENED TO HAVE SOME FREE TIME, SO I COMPLIED. THAT'S IT.
WELL, THANK YOU FOR YOUR HARD WORK.
CHIRA (GLANCE)
...
...GOOD THING I DID TOO...
WHILE I WON'T COMMENT ON THE CONTENTS OF THIS INANE EXAM ITSELF...
...DON'T YOU THINK THERE'S TOO MUCH CHATTER AMONG THE STUDENTS?
ざわ
ZAWA (CHATTER)
ざわ
ZAWA
ざわ
ZAWA
HEY! DON'T FORGET, THIS IS AN END-OF-TERM EXAM!
THIS TEST IS SUPPOSED TO MEASURE THEIR INDI-VIDUAL "LUCK LEVELS," RIGHT?
WON'T ALL THIS MINGLING SKEW THEIR SCORES?
OH, IT'S FINE.

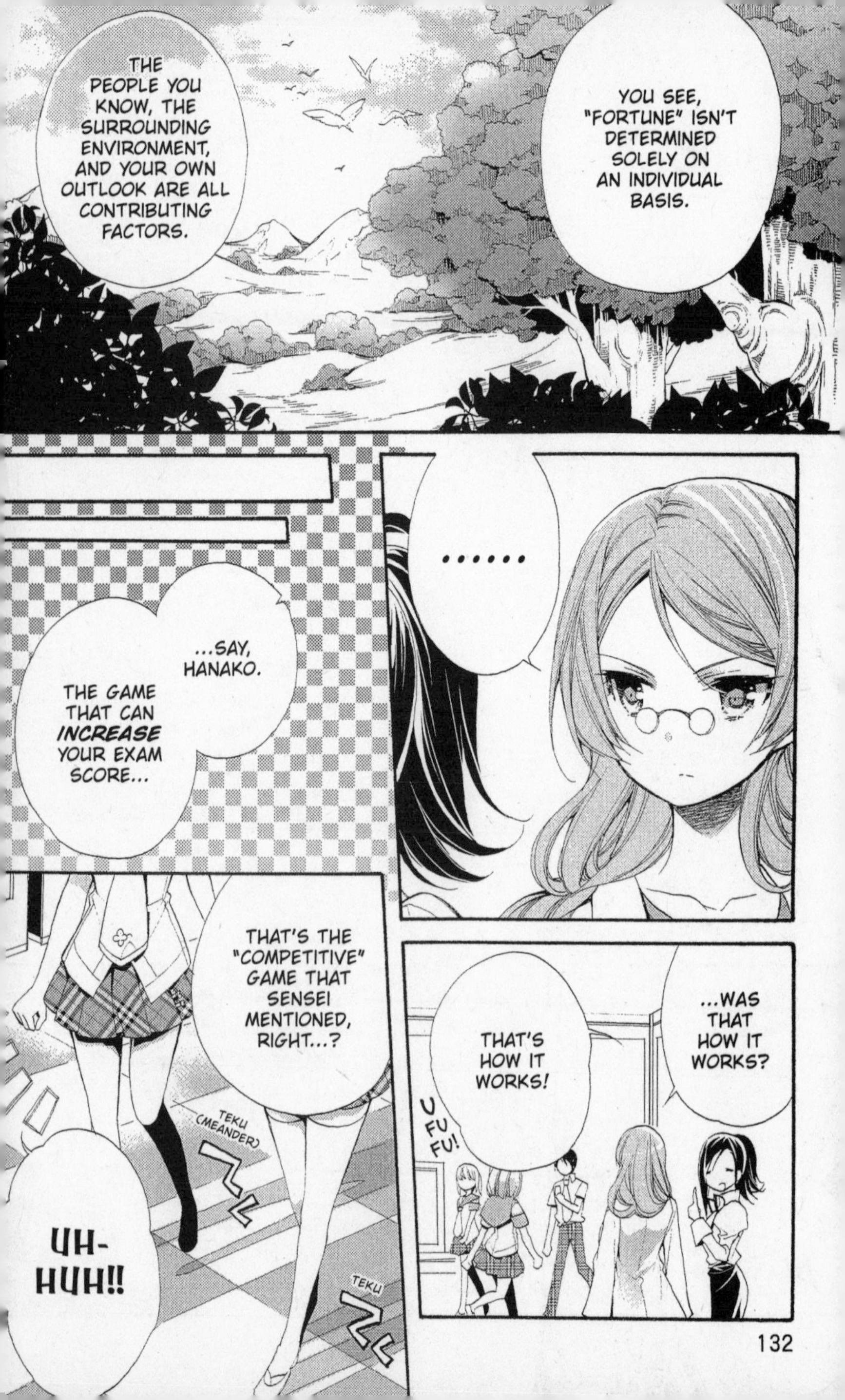

YOU SEE, "FORTUNE" ISN'T DETERMINED SOLELY ON AN INDIVIDUAL BASIS.
THE PEOPLE YOU KNOW, THE SURROUNDING ENVIRONMENT, AND YOUR OWN OUTLOOK ARE ALL CONTRIBUTING FACTORS.
......
...SAY, HANAKO.
THE GAME THAT CAN *INCREASE* YOUR EXAM SCORE...
...WAS THAT HOW IT WORKS?
THAT'S HOW IT WORKS!
UFUFU!
THAT'S THE "COMPETITIVE" GAME THAT SENSEI MENTIONED, RIGHT...?
TEKU (MEANDER)
UH-HUH!!
TEKU

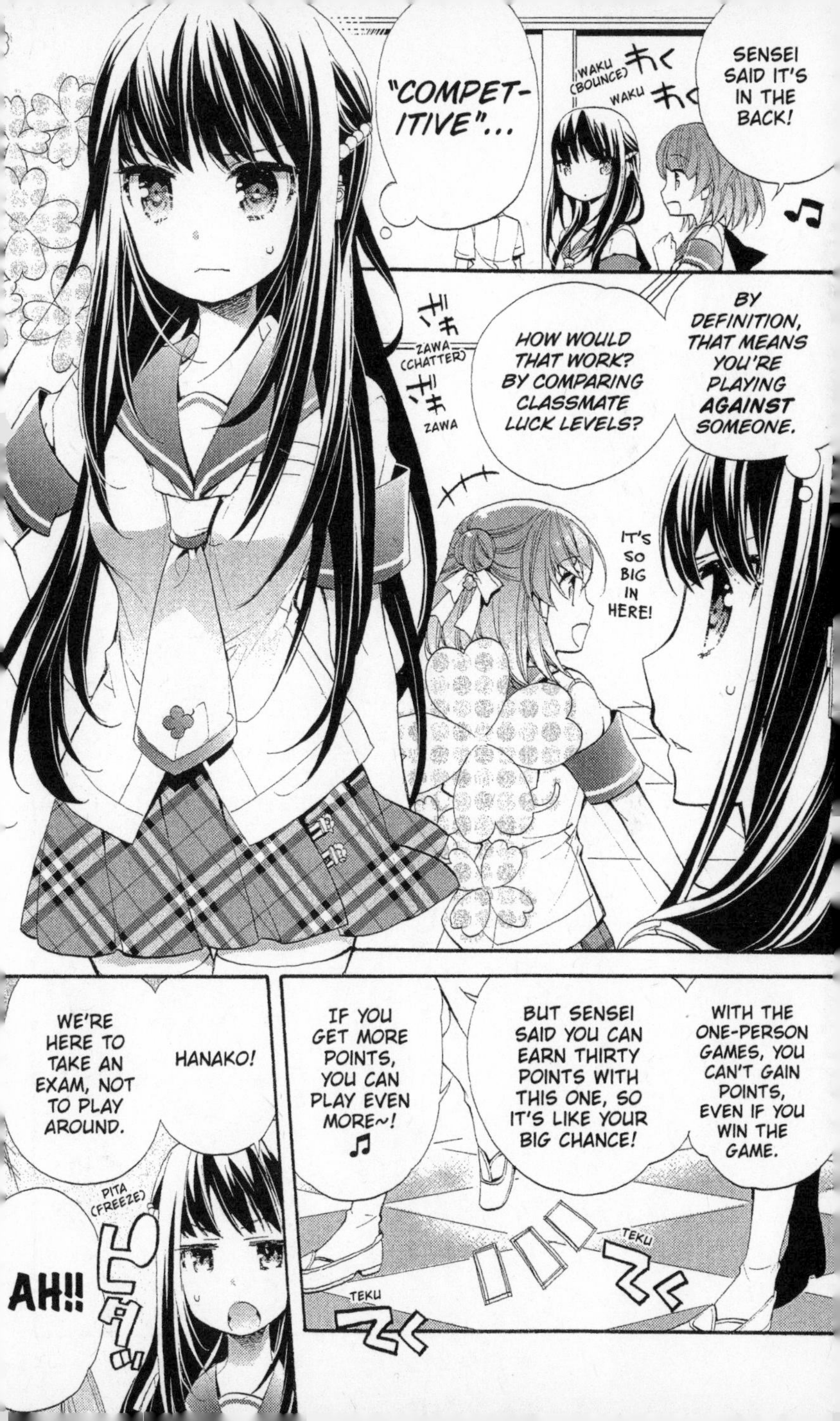
WAKU (BOUNCE) わく
WAKU わく
SENSEI SAID IT'S IN THE BACK!
"COMPETITIVE"...
BY DEFINITION, THAT MEANS YOU'RE PLAYING AGAINST SOMEONE.
HOW WOULD THAT WORK? BY COMPARING CLASSMATE LUCK LEVELS?
ZAWA (CHATTER)
ZAWA
IT'S SO BIG IN HERE!
WITH THE ONE-PERSON GAMES, YOU CAN'T GAIN POINTS, EVEN IF YOU WIN THE GAME.
BUT SENSEI SAID YOU CAN EARN THIRTY POINTS WITH THIS ONE, SO IT'S LIKE YOUR BIG CHANCE!
IF YOU GET MORE POINTS, YOU CAN PLAY EVEN MORE~! ♫
TEKU
TEKU
HANAKO!
WE'RE HERE TO TAKE AN EXAM, NOT TO PLAY AROUND.
PITA (FREEZE)
AH!!

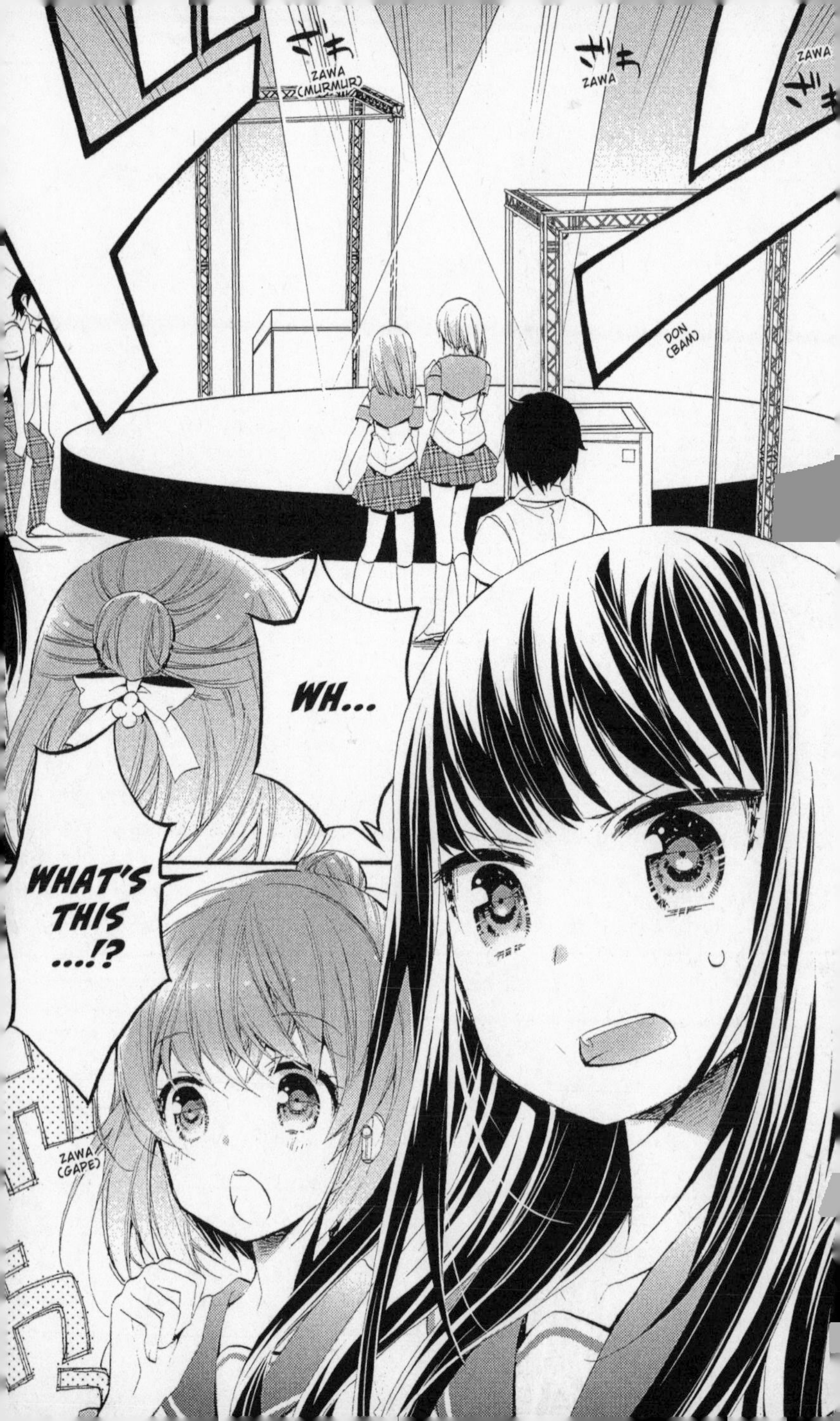
ZAWA
ざわ
ZAWA
ざわ
ZAWA (MURMUR)
DON (BAM)
WH...
WHAT'S THIS ....!?
ZAWA (GAPE)

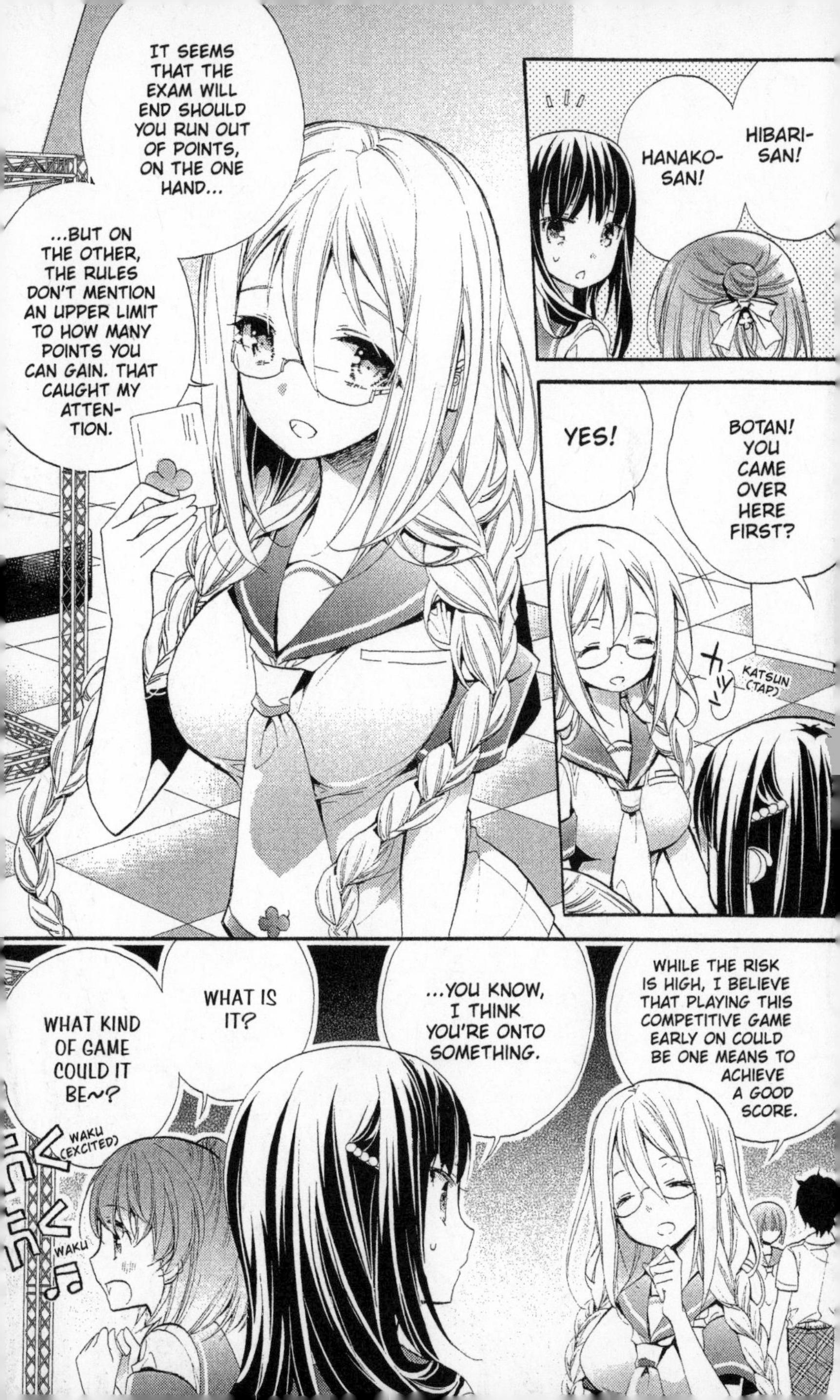
HIBARI-SAN!
HANAKO-SAN!
BOTAN! YOU CAME OVER HERE FIRST?
YES!
KATSUN (TAP)
IT SEEMS THAT THE EXAM WILL END SHOULD YOU RUN OUT OF POINTS, ON THE ONE HAND...
...BUT ON THE OTHER, THE RULES DON'T MENTION AN UPPER LIMIT TO HOW MANY POINTS YOU CAN GAIN. THAT CAUGHT MY ATTEN-TION.
WHILE THE RISK IS HIGH, I BELIEVE THAT PLAYING THIS COMPETITIVE GAME EARLY ON COULD BE ONE MEANS TO ACHIEVE A GOOD SCORE.
...YOU KNOW, I THINK YOU'RE ONTO SOMETHING.
WHAT IS IT?
WHAT KIND OF GAME COULD IT BE~?
WAKU (EXCITED)
WAKU

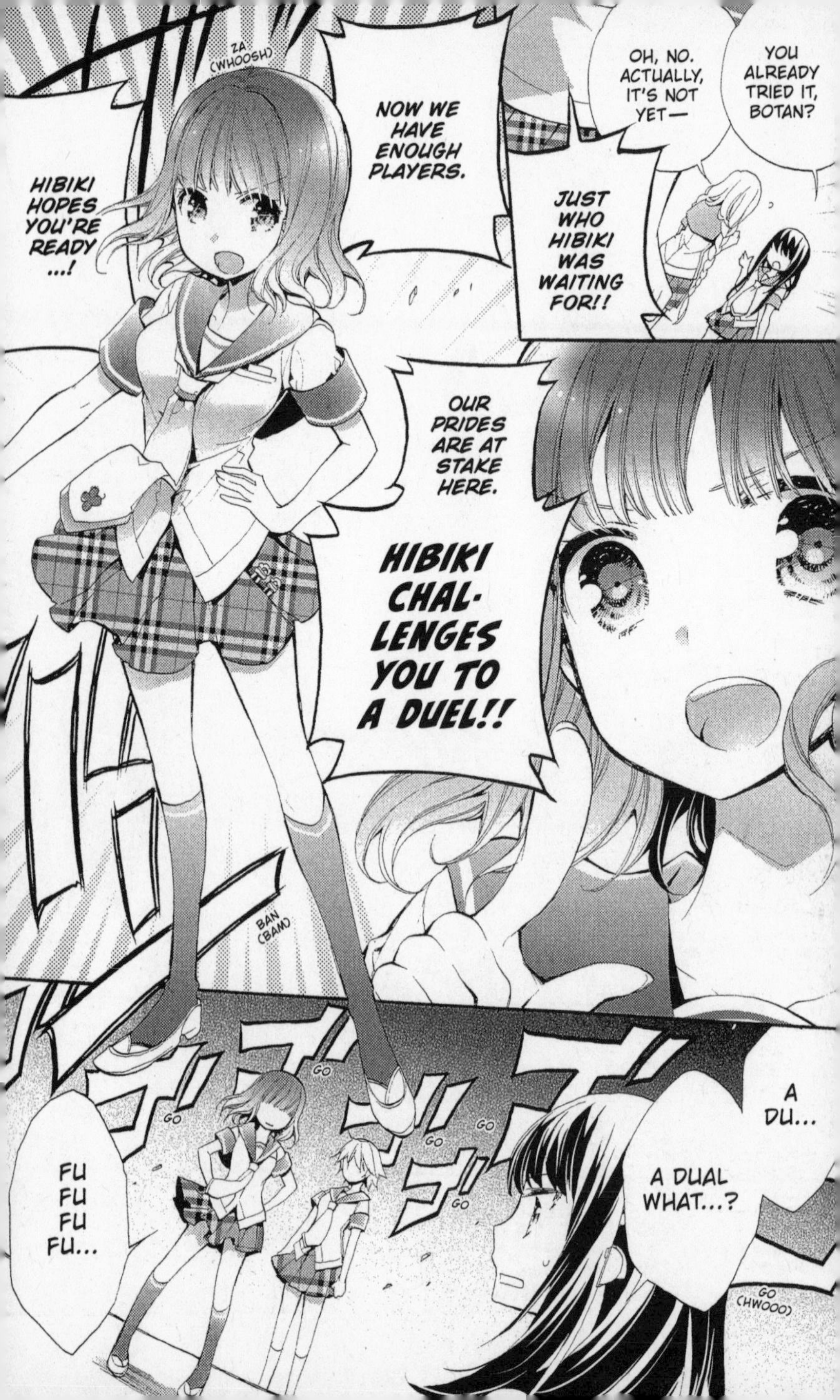
YOU ALREADY TRIED IT, BOTAN?
OH, NO. ACTUALLY, IT'S NOT YET—
JUST WHO HIBIKI WAS WAITING FOR!!
OUR PRIDES ARE AT STAKE HERE.
HIBIKI CHAL-LENGES YOU TO A DUEL!!
ZA (WHOOSH)
NOW WE HAVE ENOUGH PLAYERS.
HIBIKI HOPES YOU'RE READY ...!
BAN (BAM)
A DU...
A DUAL WHAT...?
GO (HWOOO)
GO
GO
GO
GO
GO
FU FU FU FU...

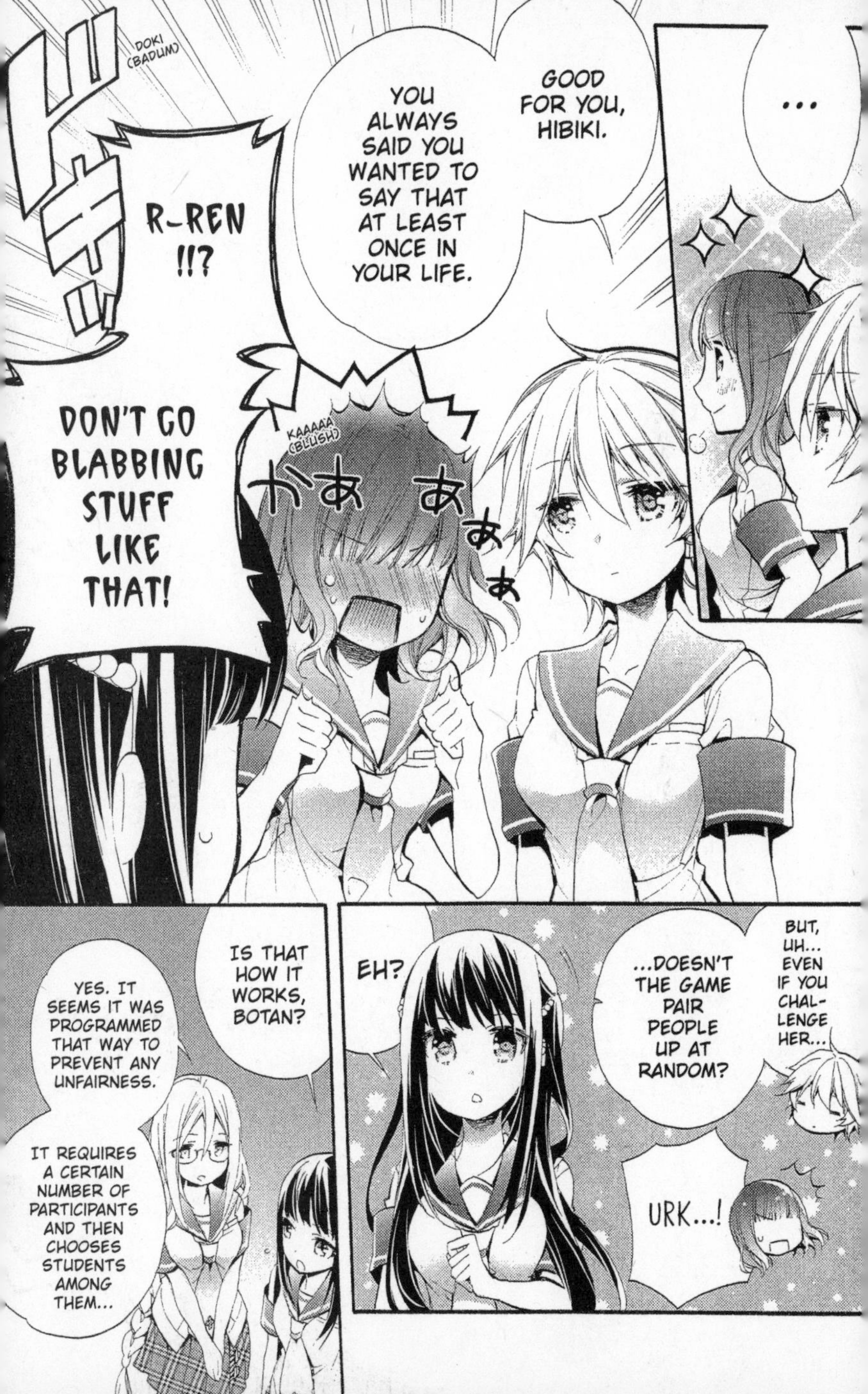
...
GOOD FOR YOU, HIBIKI.
YOU ALWAYS SAID YOU WANTED TO SAY THAT AT LEAST ONCE IN YOUR LIFE.
DOKI (BADUM)
R-REN !!?
KAAAAA (BLUSH)
DON'T GO BLABBING STUFF LIKE THAT!
BUT, UH... EVEN IF YOU CHAL-LENGE HER...
...DOESN'T THE GAME PAIR PEOPLE UP AT RANDOM?
URK...!
EH?
IS THAT HOW IT WORKS, BOTAN?
YES. IT SEEMS IT WAS PROGRAMMED THAT WAY TO PREVENT ANY UNFAIRNESS.
IT REQUIRES A CERTAIN NUMBER OF PARTICIPANTS AND THEN CHOOSES STUDENTS AMONG THEM...

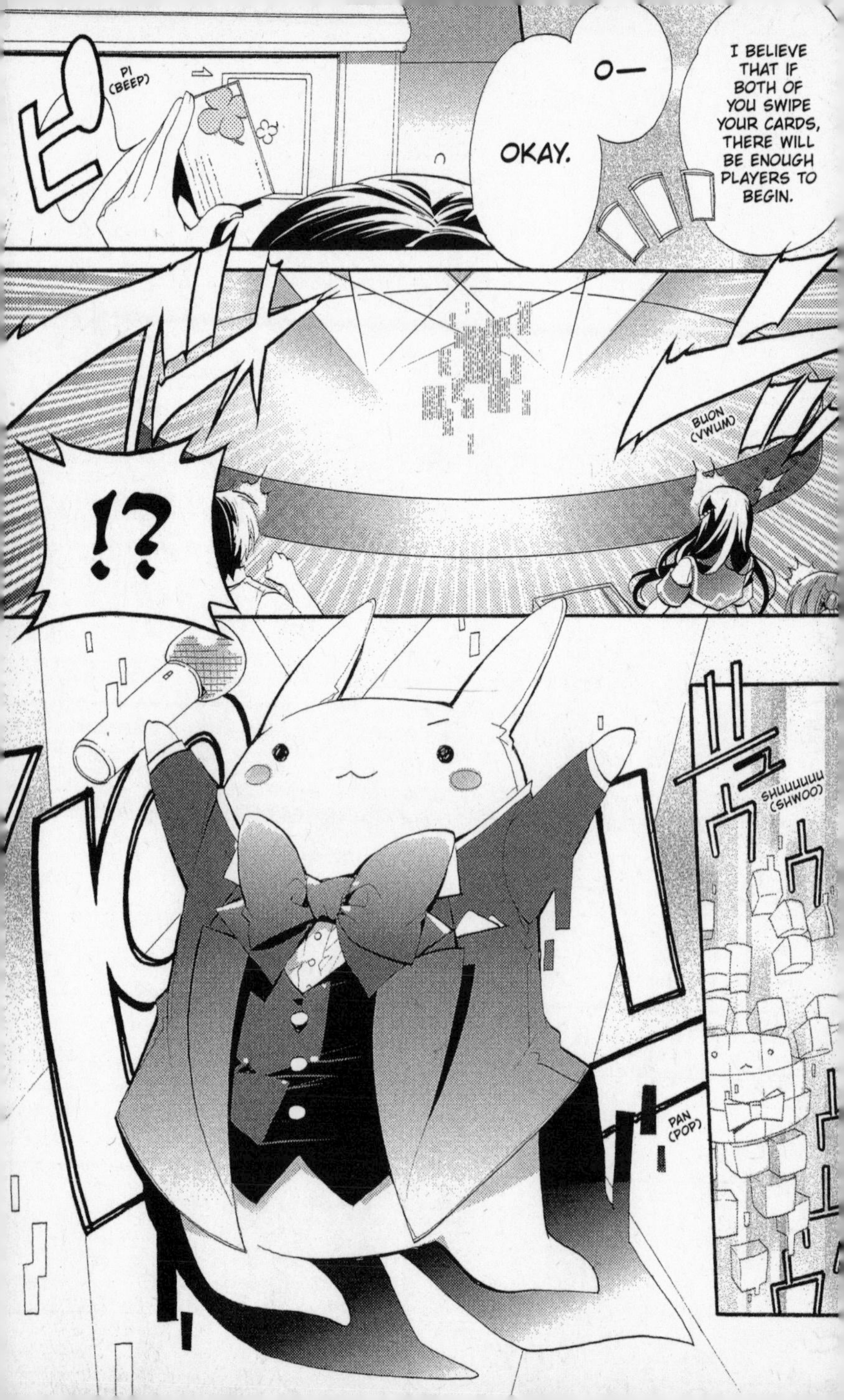
I BELIEVE THAT IF BOTH OF YOU SWIPE YOUR CARDS, THERE WILL BE ENOUGH PLAYERS TO BEGIN.
O—
OKAY.
PI (BEEP)
BUON (VWUM)
!?
SHUUUUUU (SHWOO)
PAN (POP)

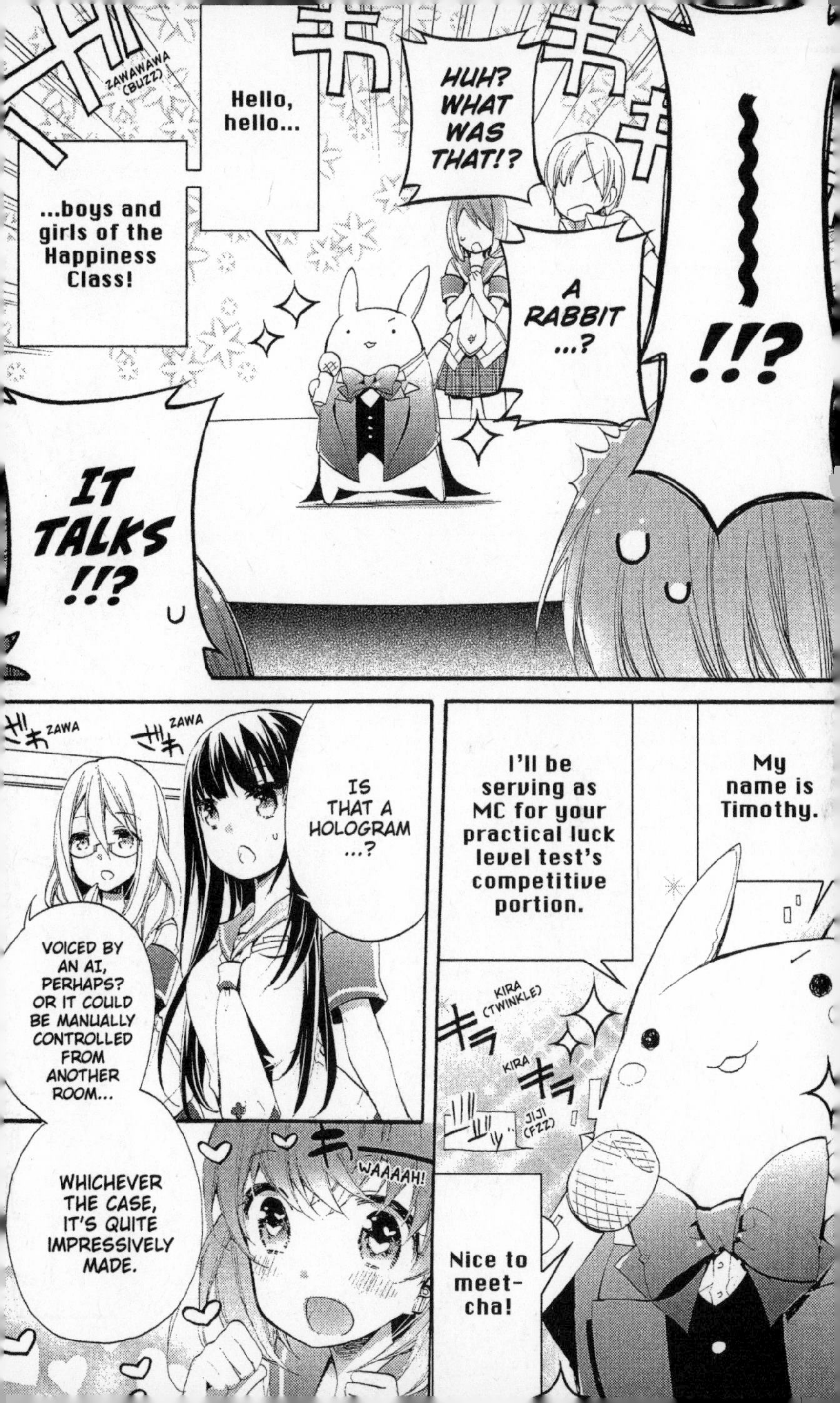
!!?
HUH? WHAT WAS THAT!?
A RABBIT ...?
ZAWAWAWA (BUZZ)
Hello, hello...
...boys and girls of the Happiness Class!
IT TALKS !!?
My name is Timothy.
I'll be serving as MC for your practical luck level test's competitive portion.
KIRA (TWINKLE)
KIRA
JIJI (FZZ)
Nice to meet-cha!
ZAWA
ZAWA
IS THAT A HOLOGRAM ...?
VOICED BY AN AI, PERHAPS? OR IT COULD BE MANUALLY CONTROLLED FROM ANOTHER ROOM...
WAAAAH!
WHICHEVER THE CASE, IT'S QUITE IMPRESSIVELY MADE.

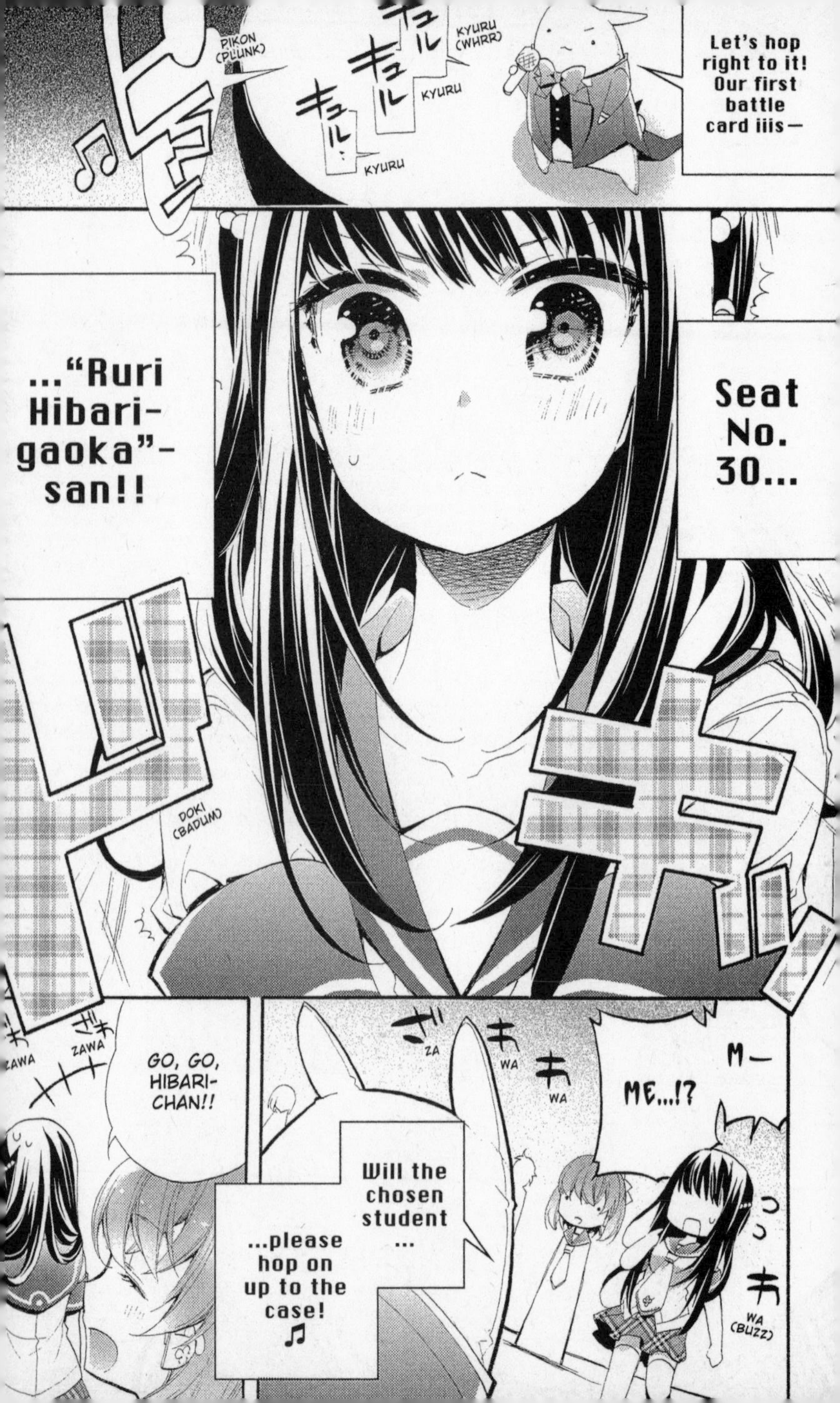

Let's hop right to it! Our first battle card iiis—
KYURU (WHRR)
KYURU
KYURU
PIKON (PLUNK)
Seat No. 30...
..."Ruri Hibari-gaoka"-san!!
DOKI (BADUM)
M—
ME...!?
ZA
WA
WA
Will the chosen student ...
...please hop on up to the case! ♫
WA (BUZZ)
GO, GO, HIBARI-CHAN!!
ZAWA
ZAWA

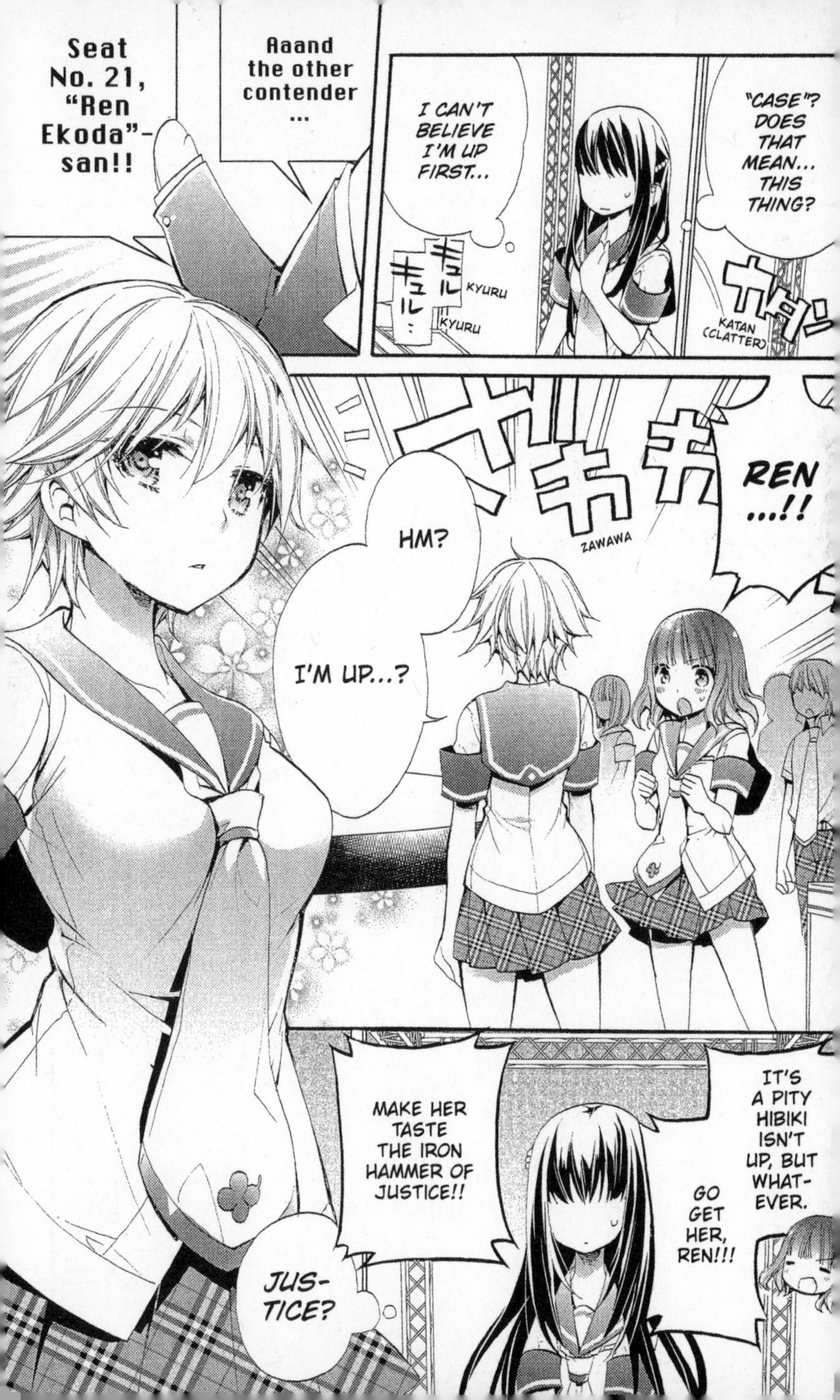
"CASE"? DOES THAT MEAN... THIS THING?
KATAN (CLATTER)
I CAN'T BELIEVE I'M UP FIRST...
KYURU KYURU
Aaand the other contender ...
Seat No. 21, "Ren Ekoda"-san!!
REN ...!!
ZAWAWA
HM?
I'M UP...?
IT'S A PITY HIBIKI ISN'T UP, BUT WHATEVER.
GO GET HER, REN!!!
MAKE HER TASTE THE IRON HAMMER OF JUSTICE!!
JUSTICE?

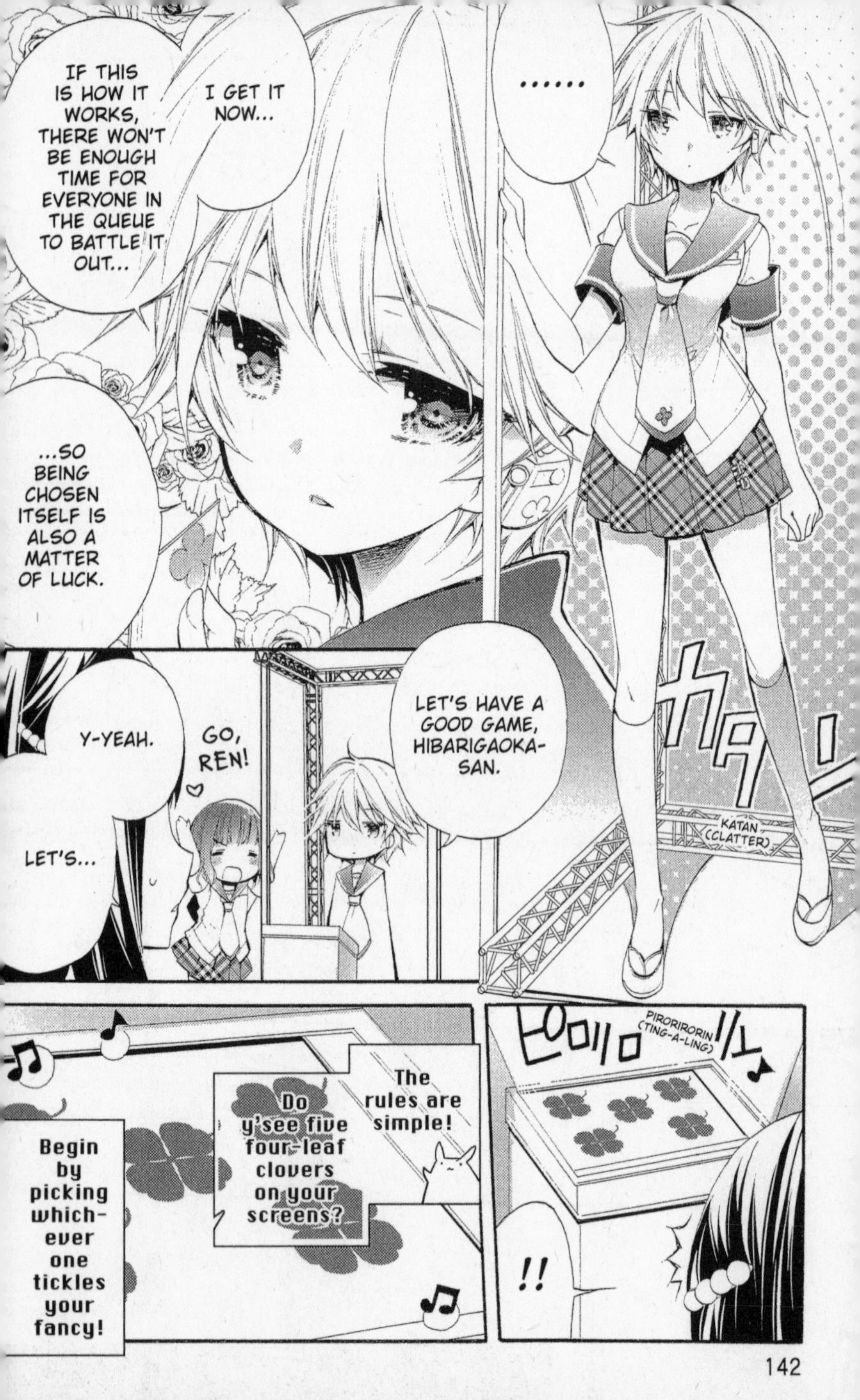
......
カタン
KATAN (CLATTER)
I GET IT NOW...
IF THIS IS HOW IT WORKS, THERE WON'T BE ENOUGH TIME FOR EVERYONE IN THE QUEUE TO BATTLE IT OUT...
...SO BEING CHOSEN ITSELF IS ALSO A MATTER OF LUCK.
LET'S HAVE A GOOD GAME, HIBARIGAOKA-SAN.
GO, REN!
Y-YEAH.
LET'S...
PIRORIRORIN (TING-A-LING)
!!
The rules are simple!
Do y'see five four-leaf clovers on your screens?
Begin by picking whichever one tickles your fancy!

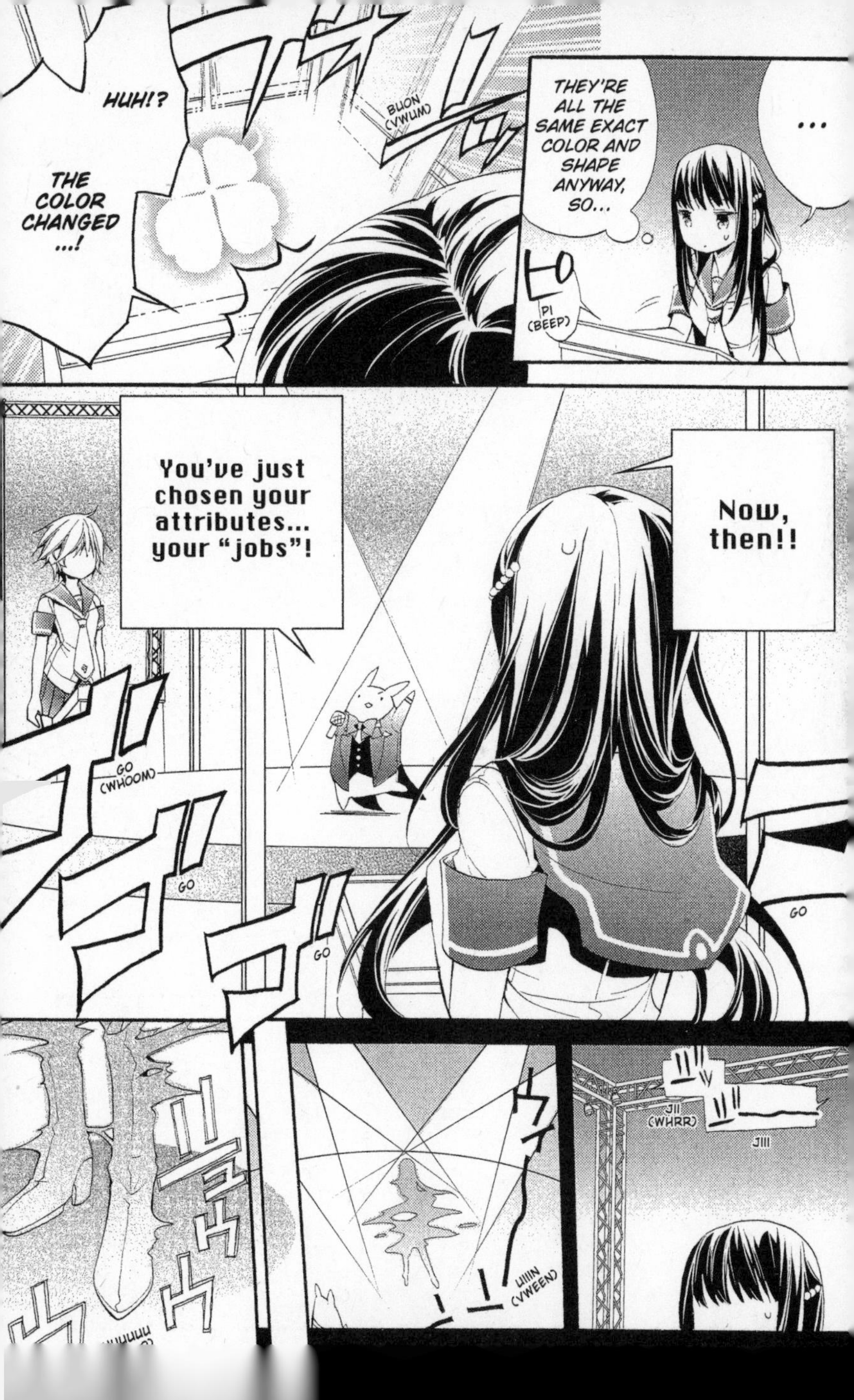
...
THEY'RE ALL THE SAME EXACT COLOR AND SHAPE ANYWAY, SO...
PI (BEEP)
BUON (VWUM)
HUH!?
THE COLOR CHANGED ...!
Now, then!!
You've just chosen your attributes... your "jobs"!
GO
GO
GO (WHOOM)
GO
JII (WHRR)
JIII
UIIIN (VWEEN)

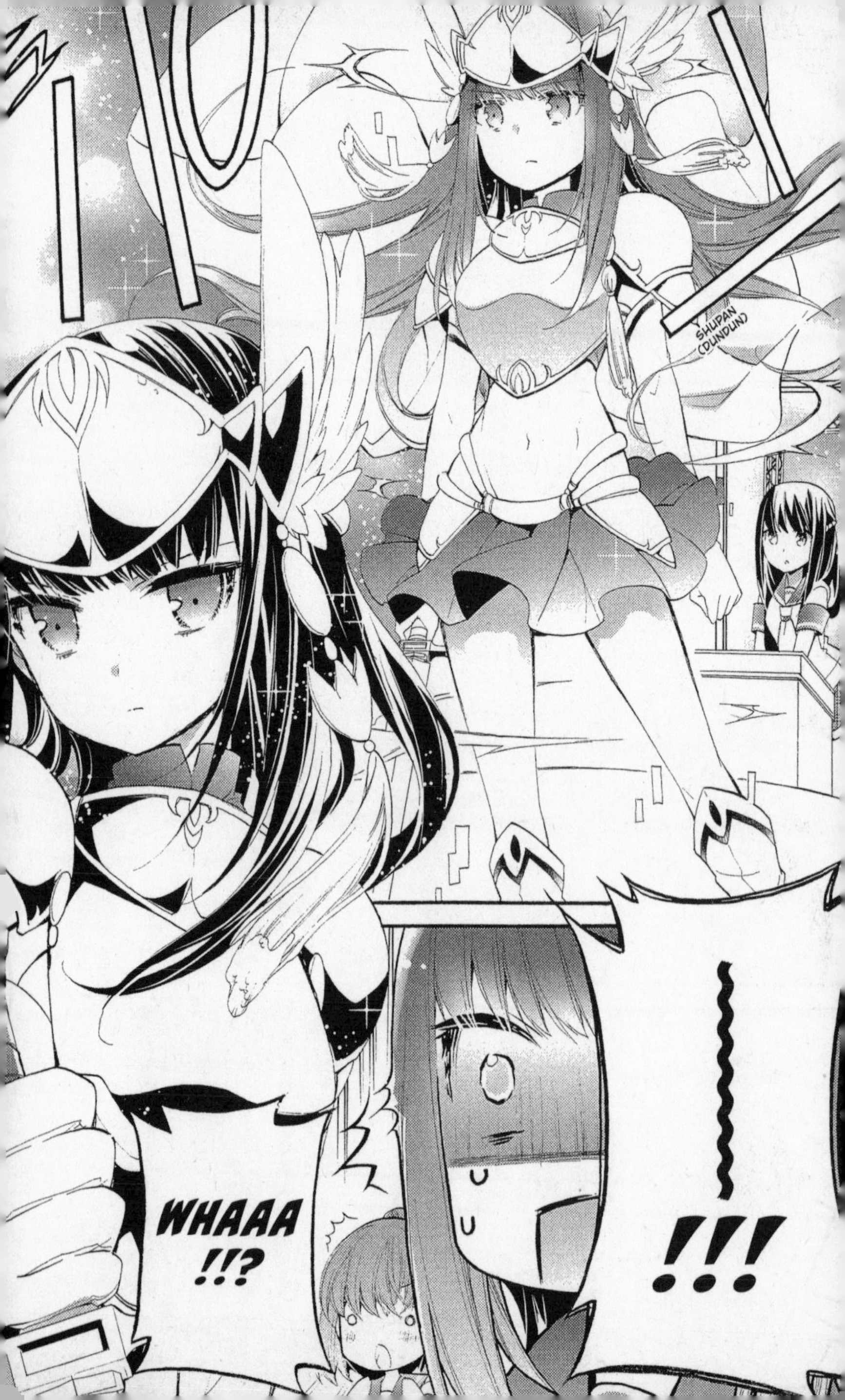
SHUPAN (DUNDUN)
!!!
WHAAA !!?

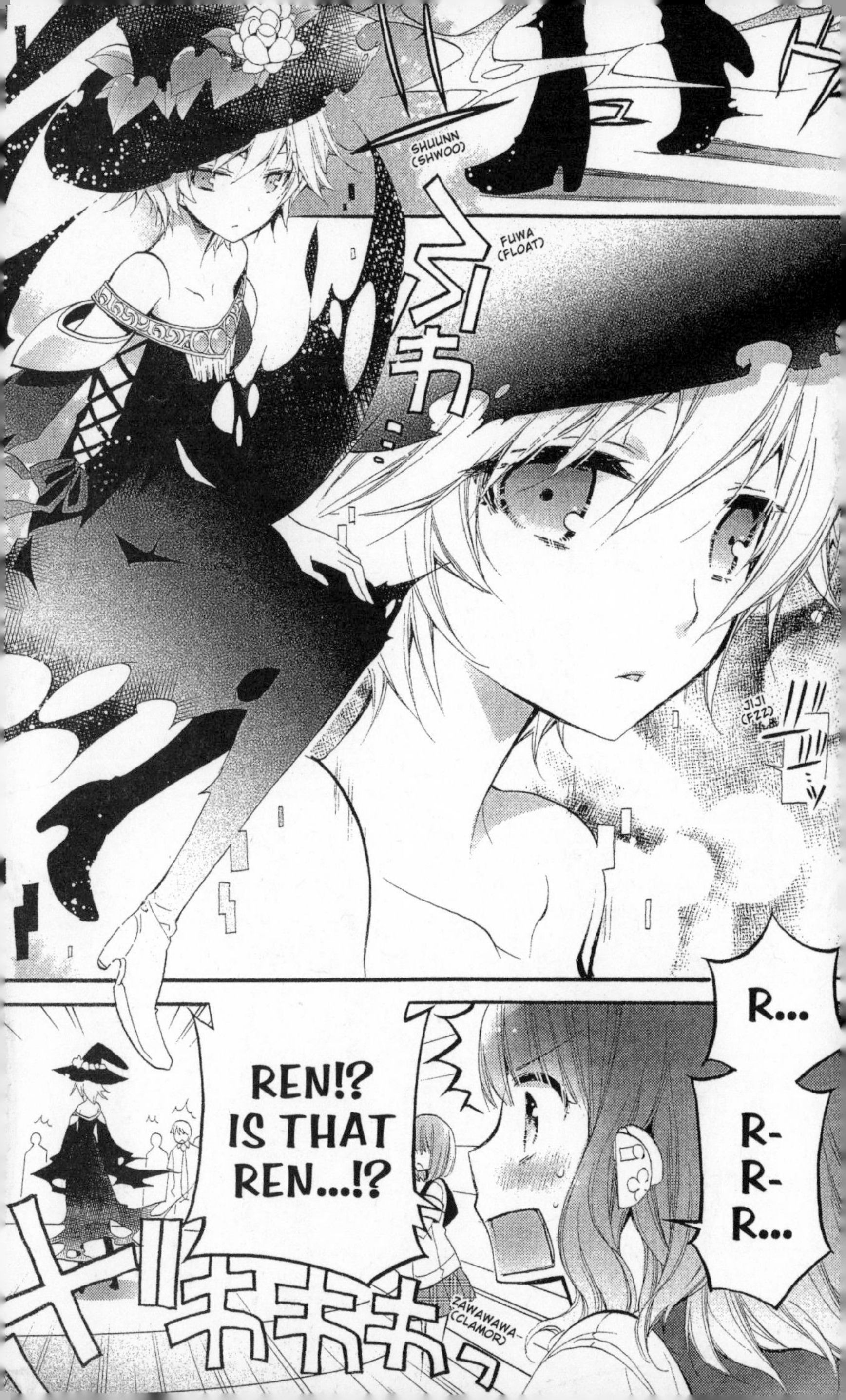
SHUUNN (SHWOO)
FUWA (FLOAT)
JIJI (FZZ)
R...
R-R-R-R...
REN!? IS THAT REN...!?
ZAWAWAWA (CLAMOR)

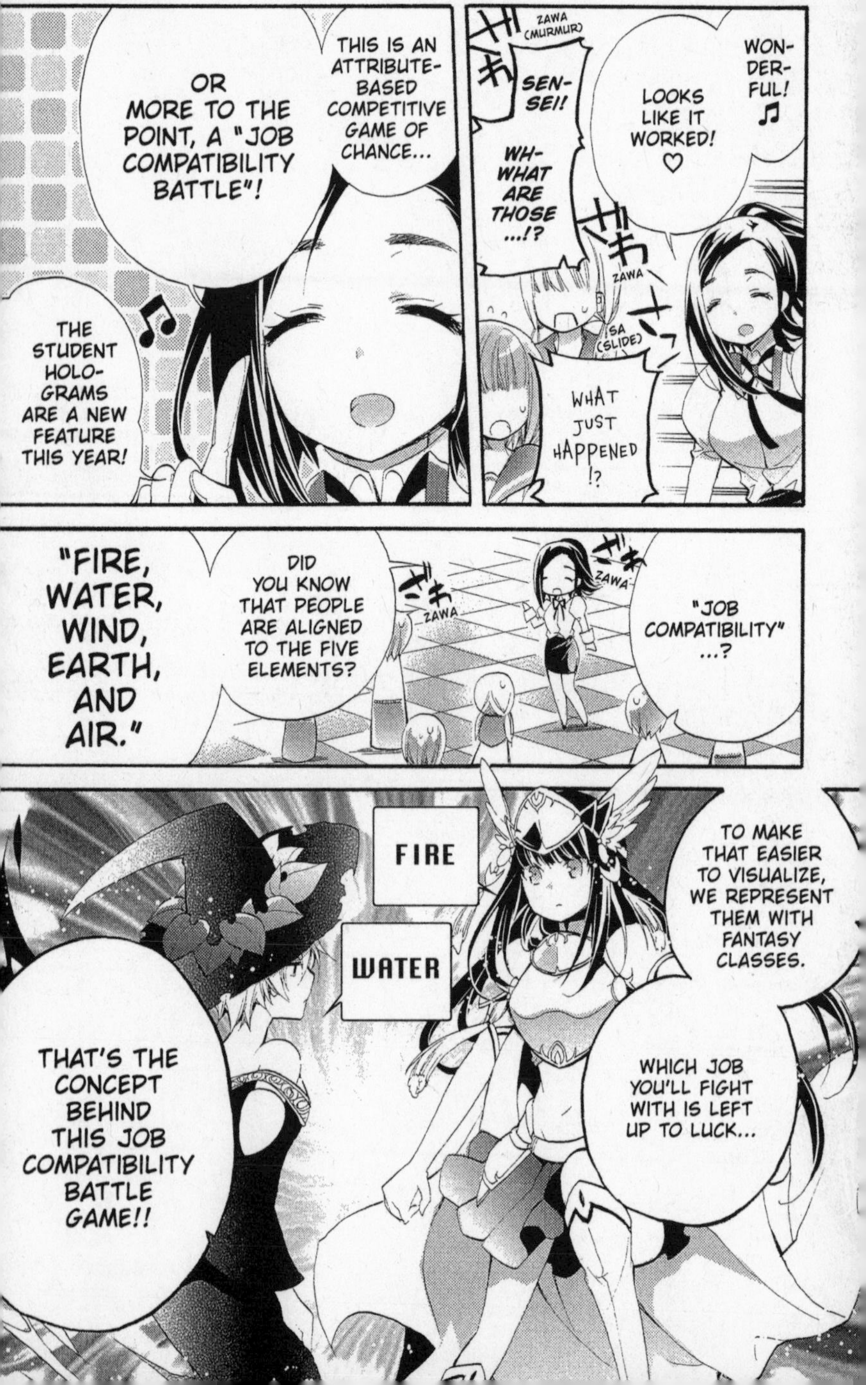
WON-DER-FUL! ♫
LOOKS LIKE IT WORKED! ♡
ZAWA (MURMUR)
SEN-SEI!
WH-WHAT ARE THOSE ...!?
ZAWA
SA (SLIDE)
WHAT JUST HAPPENED !?
THIS IS AN ATTRIBUTE-BASED COMPETITIVE GAME OF CHANCE...
OR MORE TO THE POINT, A "JOB COMPATIBILITY BATTLE"!
THE STUDENT HOLO-GRAMS ARE A NEW FEATURE THIS YEAR!
"JOB COMPATIBILITY" ...?
ZAWA
ZAWA
DID YOU KNOW THAT PEOPLE ARE ALIGNED TO THE FIVE ELEMENTS?
"FIRE, WATER, WIND, EARTH, AND AIR."
TO MAKE THAT EASIER TO VISUALIZE, WE REPRESENT THEM WITH FANTASY CLASSES.
FIRE
WATER
WHICH JOB YOU'LL FIGHT WITH IS LEFT UP TO LUCK...
THAT'S THE CONCEPT BEHIND THIS JOB COMPATIBILITY BATTLE GAME!!

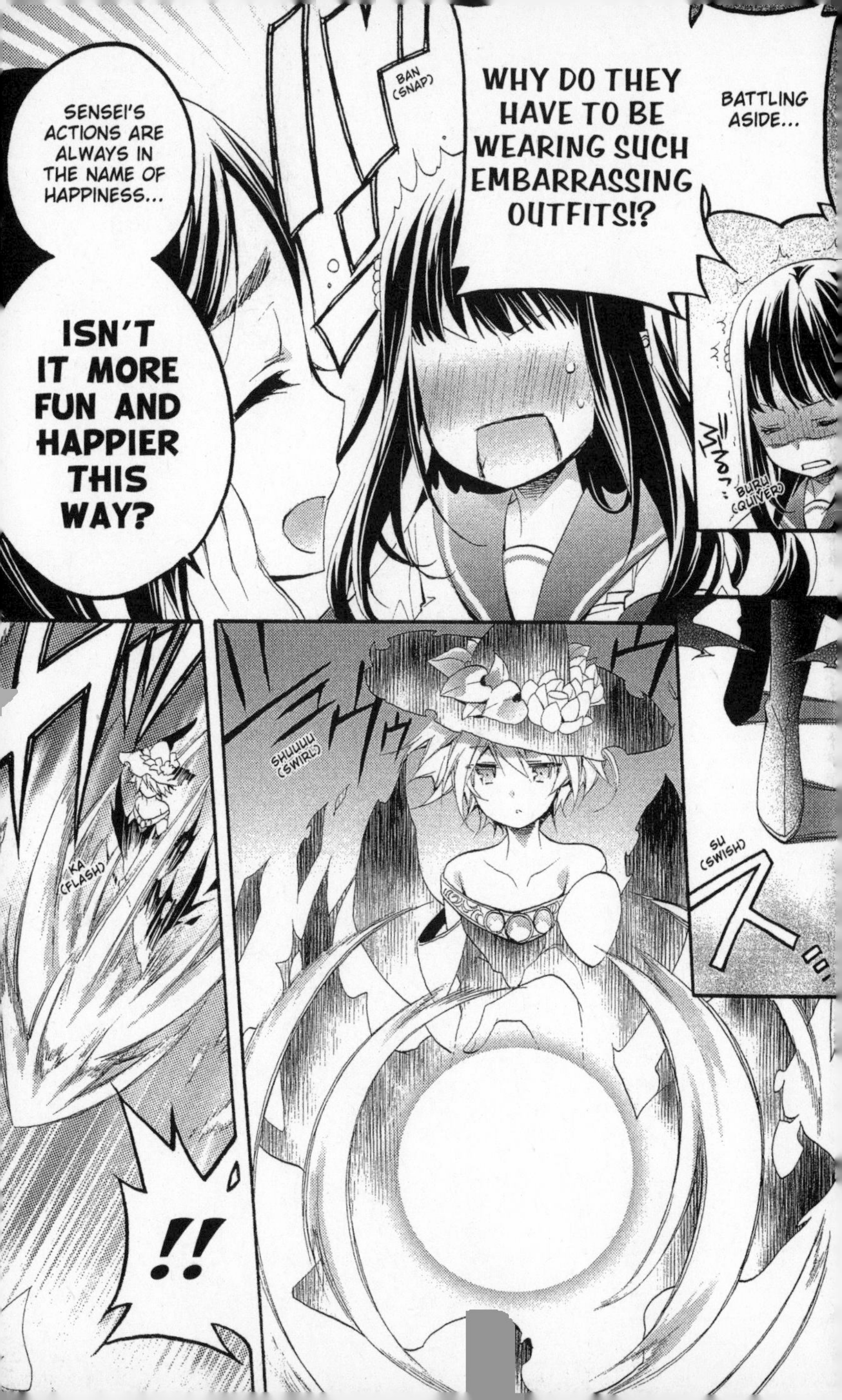
BATTLING ASIDE...
WHY DO THEY HAVE TO BE WEARING SUCH EMBARRASSING OUTFITS!?
BAN (SNAP)
BURU (QUIVER)
SENSEI'S ACTIONS ARE ALWAYS IN THE NAME OF HAPPINESS...
ISN'T IT MORE FUN AND HAPPIER THIS WAY?
SU (SWISH)
SHUUUU (SWIRL)
KA (FLASH)
!!

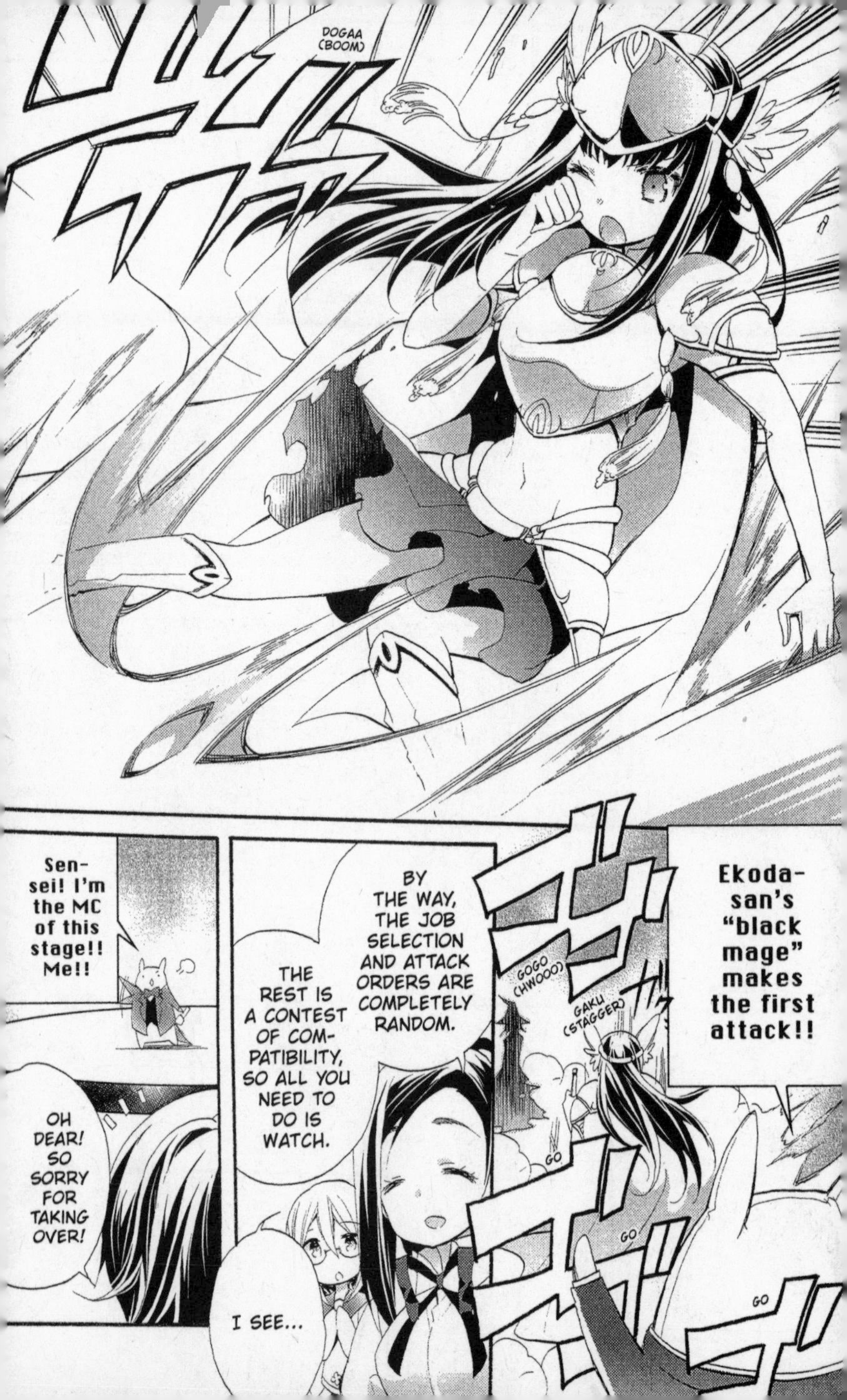

DOGAA (BOOM)
Ekoda-san's "black mage" makes the first attack!!
GOGO (HWOOO)
GAKU (STAGGER)
GO
GO
GO
BY THE WAY, THE JOB SELECTION AND ATTACK ORDERS ARE COMPLETELY RANDOM.
THE REST IS A CONTEST OF COMPATIBILITY, SO ALL YOU NEED TO DO IS WATCH.
I SEE...
Sensei! I'm the MC of this stage!! Me!!
OH DEAR! SO SORRY FOR TAKING OVER!

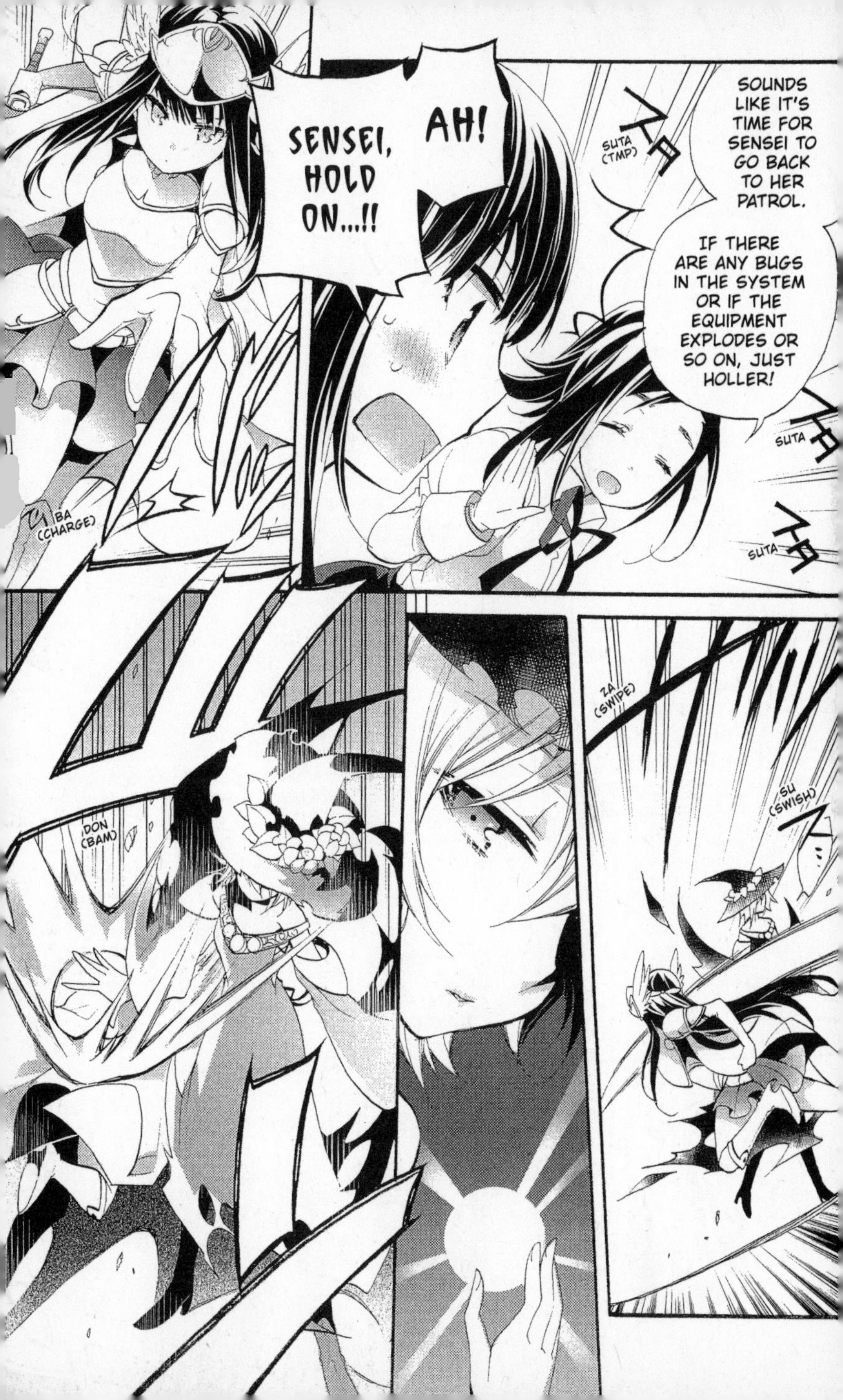
SUTA (TMP)
SOUNDS LIKE IT'S TIME FOR SENSEI TO GO BACK TO HER PATROL.
IF THERE ARE ANY BUGS IN THE SYSTEM OR IF THE EQUIPMENT EXPLODES OR SO ON, JUST HOLLER!
SUTA
SUTA
AH!
SENSEI, HOLD ON...!!
BA (CHARGE)
ZA (SWIPE)
SU (SWISH)
DON (BAM)

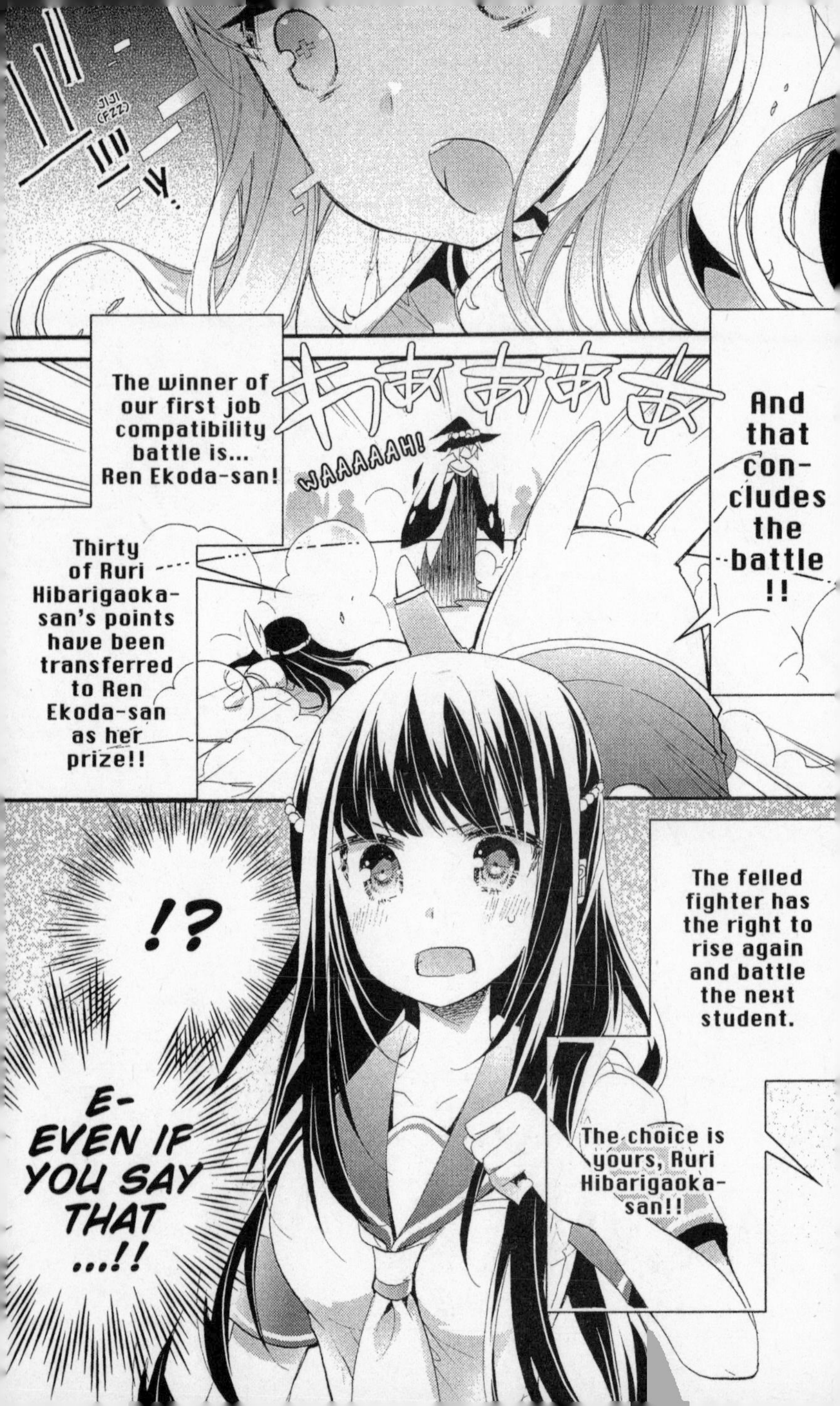
JIJI (FZZ)
And that concludes the battle!!
The winner of our first job compatibility battle is... Ren Ekoda-san!
わあああああ
WAAAAAAH!
Thirty of Ruri Hibarigaoka-san's points have been transferred to Ren Ekoda-san as her prize!!
The felled fighter has the right to rise again and battle the next student.
The choice is yours, Ruri Hibarigaoka-san!!
!?
E-EVEN IF YOU SAY THAT...!!

AnneHappy
unhappy go lucky!

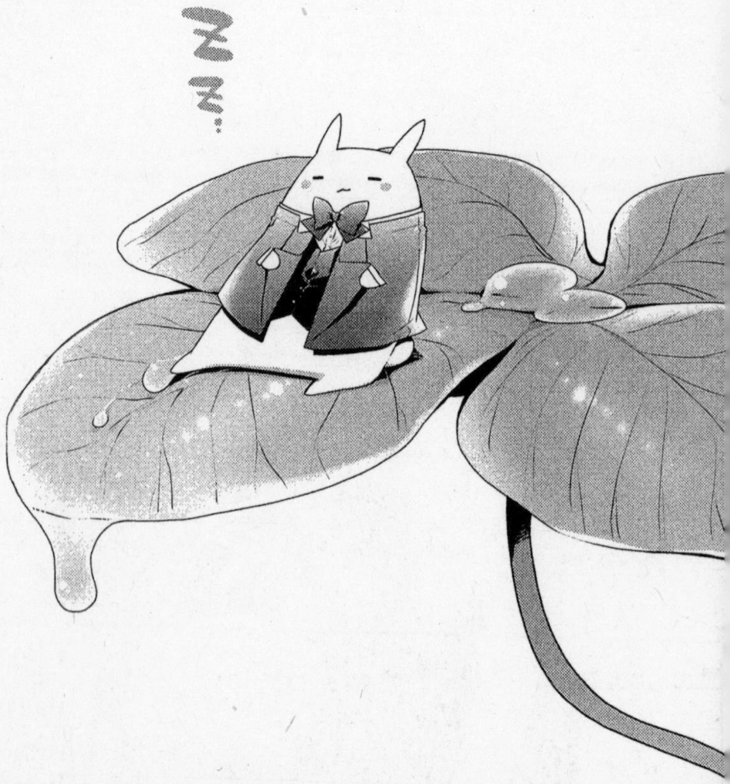
Z z..

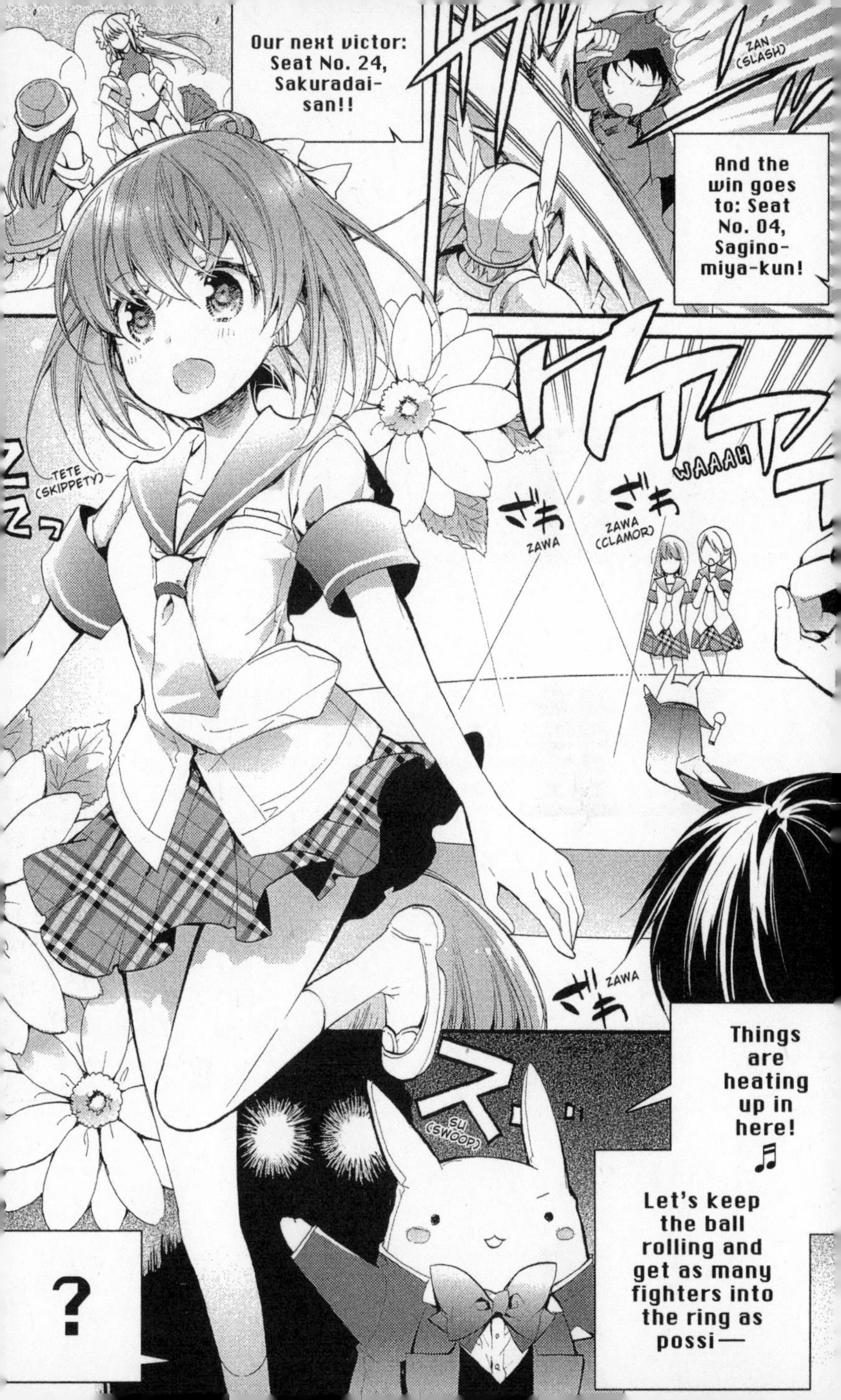

ZAN (SLASH)
And the win goes to: Seat No. 04, Sagino-miya-kun!
Our next victor: Seat No. 24, Sakuradai-san!!
WAAAH
ざわ ざわ
ZAWA (CLAMOR)
ZAWA
TETE (SKIPPETY)
ざわ
ZAWA
Things are heating up in here! ♫
Let's keep the ball rolling and get as many fighters into the ring as possi—
SU (SWOOP)
?

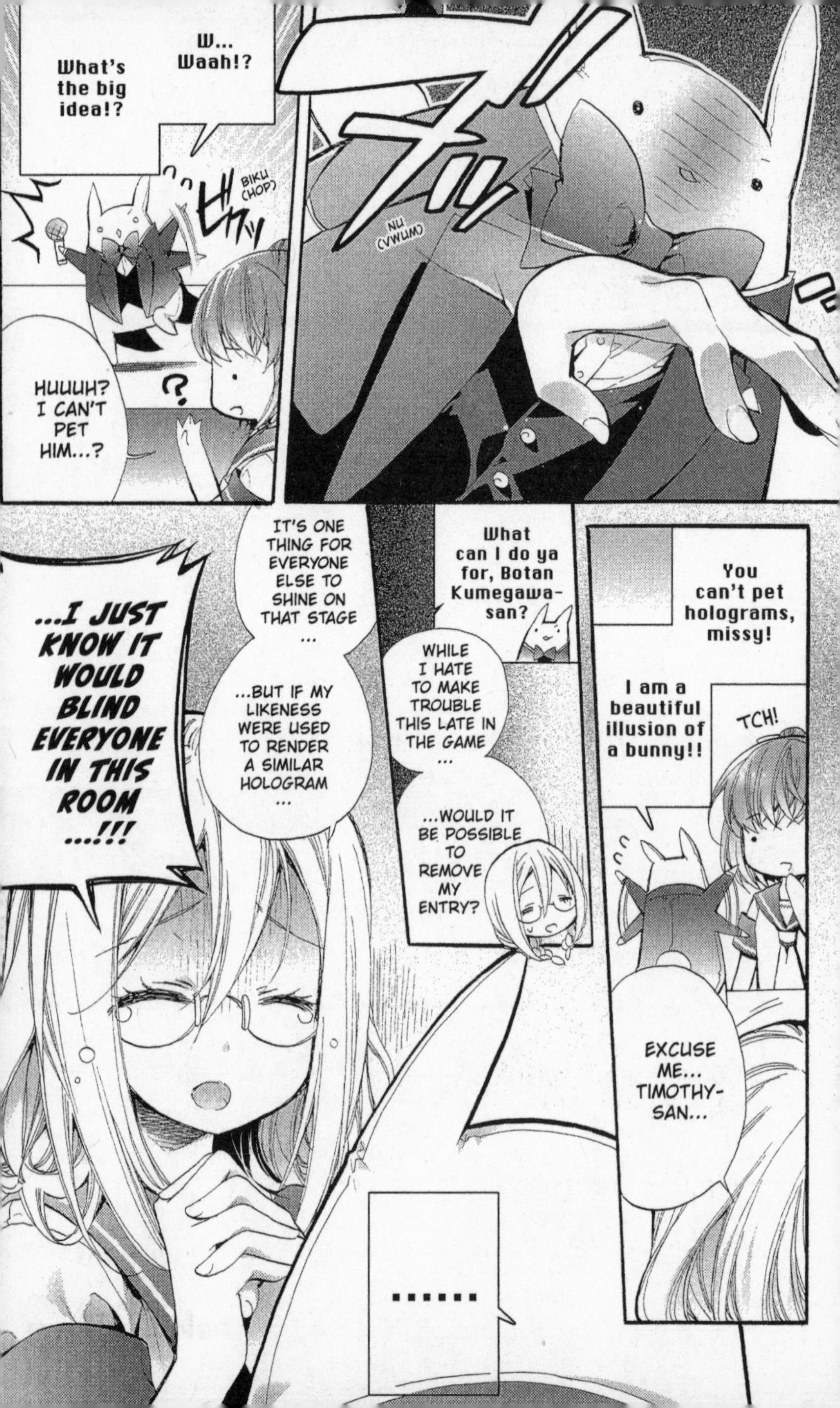
NU (VWUM)
W... Waah!?
What's the big idea!?
BIKU (HOP)
HUUUH? I CAN'T PET HIM...?
You can't pet holograms, missy!
I am a beautiful illusion of a bunny!!
TCH!
EXCUSE ME... TIMOTHY-SAN...
What can I do ya for, Botan Kumegawa-san?
WHILE I HATE TO MAKE TROUBLE THIS LATE IN THE GAME...
...WOULD IT BE POSSIBLE TO REMOVE MY ENTRY?
IT'S ONE THING FOR EVERYONE ELSE TO SHINE ON THAT STAGE...
...BUT IF MY LIKENESS WERE USED TO RENDER A SIMILAR HOLOGRAM...
...I JUST KNOW IT WOULD BLIND EVERYONE IN THIS ROOM...!!!
......

HANAKO HIBARI BOTAN
HP 875 757 42
MP 96 0 2525
UNLUCKY UNENVIED UNHEALTHY
Lucky. 22

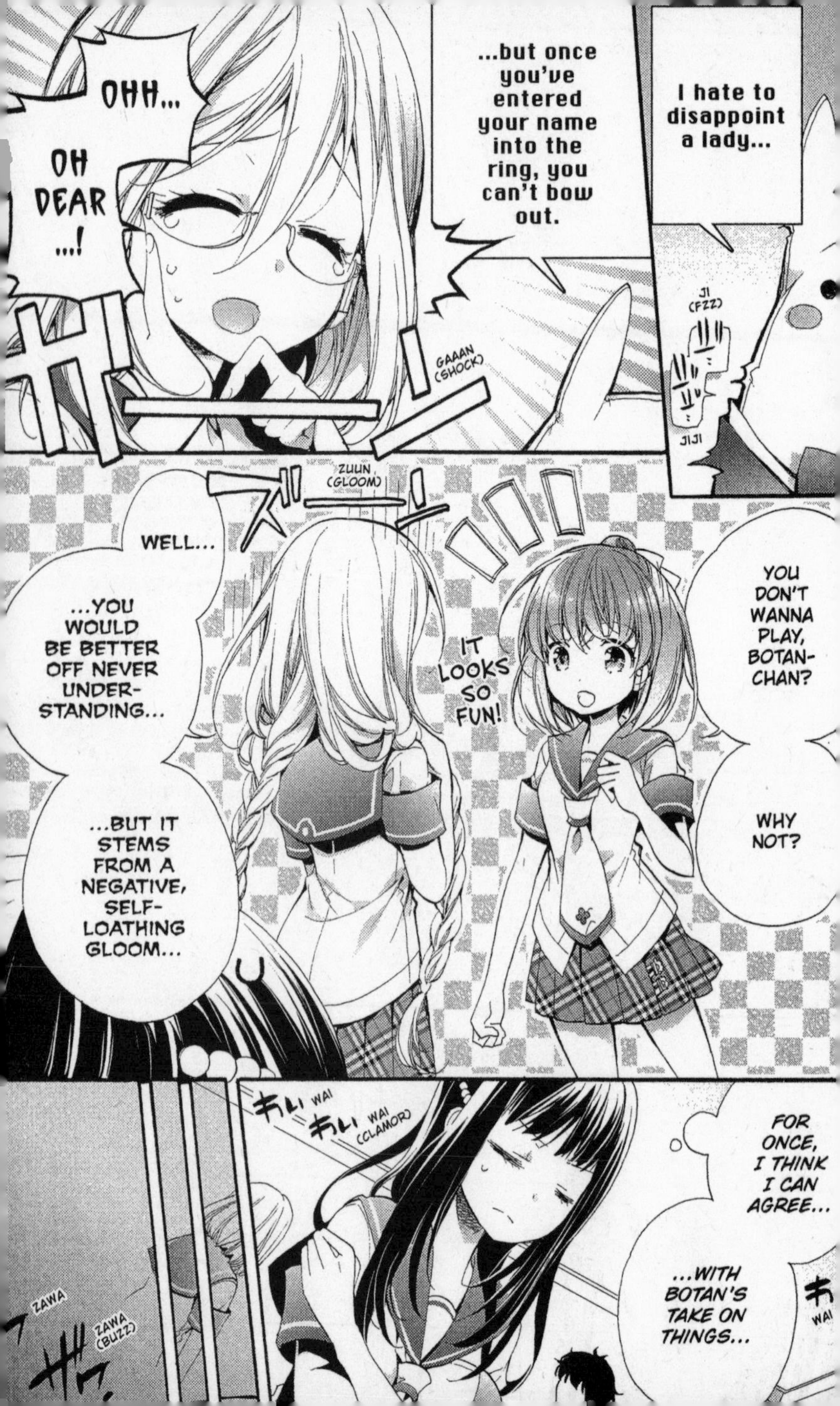
I hate to disappoint a lady...
JI (FZZ)
JIJI
...but once you've entered your name into the ring, you can't bow out.
OHH...
OH DEAR ...!
GAAAN (SHOCK)
ZUUN (GLOOM)
YOU DON'T WANNA PLAY, BOTAN-CHAN?
WHY NOT?
IT LOOKS SO FUN!
WELL...
...YOU WOULD BE BETTER OFF NEVER UNDER-STANDING...
...BUT IT STEMS FROM A NEGATIVE, SELF-LOATHING GLOOM...
WAI
FOR ONCE, I THINK I CAN AGREE...
...WITH BOTAN'S TAKE ON THINGS...
WAI WAI (CLAMOR)
ZAWA ZAWA (BUZZ)

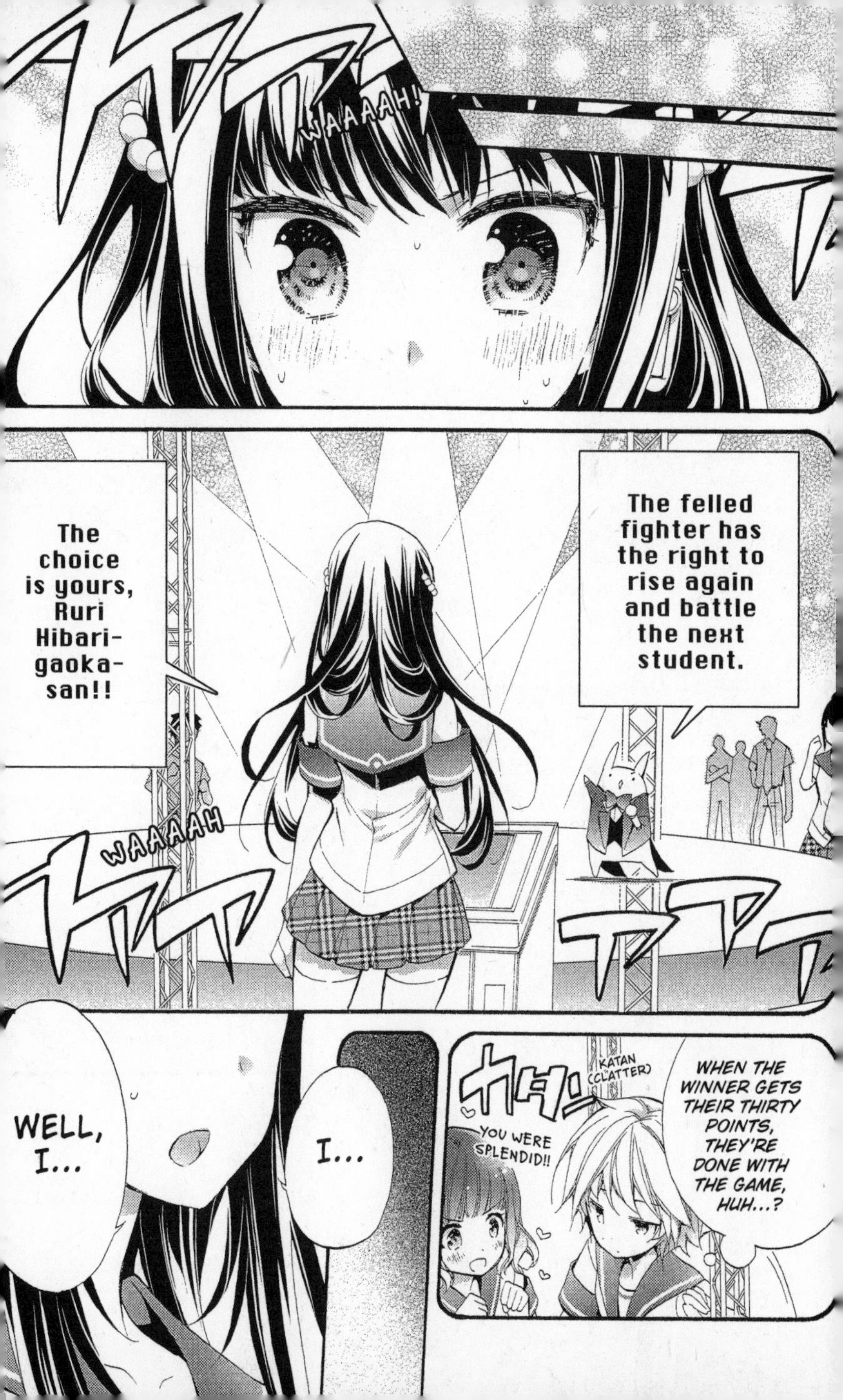
WAAAAH!
The felled fighter has the right to rise again and battle the next student.
The choice is yours, Ruri Hibari-gaoka-san!!
WAAAAH
KATAN (CLATTER)
WHEN THE WINNER GETS THEIR THIRTY POINTS, THEY'RE DONE WITH THE GAME, HUH...?
YOU WERE SPLENDID!!
I...
WELL, I...

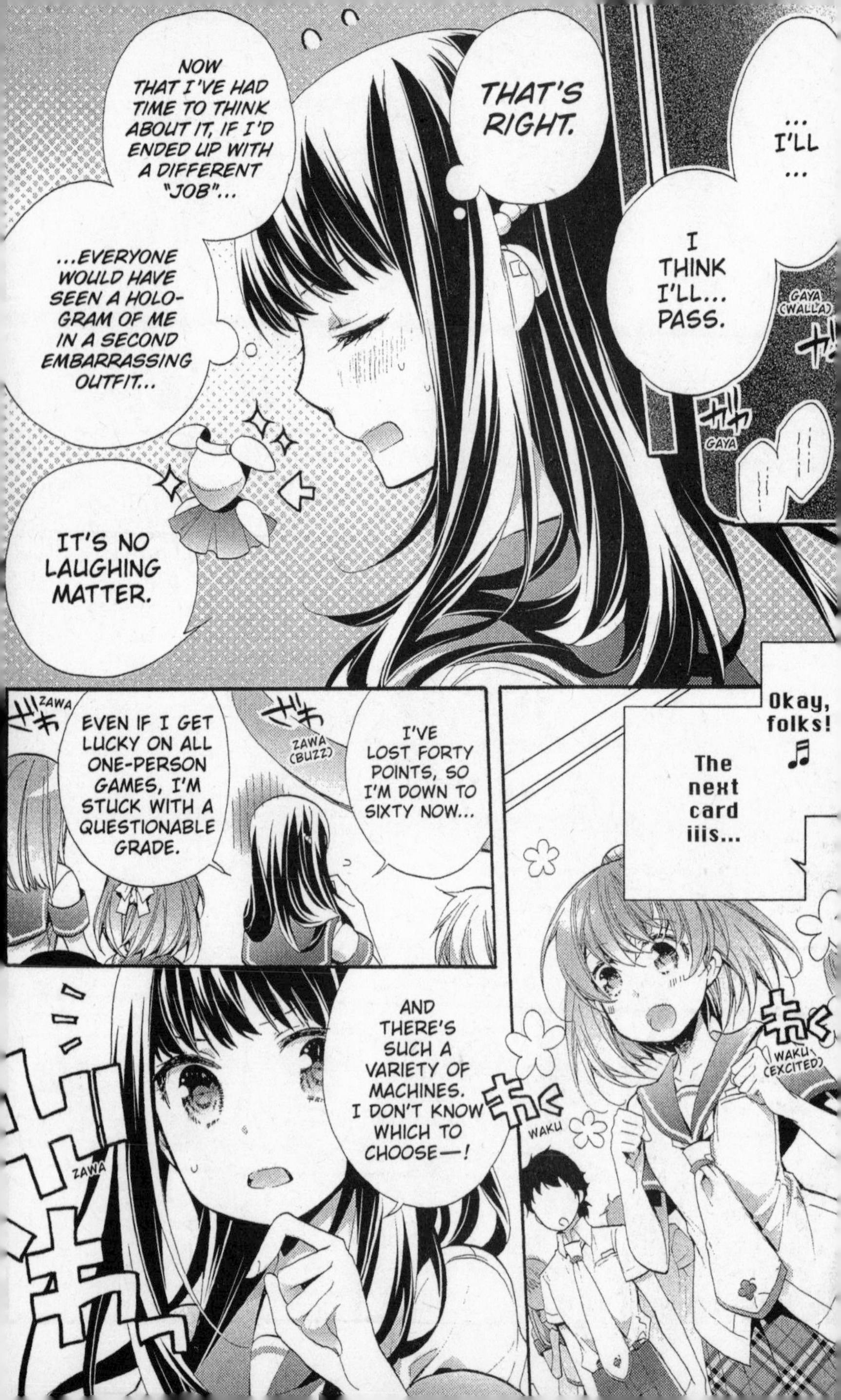

... I'LL ...
I THINK I'LL... PASS.
GAYA (WALLA)
GAYA
THAT'S RIGHT.
NOW THAT I'VE HAD TIME TO THINK ABOUT IT, IF I'D ENDED UP WITH A DIFFERENT "JOB"...
...EVERYONE WOULD HAVE SEEN A HOLO-GRAM OF ME IN A SECOND EMBARRASSING OUTFIT...
IT'S NO LAUGHING MATTER.
Okay, folks! ♫
The next card iiis...
WAKU (EXCITED)
WAKU
I'VE LOST FORTY POINTS, SO I'M DOWN TO SIXTY NOW...
ZAWA (BUZZ)
EVEN IF I GET LUCKY ON ALL ONE-PERSON GAMES, I'M STUCK WITH A QUESTIONABLE GRADE.
ZAWA
AND THERE'S SUCH A VARIETY OF MACHINES. I DON'T KNOW WHICH TO CHOOSE—!
ZAWA

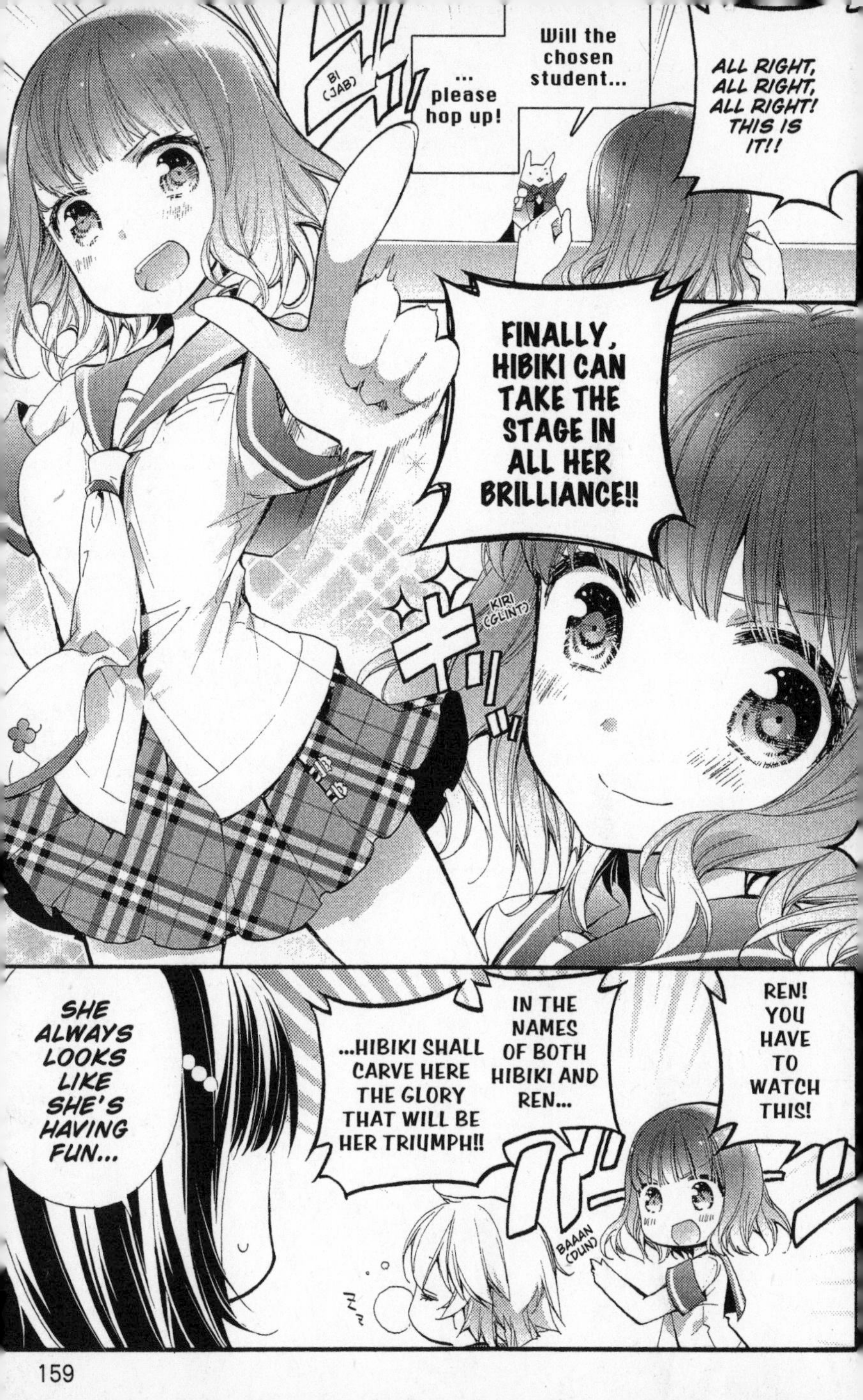
ALL RIGHT, ALL RIGHT, ALL RIGHT! THIS IS IT!!
Will the chosen student...
... please hop up!
BI (JAB)
FINALLY, HIBIKI CAN TAKE THE STAGE IN ALL HER BRILLIANCE!!
KIRI (GLINT)
REN! YOU HAVE TO WATCH THIS!
BAAAN (DUN)
IN THE NAMES OF BOTH HIBIKI AND REN...
...HIBIKI SHALL CARVE HERE THE GLORY THAT WILL BE HER TRIUMPH!!
SHE ALWAYS LOOKS LIKE SHE'S HAVING FUN...

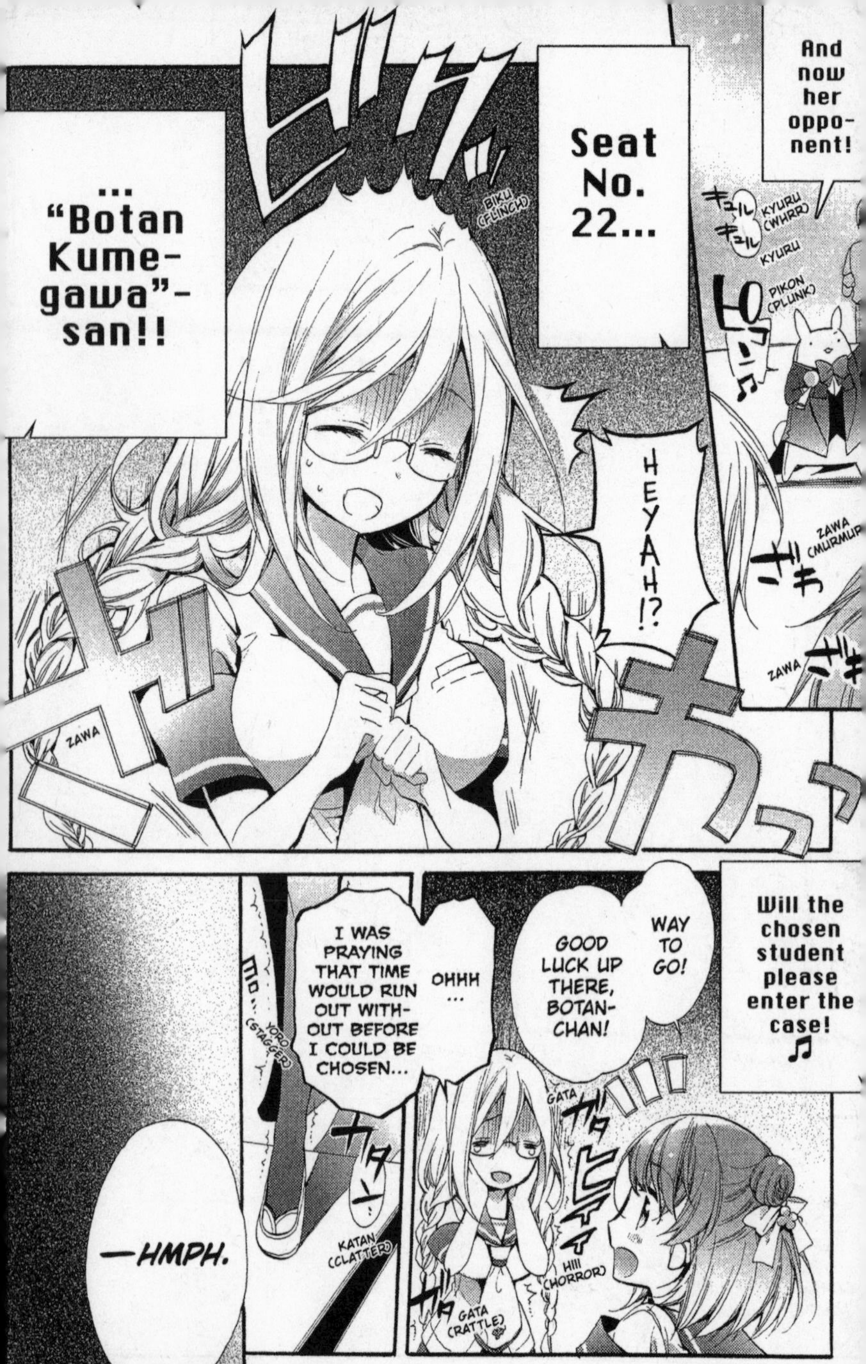
And now her oppo-nent!
KYURU (WHRR)
KYURU
PIKON (PLUNK)
ZAWA (MURMUR)
ZAWA
Seat No. 22...
... "Botan Kume-gawa"-san!!
BIKU (FLINCH)
HEYAH!?
ZAWA
Will the chosen student please enter the case! ♫
WAY TO GO!
GOOD LUCK UP THERE, BOTAN-CHAN!
GATA
HIII (HORROR)
GATA (RATTLE)
OHHH ...
I WAS PRAYING THAT TIME WOULD RUN OUT WITH-OUT BEFORE I COULD BE CHOSEN...
YORO (STAGGER)
KATAN (CLATTER)
—HMPH.

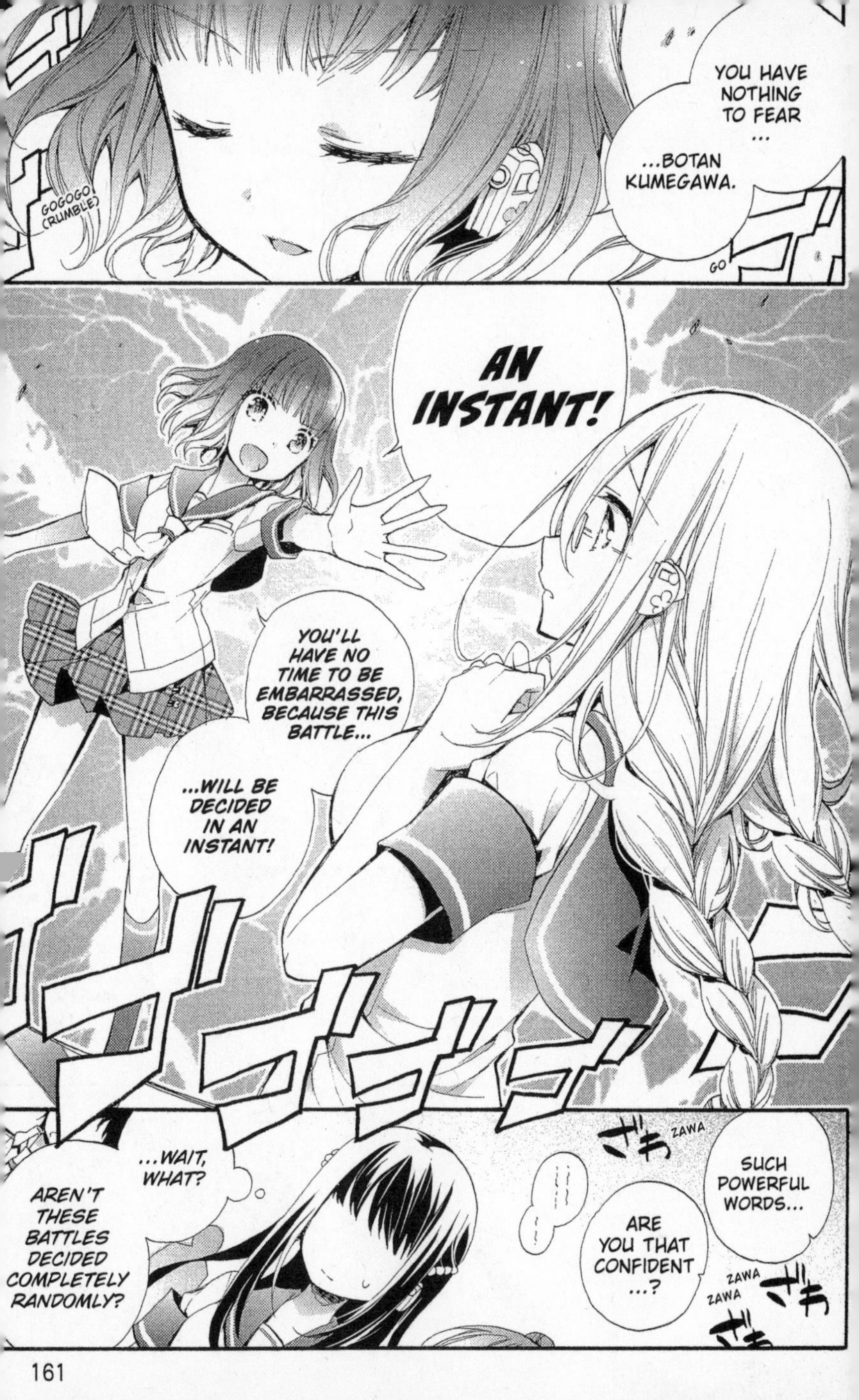
YOU HAVE NOTHING TO FEAR ...
...BOTAN KUMEGAWA.
GO
GOGOGO (RUMBLE)
YOU'LL HAVE NO TIME TO BE EMBARRASSED, BECAUSE THIS BATTLE...
...WILL BE DECIDED IN AN INSTANT!
AN INSTANT!
ZAWA
SUCH POWERFUL WORDS...
ARE YOU THAT CONFIDENT ...?
ZAWA ZAWA
...WAIT, WHAT?
AREN'T THESE BATTLES DECIDED COMPLETELY RANDOMLY?

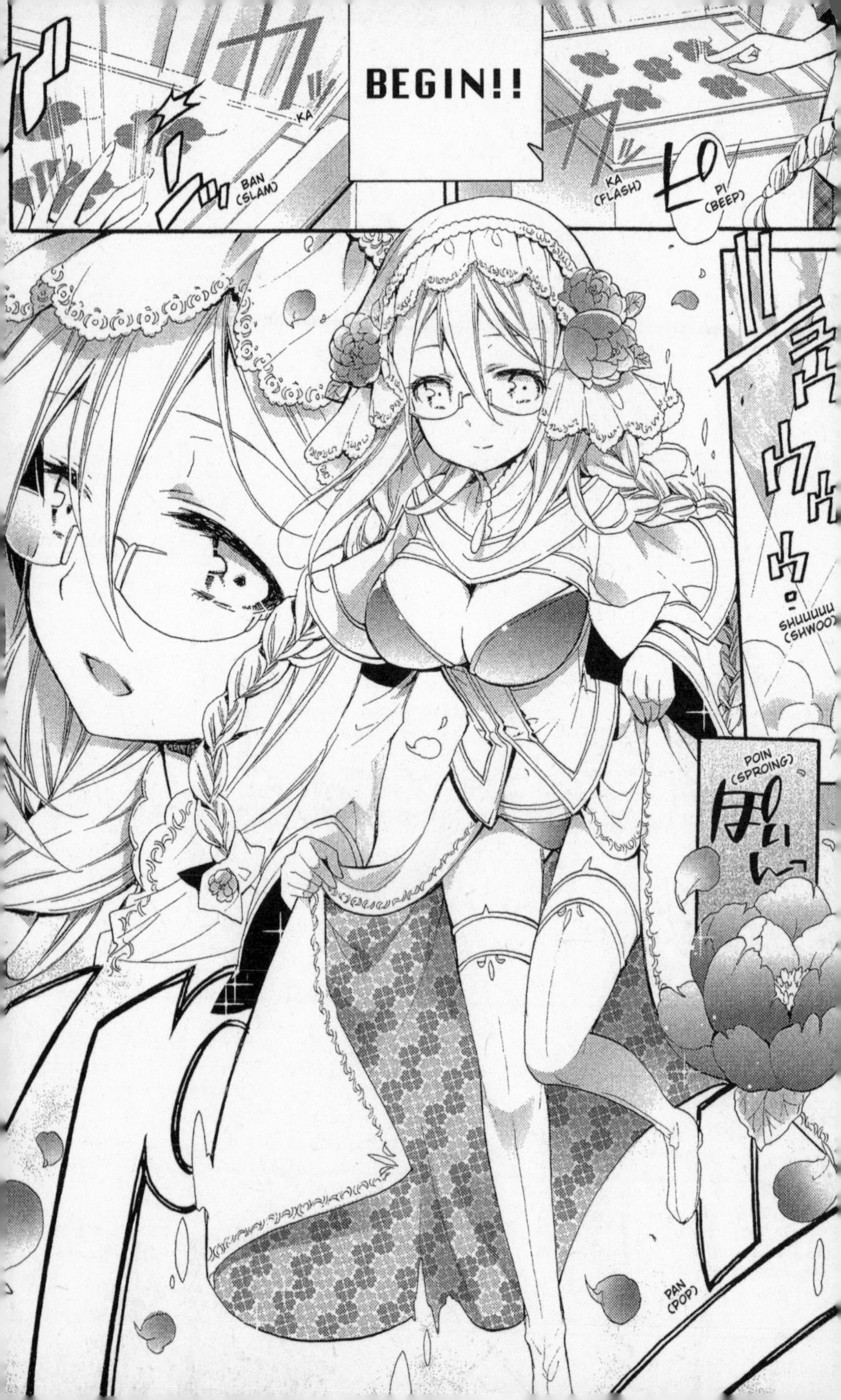

PI (BEEP)
KA (FLASH)
BEGIN!!
KA
BAN (SLAM)
SHUUUUU (SHWOO)
POIN (SPROING)
PAN (POP)

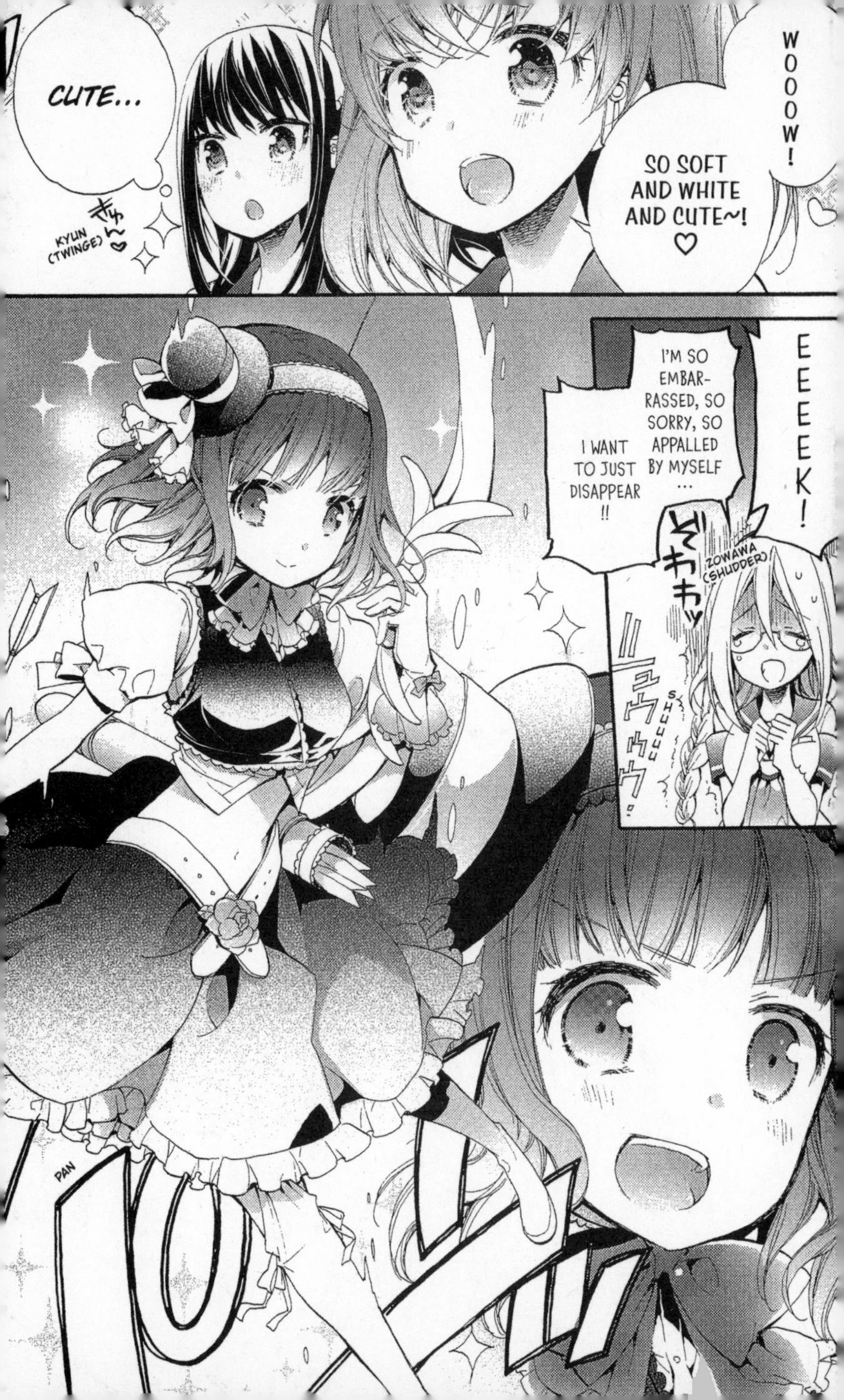
WOOOOW!
SO SOFT AND WHITE AND CUTE~! ♡
CUTE...
KYUN (TWINGE)
EEEEEK!
I'M SO EMBARRASSED, SO SORRY, SO APPALLED BY MYSELF...
I WANT TO JUST DISAPPEAR!!
ZOWAWA (SHUDDER)
SHUUUUU
PAN

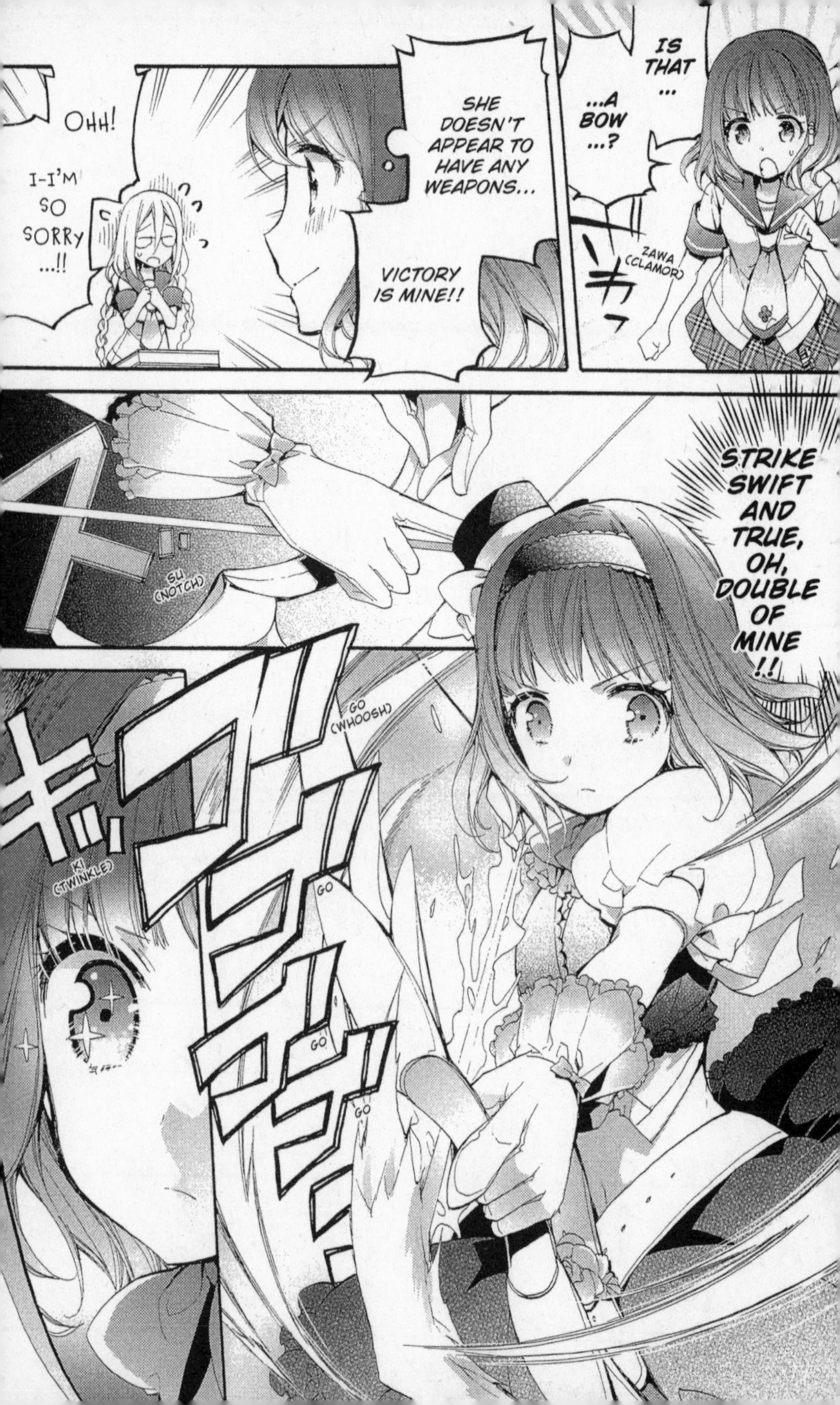
IS THAT ...
...A BOW ...?
ZAWA (CLAMOR)
SHE DOESN'T APPEAR TO HAVE ANY WEAPONS...
VICTORY IS MINE!!
OHH!
I-I'M SO SORRY ...!!
STRIKE SWIFT AND TRUE, OH, DOUBLE OF MINE!!
SU (NOTCH)
GO (WHOOSH)
KI (TWINKLE)
GO
GO
GO

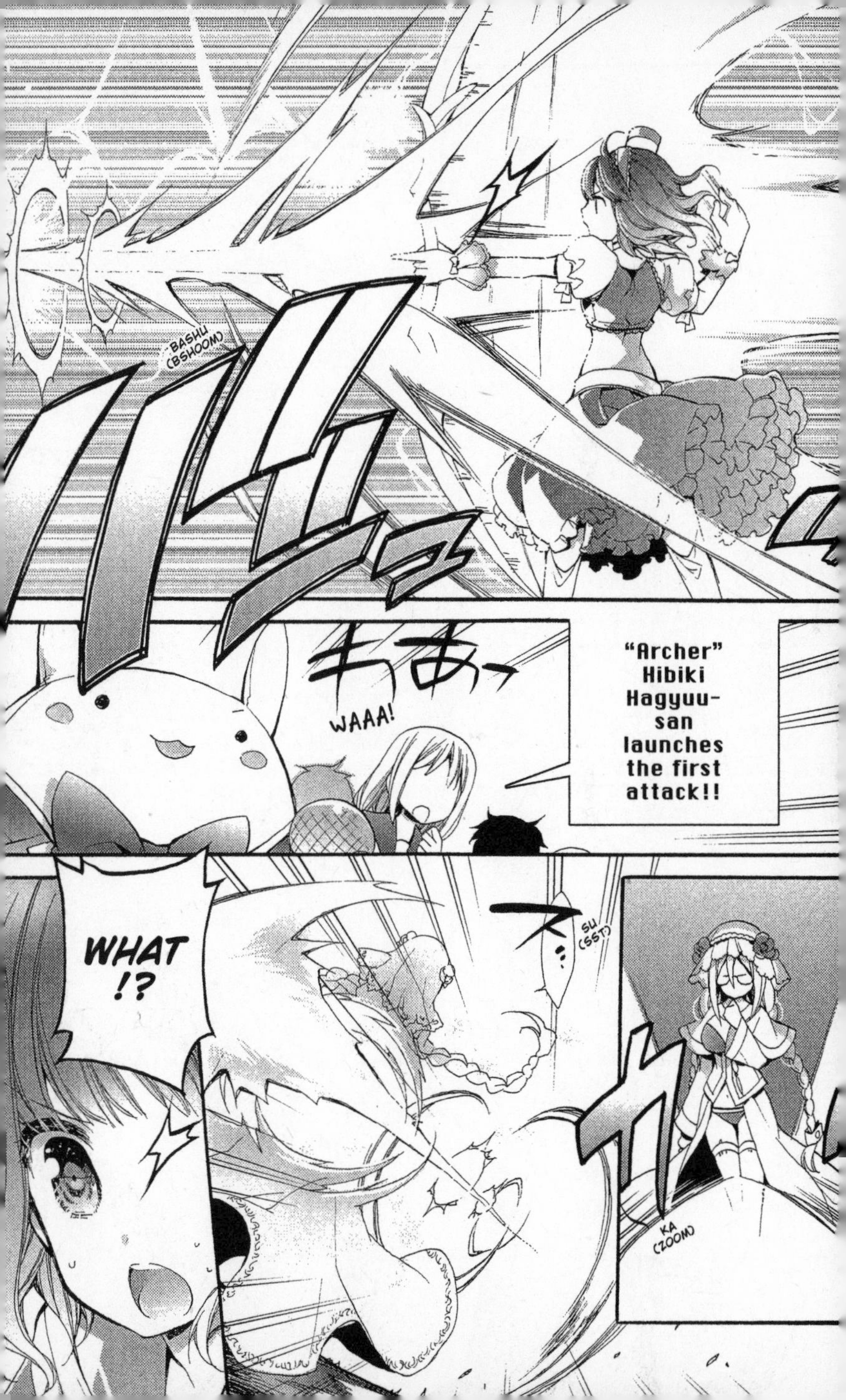
BASHU
(BSHOOM)
"Archer" Hibiki Hagyuu-san launches the first attack!!
わあっ
WAAA!
KA
(ZOOM)
SU
(SST)
WHAT!?

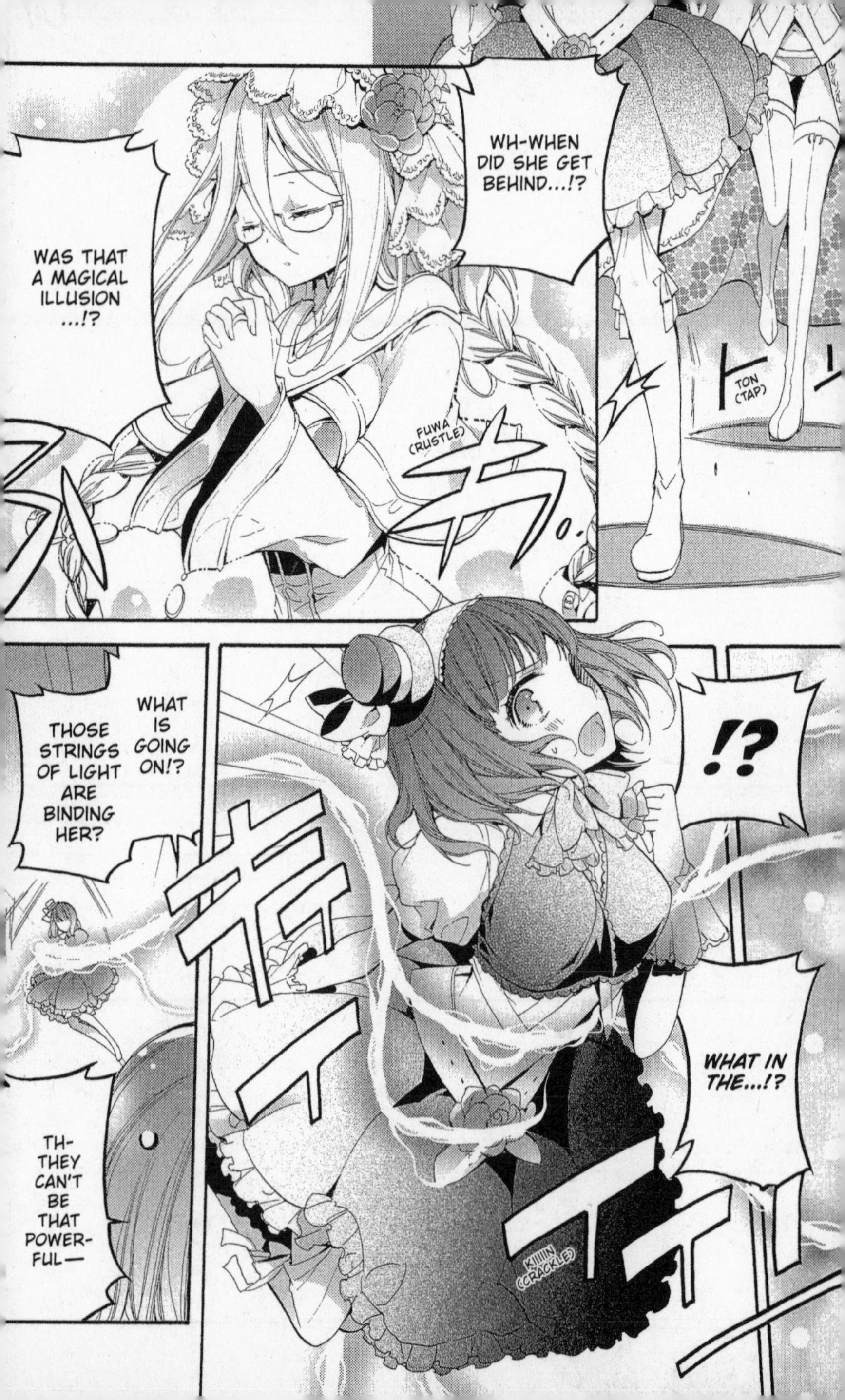

TON (TAP)
WH-WHEN DID SHE GET BEHIND...!?
WAS THAT A MAGICAL ILLUSION ...!?
FUWA (RUSTLE)
!?
WHAT IN THE...!?
KIIIIN (CRACKLE)
WHAT IS GOING ON!?
THOSE STRINGS OF LIGHT ARE BINDING HER?
TH-THEY CAN'T BE THAT POWER-FUL—

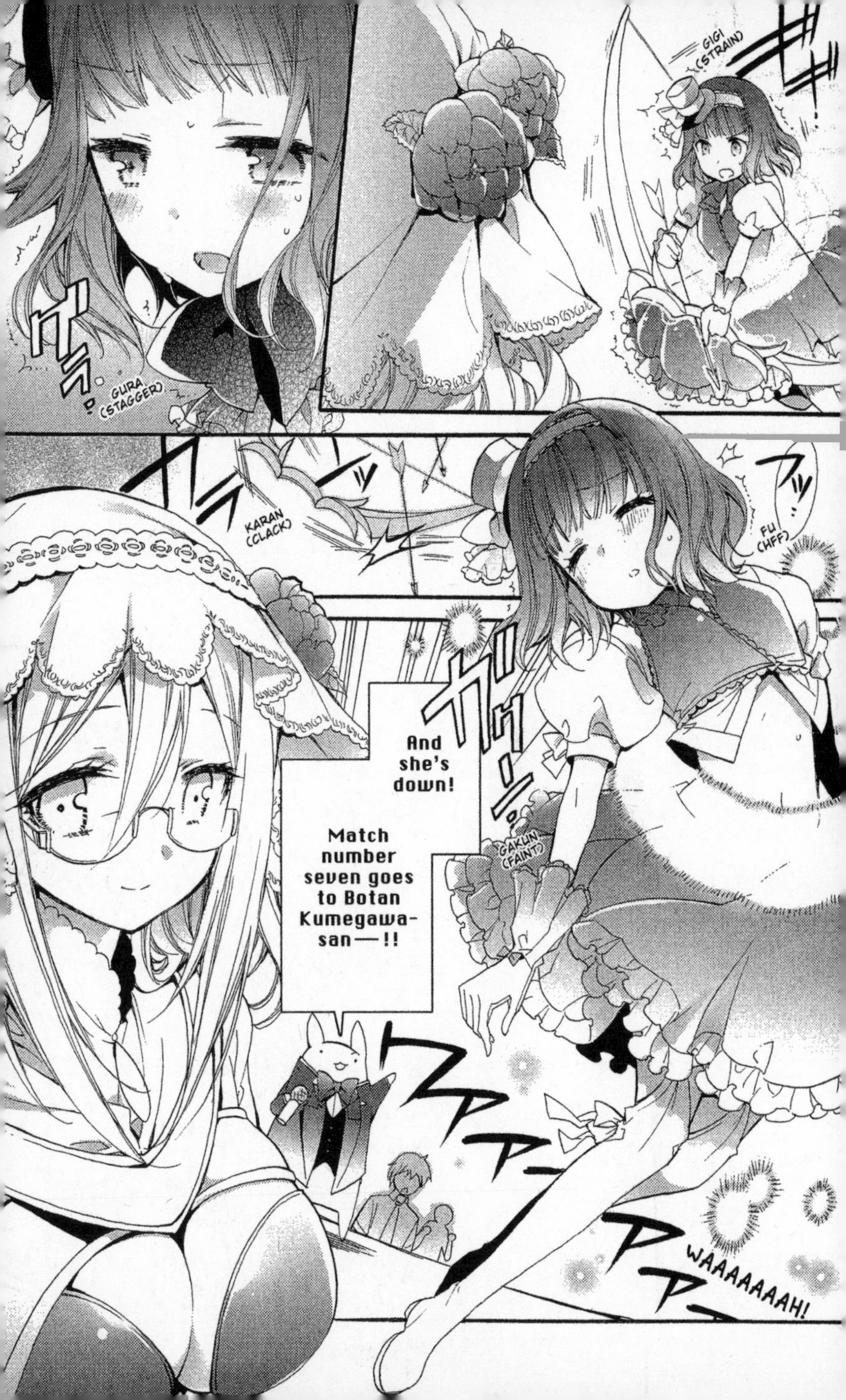
GIGI (STRAIN)
GURA (STAGGER)
FU (HFF)
KARAN (CLACK)
GAKUN (FAINT)
And she's down!
Match number seven goes to Botan Kumegawa-san—!!
WAAAAAAAH!

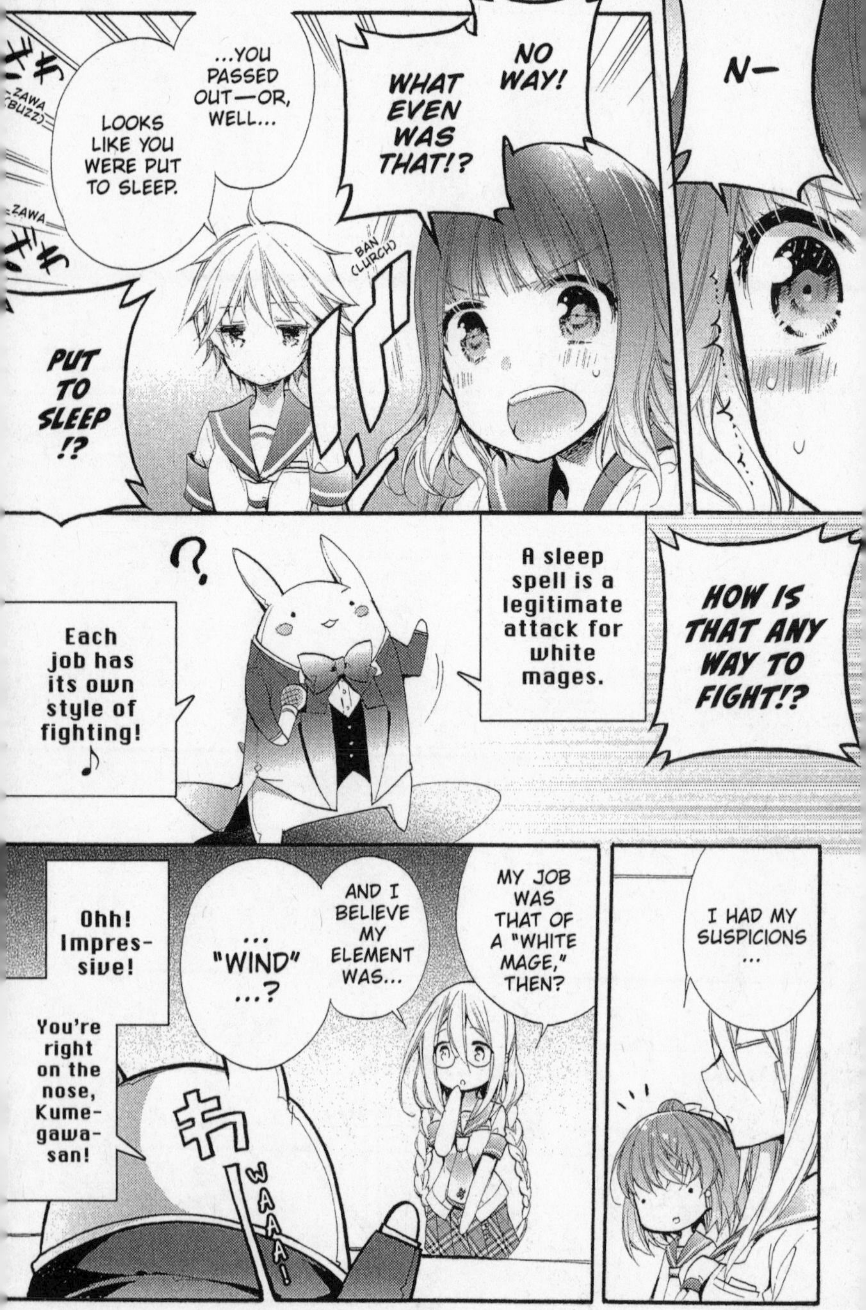
N—
NO WAY! WHAT EVEN WAS THAT!?
BAN (LURCH)
ZAWA (BUZZ)
...YOU PASSED OUT—OR, WELL... LOOKS LIKE YOU WERE PUT TO SLEEP.
ZAWA
PUT TO SLEEP!?
HOW IS THAT ANY WAY TO FIGHT!?
A sleep spell is a legitimate attack for white mages.
Each job has its own style of fighting! ♪
I HAD MY SUSPICIONS ...
MY JOB WAS THAT OF A "WHITE MAGE," THEN?
AND I BELIEVE MY ELEMENT WAS...
... "WIND" ...?
Ohh! Impres-sive!
You're right on the nose, Kume-gawa-san!
WAAAA!

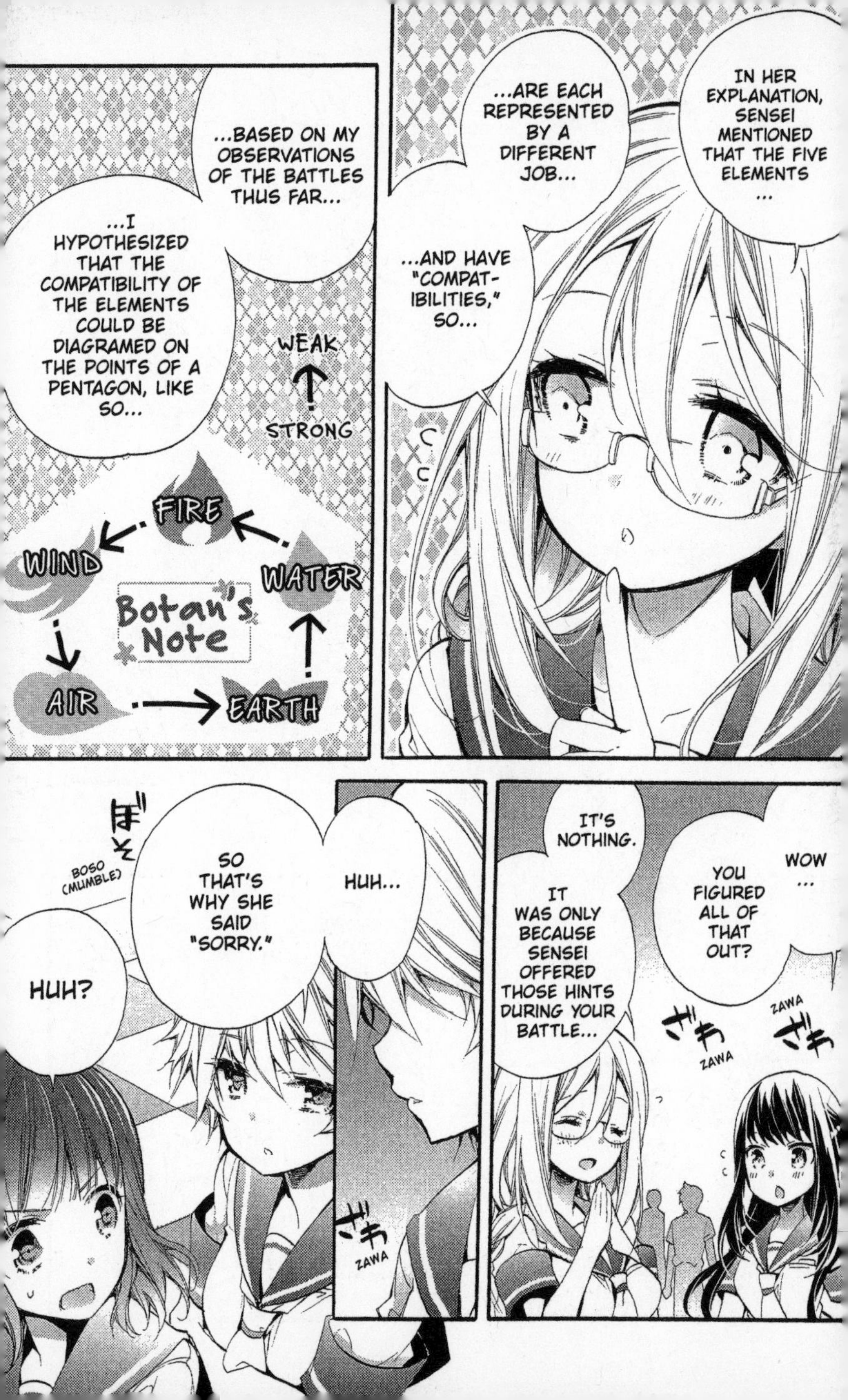
IN HER EXPLANATION, SENSEI MENTIONED THAT THE FIVE ELEMENTS ...
...ARE EACH REPRESENTED BY A DIFFERENT JOB...
...AND HAVE "COMPATIBILITIES," SO...
...BASED ON MY OBSERVATIONS OF THE BATTLES THUS FAR...
...I HYPOTHESIZED THAT THE COMPATIBILITY OF THE ELEMENTS COULD BE DIAGRAMED ON THE POINTS OF A PENTAGON, LIKE SO...
WEAK
STRONG
FIRE
WATER
WIND
Botan's Note
EARTH
AIR
WOW ...
YOU FIGURED ALL OF THAT OUT?
ざわ ZAWA
ざわ ZAWA
IT'S NOTHING.
IT WAS ONLY BECAUSE SENSEI OFFERED THOSE HINTS DURING YOUR BATTLE...
HUH...
ざわ ZAWA
SO THAT'S WHY SHE SAID "SORRY."
ぼそ
BOSO (MUMBLE)
HUH?

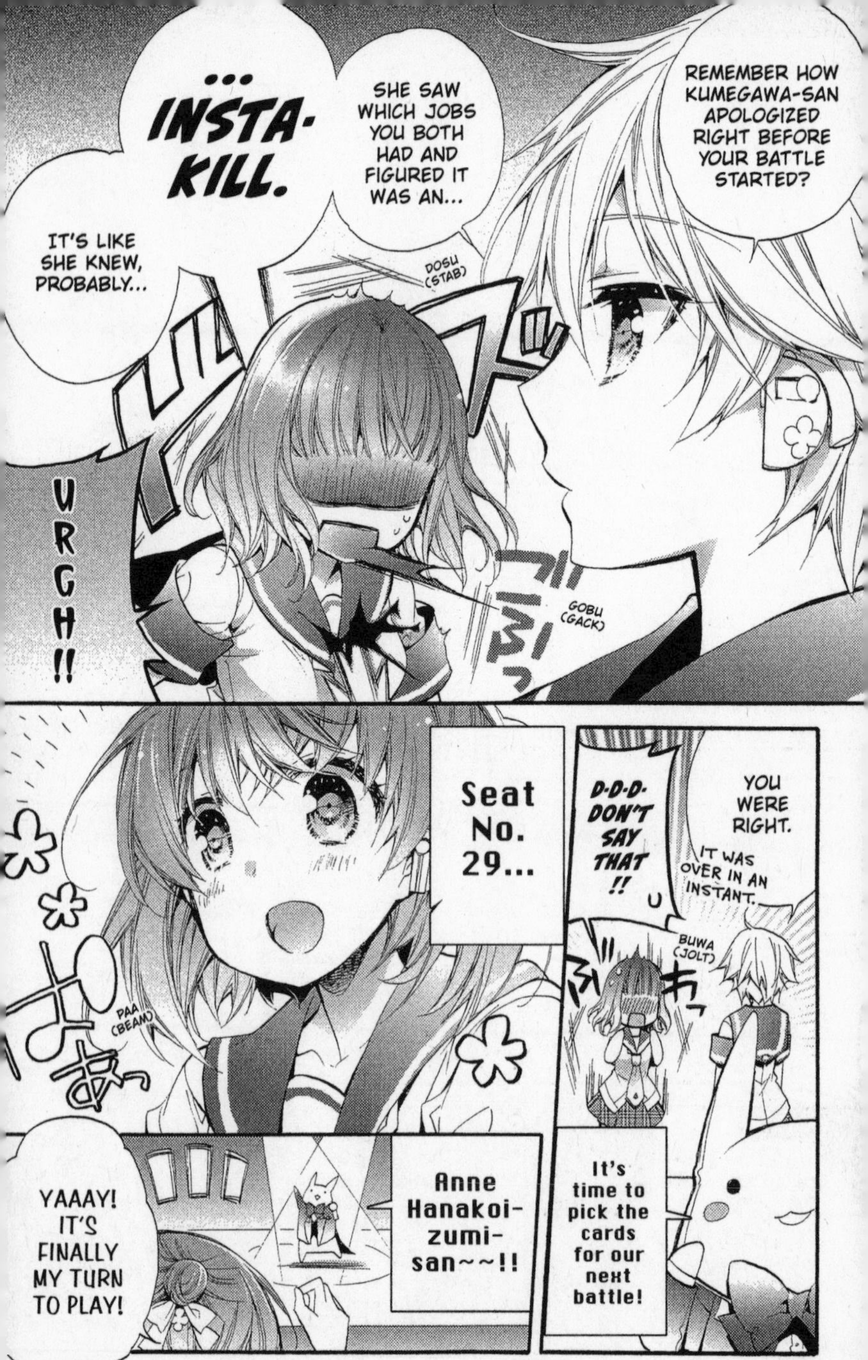
REMEMBER HOW KUMEGAWA-SAN APOLOGIZED RIGHT BEFORE YOUR BATTLE STARTED?
SHE SAW WHICH JOBS YOU BOTH HAD AND FIGURED IT WAS AN...
...INSTA-KILL.
DOSU (STAB)
IT'S LIKE SHE KNEW, PROBABLY...
GOBU (GACK)
URGH!!
YOU WERE RIGHT.
IT WAS OVER IN AN INSTANT.
D-D-D-DON'T SAY THAT!!
BUWA (JOLT)
Seat No. 29...
PAA (BEAM)
It's time to pick the cards for our next battle!
Anne Hanakoi-zumi-san~~!!
YAAAY! IT'S FINALLY MY TURN TO PLAY!

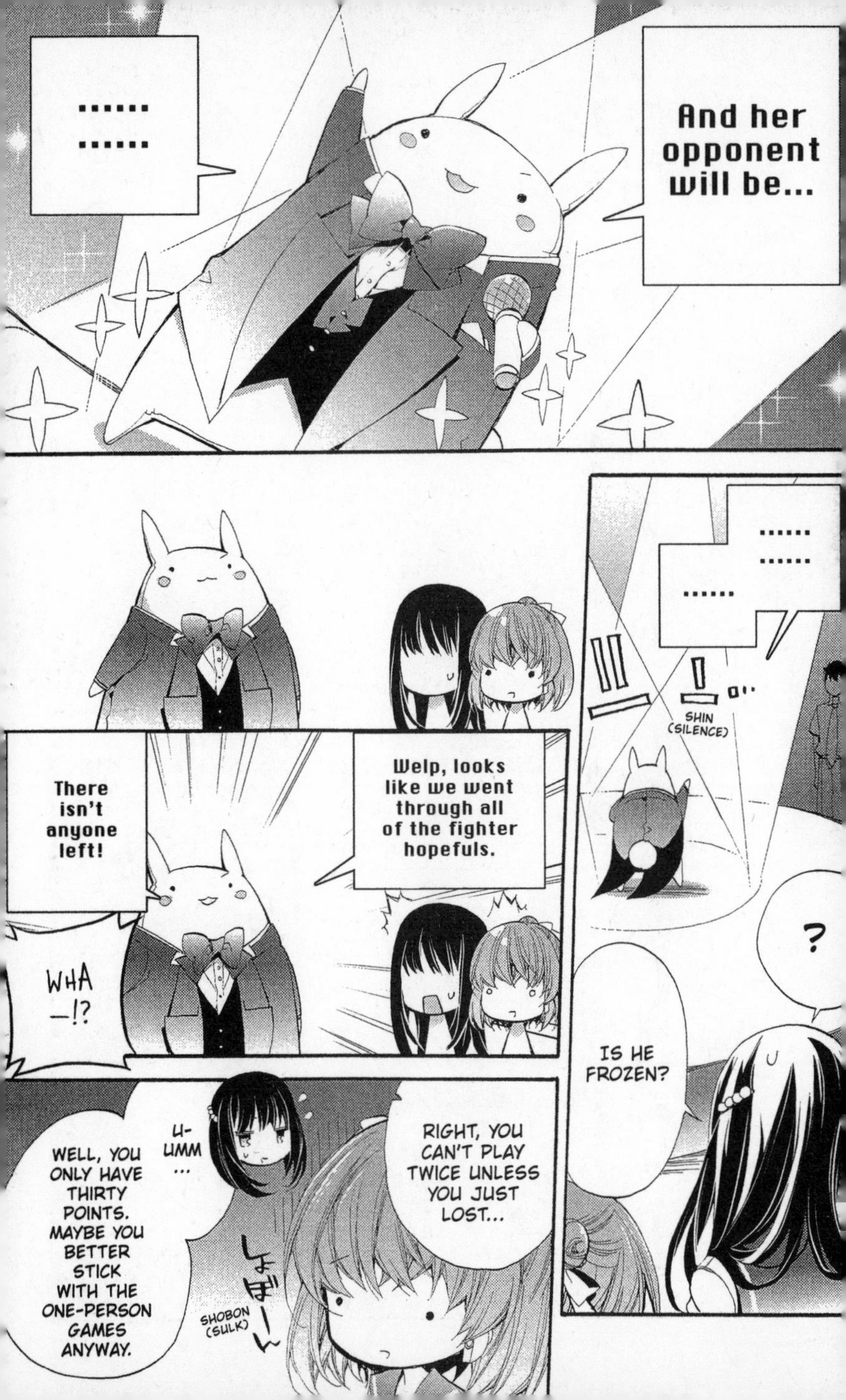
And her opponent will be...
......
......
......
......
......
SHIN (SILENCE)
?
IS HE FROZEN?
Welp, looks like we went through all of the fighter hopefuls.
There isn't anyone left!
WHA—!?
RIGHT, YOU CAN'T PLAY TWICE UNLESS YOU JUST LOST...
U-UMM...
WELL, YOU ONLY HAVE THIRTY POINTS. MAYBE YOU BETTER STICK WITH THE ONE-PERSON GAMES ANYWAY.
SHOBON (SULK)

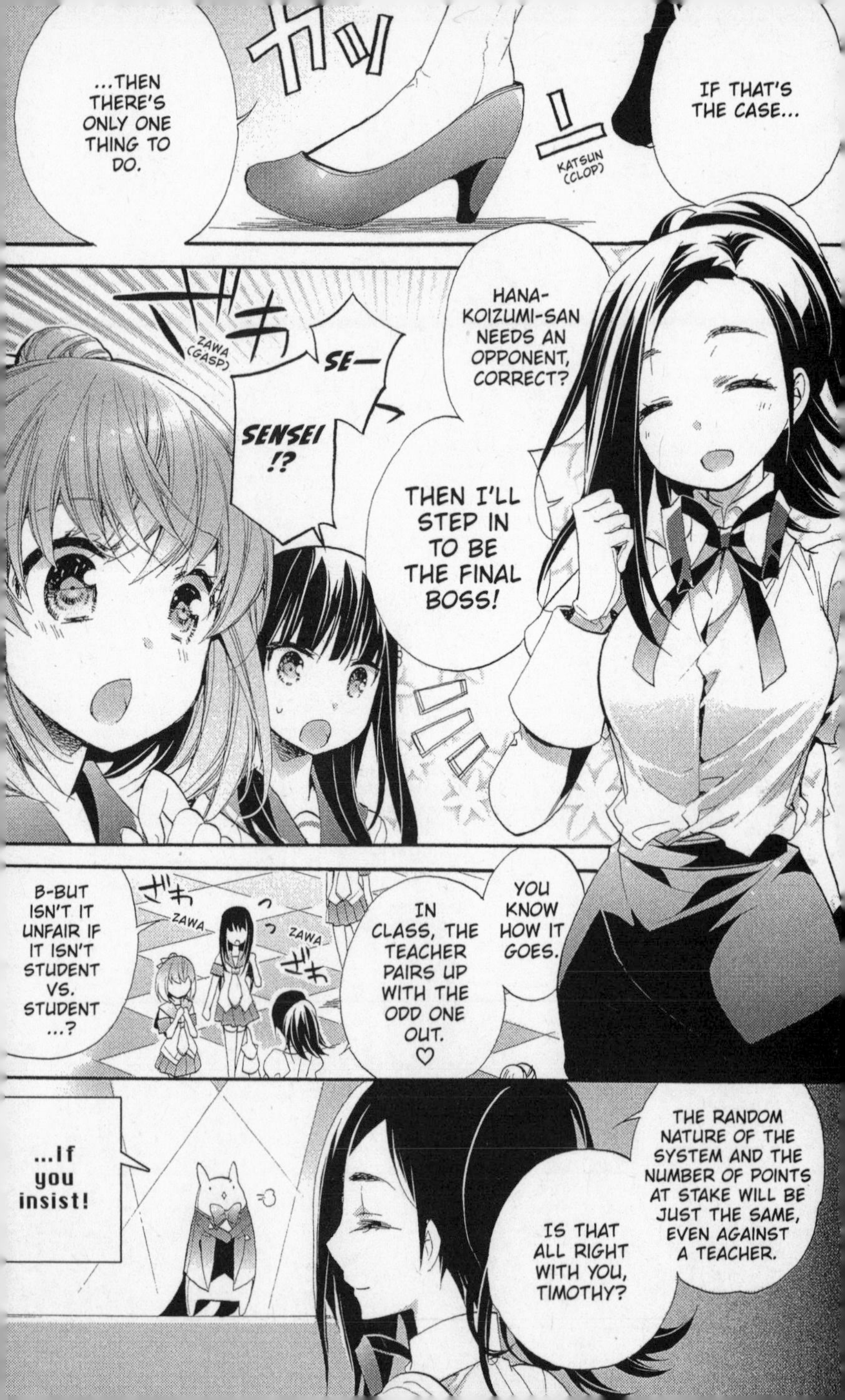
IF THAT'S THE CASE...
KATSUN (CLOP)
...THEN THERE'S ONLY ONE THING TO DO.
HANA-KOIZUMI-SAN NEEDS AN OPPONENT, CORRECT?
THEN I'LL STEP IN TO BE THE FINAL BOSS!
ZAWA (GASP)
SE—
SENSEI !?
YOU KNOW HOW IT GOES.
IN CLASS, THE TEACHER PAIRS UP WITH THE ODD ONE OUT. ♡
ZAWA
ZAWA
B-BUT ISN'T IT UNFAIR IF IT ISN'T STUDENT VS. STUDENT ...?
THE RANDOM NATURE OF THE SYSTEM AND THE NUMBER OF POINTS AT STAKE WILL BE JUST THE SAME, EVEN AGAINST A TEACHER.
IS THAT ALL RIGHT WITH YOU, TIMOTHY?
...If you insist!

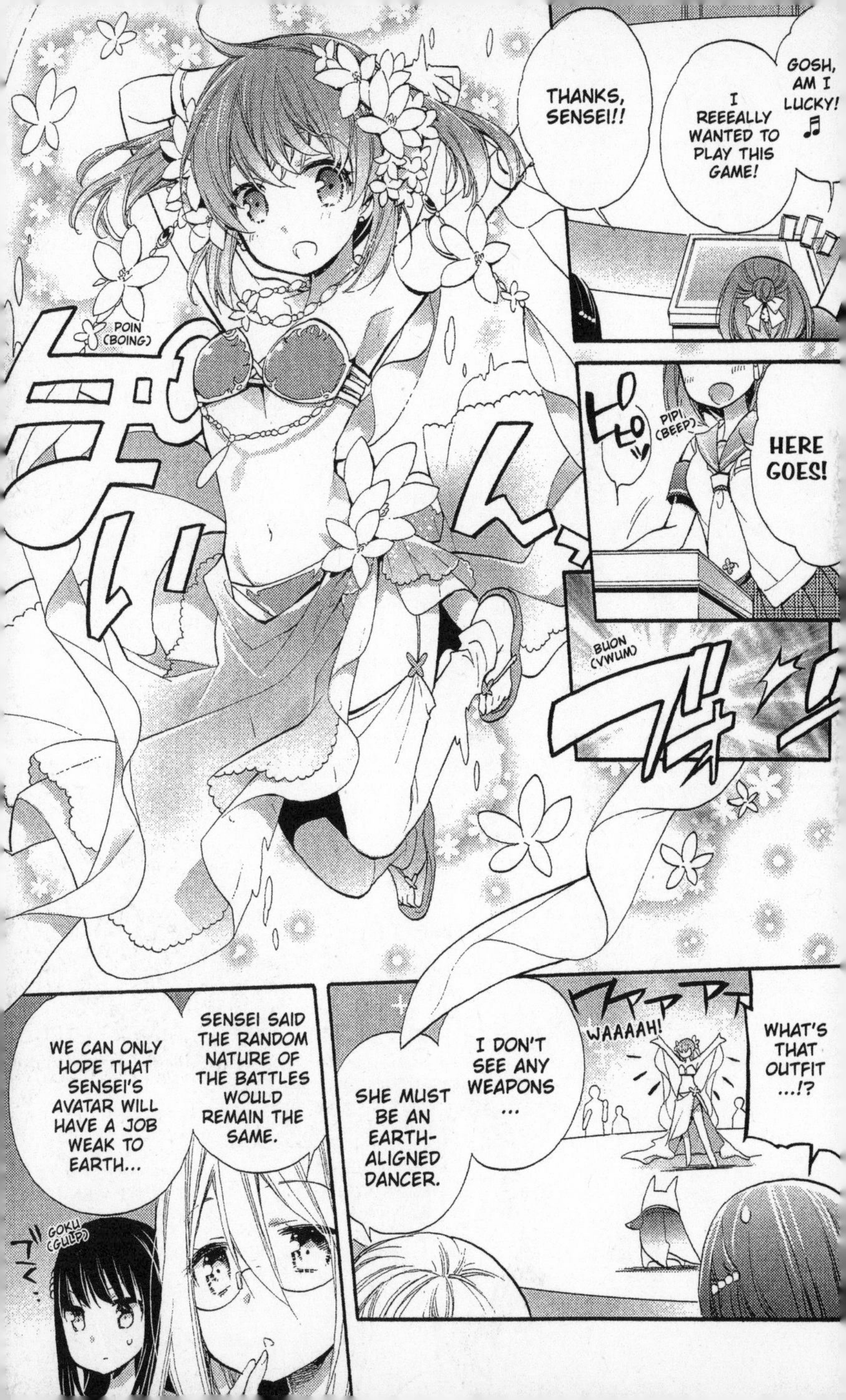
GOSH, AM I LUCKY! ♪
I REEEALLY WANTED TO PLAY THIS GAME!
THANKS, SENSEI!!
HERE GOES!
PIPI (BEEP)
BUON (VWUM)
POIN (BOING)
WHAT'S THAT OUTFIT ...!?
WAAAAH!
I DON'T SEE ANY WEAPONS ...
SHE MUST BE AN EARTH-ALIGNED DANCER.
SENSEI SAID THE RANDOM NATURE OF THE BATTLES WOULD REMAIN THE SAME.
WE CAN ONLY HOPE THAT SENSEI'S AVATAR WILL HAVE A JOB WEAK TO EARTH...
GOKU (GULP)

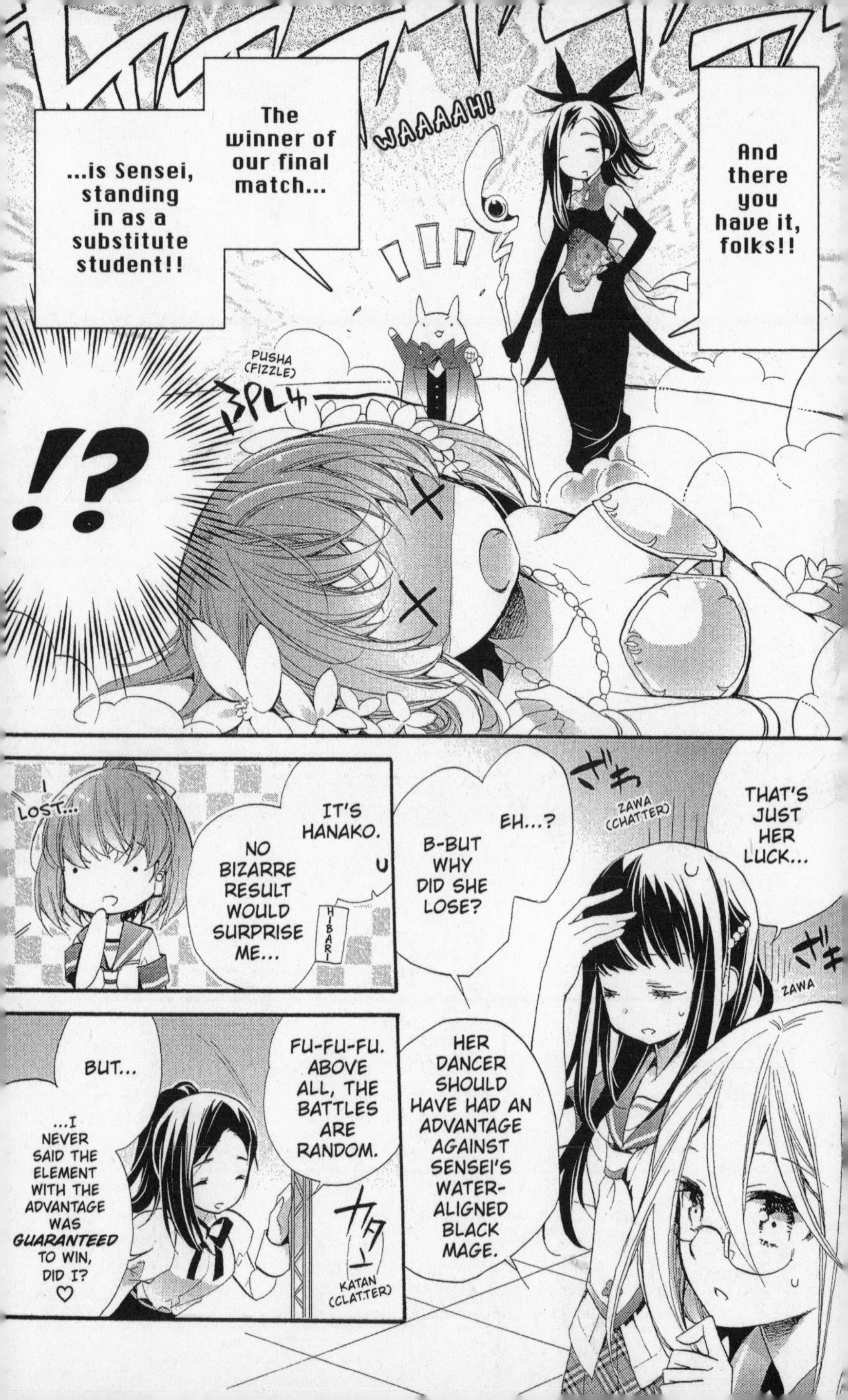
And there you have it, folks!!
The winner of our final match...
...is Sensei, standing in as a substitute student!!
WAAAAH!
PUSHA (FIZZLE)
!?
ZAWA (CHATTER)
THAT'S JUST HER LUCK...
ZAWA
EH...?
B-BUT WHY DID SHE LOSE?
IT'S HANAKO.
NO BIZARRE RESULT WOULD SURPRISE ME...
HIBARI
I LOST...
HER DANCER SHOULD HAVE HAD AN ADVANTAGE AGAINST SENSEI'S WATER-ALIGNED BLACK MAGE.
FU-FU-FU. ABOVE ALL, THE BATTLES ARE RANDOM.
KATAN (CLATTER)
BUT...
...I NEVER SAID THE ELEMENT WITH THE ADVANTAGE WAS GUARANTEED TO WIN, DID I? ♡

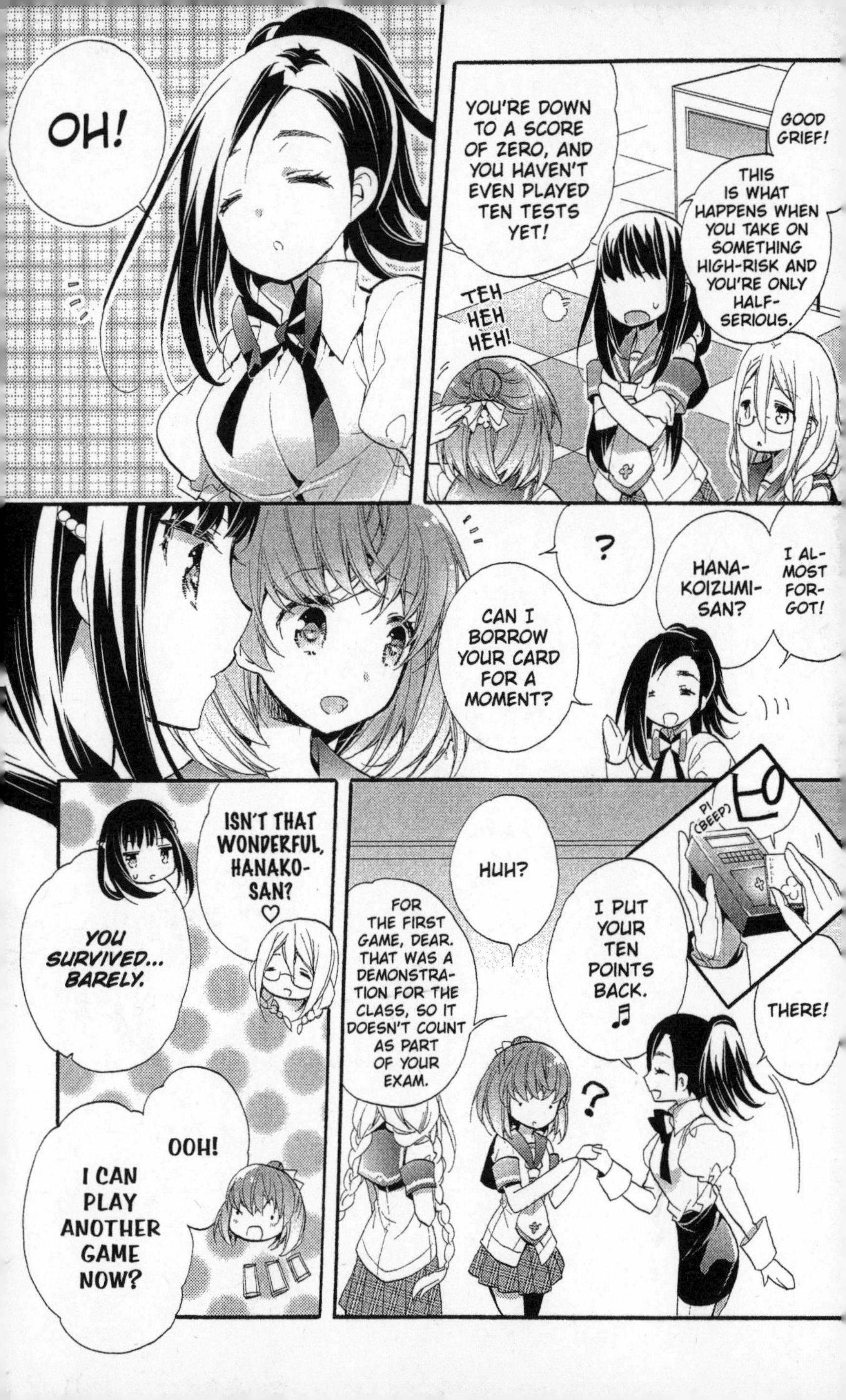
GOOD GRIEF!
THIS IS WHAT HAPPENS WHEN YOU TAKE ON SOMETHING HIGH-RISK AND YOU'RE ONLY HALF-SERIOUS.
YOU'RE DOWN TO A SCORE OF ZERO, AND YOU HAVEN'T EVEN PLAYED TEN TESTS YET!
TEH HEH HEH!
OH!
I AL-MOST FOR-GOT!
HANA-KOIZUMI-SAN?
?
CAN I BORROW YOUR CARD FOR A MOMENT?
PI (BEEP)
THERE!
I PUT YOUR TEN POINTS BACK. ♫
HUH?
FOR THE FIRST GAME, DEAR. THAT WAS A DEMONSTRA-TION FOR THE CLASS, SO IT DOESN'T COUNT AS PART OF YOUR EXAM.
?
ISN'T THAT WONDERFUL, HANAKO-SAN? ♡
YOU SURVIVED... BARELY.
OOH!
I CAN PLAY ANOTHER GAME NOW?

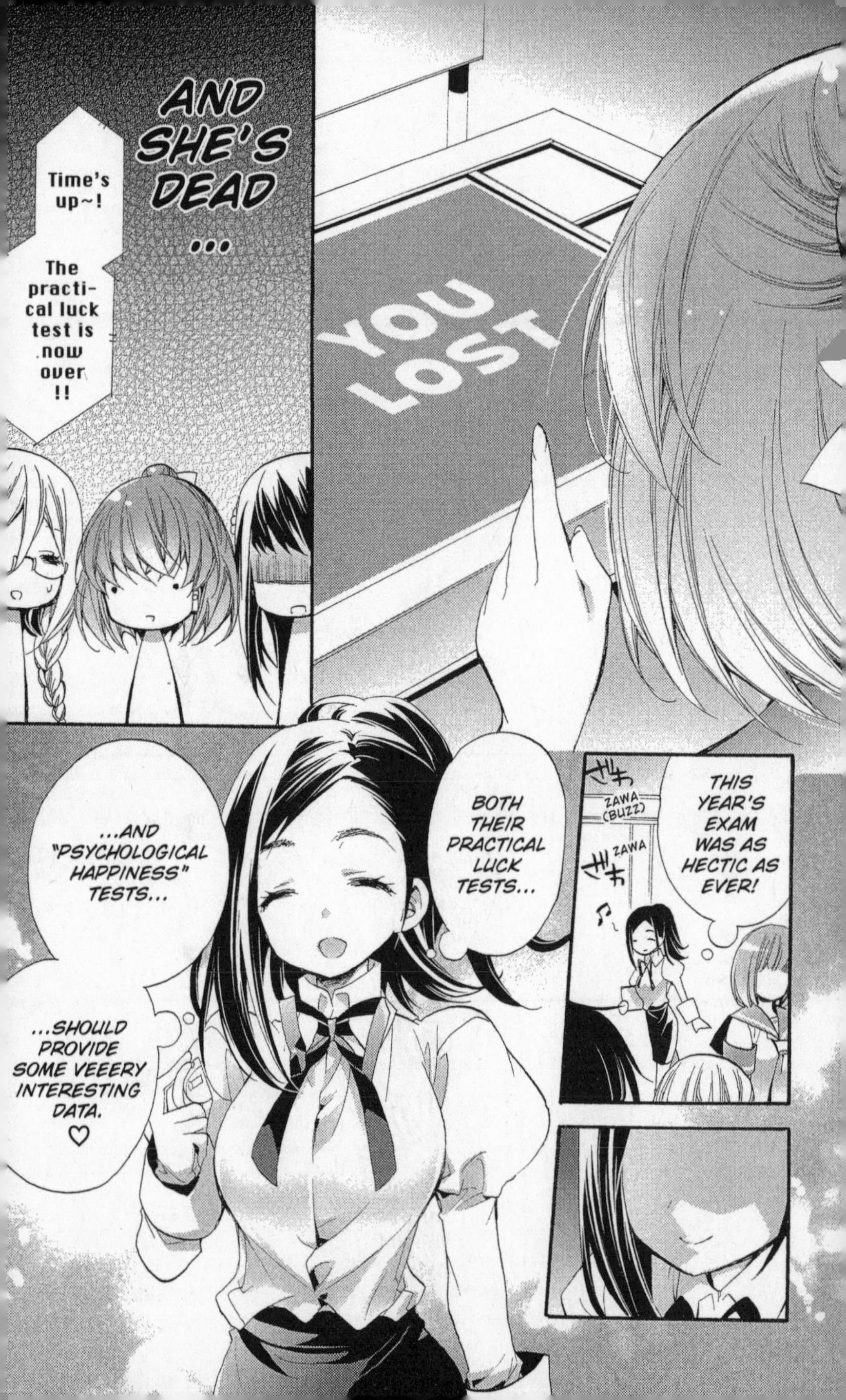
YOU LOST
AND SHE'S DEAD...
Time's up~!
The practical luck test is now over!!
ざわ
ZAWA (BUZZ)
ざわ
ZAWA
THIS YEAR'S EXAM WAS AS HECTIC AS EVER!
BOTH THEIR PRACTICAL LUCK TESTS...
...AND "PSYCHOLOGICAL HAPPINESS" TESTS...
...SHOULD PROVIDE SOME VEEERY INTERESTING DATA. ♡

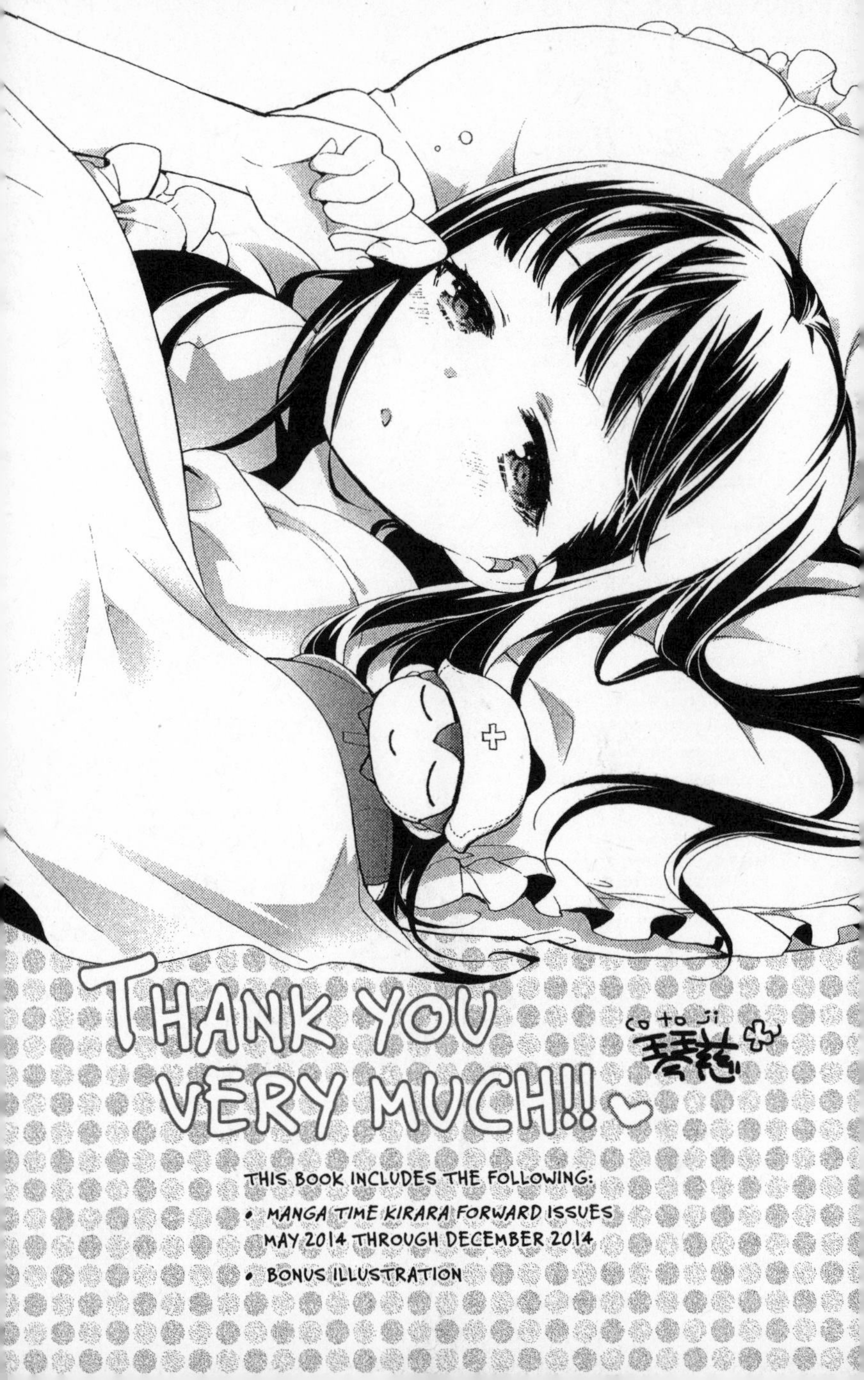

THANK YOU VERY MUCH!!

co to ji 琴慈

THIS BOOK INCLUDES THE FOLLOWING:

- MANGA TIME KIRARA FORWARD ISSUES MAY 2014 THROUGH DECEMBER 2014
- BONUS ILLUSTRATION

COTOJI

Translation: Amanda Haley
Lettering: Rochelle Gancio

ANNE HAPPY ♪ VOL. 3
© 2014 Cotoji. All rights reserved. First published in Japan in 2014 by HOUBUNSHA CO., LTD., TOKYO. English translation rights in United States, Canada, and United Kingdom arranged with HOUBUNSHA CO., LTD through Tuttle-Mori Agency, Inc., TOKYO.

English translation © 2016 by Yen Press, LLC

Yen Press
1290 Avenue of the Americas
New York, NY 10104

Visit us at yenpress.com
facebook.com/yenpress
twitter.com/yenpress
yenpress.tumblr.com
instagram.com/yenpress

First Yen Press Edition: November 2016

Yen Press is an imprint of Yen Press, LLC.
The Yen Press name and logo are trademarks of Yen Press, LLC.

The publisher is not responsible for websites (or their content) that are not owned by the publisher.

Library of Congress Control Number: 2016931012

ISBNs: 978-0-316-31785-6 (paperback)
        978-0-316-31786-3 (ebook)

10 9 8 7 6 5 4 3 2 1

BVG

Printed in the United States of America